Cotito

«Cuando parecía que nos encaminábamos a recuperar algo de cordura en este país maltrecho, y a lograr cierta madurez institucional, debajo de las piedras reaparece el monstruo endémico del juega vivo para recordarnos que por comodidad, por omisión y por complacencia siempre hemos permitido que los sinvergüenzas terminen por imponer la ley de la impunidad y que los delincuentes...disfruten sus [fechorías] con la desfachatez de los cínicos perpetuos.»

—«Hoy por Hoy», *La Prensa*, 5 de marzo, 2015

Carlos H. Cuestas Gómez, J.D.

Cotito

Chronicle of a Forgotten Crime

Revised English Edition

Translated from the Spanish and edited
with new material and a Foreword by
David M. Fishlow

Altozano Press
Volcán, Chiriquí – Panamá
2015

REVISED ENGLISH EDITION
ALTOZANO PRESS BY ARRANGEMENT WITH THE AUTHOR
ISBN 978-9962-05-914-1
TRANSLATION, ADDITIONAL MATERIAL ©MMXIII, MMXV DAVID M. FISHLOW
ALL RIGHTS RESERVED   PRINTED IN USA   7 9 10 8 6   19 18 17 16
SET IN GEORGIA 9.5/13, WITH DISPLAY IN ROCKWELL AND TREBUCHET

FIRST ENGLISH EDITION
ALTOZANO PRESS 2013 — ISBN 978-9962-05-100-8

ORIGINAL SPANISH EDITION
COTITO: CRÓNICA DE UN CRIMEN OLVIDADO / CARLOS H. CUESTAS G.
PUBLISHED BY THE AUTHOR ©MCMXCIII
PRINTED IN PANAMA BY LITHO EDITORIAL CHEN
TODOS LOS DERECHOS RESERVADOS

Queda terminantemente prohibida —salvo excepción prevista en la ley o breves y debidamente atribuidas citaciones en la prensa u obras de investigación— cualquier forma de reproducción, distribución, comunicación pública o transformación de esta obra sin contar con la previa autorización escrita de los respectivos titulares de la propiedad intelectual. Hechos los depósitos legales, RP Ley 47/1946 § 151, USA 17 U.S.C. § 407.

THE EDITOR INVITES INQUIRIES AND COMMENTS
DAVID@FISHLOW.COM

PUBLISHER'S CIP

Cuestas Gómez, Carlos H[umberto], 1953 – 20 .
[Cotito: Crónica de un crimen olvidado. English.]
Cotito: Chronicle of a forgotten crime / Carlos H. Cuestas Gómez, J.D. Translated from the Spanish and edited with new material and a Foreword by David M. Fishlow — Revised English ed.
illus., lxxxiv,254 pp. 20 cm.
Contains index, bibliographic references.
ISBN: 978-9962-05-914-1
1. Police shootings — Panama — Cotito. 2. Massacres — Panama — Cotito. 3. Agricultural colonies — Panama — Cotito. 4. Civil–military relations — Panama — History. 5. Panama — Politics and government — 1903–46 — Moral and ethical aspects. 6. Panama — Immigration, Swiss. 7. Panama — Presidents — Arias Madrid, Arnulfo 1901–88. 8. Hassán R., Aristides Iván, [date]. 9. Lehner, Karl 1888–1941. 10. Divine, Father M. J. c1877–1965 — Followers — Panama.
I. Title. II. Orig. title. III. Fishlow, David M[ichael], 1943 – 20 .

LCCN 2015494706 HV 8168.C67 C8413 2015   364.132'7287'11'2 – dc23 BiNal Pmá: 972.87 C754

1ST Eng. ed. — ISBN 978-9962-05-100-8 LCCN 2013478445 BiNal Pmá: 972.87 C676
Sp. ed. — LCCN 94-18350 HV 8168.C67 C84 1993 — BiNal Pmá: 972.87 C754

| *Author's Dedication*

A CHEFITA, MADRE amantísima, con profundo amor en su recuerdo.

| *Editor's Dedication*

TO THE MEMORY OF—

THE *SUIZOS,* most of whom lived by their principles until they died, and

BRO. ÆLRED WETLI OBL. O.S.B., 1912–2009, another *Suizo* from Wisconsin who did the same, striving from 1963 until his death to awaken the spirit of inquiry in Volcán, but whose library, alas, I could not save from the ecclesiastical predators.

Y A GIOVANNI FUENTES TORRES y Yariela Samaniego de Fuentes, quienes ya saben por qué, y a Yohanis, Yelenis, Alexandra y Giovanni David, quienes algún día lo sabrán.

| Author's acknowledgments

TO ALL THOSE individuals and institutions who in one way or another made the accomplishment of this work possible, especially, to Annette Pasco, Josef Probst, Franz Hunkeler, Carlos García de Paredes, Magela Cabrera, Isabel Valsevicius, Juan David Morgan Jr., Jorge Fábrega P., Mirtha O. Navarro, Vicenta Ibarra and Doris O. Jaén D. In addition, to José Félix Estribí and Dora Batista, who accompanied me to Cotito to learn about the object of this inquiry in the place where the events occurred.

Finally, to Carmela, Riccardo, Raffaella and to Graciela Mojica, for their infinite patience.

| Editor's acknowledgments

OSVALDO IVÁN FLORES (1959–2016) first showed me the Spanish text of this book and then lent it to me, and has taught me much about the local history of my adopted home.

His family has for nineteen years shown me a kind of hospitality the Swiss colonists would have understood. Dr^a. Berta Ramona Thayer Fábrega first introduced me more than fifteen years ago to the Cotito story and lent me the Hassán book, leading to my first encounter with Albert Schmieder and the late Walter Morf. She lent it to me again in time for the preparation of this new English edition, and shared details from her extensive knowledge of the issue and Panamanian politics.

Albert Schmieder and Rosario Laws de Schmieder provided information from memory, documents and photographs unavailable anywhere else, corrected errors of fact, and offered perspective, support, friendship and hospitality. The late Yvonne Worrell Pover answered many questions and provided photos.

Appendices A and B were translated from Political Department (foreign ministry) files in the Schweizerisches Bundesarchiv at Bern by *Frau* Barbara Traber, whose research and translations were crucial. Having translated Trudi Häusle Worrell's memoir from English to German, *Frau* Traber could add details about Trudi's character, Swiss geography, and the spelling of Swiss family names, which I had botched in my effort to correct the Spanish. All other translations, except as noted, are mine. *Monsieur* Serge Basilewsky of Cannes helped obtain other material in Europe.

The detail from the original cover is by the eminent political cartoonist Victor Ramos, known in Panama as "Vic." *Sra.* Romelia *Vda. de* Hils in Volcán gave me free access to her family albums. *Sr.* Werner C. Senn of Volcán provided clippings, photos, reminiscences and helped identify photos. Historical photographs originally from Panamanian government sources were republished many times in newspapers in Panama and Cuba in 1941; again in 1982 and 1987 in *Holocausto en Panamá* (whose accuracy and documentation are woefully inadequate, and which bears no copyright notice); and again in the daily press in 1984; and are hence presumed to be in the public domain. Prof. Max Paul Friedman provided the Camp Kenedy photos from the U.S. National Archives. All other illustrations are published with permission or presumed to be in the public domain.

My cousin Deborah Claire Weiner (Goldstein) untangled my syntax, clarified my argument, exposed my inadequacies as a typesetter, and tried unsuccessfully to modernize my style.

Don Jorge Cedeño Anguizola kept asking *¿Cuándo?*, and *Sra.* Amaryllis Mabel Villarreal de Santamaría kept everything else going *mientras*.

By way of prologue

[PREFACE TO THE 1993 SPANISH EDITION]

JORGE KAM RÍOS
CORRESPONDENT OF THE PANAMANIAN
AND COLOMBIAN ACADEMIES OF HISTORY

IT IS EASY TO WRITE the history of yesterday for the reader of today, but to write the history of today for the reader of today ... . The history of past misdeeds and the history of misdeeds as they continue to unfold on the Isthmus of Panama are replete with instances of errors committed within the borders of the Republic, and there is no reason to believe that these will cease to occur.

So it was that, in early days, Balboa was beheaded by his father-in-law Pedrarias, and all the indications are that envy and revenge tinged the incident. In the nineteenth century, local separatist movements—including the eternal, internecine Colombian wars—produced the lynching of Pedro Prestán, a case that remains only half-solved.

But the examples of injustice presented by the twentieth century are more distressing to us, perhaps because we are closer to them in time, for the history of the century is contemporaneous with the history of events since the birth of the Republic: the death of Victoriano Lorenzo (although in this century, it occurred before the actual founding of the Republic [1903]), the death of Remón,* of Miró,* of Araúz, of Falconett and Mendizábal, of Spadafora, to mention just a few. They all have a common denominator: they were only half-solved and they were all affected by the existence of individuals and institutions that tend to protect the guilty to the detriment of the victims and those who have disappeared. And, in this respect, we historians do little to salvage their memory for the community at large.

All the foregoing reminds us of a prologue by Carlos Manuel Gasteázoro dated 1954, where he noted that it is almost unheard of in Panama for "government officials to make a serious effort to examine our history, much less to adopt this effort as their vocation." Almost forty years later, we may assert that this remains true; only the historians, men like Dr. Carlos Cuestas (jurist, lawyer and scholar), try to salvage events from the labyrinth of history that the criminal hand wishes to keep buried beneath a rocky layer of earth; whence, perhaps his other works: *Memoria de un fiscal: El escándalo de la Caja del Seguro Social; El histórico combate de San Pablo; Soldados americanos en Chiriquí*.[†] At this juncture, Cuestas surprises us with a new work in which, beyond making a heuristic effort, he rewards the reader with a hermeneutic one, giving us his *Cotito: Chronicle of a Forgotten Crime*.

It may be noted that the historiography of Panama in the twentieth century is usually limited, directly or indirectly, to the Canal Zone or to [political] leaders. In this sense, the work of Dr. Cuestas departs from tradition, conveying to us, throughout his six chapters, —with objectivity, clarity and balance,—a historical episode that, for obscure reasons is only today beginning to be clarified. For the first time, [the historiography of] the slaughter of the Swiss–German colonists at Cotito breaks away from the tendentious, politicized and yellow–journalistic style and is presented in a more objective dimension: the disgraceful action carried out against men, women and

---

* See p. 69, n. *, *infra*.

† [*The Scandal of the Social Security Fund: Memoir of a Prosecutor; The Historic Battle of San Pablo; American Soldiers in Chiriquí*.]

children one morning on July 7, 1941; an incident occurring in the region of Chiriquí where fanaticism and intolerance, the fruits of ignorance, boiled over.

Carlos Cuestas has managed to dig out of the published, unpublished and oral sources the motives of those guilty of this lamentable multiple crime; in the same way, he relates the irrational conduct of Captain Antonio Huff who, "beyond the call of duty," erupts in fury against the "hospitable" Swiss–German colonists—their fanaticism and ideals, perhaps extreme—who, led by Karl Lehner—a man rooted in his religious principles—resisted only passively, provoking a clash between senselessness and intransigence, with the result described in this work: twelve dead, of whom nine were men and three women, eight of them Swiss and four German.

As Carlos says: those were times of institutional renewal, of intolerance, of political persecutions, of uprisings and repression. They were also times of war, of racial prejudice, of harassment of minorities enacted into law, from 1904 on, in legislation and executive orders and in the Constitution adopted in 1941.

In this instance, Christians were massacred, and it is a chronicle of yesterday for today, as well as a chronicle of today for today, which Dr. Carlos Cuestas enables us to recall.

| Contents

	Editor's foreword	xvii
		How this edition came to be	xxi
		The panamanian political context	xliv
		Efforts to 'improve the race'	xliv
		The u.s. demands anti-german measures	lvi
		Cotito an issue in 1984: Goofy politics in a sham election	lxvi
	Author's introduction	lxxx
I	A swiss religious commune	1
1	Switzerland during the nineteen-thirties	1
2	The founding of the commune	2
3	The cult of father divine	6
4	The commune's problems	11
5	Karl schmieder's farm	15
6	An emissary to Panama	21
7	A group immigrant visa	25
8	The journey to panama	26
9	Cotito in 1939	30
10	The german neighbors	33
11	The organization of the colony	37
12	Relations with the Panamanian neighbors	44
II	The year 1941 in Panama	51
1	The presidency of arnulfo arias madrid: 1940-41	51

		2 | Arnulfo Arias, unopposed candidate	54
		3 | The armed uprisings	56
		4 | The militarization of the national police	58
		5 | The military reorganization of Gómez Ayau	61
		6 | The national police in Chiriquí	67
		7 | Religious intolerance: the case of the Seventh-Day Adventists	71

III | *The slaughter at Cotito* — 77

1 | The immediate antecedents — 77
2 | Captain Huff's service of notice — 78
3 | Supposed Nazi spies in Cotito — 85
4 | Attempts to avoid tragedy — 87
5 | A military operation against unarmed colonists — 88
6 | July 7, 1941 — 90
7 | The result of the police attack — 98
8 | The cover-up work begins — 102
9 | The official story — 104
10 | A compromising telegram — 107
11 | The reaction — 109
  | A cable to Berlin — 109
  | The American intelligence reports — 111
  | The protest of Wilhelm Probst — 114
  | José Guillermo Batalla's letter — 116

IV | *A twelve-year investigation* — 121

1 | A criminal investigation report disappears — 121
2 | Prosecutor Gómez's preliminary investigation — 123
3 | The prosecutor *vs.* the chief of police — 125
4 | Prosecutor Gómez is removed — 127
5 | The colonists' alleged arsenal — 130
6 | The torturous path of a criminal prosecution — 134
7 | Swiss-German recrimination — 138
  | The investigation of the Mixed Commission — 138
  | German claims — 144
  | Swiss claims — 146
8 | A delayed acquittal — 149

V	*The disposition of the commune's property*	**157**
1	The survivors	157
2	Measures to secure the assets	158
	The intervention of the mixed commission	158
	The actions of the survivors	159
3	The problems of inheritance	162
	Alfred Waser's stewardship	163
	The return of Gustav Haug	164
4	The sale of the Cotito farm	168
5	The Müllers' reservations	170
6	Cotito today	171

VI	*'Holocaust' in panama, or,*	
	a hoax distorting the truth	**174**
1	The origins of a deceptive book	177
2	A failed electoral strategy	180
3	Salvaging historical truth	185

| | *Epilogue* | **193** |

	Appendices	**195**
A	My experiences with the 'molch' colony	195
B	Deposition regarding infant Virgilio Columbio Rieser, born Sept. 21, 1938	219
C	Trudi Häusle Worrell's Cotito memoir, *Bridge on the Chiriquí Viejo*	221

	Bibliography	**231**
	Archival collections	231
	Works cited	231
	Books and articles	231
	Interviews and conversations	233
	Judicial decisions and orders	233
	Correspondence	233
	Government documents	234
	Newspapers	235
	Cited by editor	235
	Index	**236**

Illustrations*

Uncle pleads for information	xvi
The cover of *Holocausto en Panamá*	xxv
Albert Schmieder, 1941	xxxiv
Walter Morf, 1941	xxxiv
Albert Schmieder visits the site of the colony, 2013	xxxv
President Arnulfo Arias Madrid, 1941	xlvi
German internees, Camp Kenedy, Texas	liii
The Cotito farm. ca. 1940	lxxx
David, capital of the province of Chiriquí, ca. 1941	lxxxiv
Penninah, the first Mother Divine	8
Father Divine and the second Mother Divine	8
Werner Robert (Böps) Müller, 1994	10
Gretel, Karl Jr., Albert at home in Cotito, 1938	17
The Schmieders' 1928 passport	19
The post office, a community center	22
The Volcán post office, interior, late 1940's	23
Trudi Häusle's map of the journey, 1993	27
Immigrant hunter and *macho de monte*	31
The Schmieder family home in Schramberg	32
A view of Schramberg, home of the Brauchles, Hilses, Schapers, and Schmieders, 1950	33
Frau Lydia Brauchle, Gertrudis Hils, early 1940's	34
The *Bienenhaus*	35
Karl Lehner	36
Heinrich Ott	37
Felling timber with axes	39
Trudi Häusle's sketch of a timber-felling operation	40
Sawing timbers into planks	40
The bridge under consruction	41

---

* Illustrations were selected and captions supplied by the Editor.

ILLUSTRATIONS

THE COMPLETED BRIDGE, 1940	42
THE *BANANENHAUS*	43
BANANA HARVEST, CHIRIQUÍ, LATE 1930'S	50
LT. COL. FERNANDO GÓMEZ AYAU	59
THE SCHMIEDERS' FARMSTEAD, LATE 1930'S	76
CAPT. ANTONIO HUFF, CA. 1941	79
THE HILS FAMILY, EARLY 1940'S	82
LUCAS GARCÉS DISPLAYS FACE WOUND, 1941	92
CASUALTY LIST, SWISS ARCHIVES	95
GOTTFRIED WERREN AND PAUL HÄUSLE, CA. 1939-40	96
PAUL HAÜSLE, CA. 1938	98
ELFRIEDE MORF (MOTHER), CA. 1938	98
WERNER MÜLLER, CA. 1938	99
LONI MORF, 1941	100
DEATH SQUAD: POLICE POSE FOR PROUD PHOTOGRAPH	101
POLICE PHOTO OF BOGUS ARMS CACHE	102
ROBERT MÜLLER DISPLAYS HIS WOUNDS, 1994	113
THE FIRST PROSECUTOR, ABEL GÓMEZ ARAÚZ	122
WIDOW AND ORPHANS IN THE CARE OF THE NUNS	162
SOPHIE MÜLLER WITH SWISS NEIGHBOR BRÜNNHILDE SENN	164
ALBERT SCHMIEDER MEETS TRUDI HÄUSLE'S DAUGHTER, 1945	165
ROBERT MÜLLER WITH HIS TRUCK, CA. 1950	166
THE SURVIVORS IN MIDDLE AGE	168
SURVEY OF THE COTITO FARM, 1954	174
HITLER CONGRATULATES ARIAS, OCT. 18, 1940	175
HASSÁN BEGINS HIS FIRST EXHUMATION, 1980	176
THE GRAVE AS IT APPEARED IN 1993	176
ALOIS HARTMANN IN FRONT OF HIS CABIN, CA. 1915	185
EARLIEST KNOWN PHOTO OF THE GRAVE	186
THE GRAVE OF THE VICTIMS, COTITO, 2013	187
MARTHA AND FRITZ SCHAPPER, CA. 1962	189
HARTMANN FAMILY, 1920'S	190
THE SCHMIEDERS WITH KARL SR.'S MOTHER AND STEPFATHER	200
NIEDERBERGER, THE SCHMIEDERS, GUSTAV HAUG, CA. 1941	205
THE SCHMIEDERS VISIT THE BRAUCHLES, CA. 1939	211
HAUGS, SCHMIEDERS, HILSES, LYDIA BRAUCHLE, CA. 1946	218
VIOLA WEHRLI, CA. 1938 AND CA. 1941	220
MEMORIAL PLAQUE	252

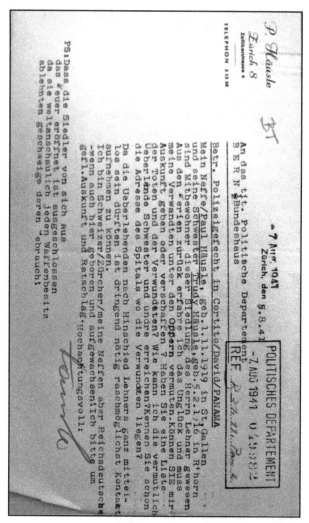

SCHWEIZERISCHES BUNDESARCHIV, BERN—PHOTO BARBARA TRABER

August 5, 1941, a month after the massacre, Mr. P. Häusle of Zollikerstrasse № 6, Zürich 8, writes frantically to the ministry of foreign affairs at Bern, seeking information about his niece Trudi and nephew Paul, members of Lehner's commune at 'Cortito' in Panama. He asks for casualty lists and the 'address where the wounded are being cared for.' Paul was already dead, the first casualty of the massacre. Trudi was alive but badly wounded.

We must come down from our heights and leave our straight paths for the byways and low places of life if we would learn truths by strong contrasts; and in hovels, in forecastles, and among our own outcasts in foreign lands, see what has been wrought upon our fellow-creatures by accident, hardship, or vice.

—RICHARD HENRY DANA JR.,
Two Years Before The Mast

| EDITOR'S FOREWORD*

THE BOOK THAT follows is a tale of folly degenerating into madness. All human stories involve some degree of folly, and many are tales of madness, but the events culminating in the tragedy of July 7, 1941, in a remote settlement in the highlands of Chiriquí, were marked by a singular abundance of both.

The greatest folly may have been committed by the naïve Swiss idealists who followed a genuine madman, apostle of a screwball

---

* The views expressed in this Foreword are *exclusively* those of the Editor of this edition. The Author of the original Spanish text of *Cotito* bears no responsibility for them.

Except in this Foreword, in the Appendices and in the captions for the illustrations (all included for the first time in the first English edition), all insertions in the text, footnotes and endnotes added by the translator/editor, are enclosed in [brackets].

North American cult religion, into South American exile at the end of 1938. These idealists were convinced they would be able, with goodwill and machetes alone, to tame the virgin cloud forest and live on the fruits of their labors in an earthly paradise of their own making, insulated from the poverty of depression–era Europe and the maelstrom of a world war that had already begun.

In 1940, when the Swiss proved unequal to the task of clearing the jungle, planting and harvesting their crops, when living their idyll proved more daunting than they had imagined, German settlers—with whom they shared a language and who had preceded them to Chiriquí in 1928—took them in, sheltered and fed them. Since no good deed goes unpunished, some of these hospitable Germans would also fall victim—in the most literal sense—to the folly of their guests, the madness of their leader and the lunacy of the police.

At the time, Panama was governed—to the extent it was governed at all—by a failing president, Arnulfo Arias Madrid, an uncompromising nationalist who took office in October, 1940. By mid–1941, his radical populist supporters were struggling to keep his government afloat, while the conservative oligarchy, the fractious paramilitary police, and the President's own elder brother Harmodio—himself a former President and Arnulfo's mentor—connived with the United States to sink it. Dazzled by the Nazi and Fascist dictatorships of the nineteen–thirties and the delusory sense of order and prosperity they had created, President Arnulfo Arias committed the greatest political folly imaginable: he assumed he could take on all three of his foes—the oligarchy, the police and the United States—and complete his first term in the Palace of the Herons. He failed and was deposed, as would happen for the second time in 1951.

Having lost a third election in 1964, Arnulfo Arias ran for the fourth time and won in 1968, tried to begin his third term, and was again deposed. In 1984, he ran for the fifth time in forty–five years, only to see his victory snatched away by naked manipulation of the vote count. Altogether, Arias won four of five elections by fair means and foul, but he was never allowed to complete (in one instance, even to begin) any of his terms in office.

And in 1941, as always, every folly, every madness endemic to the United States reached Panama in exaggerated and perverted form. From 1903 on, at least until 1999, the United States had treated Panama as a protectorate—in 1928, Calvin Coolidge called it an "outlying possession" of the United States[1]—although from 1936 on, the protectorate status was a fact of life, not a formally acknowledged relationship. Now, in 1940–41, as prewar, anti–German hysteria engulfed the U.S. government, and the Arias government tottered, the United States still exerted enormous influence over Panama.

Before World War II, in most of Latin America, German refugees from poverty and from Hitler—including Jews fleeing persecution and certain death—were quietly farming, running businesses, or just scratching out a meager living. In the smaller countries, these Germans living abroad would soon be rounded up at the behest of the United States, held in the notorious Camp Empire at Balboa in the Panama Canal Zone, and then shipped off to prison camps in Texas; some would be repatriated to Germany. Internment of innocent, anti–Nazi refugees who had fled Germany was a particular folly all over the continent, but such roundups had occurred in Panama before.

In April, 1918, when the Canal was just four years old, and the Republic just fifteen, the Panamanian government for the first time rounded up all the German men it could find and turned them over to the Americans for internment in New York. This would later (1940–41) be cited as precedent justifying a radical new policy: seizing aliens in a non–belligerent country—Panama—and delivering them over to another non–belligerent—the United States—for internment.[2]

By the end of World War II, some 4,058 Germans, 2,264 Japanese, and 288 Italians[3] had been forcibly deported from Latin America and interned in the United States. "With only eight of the 4,058 German deportees even allegedly involved in espionage, and the record of sabotage 'practically nil,' according to the FBI, spying and sabotage were red herrings...."[4] This particular folly would feed the madness in Panama in 1941.

xix

As war raged in Europe, the U.S. was insisting that the Panamanians root out the "Nazi fifth–column," even though the putative threat of sabotage to the Canal was largely illusory. It also demanded what Arias considered further concessions of Panamanian sovereignty. Arias remained obdurate, but the upper classes and the paramilitary police—a political force in their own right—responded willingly to Gringo folly: the President's domestic enemies were happy to paint him as an eccentric tool of the Nazis.

With the hunt for spies and fifth–columnists reaching such levels of chaotic intensity in most of the continent, what hope could there have been for a handful of German–speaking Swiss pacifists in Chiriquí who refused to comply with direct orders from the police to report for yet another registration of foreigners living in Panama? What semi–literate Panamanian cop knew the difference between *Suiza* and *Suecia*,[*] for that matter, let alone the difference between *Suizos-Alemanes* (German–speaking Swiss) and *Alemanes* who were indeed Germans, between *Reichsdeutschen* from Germany proper and *Auslandsdeutschen*, Germans born abroad, refugees or expatriates moved to emigrate by economics, conscience or *Wanderlust*? The governments of Latin America often joined the posse so that privileged locals could take possession of internees' property. Nobody—not the Nazi–hunters in the U.S., much less the Latin Americans—sought to distinguish supporters of the Nazis—who might conceivably have engaged in espionage or terrorism on behalf of the *Reich*—from refugees who had abandoned Germany because they opposed Hitler or had already suffered at the hands of his henchmen.

Typical of the many ambiguities of citizenship and nationality, and the irrelevance of one's support for, or opposition to, the *Reich*, was the instance of Paul Häusle, the first to fall before the hail of bullets at Cotito. He was an orphaned German national, born and raised in neutral Switzerland. He had come to Panama as a religious pacifist, only to be accused *posthumously* of Nazi terrorism. He was

---

[*] Switzerland and Sweden, respectively.

killed by a local Panamanian policeman who probably had only a vague notion of his alleged misdeeds and probably had no idea whether he was a German citizen or a Swiss, a Hottentot or an Eskimo.

And in Panama, the contemptible, uninformed, sensationalist daily press—so formative of the national psyche in that era before television (not that the television news of the present day is much better), that era when, as now, each newspaper was merely the propaganda organ of the family or faction that controlled it—was only too eager to indulge in its usual folly, to feed the madness, rushing to publish whatever nonsense of the moment, whatever falsehoods and justifications for murder, were fed to it.

This was the Panama of 1941. Folly everywhere, often descending into madness.

| HOW THIS EDITION CAME TO BE

THIS EDITION BEGAN as a simple translation project, but it became much more than that for me, and—invoking the privilege of the self–published, subject to no editorial constraints but my own—I will try the reader's patience by relating how the Cotito story came to have a grip on me.

I first came to Panama in 1964, a sincere, well-intentioned, but naïve and ineffectual, volunteer in the U.S. Peace Corps, then in its infancy. When we arrived, the word *¡Volveremos!* ("We shall return!") was painted everywhere on the asphalt of streets and highways, but what did we benighted volunteers know or care about the *Arnulfistas,* whose hero Arnulfo Arias had just lost the 1964 election to Marco Aurelio Robles? The losers revived a slogan they had first adopted when Arnulfo was deposed (for the second time) in 1951. There was history in those graffiti, but we were "above" politics, ignorant, and oblivious to reality.

In that era, Panama City had not yet become the perpetual traffic–jam it is today, freeways—deteriorating before they open and immediately choked beyond their capacity when they do—snaking around half–empty, high–rise apartment buildings thrown up by speculators and money–launderers. The condos had not yet cut the city off from the bay. Idlers in the open-air cafés on Avenida Balboa could still see President Robles's little caravan of three matching blue Fords tearing along the *malecón* (perhaps on pressing affairs of state, or perhaps carrying *El Rifle* to a nooner or a *cinq-à-sept*). Back then, Bellavista was the most relaxed—though by no means the most colorful—part of town.

Parque Urraca was a shaded refuge from the relentless tropical heat and from the traffic of those days. Buses (local fare: 5¢) of every vintage, size and shape, color-coded by route (blue and gray with a red stripe to Río Abajo, yellow and white with a black stripe to Colón, gray with a red stripe to Alcalde Díaz) filled the crowded streets. The drivers, who paid a daily rental for the buses and lived on what was left over, jockeyed and honked as they competed at every stop for passengers and their nickels. *Chivas* and *gallineras*, buses and tiny Hillman Minx taxis (fare: 35¢) outnumbered private cars on Avenida Central and its Vía España extension. The infamous "Red Devils" were everywhere, but had not yet become the daily indignity suffered by commuters who would do anything to avoid them, anything to get some kind of jalopy on the ever more-congested streets.* New car imports were not yet the geometrically exploding plague of today.

---

* *Chivas* ("nanny goats") was a generic slang name for all sorts of little buses, station wagons and vans that served the suburbs of the capital and the towns and villages of the interior. The traditional *chiva*: a wooden body with facing benches along its length, built onto a low-slung, 1930's-era truck chassis, was specifically called a *gallinera* (chicken coop). Only a handful of them could still be seen in Panama City after 1960. The *Diablos Rojos*, "Red Devils," were the retired, worn-out Thomas school buses from the U.S., repainted red and fantastically decorated with painted scenes, slogans, tassels, deedly balls and colored lights. They were the principal means of public transportation for decades, overcrowded, ill maintained, and driven recklessly over streets full of potholes, cooled only by the air that manages to get through the small windows designed to keep kindergartners from falling out. When the inevitable downpours arrived, up would go the windows, and the heat would be stifling. After a few years of mistreatment on the streets of Panama City, the *Diablos* have a distressing tendency to lose their rear axle assemblies in traffic. Now being phased out in the capital, many of the retired wrecks are reappearing in the towns of the interior.

When the Canal was built, Panama City had been a small town of fewer than forty thousand inhabitants, but by the early nineteen-sixties, it had become home to half-a-million; in 1964, the population of the entire Republic had just inched past a million, having doubled in the sixty years since independence. (It would double again in the next thirty years, and nearly double again in the following twenty.) The middle- and upper-class slivers of the population, even a smaller fraction of the whole than they are today, still lived in modest two-story villas on Bellavista's shady streets, but were beginning to move on, abandoning it bit by bit to the dentists' and lawyers' offices and fly-by-night universities. There was even a quiet bookstore on the corner of 35th and Perú. The Cine Bellavista, later an evangelical church and then a bridal shop, showed the latest James Bond extravaganzas. When the President came in, they would stop the film, and you had to stand up. The peddlers in the tumultuous market street of *Salsipuedes* did a thriving business a little further downtown, but after January 9, some bars barred Gringos.

The health and finance ministries stood proud in their spanking new white towers (still a novelty) beside the stately turn-of-the-century elegance of the Ministry of Foreign Relations and the Spanish embassy, which amiably faced each other off across Parque Porras. Near the equally proud tower of the National Lottery stood the traditional small, white office of the state prosecutor—then as now, modest and dignified on the outside, a politicized mess on the inside—surrounded by its garden, on Avenida Perú. The Hotel Continental and the Hilton, winner of architectural prizes when built in 1956, with its Wurlitzer in the bar, were what passed for glitz in those days. Moneyed refugees from the Cuban revolution of 1959 ordered a *mentirita* ("a little lie") instead of a *Cuba libre* because Cuba was no longer *libre*. Visitors on a budget stayed in the small, spare hotels in Bellavista and Calidonia, often run by Spaniards or Arab immigrants.

But that was then. The Republic was only sixty years old, the Canal only fifty (and I was only twenty). Piled atop the turbulent history of the nineteen-thirties, -forties and -fifties, the civil disorders of January, 1964, were still a fresh wound. The boulevard separating *la Zona* from Panama City proper had always been called *Avenida 4 de Julio*. It became, for a few months after November 22, 1963, *Avenida Presidente Kennedy*. Then, before even a year had passed, came the political riots of January 9, 1964, and thenceforth it would be known as *Avenida de los Mártires,* honoring the twenty-four Panamanians who died between the 9th and the 13th. Panama would yet have to endure another thirty-five years of the sempiternal conflict over the existence of the U.S. Canal Zone.

Starting in 1968, when Arnulfo Arias was ousted in a coup for the third time, the country "without an army" began twenty-one years of military dictatorship, followed in 1989 by a U.S. invasion. Then came the nineteen-nineties, ten years of moderately competent civilian government under two presidents neither of whom did much to restrain—who rather joined—the kleptocrats who had profited from the dictatorship. The civilian presidents did restore some semblance of civil liberties, but only within the enduring limitations imposed by the grinding, clanking incompetence of the criminal justice apparatus and the preposterous libel and defamation laws.*

IN THE MID-nineteen-nineties, I was back, again living in Panama. Airline schedules still made it impossible to get from the U.S. to the little farm in Chiriquí I had bought in 1993, imposing an overnight stay in a city I would rather have breezed through in a blur *en route* to paradise, defined as the Chiriquí highlands where the events in this book took place. Bellavista by then had declined into dowdiness, but I still loved it: the brash, new parts of the city—pale imitations of Miami without the beach or the glitter—held little attraction.

---

* Even today, three-quarters of prisoners in jail have never been formally tried or definitively sentenced by a judge, and never will be; eventually they will be released on a *habeas corpus,* having served the "max" to which they might have been sentenced had they actually been convicted and sentenced. The Supreme Court wallows in confusion and corruption. In the meantime, the criminal defamation suits filed by politicians against each other—each championing his "honor" where but little exists, freezing each other's assets and persecuting the press—remain the biggest waste of time in the judicial system. Truth is no defense.

One morning in 1997 or 1998, having just arrived from the U.S., I was sitting at the lunch counter of the Veracruz, one of the small hotels remaining on Avenida Perú, between Bellavista and Calidonia. There I was with a dish of chilled papaya and a *tortilla de huevo* for breakfast, drinking superb coffee from a real *espresso* machine, my nose in a book. Panama is not a country of readers, let alone publishers. Even the airport lacks a bookstore last I checked; although there are two medium-sized ones in the capital nowadays, they have limited selections. The modest one I remember on Calle 35 and Avenida Perú has long since vanished. Drug and department stores sell a few books, but their shelf space is mostly devoted to the second-rate, locally written textbooks the Ministry of Education imposes on those few students whose parents can afford to buy them, along with the Argentine, Brazilian, Colombian and Mexican novels of the day, and the usual translations of Jacqueline Suzanne, Deepak Chopra and *Caldo de gallina para el alma*. Public lending libraries are rarely encountered and seldom survive more than a year or two.

The cover of the book I was reading at the lunch counter.

Only thanks to a friend had I encountered an out-of-print gem—deeply flawed, but a jewel nonetheless—an odd little book whose title translates as *Holocaust in Panama*,[5] by Aristides Iván Hassán R.,* (as I learned later) a retired colonel who had served

---

* After the military *coup d'état* (in Spanish, *golpe de estado*) of October 11, 1968, coup leader Boris Martínez abandoned the attempt to co-opt civil-

Continued→

briefly as the figurehead *comandante* of the National Guard. Its subject was the supposed 1941 massacre of two agricultural colonies in the then nearly trackless highland forests of Chiriquí: one at Cotito, between El Hato del Volcán (as it was then known) and the Costa Rican border; and another, this one supposedly Jewish, at Sierra de Palo Alto, near Boquete, on the opposite slope of the Volcán Barú. I suppose that *if* such a Jewish colony had ever existed, it might have been called a *kibbutz*.

The dubious use in the title of *Holocaust*, a term so often and so loosely tossed about; the lurid cover with its childish graphics—a crudely drawn Nazi standard hoist o'er Chiriquí, with the swastika backwards; a human skull suspended somehow on or near the flagpole; and a Star of David ominously floating vaguely over the Caribbean somewhere north of the Darién—gave the cheap little volume the appearance of another nutty propaganda pamphlet. It was indifferently edited, badly printed (in neighboring Colombia) on the cheapest of paper, and the blurry photographs crudely reproduced seemed to have been taken from the far end of a dark tunnel. With its breathless, detailed transcriptions—lacking any credible attribution[*]—of satanic rites conducted in the basement of President Arnul-

---

← *Continued from prev. page.*
ians into his revolutionary government, and opted for direct military control under a two–"member" (the term a source of endless hilarity) military *junta*. Martínez perceived Lt. Col. Hassán, a former deputy chief of the traffic bureau, as a non-entity willing to serve as the *junta*'s titular commander of the armed forces. Ostensibly on the basis of seniority, Martínez named Hassán *comandante* of the *Guardia Nacional,* retaining the real authority for himself as head of the General Staff (*Estado Mayor*). A couple of months later, in December, 1968, the once–unknown Omar Torrijos Herrera consolidated his power as military dictator of Panama. Torrijos named himself to succeed Hassán as *comandante*, Hassán was retired, and Martínez, original leader of the coup, soon got the boot. R. M. Koster and Guillermo Sánchez Borbón, *In the Time of the Tyrants* (1990), pp. 74, 76.

[*] Buried in Hassán's Appendix to Part 7 (p. 237, n. 6) is a particularly odd attribution: "All the information obtained in [*sic*, not "for"] this book, down to the smallest detail—on the mysterious police detachment, its members, its instructions, their oath of initiation, their nightmare graduation in the basement of Dr. Arias's house, the murders committed—was confessed to us by Mr. Julio César González." Alas, if *Don* Julio César existed, he was delu-

Continued→

fo Arias's private home, *Holocausto en Panamá* made for a great "read," not because it was so good, but because it was so dreadful, a bizarre curiosity rather than a source of illumination. The meager text was padded out to more than 260 pages by the use of widely leaded twelve–point type, double–spaces separating the short, deeply indented paragraphs. There were full-page photographs of nothing in particular and largely irrelevant photocopied documents. Purportedly a work of history, it contained page after page of invented dialogue, supposititious conversations that could never have taken place. Even if such conversations had been overheard by Hassán or any reliable informant, few of them would have been worth reporting in a book published forty years later.

Even Hassán's smug report of his first, ghastly exhumation of the common grave at Cotito on October 31, 1980, and his grisly photographs of the jumbled teeth and bones of known individuals, still hold a certain morbid fascination. Both that exhumation and another he staged for CNN in 1984, as part of that year's bizarre presidential election campaign, were utterly pointless, because for forty years, ever since 1941, the precise names of the individuals buried there, and the nature of their demise, had been known and recorded in the official records of three countries.

Without knowing a word of either German or French or the elements of geography, Hassán attempts to introduce his Spanish readers to the niceties of European discourse. Sometimes his "explanations" are hilarious. "Magderburgo *[sic]*,...East Prussia and Upper Silesia," he relates, are among the *cities* of Germany. Silly details receive much attention: the Panamanian consulate in Hamburg

---

← *Continued from prev. page.*
sional. Hassán also names (in a photo caption, p. 56), another gentleman— one Manuel Antonio Serracín, "*cédula* 4–AV–78–721 born April 21, 1901"— as the source for the existence of a German–Jewish colony at Palo Alto. Serracín is reported by Hassán to have met Arnulfo Arias in 1940, and to have become the caretaker for one of Arias's Chiriquí properties. Serracín would have been in his early 80's at the time Hassán was conducting his "research"; the particular crimes Hassán alleges González and Serracín "revealed" never were committed.

was in the basement of the "Hamburgo–America Line" on the "calle Hermann," a helpful parenthesis indicating that this is Hassán's rendition of the German "(Hermann Strasser [sic])." The Panamanian embassy in Berlin was located on the "Kurt Fusten Dan, which in German means [per Hassán] "Prince Kurt Avenue." In fact the main boulevard of Berlin is the *Kurfürstendamm,* which follows the route of the *Damm,* the causeway that centuries ago traversed the swamp on which Berlin is built, and was named for the *Kurfürsten* ("Prince-Electors") of Brandenburg.[6]

A typical, full page (such as this example, in literal English translation from Hassán's Spanish) is devoted to fluff worthy of a C– high school term paper:

> It was a cold afternoon on Oct. 23, 1939, a harbinger of the beginning of winter in Paris. A young man on a bicycle rides through the streets, whistling the melody of a popular Maurice Chevalier (a popular melody) song [repetition and misidentification *sic*] to amuse himself during the tedious daily routine of delivering *"los [sic] te-légrammes [sic]* (cables)" of *"le bureau de poste* (Post Office)." Looking at the address indicated, he sees the building number dix (10). He parks and runs to pull the chain at the door to announce his arrival with the enthusiasm appropriate to his youth.
>
> "*Pour [sic] Dieu…*(*Por Dios*)." There is an exclamation from inside in a female voice denoting a certain age.
>
> "Gar[ç]on (Muchacho)," says the woman, "you will break my eardrums." The boy limits himself to a malicious grin; this is a game he is used to playing as a reward for the daily pedaling of his bicycle. He gives her the usual receipt so that she can acknowledge receipt of the envelope containing the "telégramme *[sic]*." She with an unpleasant expression on her face, says:
>
> "Merci, Demon *[sic]* (Gracias, Demonio)"…[7]

What this meretricious passage contributes toward establishing responsibility for the real massacre of Swiss pacifists at Cotito or substantiating a supposed massacre of Jews at Boquete remains unclear, but so it goes for pages: the maid takes the telegram to an official. The official opens it. He summons an assistant, whose father once owned a famous jewelry store in Panama. ... ¡Et cétera, et cétera, et cétera!

Such literary rubbish would be harmless enough *if* this polemical and tendentious book did not advance a maliciously concocted tale of two massacres, one entirely fictitious. In a direct quotation, completely fabricated by Hassán, President Arias tells his homicidal henchmen he has received, through German "Ambassador" Hans von Winter,

> an autograph letter from our spiritual guide, Adolf Hitler, in which he recommends that I proceed according to my own best judgment with the plan for the elimination of the two Jewish groups in Chiriquí; he asks that we take all necessary security measures so that nobody, absolutely nobody, suspects this operation. He makes reference to the United States security services in Panama.[8]

In other words, President Arnulfo Arias Madrid, a Nazi obeying direct instructions from the *Führer*, ordered the dual massacre of Jews at Palo Alto and Cotito, but the settlers at Cotito were Swiss immigrants mistaken for Jews and murdered by mistake, so exactly which Jews Arias was planning to annihilate remains a mystery.

Hassán writes that earlier, in 1922, two settlements—each composed of twenty-five German families, limited by the Panamanian government to Roman Catholics—had been established, one at Capira, near Panama City; and the other at La Elvira, in the neighborhood of Boquete, Chiriquí.[9] Before long, a dire secret emerged:

> [D]uring the course of the development of the [La Elvira] settlement [near Boquete], a difference of faith was detected among a large number of the 25 families, which was not the credo established as a condition for entry into our country. But the malicious intention to denounce them did not exist among the group, as they were companions who shared their fate, and offered each other mutual protection."[10]

Hassán says that by 1926, however, the settlements at both Capira, in Central Panama, and La Elvira, in Chiriquí, had collapsed. A few of the families who had settled at La Elvira—hidden members of that accursèd race without a homeland—decided to relocate to two new settlements, one nearby at Palo Alto, not far from Boquete, and another at Cotito, near Volcán. Of course, (like all Jews?) they kept to themselves:

> With respect to the relations [of those who relocated] with the rest of the neighbors, they were minimal; they remained distant in order to conceal their real problem: their Creed. At that time, their religion was the motive for rejection everywhere on the planet; they were outcast,* they received the same treatment as Gypsies, and even worse; because in the history of the Christian world they bore the sin of having been the people who denounced the son of God. (Our country, especially [says Hassán], conserves the religious education inherited from colonial times, this belief deeply rooted in the interior of the country.)
>
> We know also that all the members [of this people] had been on a long pilgrimage because they had no homeland, leaving behind them, in the course of time, insults and opprobrium that made their road to the vindication of their destiny more difficult. Of the millions that they numbered around the world, not all were so solvent as some businessmen of our region; there were among them in their scattered society those from every stratum of society, the class of the poor being of interest to us here.[11]

Ominously, Hassán warns that—

> [d]uring those years of peace, tranquility and work, they did not imagine how a strange movement, a phenome-

---

* *"estaban a la zaga"*

non originating in Germany, its place of origin [redundancy *sic*], was blossoming among human nature, the product of a post-war that established in a false Messiah a shadowy future for humanity and for some of whose disciples an end in our Province of Chiriquí.[12]

Incomprehensible nonsense, for if the "false Messiah" was Hitler, these mysterious "disciples" of the *Führer* who would come to "an end in our Province of Chiriquí" would have to have been the Jews at Palo Alto and the Swiss settlers at Cotito, but neither of these could have been described as disciples of Hitler's. If the disciples were some Nazi sympathizers in Panama, according to Hassán himself these never came to their end in Chiriquí. By page 193, the German–Jewish settlers who had relocated to Cotito in 1926 are not Jews but Swiss emigrants who had arrived in 1939, murdered in 1941 on Schmieder's farm "by mistake,"[13] having been confused with another Jewish colony somewhere else, perhaps at Piedra Candela. What happened to the hidden Jews who sneaked into the country in 1922 and relocated to Cotito in 1926 is never explained.

The first attack, which Hassán says was intended to exterminate "the real" Jewish colony at Palo Alto, was supposedly a bloodbath complete with women and girls "raped like bitches," murder and mayhem. Narrated as eyewitness history, with bodies flying through the air, Nazi-oid Panamanians spitting on Jewish cadavers and growling (Hassán's mangled version of) German expletives, it contains cross–references to non–existent photos of a mass grave near Boquete, the photos non-existent because the grave never existed.[14] The putative culprits: the German ambassador himself, the Guatemalan imported by Arias as commander of the police, and several "German" sympathizers of the Nazis, including Josef Niederberger (who was in fact Swiss), Frank Tedman (in reality a Canadian from Boquete) and Luis Hartmann, (a Moravian Czech from Santa Clara and a good friend of the Swiss), the latter three somewhat—but only somewhat—squeamish about the police excesses they witnessed.

This chapter, the heart of the book, is utterly without attribution, either in the text or in Hassán's hodgepodge of an Appendix, which contains many vague attributions and a random collection of photocopied archival documents, fragmentary and largely irrelevant,* but completely lacks references for Part 9, the tale of a massacre of Jews at Palo Alto. The appendices to "Parts 10 and 11," which chronicle—with breathless, blow–by–blow narration and what is claimed to be verbatim dialogue—the second attack, the massacre of the colony at Cotito, cite completely irrelevant documents.[15]

The whole story is incoherent fantasy.[16] All this slaughter ordered by Arias in response to a hand–written, 1941 *Führerbefehl* from the man famous for never putting anything in writing? The Germans had rolled into Austria in April, 1938; the conflagration of the *Kristallnacht* had occurred on November 9 (just two months before the real *Suizos* of Cotito set sail from Genoa for Panama). The Germans had seized Czechoslovakia on March 15, 1939, and invaded Poland in September. Eight months after the invasion of Poland, in May, 1940, the *Reichswehr* had begun blitzing its way across Western Europe. In the Germany of 1941, the infamous Nuremberg decrees of 1935 were already history. Concentration camps were a reality across Germany and the conquered territories; experiments in mass extermination were already underway. On June 22, 1941 *(precisely fifteen days before the real massacre at Cotito),* Hitler had hurled 4.5 million German troops into what was ultimately a suicidal invasion of the Soviet Union.

Could any rational reader believe that Hitler—so occupied with a two–front war and the real, systematic extermination of millions of Jews, Gypsies, Jehovah's Witnesses and political enemies—chose

---

* Six–and–a–half pages, 239–46, are devoted to facsimiles of a tedious 1977–78 exchange, thirty years after the massacre(s), between Panamanian officials and a punctilious German diplomat named Karl Spittler, who was hoping to locate a copy of the Panamanian declaration of war against Germany, and information on the internment of German citizens during the conflict. The German historian's interest in "the fate of the Germans" was genuine, but the Panamanian responses reproduced at such length by Hassán were of no more value, in 1978, than they had been in the days of the Mixed Commission of 1941, and were irrelevant to the tale of Hassán's "holocaust." But Hassán was a military author: when in doubt, append as many c.y.a. photocopies as you can find, secure in the knowledge that no one will read them!

two tiny, obscure, Jewish agricultural communes (which never existed) in the mountains of Chiriquí as a testing ground for his plan to annihilate the Jews of Europe? Or perhaps this was the forerunner of a plan for all the Jews of Latin America? It would be—if the subject were not so grim—an equally hilarious notion to assert that Hitler might have relied on a *mestizo*, a *Mischling* like Arnulfo Arias, to implement his ethnic cleansing of the Western Hemisphere.

I knew from the fragmentary oral accounts often to be heard in Volcán that some kind of mass killing had indeed occurred at Cotito on the eve of World War II, but Hassan's explanations for that shooting seemed nonsensical, and the tale of an earlier "holocaust" near Boquete was a new one on me. It seemed unlikely, as I read this weird book, that Jews from Germany would have set up a kibbutz at Palo Alto without anybody's—even the Panamanian Jewish community's—have remembered it; anybody, that is, except for Hassan's alleged *campesino* informant, elderly, perhaps confused, and without a doubt misinformed. That there were a few families of Sephardic origin in the coffee business in the area—the Sittóns and the Duráns the best known—is a matter of record, but a *massacred German–Jewish agricultural colony* no one else remembers?

It was apparent, as I sat at the lunch counter, that the true author of Hassan's book must have been either one of that infinite number of monkeys with their infinite number of typewriters *en route* to Shakespeare's sonnets, or a lunatic obsessed with Jews to the point of gibbering madness, but what the true story was, I continued to wonder.

AS I SAT READING, there occurred one of those coincidences that make even a rationalist like me suspect a whimsical Providence pokes a meddlesome finger into our quotidian affairs. A few seats to my right at the otherwise–empty counter were three middle–aged people of indeterminate nationality. They were speaking English and sounded as if they might have been from the States, but there was something vaguely European rather than American or Latin American about their accents; they were discussing an impending visit to family in Chiriquí, so perhaps they were Panamanians who had emigrated to the States. My eavesdropper's curiosity must have been obvious, and they seemed to be taking a furtive interest in my reading-matter.

Then, one of the two gentlemen, by way of initiating a friendly conversation, asked me what book I was reading. Of course, I launched into one of my lamentable displays of pedantry, but this time I would get my comeuppance. Patiently and, I am sure, condescendingly, I explained that it was a very interesting, but obviously not very reliable, book about the murder of some Swiss farmers in Chiriquí fifty years previously, that I had lived in the area for a few years and was very interested in learning more about it.

COURTESY YVONNE WORRELL POVER
Walter Morf in the care of the nuns after the massacre, 1941; detail from group picture (p. 162, *infra*).

Smiling enigmatically, the gentleman said he knew the book, as well as something about the incident at Cotito. He suggested I take a look at one of the photographs in it. Mystified, I complied. A barely-legible caption identified young Albert Schmieder, one of the few survivors of the Cotito massacre.

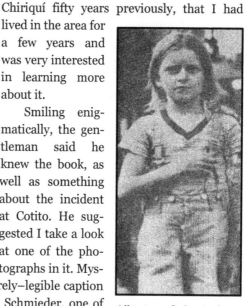

Albert Schmieder, (known as "Benni" in childhood) as he was pictured in *Holocausto en Panamá*. Detail from a group picture in *Panamá-América*, July 14, 1941.

"This is my wife Elvi, and this is Albert Schmieder," said the gentleman in the coffee shop—who, it turned out, was Walter Morf—"We all live in the States, but we are heading out to visit our family and our friends in Volcán and Santa Clara."

¡*Plap!* is the sound of *Condorito*, the wise-guy, comic-strip condor in flip-flop sandals, as he hits the floor, bowled over by some stunning punch-line revelation in the final frame of every episode. I was dumbfounded, and, as might be imagined, the conversation that followed was animated, but in the end, the story was too long and complex to tell there at the lunch counter. Albert Schmieder and Walter Morf, who had between them lost parents and siblings in the massacre, had long before given up trying to explain the complex truth to casual acquaintances.

Walter and Elvi Morf and Albert Schmieder visited me on my little farm outside Volcán a few days later. The Panamanian lawyer who had lent me the Hassán book was also visiting in Volcán, and we all had some lively conversations about the Cotito massacre. Albert and Walter could confirm that the *Suizos* were anything but Jews, that they followed rather the teachings of the Christian mystic Father Divine, but our brief conversation was not a formal interview. Left unanswered were many questions about how the *Suizos* had come to Chiriquí, how they were related to all the Panamanian families with German surnames still living in this area, and what had actually happened in 1941. Walter was of Swiss extraction, but had been born in the States. Albert was of German extraction, not Swiss, but was born in Panama. It was all so complex. When my lawyer friend left for Panama City, I returned her copy of the Hassán book.

PHOTO BY THE EDITOR

Albert Schmieder on a visit to the site of the colony, 2013.

The years passed and I lost track of the Morfs and Albert Schmieder. One of them had jotted down (on a scrap of my notepaper left over from my days in the New York State Attorney General's office) the title of a German book, *Die*

Brücke am Chiriquí Viejo ["The Bridge on the Chiriquí Viejo"] by Trudi Häusle Worrell,[17] but in those pre–Internet, pre–Amazon days I never tracked it down. I always meant to ask Helmut Hils—from whom I bought my gasoline in Volcán, and who at the time of the massacre had been a 16–year–old, German–speaking neighbor—about "Cotito," but he passed away recently and by the time my interest in Cotito was renewed, it was too late to talk to him. I never pressed my lawyer friend about her presence, in the course of the bizarre election campaign of 1984, at the second, pointless exhumation of bones from the grave at Cotito. I remained uninformed and confused about the incident.

And then, nearly fifteen years later, in 2010, Iván Flores, publisher of the little *Chiriquí Libre* monthly, showed me the dog–eared photocopy of another out–of–print book he had dug up somewhere. It was a recounting of the Cotito story by Dr. Carlos H. Cuestas Gómez, a Panamanian lawyer–historian, a native of Chiriquí and grandson of the first prosecutor in the Cotito case. Dr. Cuestas had exhaustively studied the legal aftermath of the episode. Iván Flores (and his collaborator David Dell) had used his book as the source for an article in their *Chiriquí Libre* newspaper. I borrowed the dog–eared photocopy of *Cotito: Crónica de un crimen olvidado* from Iván, and I fear I still have not returned it!

I READ IT THROUGH twice, fascinated by what was obviously a reliable account—as far as it went— of the 1941 massacre at Cotito, and equally fascinated by the author's virtual annihilation of the *Holocausto* book I had read fifteen years earlier. Here in *Cotito* were the answers to virtually all my questions. A massacre had indeed been perpetrated, but the victims were Swiss–German agricultural colonists and their German host. The enigmatic Christian religious fanatics and somewhat confused young people were not Jews, but rather long–distance followers of the African–American cult figure George Baker, alias "Father Divine." With their long beards and tire–tread sandals, laboriously hacking their communal, agrarian, vegetarian, terrestrial paradise out of the humid tropical forest, they would indeed suffer a very real tragedy, unrelated to any so–called holocaust, for reasons unconnected in any way with Judaism or Jewry.*

Cotito reveals that Hassán's version, an irresponsible attack on Arnulfo Arias, did not even approximate the truth (although the book was republished in English in 1987)[†] but the crude hoax Hassán and his military sponsors perpetrated in 1982–84 had an enduring, long–term effect, as is related in Chapter VI of the book now in the reader's hands.

Reading for the second time the photocopy of *Cotito,* it struck me that for the English–speaking immigrants[‡] now so numerous in the Chiriquí highlands—who have always been so numerous throughout Panama—who know so little, and in many cases seem to care so little about the history of this country and its traditions, it could be of much interest. For them it might be enlightening, a window into what Chiriquí was like before the forests were denuded and the four–lane roads were built and the gated communities and half–built *aparthotels* had turned much of the once–lovely town of Boquete, now full of hamburger joints and package–forwarding offices to accommodate the foreigners, into an exurban sprawl cloven by a figurative cultural fence dividing locals from immigrants. Hassán's fabrications had been translated into English, but *Cotito,* a true account of real events, existed only in Spanish. I decided to do the translation.

The original *Cotito* is not a lengthy book—a hundred-fifty pages or so, like *Holocaust in Panamá* set in large type with short, widely spaced paragraphs; in translation, with the addition of fifty illustrations, lengthy footnotes and an index, it runs to something over two hundred, to which I prefaced this Foreword.)

---

* *Judaism,* the Jewish religion; *Jewry,* the Jewish people.

† Ironically this attack on Arnulfo Arias was printed on the presses of the [Harmodio] Arias family's own publishing company, then in the hands of the military dictatorship. The Ariases would not recover their publishing company until the restoration of elected government in 1989.

‡ The immigrants who have a few bucks, or wish they had, prefer to be known as "ex–pats" in the tradition of the British *raj.*

I admit to a few doubts about the content. It may not be a soaring work of high literature; if it were, it would have deserved a better translator. Dr. Cuestas did not have the opportunity to review additional records, largely in German with a few in French, either to be found in Swiss government archives at Bern or available from the families of the colonists. Convinced as I was that *Cotito* deserved a wider audience, I also believed it was a bare–bones story, a reliable armature on which to round out a three–dimensional figure, and I believed there was more to be said.

For one thing, although Dr. Cuestas's *Cotito* was a meticulous recounting of the judicial and diplomatic records available in Panama, the recounting in Chapter IV of the protracted judicial proceedings might be of interest only to legal buffs, excessively detailed for the general reader, not least because in the end the interminable proceedings came to naught. *Cotito* relates but little of the character of the *Suizos,* their individual personalities, their motivations or the nature of their devotion to their cult.

It definitely relied too heavily on the muddled recollections of one of the survivors: the man born Werner Robert Müller, known in later life as Roberto Miller, a somewhat unreliable witness, though the only survivor available to Dr. Cuestas at the time. More significantly, *Cotito* did not address rumors about child abuse and the likely causes of three separate infant deaths in the colony.

For Dr. Cuestas's Panamanian audience, the complex story of the rise and fall—and rise and fall and rise and fall—of Arnulfo Arias, and his involvement—or not!—in the massacre, might not have required much explanation, but the account in *Cotito* is a little cryptic for a foreign readership. The full story of the U.S.–driven campaign against German emigrants to Latin America on the eve of the world war would not be told until 2003. The connection between that campaign and the pressure cooker of Panamanian politics in 1941 had not yet been fully recognized.

I also questioned the Author's acceptance in Chapter VI of assumptions about what might have been Hassán's, or his military patrons', motivation for publishing *Holocausto en Panamá,* although in retrospect, I recognize that it was the military, not the historian, who clung to delusional theories based on archaic stereotypes, and that the historian merely sought to explain their obsession.

Whatever its minor failings, however, *Cotito* was the painstaking and evenhanded exposition of a catastrophe that might easily have been forgotten. It is implicitly a plea for toleration, due process, guarantees of liberty in matters of conscience and a warning about the dangers inherent in allowing the exercise of naked force by a reckless, ill–trained police force free from the constraints that an irresponsible bureaucracy and a feeble, disorganized judiciary, have so often failed to impose.*

Obtaining the Author's permission and completing the translation were relatively easy. A phone call to the Supreme Court switchboard put me in touch with Dr. Cuestas, the high court's secretary–general, and his response was something in the nature of "You want to translate my book and publish it in English? Be my guest!"

A LITTLE MORE DIFFICULT than obtaining permission and completing the direct translation of a short book was following up on the many leads to additional information that emerged in this age of Internet research, the instantaneous transmission of scanned documents, cheap international phone calls, and courier services that substitute for the pitiful Panamanian postal service. That is the reason why this extensive Foreword, and the many insertions, footnotes and endnotes in the translation itself, appear to me to be justified.

Years later, I encountered the question Dr. Cuestas had put in a letter to Walter Morf: "Do you think *Cotito* is really a good book? Do you think it could be translated and published for American readers?"[18] That translation has now been published.

---

* Readers entirely unfamiliar with the story of the Cotito massacre might wish at this point to turn to Chapter I, returning to the Foreword later for additional background on the political context of the massacre, the individuals involved, and further consideration of the many questions raised. The Foreword will perhaps be more easily followed by the reader who has some familiarity with the events.

THERE IS—IN ADDITION to the unanswerable question of whether Arnulfo Arias directly ordered the 1941 massacre, thoroughly explored in *Cotito*—another that must remain unanswered forever. Living with "Cotito" during the translation and editing of this book, I come back to it always: *even if the tragic shooting had never occurred, would the colony have survived for very long anyway?* Leaving aside the spiritual or religious aspirations of the settlers, their varying degrees of devotion to the strange and still shadowy Lehner, in guessing what the real life expectancy of the colony might have been, one must also consider the sheer magnitude of the task the colonists had undertaken in such innocence.

The farm the Schmieders had built, and on which the Swiss took refuge—often described as "prosperous"—was an expanse of banana orchards, requiring little care once planted, and extensive pastureland laboriously cleared by slash and burn techniques. Maintaining such pastureland in Chiriquí, where the weeds are better suited to the subtropical climate than the grasses planted for fodder, then required constant mowing with machetes, a tedious, back-breaking, never–ending task. There were also a few tiny, rough-hewn, unpainted, wooden buildings whose windows had lace curtains but no glass. Schmieder and his wife could indeed produce beef, cheese, butter, honey, bananas, a few fruits and vegetables, but it was a four-hour horseback ride to El Hato, the "nearest" hamlet, and local markets were practically non–existent. Despite the few cents to be made on each quarter of a kilo of cheese sold, the few and distant neighbors had their own bananas and chickens, thank you. Some traders might buy cattle in the highlands and ship it to Panama City along the coast by boat from Pedregal, the Chiriquí port of embarkation, a three– or four–day voyage, following a trail–drive and truck haul of thirty-five or forty miles over forest trails and hideous roads.

Despite romantic descriptions to the contrary, neither the German settlers nor the Swiss colonists who arrived a decade later were, in the main, sturdy yeomen or hardy pioneers by nature. Their ancestors had cleared the dense primeval forests from the verdant pastures of their European homelands centuries before they were born.

Karl Schmieder, the German settler who sheltered the Swiss after they abandoned their initial effort at Piedra de Candela, had toiled for a decade in Panama at hacking—literally—a farm out of the wilderness, but in Germany, Schmieder had been a bookkeeper in a pottery factory. The Swiss Heinrich Ott was a carpenter by trade, but he was advanced in years. Morf was a hotelier who had suffered injuries that affected his mental faculties. Gottfried Werren was past 60. Sophie Müller was unpredictable and according to most reports, unreliable.

Of the twenty-three members of the colony, there were, in addition to Karl Schmieder, only three young men (Paul Häusle, Helmut Brauchle and Werner Müller) and four young women (Friedy Morf, Cornelia and Klärli Werren, and Trudi Häusle) to whom the bulk of the heavy labor fell, and one of them was pregnant during most of the brief life of the colony. Six of the colonists (Albert Jr., Walter and Loni Morf; "Böps" Müller; Karl Jr. and "Benni" Schmieder) were children, the younger ones good perhaps for carrying captured possums across the river and releasing them, but too small to wield a machete for hours on end. And yet initially, this group had intended to clear, plant and farm five hundred hectares of land at Candela, yet another four hours' march from Cotito, which was already—as Albert Morf wrote to his mother in 1938—"at the end of the world."[19]

Little—in fact virtually nothing—is known of Karl Lehner's history[*] before he became the leader of a devoted sect, but he was older and appears to have been genuinely insane. His theories were at best eccentric, and there exists compelling evidence that he engaged in child abuse and infanticide. Lehner labored alongside the others, but he also filled their heads with arrant, inconsistent nonsense. For example, once the settlers surrendered to Schmieder's care, they also produced chicken and beef, though they would eat no meat; and

---

[*] Viola Wehrli would tell her daughter Erica in later years that she believed Lehner had caused the deaths of his previous family, and was directly responsible for the death of the infant Virgilio, who disappeared just before the colonists' departure from Switzerland. Ed.'s intv. with Erica Witzig–Fassler, Volcán, Feb. 2015.

cheese and honey for sale, all the while refusing, supposedly, to engage in trade.

Once the money brought from Europe had run out, even essential cash purchases—of tools, clothing, flour (no wheat is grown in Panama), even barbed wire and fencing staples, kerosene or cooking oil—could pose a nearly insurmountable obstacle to achieving even a modicum of comfort. Isolation favors contemplation, but not the education of one's children, especially when the author of just about the only books available for home schooling was Father Divine. It is not hard to understand Margarethe Schmieder's skepticism or Gustav Haug's early and bitter disillusionment.

Could these naïve idealists have had any idea of what was involved in felling a single tree ten feet in diameter with axes and sweat? As peaceful as the forest was, during the settlers' efforts at Candela in the first year, only hunting and gathering were available to them for obtaining food, and they would kill no animal; hence, they could rely only on gathered fruit and the supplies they could carry in. For protection against torrential tropical downpours, they had only the rude shelters they could build with palm-leaf thatch or galvanized roofing carried miles on horseback. They had not known of the distances to be traveled on foot just to arrive at their worksites, the trails to be cleared and the seed to be brought in, a sack at a time, on packhorses or their own backs. They soon learned of the hazards from venomous snakes and insects, treacherous mud and the steep *barrancos* that endanger livestock, the unproductive nature of the undersized native cattle then the norm in Chiriquí.* ... But they hadn't had a clue when they "signed on"...

---

* The devastating effect of the deforestation of Panama in favor of grazing land—a practice in which the *Suizos* and their German neighbors happily engaged—and the futility of relying on the cattle industry to alleviate the condition of the masses of rural poor, is studied and strikingly chronicled by Stanley Heckadon Moreno in *De selvas a potreros: La colonización santeña en Panamá ["From Jungles to Pastures: the Settlement of Panama by Los Santos Natives"] 1850–1980* (2009). "Deforestation did away with the dry forests of the Pacific coast and a good part of the humid forests of the Caribbean coast, the coastal and highland cloud forests, and especially the mangroves. Nevertheless, this profound transformation of nature did not reduce

Continued→

In the midst of their first real rainy season, the *Suizos* moved to Cotito, only after having attempted farming in what was virgin forest at Candela and at Cotón on the Costa Rican side of the border. These peripatetic adventures simply cannot have produced much in the way of food or other sustenance. The condition of the settlers brings to mind the recollection of another German pioneer in Ecuador who said "he had survived thirty years of Amazon existence"—with the attendant "insect plagues and failed harvests"—"partly by eating ten thousand bananas."[20] Years later, the no–longer young women, gathered at a birthday or other reunion, would confide to Rosario Laws—the Panamanian teacher from Dolega whom Albert Schmieder had met and married in the United States—that when the settlers accepted Karl Schmieder's invitation to stay at Cotito, they were *hungry*. And often soaking wet, cold, and whether they accepted the reality or not, exhausted. The milk mixed with honey Karl and Gretel could provide—fruits of their own arduous labor—were truly milk and honey to the colonists. The basic diet of beans and cheese, vegetables and fruit, was sheer manna in the desert. Trudi Häusle recalls the gallons of milk consumed daily by twenty-three people with little else on the table; each pail of fresh milk carried through the thick mud of the rainy season from corral to spring house to dining table can weigh thirty or forty pounds. And despite the nostalgic recollections of sympathetic friends and neighbors, there was ample evidence of considerable internal strife within the colony.

The Cotito colony lasted from January 1, 1939, their first day in Panama, to July 7, 1941: two years, six months and seven days. Two rainy seasons, three dry. Two–and–a–half years of grueling labor, including the building of a substantial bridge over a torrential river; years of sleeping on home-made reclining chairs, packed into tiny cabins (later remembered as substantial houses), two years of restless young people living without news or substantial contact with the outside world, with strangely constrained sex lives, some of the

---

← *Continued from prev. page.*
the poverty of the people. ... Behind these changes in land use are hidden [both] poverty and scientific and technological backwardness." Pp. 12–13.

adults turning a blind eye to, or aiding in, genuine abuse of their own children. How long could this idyll have lasted, even if the tragedy had been averted? One must wonder whether, in the brief life of the colony, these idealists had not, simply put, bitten off more than they could chew. Was Cotito heaven on earth? Or was it, as one survivor later said, "a big lie"? We can only conjecture, but perhaps we should not accept overly romantic notions.

| THE PANAMANIAN POLITICAL CONTEXT*

| EFFORTS TO 'IMPROVE THE RACE'

THE SWISS COLONY at Cotito was only one in a series of attempts at settling European farmers on the land in Panama. From independence on, successive Panamanian governments had toyed with the idea of settlements, especially in Chiriquí.

Even then–Agriculture Minister Arnulfo Arias, floundering in 1936 as he would flounder for the rest of his life, trying to figure out how he felt about the European races,

> had worked out an appropriate project for colonization of ten families which was encouraged by the Swiss government.† The Cabinet gave its blessing to the proposal,

---

* As the specific attributions in the endnotes make clear, this section draws heavily on the work of two scholars: Walter LaFeber, whose *Panama Canal: The Crisis in Historical Perspective* (1978, 1989), is the best history of Panama—from independence in 1903 to the end of the military dictatorship in 1989—that I have encountered; and Max Paul Friedman, the title of whose *Nazis and Good Neighbors: The United States Campaign against the Germans of Latin America in World War II* (2003), speaks for itself.

† In Aug., 1934, Arnulfo, then chief of the Dept. of Health and Welfare (*Sanidad y Beneficencia*) lamented, in the dept.'s *Boletín,* that Panama's population had only reached 483,780 in the 31 years since Independence, and that immigrants had been primarily from "undesirable...parasitical races:" "Chinese, Japanese, Syrians, Turks, East Indians, Aryan Indians, Dravidians and blacks from the Antilles and the Guianas...," leading most Panamanians to favor "eugenic...measures against the degeneration of the race:"..."repatriation or expulsion, systematic sterilization..." "Terrified [*"con espanto"* w]e have viewed an English-speaking black cloud occupy new neighborhoods of our principal city and extend into the suburbs...; and on

Continued→

but put Arias under financial restraints. Whether it was a result of these, or the opposition of the other ministers involved, is no longer known, but the project was not discussed further.[21]

ARNULFO'S SUPPORT for the immigration of Swiss settlers in 1936, when he was a cabinet secretary (later called ministers), might cast some doubt on the assertion that he later ordered the massacre at Cotito, but consistency of character was never among Arias's salient characteristics.

PHOTO: DAVID E. SCHERMAN
President Arnulfo Arias Madrid in 1941.

Did the folly of inconsistency and his own racial insecurity descend, by the time he became president in 1940, into the madness of homicide? As R. M. Koster and Guillermo Sánchez Borbón—the historians of dictatorship in Panama—observed years later, the man's folly was manifest, his madness incipient:

> No Panamanian president did so many things the country needed so quickly [especially in the field of social welfare], but his method was so spasmodic, his other measures so ill considered (not to say insane), that when

---

← Continued from prev. page.
every corner of our villages, towns and cities a yellow stain that has employed its penny-ante *["de cuartillo"]* business methods and its diet of rice and 'chop suey,' to wrest businesses from the hands of Panamanians..." Depto. de Sanidad y Beneficiencia, «Boletín sanitario,» I:3 (ago. 1934), pp. 4-7.

Arnulfo's goal was to "to attract a healthy immigration that would populate its countryside..." [*"atraer una migración sana que pueble sus campos"*]. Cabinet minutes, Feb. 20, 1936, in 1936 ACTAS DEL CONSEJO DE GABINETE, Harmodio Arias Adm., *Archivos Nacionales*, q. Holger M. Meding, *Panama: Staat und Nation im Wandel [State and Nation in Flux]*, 1903–1941 (2002).

The Ed. thanks Dr. Jorge Motta for locating the *Boletín* article in the *Archivos Nacionales* and Dr. Daniel Pichel for supplying it.

he was stripped of office a year after he had assumed it, most Panamanians heaved a sigh of relief. ... Power deranged him. It was as if he craved restraint but could not fully govern his own actions.[22]

The popular journalist John Gunther,* commissioned to study attitudes in Latin America, had written,

> Panama [under Arias] has the closest thing to a totalitarian government—Paraguay excepted—that is to be found in the Western Hemisphere. It is ruled by a Harvard–trained neurotic.[23]

Was the massacre at Cotito one of Arnulfo's spasmodic, ill–considered (not to say insane) measures? In the end, we can still only speculate about whether he was its direct author. The nature of the shooting would imply—*res ipse loquitur*†—that the police were under orders, or at the very least authorized, to use extraordinary force, but we still do *not* know, and probably never will, whether Arias was directly responsible for those orders. And yet, while there is no smoking gun, there are many reasons to believe he might have been, either actively on his own initiative, or passively under mutinous pressure from the police. That he was an apologist for the shooting after the fact is a matter of record.

Whatever the case, whether the shooting was authorized by the President; or was rather the result of vicious cruelty or negligence by the commanding officer, Captain Antonio Huff; or the drunkenness of the police detachment; or was the work of some officer high in the chain of command—perhaps Lt. Col. Gómez Ayau or Major Abel Quintero—it was in any case the product, though a grotesque perversion, of policies that the United States sought at the time to impose on Panama. The policies were folly. The result was madness.

---

* Legend has it that Gunther did his research in Panama from the spacious, white-columned verandah of the Tivoli Hotel in the Canal Zone, gazing down on the turbulent city below. Koster & Sánchez Borbón, p. 177.

† *"The thing speaks for itself,"* a legal phrase referring to facts so obvious as to be considered proven even without presentation of evidence.

ACCIÓN COMUNAL WAS a nationalist movement founded in the nineteen–twenties as an alternative to three decades of chaotic rule by the land–owners and tycoons who made up the Panamanian establishment. There was a strong racist strain in its doctrine,[24] and "[l]ike Ku Klux Klansmen," the members of *Acción Comunal* "wore sheets to meetings."[25] By the thirties, it was led by Harmodio and Arnulfo Arias Madrid, brothers and sons of the *mestizo* upper middle class from the hinterland of Penonomé in the province of Coclé, who had each achieved professional success. The elder Harmodio was a lawyer *cum* newspaper publisher trained at Cambridge and the London School of Economics; Arnulfo a Harvard– and University of Chicago–trained physician and coffee planter.[26] Harmodio became, briefly, acting president in a January 2, 1931, *coup d'état,* tacitly supported by the United States, that ousted President Florencio Arosemena. When Arosemena's vice president, Ricardo Alfaro, returned from the U.S.,[27] Harmodio yielded the presidency for the nonce, but was elected in his own right in 1932.[28]

The younger Arnulfo served as Minister of Commerce and Agriculture and as Minister of Health and Social Welfare; Harmodio named him ambassador to the French Third Republic and to Mussolini's Fascist Italy. The young Arnulfo came to admire the Italian Fascism and German National Socialism he saw firsthand as ambassador. The title *El Caudillo,* as Arnulfo later styled himself, and *El Hombre,* as he was often called, had in Spanish a ring similar to the titles of *der Führer* and *il Duce*, and aped those of *Caudillo* and *Generalísimo* Francisco Franco in Spain.[29] It was said that Hitler had received Arnulfo in 1937,[30] when reconstruction of the German economy—with the emphasis on guns, not butter—was in full swing.

Mussolini was reputed to have made the Italian "trains run on time." In those pre–war days, Panama still had two railroads. One was the century–old artery crossing the Isthmus parallel to the Canal—now recently restored to regular service. The other—also built with U.S. capital and operated by the *bananeras* on two hundred fifty miles of track in Chiriquí—is now long gone. But "making the trains run on time" did not, of course, refer to railroad timetables alone. Mussolini's example was important for Panama, Arnulfo believed, because *il Duce* had managed to instill in a lackadaisical, sun–loving, southern people the work ethic, an appreciation for precision and order. In the mid–nineteen–thirties, Hitler and Mussolini seemed—to those blindest of the blind, those who would not see—to have discovered the secret for restoring poor, disorganized, politically and socially tumultuous countries to efficiency, strength and prosperity. All you had to do to accomplish the same goals in tropical Panama would be to find a couple of ethnic scapegoats to rally the masses and to provide a rationale for drastic reform measures; rail against foreign exploitation, both real and imaginary, to divert attention from the failings of the governing class; provide employment and social services for the desperate masses; militarize the police and bring them under the strict and exclusive control of the presidency; exterminating with ruthless severity anybody who did not conform to the will of the leader.

During his presidency, Harmodio Arias had groomed younger brother Arnulfo as the heir apparent, appointing him cabinet minister and ambassador, but in 1936 Arnulfo was constitutionally barred by consanguinity from an immediate succession. Juan Demóstenes Arosemena ran, won, and died in office, leaving Arias loyalist Samuel Augusto Boyd as acting president for the remainder of the 1936–40 term. In 1940, Boyd annointed Arnulfo the Government's candidate. His opponent was Ricardo Alfaro, the respected diplomat to whom Harmodio had yielded the presidency after the coup of 1931. Like Harmodio Arias, by 1940 Alfaro had come to oppose Arnulfo's erratic policies.

Opposition to Arias's racist demagoguery and stubborn refusal to cooperate with U.S. policy in Panama created plenty of vocal support for Alfaro,[31] but the strong-arm methods used by the incumbent Boyd in support of Arnulfo Arias ultimately led Alfaro's party to boycott the elections, handing *El Hombre* a 107,750–to–3,022 "landslide." Arias might well have won anyway, even without the strong-arm tactics and the boycott.

The new president's attitude mystified the *Yanquis*. How could anyone resent the benevolence of the country to which Panama owed its independence and the upper class, at least, owed its prosperity? There had to be a simple explanation. According to U.S. military intelligence reports filed during the 1940 campaign, Arias had remained—

> "friendly to Americans" until he became Minister to Italy in 1934; there he served intermittently until 1938. When he returned home, he led campaigns against United States– and Canadian–owned businesses in Panama, forcing National City Bank and Chase National, among others, to move their offices into the Canal Zone. Some observers [—*i.e.*, anonymous informants interviewed by U.S. intelligence agents in Panama—] linked this change to an audience with Hitler in 1937. "Those who have known him for years can offer no explanation to the change of sentiment towards the United States...other than that he has reached some understanding with the Berlin and Rome Chancelleries."[32]

Voilà! Classic bureaucratic myopia: *the only possible explanation* for Arias's pushback against U.S. treatment of Panama as a protectorate, a virtual colony of the United States, was "an understanding with the Berlin and Rome Chancelleries."

Hitler congratulated Arias on his election in a personal letter* dated October 18, 1940,

> "[appending] the wish that the abiding bonds of friendship between Germany and the Republic of Panama continue unbroken, and that during your term in office, they may, if possible, grow even stronger,"

and promised to send one Reinbeck, "a close personal friend," as "ambassador plenipotentiary and extraordinary" to attend the inauguration."[33]

Arias, however, was no mere clone of Hitler or his stooge. He had his own brand of nationalism and his own *Rassenpolitik*. Like the Nazis, he believed in dubious racial theories even more fashion-

---

* The first page of the letter is reproduced on page 175, *infra*.

able then than they are in many quarters today, but Arias's racism was of a local variety: although a firm believer in racial determinism, he ordered the races differently from the Germans.

As crazily inconsistent as Hitler, the short, dark-haired, possibly partly Jewish, dictator who idolized the tall, blond Aryan master race, Arnulfo Arias was the *mestizo* of mixed Spanish and Amerindian ancestry who actively supported the immigration of European settlers to "improve the race," and his history revealed personal insecurities about the inferiority of the genes he shared. Blacks* and Asians, Arnulfo also taught, were the *cause* of the poverty suffered, then as now, by the majority of Panamanians, rather than mere fellow sufferers. The *Arnulfistas* had little to say about the indigenous population of Panama—non–Europeans like the blacks and Asians they excoriated—but the thirty thousand "Indians" on their isolated farms in the backwoods did not represent a competing political or economic force. The *Arnulfistas* had no pragmatic "reason" to classify as enemies the very people who were here first and whose ancestry Arnulfo and Harmodio, like all *mestizo* Panamanians, shared, however attenuated by intermarriage.

Arnulfo depended for power on the *mestizo* masses, and his attempts to rid the country of blacks and Chinese were unrelenting. The *Panameñista*† populists appealed to the *mestizo* majority by se-

---

* Harmodio Arias told U.S. President Franklin Roosevelt, on a 1933 visit to the White House, that "'the Jamaicans in Panama were dangerous; that each Jamaican man slept with three women every week.' The [U.S.] President consequently urged Congress to appropriate funds for repatriating 'some of the aliens,' who 'constitute a serious unemployment problem for Panama,' to their home islands." LaFeber, p. 84. The concern for *mestizo* unemployment did not last.

† *Panameñismo* is an ideal political term. Like "Americanism," it is virtually devoid of meaning. The classic definition is the simplistic truism advanced by historian Ernesto J. Castillero Reyes: "Government by Panamanians for the happiness of the Panamanian people." (*Historia de Panamá* [1944], p. 201), q. LaFeber, p. 94.

Originally known as the National Revolutionary Party, it was inspired in its early days by the nationalist and racist policies described, and by Arnulfo's introduction of populist reforms such as the comprehensive Social Security health–care and retirement system. Once the military government had managed, years later, to regain sovereignty over the Canal and the Zone sur-

Continued→

lecting as their scapegoats the blacks and Asians, plus the two white elements who had cooperated since independence to dominate the country: the traditional Panamanian oligarchy known as the *rabiblancos*,* and the *Gringos*, the bad guys responsible for all Panama's misfortunes. The *Gringos* and the *rabiblancos*, both of whom detested Arnulfo Arias, would soon engineer the police coup that ousted Arias a year later. Folly, to be sure. Verging on madness.

Arnulfo Arias did not introduce these xenophobic racial tensions into Panamanian politics.† Even before Arias took office in 1940, Panamanian immigration laws, like those of the United States, were exclusionary on ethnic grounds. Arias was not the first Panamanian to rail against the West Indian (*chombo*), Asian (*chino*) and Middle

---

← *Continued from prev. page.*
rounding it, and once Panama's multi-racial nature was beyond alteration, the party's rationale was never clear. It exists to this day; Arnulfo's widow Mireya Moscoso, the former nurse who married the patient, was elected President in her own right, bearing the same red, yellow and purple banner. Though *Arnulfistas* are fervent in their devotion to *Arnulfismo* and *Panameñismo*, what specific policies such principles might imply at any given moment often remain a mystery. Like their founder, they are not immune to charges of naked corruption.

* No word in the argot of Panama demonstrates so forcefully the direct relationship between race and class as the term *rabiblanco*, universally applied to the upper class. It comes from *rabo*, tail, and *blanco*, white, and is the common name of a dove, *Leptotila verreauxi*, that ranges from South Texas—where it is also known as the "white-tailed" dove—to Argentina, and is very common in most of Panama. The ironic reference to the white tails of certain members of society need not be explained further.

† As far back as the early 1860's, Ambrose W. Thompson, the first great *Gringo* Chiriquí land hustler, had nearly succeeded in selling (non-existent) Bocas del Toro coal to Abraham Lincoln. Enticed by Thompson, Lincoln also pursued actively the establishment of colonies of emancipated slaves in Chiriquí. (Thompson envisioned the profits to be made from the U.S. government subsidies that would be involved. To the Colombian government in Bogotá, Panama was too far away to worry about, and the money to be made from the subsidized settlement of former slaves made the proposition more attractive.) The colonization project failed in large measure because of the vehement opposition of Costa Rica, which then claimed part of Chiriquí, and other Central American governments, to the importation of "Negroes" into the province. For an introduction to the subject, *see* Paul J. Scheips, "Lincoln and the Chiriquí Colonization Project" (1952).

Eastern (*turco*, the latter including Sephardic Jews from the former Ottoman empire) immigrants in Panama. The white Panamanian establishment had always shown contempt for the "lower orders," although their form of segregation was social and economic; you don't need to relegate blacks to the back of a bus no white person would dream of riding on.

The United States had long barred Asian immigration (except as coolie labor) to the mainland, and Jim Crow ruled, *de jure* in the old Confederacy and *de facto* in the rest of the nation. Neither the segregated and discriminatory U.S. Canal Zone bisecting Panama, nor the U.S.-controlled banana plantations that then dominated the export economy, provided a model for enlightened treatment of colored minorities.

At the time of independence, the entire Colombian state of Panama had had fewer than five hundred thousand inhabitants, and lacked a potential labor force adequate for such an undertaking. The West Indians—known as *Antillanos* in Spanish, or by the mildly derogatory slang term *chombos*—were first brought to Panama from the islands of the Caribbean specifically to build the trans-isthmian railroad and later the Canal, "workin' for the Yankee dolla'." They remained the preferred employees of the Canal because (except for a few thousand from French Martinique) their first language was English, and because blacks were believed to be better suited physically to hard labor in tropical conditions. Among the working poor, this importation and preferential treatment generated deep resentment.

In retail trade, the Asian and Middle Eastern immigrants who predominated, or were at least highly visible, suffered resentment simply because merchants resent all vigorous competitors and poor people tend to resent whoever sells them goods as basic as the food and clothing they must have but can ill afford.

PHOTO, CAMP CMDR. IVAN WILLIAMS, COURTESY MAX PAUL FRIEDMAN

German internees from Latin America arriving by train at Camp Kenedy, Texas, *ca.* 1939-40. The be-Stetsonned officers are from the U.S. Border Patrol. Arrested in Latin America and deliberately denied visas, they were treated upon arrival in the United States as "undocumented aliens," subject to the jurisdiction of the Immigration and Naturalization Service. In early days, guards on horseback and holding lassos herded arriving internees into the camp.

LaFeber, paraphrasing one William J. Abbot, author of a travel book on the Canal published in 1922, writes:

> Panamanians disliked North Americans...because of "their resentment at our hardly concealed contempt for them." The whiter, Spanish elite did not share these [anti–American] feelings, at least in such intensity, but "as for the casual clerk or mechanic, we Americans call him 'Spiggoty' with frank contempt for his undersize, his lack of education, and for his large proportion of Negro blood. He responds by calling North Americans 'Gringos' and hating [us] with a deep malevolent rancor that needs only a fit occasion to blaze forth in riot and in massacre."*,34

---

* LaFeber says in an apparently ironic footnote: "Abbot speculated that 'Spiggoty' came from the attempts of hackmen to lure fares by shouting

Continued→

What Arnulfo gleaned from his European experience and brought to this mix, when he ran for president in 1940, was knowledge of how to turn racial tensions to his own political advantage, how to mobilize the voting strength of the *mestizos,* using them to hold onto the power—briefly, as it turned out—*Acción Comunal* had seized from the white establishment in 1931. "Bettering," like Shylock, "the example" found in the racist policies of the Axis dictators, Arnulfo saw how the *chombos* and the *chinos* and the *turcos* and the *hindúes* could become the scapegoats for all of Panama's ills, at least those for which the *Yanquis* could not be directly blamed.

Arias may well have dreamed of a day when he could trade United States suzerainty for membership in the Greater *Reich* to come. Or, he may have been sufficiently foolish to believe that in the event of Axis victory, Panama would receive better treatment from the Nazis than it had from the Gringo*s*. How the Nazis would then have classified the *Mischlinge* (people of mixed race) like the Arias brothers can only be imagined. In the propaganda of the *Panameñistas,* however, the *Gringos* and the *rabiblancos* were too white, the *chombos* too black, the *chinos* too yellow and the *hindúes** too brown, but the *mestizo* Panamanians, like Arnulfo and poor (or formerly poor) folk from the hinterland, were fated to achieve their rightful rôle as the true masters of Panama!

IN 1939, RELATIONS between Panama and the United States were improving slightly. However, by October, 1940, when Arnulfo became president, the U.S. was increasing diplomatic pressure for fur-

---

← *Continued from prev. page.*
"Speaka–da–English." Both Abbot and LaFeber must have known this speculative etymology based on what appears to be Italian pidgin, not Spanish, is preposterous, as anyone familiar with common U.S. racial epithets will know instinctively. It is doubtless a portmanteau word combining *Spic* with the "N–word," nowadays more taboo in polite circles than was the Tetragrammaton to the ancient Hebrews.

* This in Panama's national lexicon tends to include all South Asians, as likely to be Muslims, Buddhists, Sikhs, Jains or Christians as Hindus *per se.*

ther measures to secure the hemisphere, in particular the Canal. Panama was only a reluctant partner—despite the fact that the Germans had absorbed Austria and the Sudetenland, and invaded France, the Netherlands and Belgium. "For, regardless of Nazi triumphs," LaFeber tells us,

> the same inexorable problems divided Panama and the United States. The isthmian economy, for example, remained unhealthy and unbalanced. With only primitive communications linking east[ern] and west[ern]* Panama (and the Zone posing the greatest barrier), no national market existed. Populous urban areas suffered from high unemployment and the poor farmers [including German immigrants to Chiriquí who had arrived during the previous decade and the recently arrived Swiss] were isolated in the provinces. With little incentive and less responsibility, the oligarchical families invested...overseas. To make matters worse, Washington not only refused to grant Panamanian demands that the black, English–speaking West Indians be sent home, but as planning began on the third–lock system in 1939, the United States [had] shocked the Panamanians by bringing in more Jamaican labor and repudiating a promise to open higher–level jobs on the Canal to Panamanians.35

Ever since the *Acción Comunal* populists, led by the Arias brothers, had taken power in 1931, the disdain for them harbored by the wealthy elite—traditional allies of the U.S.—and resentment of their comprehensive—for which read *expensive*—social-welfare policies, had smoldered. By the time Arnulfo was inaugurated in late 1940, the ruling classes had no more toleration for him—this cham-

---

* Those unacquainted with Panama are often unaware that the Isthmus has the form of a horizontal S lying parallel to the equator, with the Canal actually running north-to-south at roughly the mid-point. The Atlantic (Caribbean) terminus of the Canal lies slightly to the *west* of the Pacific terminus. Viewed from Panama City, the sun rises over the Pacific, to the east, and sets over the Atlantic, to the northwest.

pion of the masses who antagonized the Americans, who wanted to tax the rich to provide social services to the poor, who threatened the economic and political predominance of the upper class—than did the Roosevelt administration in Washington, eager to be rid of him. Soon, Arnulfo's own brother Harmodio joined the opposition.

An incipient rebellion was also brewing in the ragtag Corps of Police that Arias, like his predecessors, had sought to bring to heel under the harsh discipline imposed by Fernando Gómez Ayau—the Guatemalan he had brought in to reorganize and militarize the force. Arias had also embedded within the police force his own *Policía Nacional Secreta,* by statute reporting directly to the president, heightening resentment among the officer corps.[36] Resentment of Gómez Ayau was shared by the rank and file and senior officials alike. It only strengthened the links between the police and the *rabiblancos*, further threatening Arias's radical program. By July, 1941, when Arias, nine months into his presidential term, congratulated the police for the massacre at Cotito, he was already in danger of being overthrown and must have known it. The overthrow of the government by *coup d'état* would come in a matter of weeks.

> [U.S.] officials were gravely concerned about Arias's strident nationalism, and his election provided the elite with a perfect opportunity to mount a powerful antinationalist campaign.... This bid to recapture the presidency ended successfully in 1941, when several powerful Panama City landowners and merchants, working in conjunction with the United States and numerous disgruntled police [officials], ousted Arias and installed a pro–American interim régime reminiscent of the pre-1931 administrations.[37]

| THE U.S. DEMANDS ANTI-GERMAN MEASURES

THE EXTRAORDINARY PRESSURES brought to bear on all the governments of Latin America by the United States, not yet in the war but already in an anti–German frenzy, exacerbated the chaos during the 1939–41 lifetime of the Swiss colony at Cotito. Despite Arnulfo's reluctance, however, Panama was also in an anti–Nazi frenzy, fed by the oligarchy, the press it controlled, and the American tribunes ruling behind the scenes from the grand Canal administration building on its panoramic hilltop and the scruffy, old wooden Embassy downtown. However autocratic and erratic Arnulfo Arias might have been as president, his sympathies had little effect. The generalized fear of Nazi organizing among German emigrants in Latin America, and the threat of espionage, were intensified even further in Panama, bisected by the Canal.

The result was a series of almost random measures taken by the police, at the behest of the upper classes, against nationals of Axis countries living in the Zone and in the Republic. Meanwhile the colonists at Cotito, isolated in the forests of Chiriquí and subject to the will of Karl Lehner, fanatical leader of the community, stubbornly resisted the measures that the Panamanian government, inspired by this anti–subversive pressure from the United States, sought to impose.

At the same time, however, Arias antagonized the Roosevelt administration by resisting other American demands he believed impinged on Panamanian sovereignty. Arias refused the urgent request for 999-year leases—just one year less than the Third *Reich*'s estimate of its own life expectancy—on a hundred additional military bases to be created outside the Canal Zone, or for the arming of the Panamanian-flag merchant fleet. His stubbornness had its negative effect in Washington.

"Secretary of War Henry Stimson wrote in his diary, 'Roosevelt...told me of his troubles with Arias and told [Secretary of State Cordell] Hull to try some strong arm methods on him.'"[38] When Arias was deposed, Stimson would write, "It was a great relief to us."[39]

The decision to round up Germans, to set up transit camps in the Canal Zone*—where Arias was powerless—and to ship the internees from the Zone to the United States for the duration, contributed to the frenzy in Panama. In August, 1940, a year before the

---

* Readers unfamiliar with Panama's past might need to be reminded of the difference at the time between the "Panama Canal Zone," a territory entirely under the direct control of the United States, and the rest of the country, the Republic of Panamá, in theory at least, sovereign in its own land.

Cotito massacre, and sixteen months before the U.S. became a belligerent, Secretary Stimson announced that eighty-one Axis "agents" had been arrested and would soon be deported to the United States for internment. The next day, he announced a revision: they weren't agents after all, but German nationals whose "papers weren't in order."[40]

The transit camp at Balboa, easily observed by the Panamanian public and police, was indeed "no country club."

> [P]hysical conditions of internment in the United States...came as a relief to those deportees who had been transferred from Latin American camps and jails, including U.S.–administered Camp Empire at Balboa...a transit camp for deportees from all over Latin America. [It was r]un by military men responsible for defending the primary target in the Western Hemisphere. ... The first arrivals went two weeks without bathing and saw their Red Cross packages plundered by U.S. soldiers. Many of the internees were mature or older men from the white-collar professions, unaccustomed to hard physical labor, ...ordered to clear thick brush with machetes in the intense midday heat. Working in their underwear, they swallowed salt tablets every half-hour under the gaze of occasionally brutal guards. Sickness, exhaustion and ringworm were common. One internee suffered a heart attack; another lost fifty pounds. Roaming police dogs attacked Alfredo Brauer and forced him up against the barbed-wire fence, lacerating him so badly he spent a week in the hospital.[41]

The German-owned *Sociedad Colombo–Alemana de Transportes Aéreos* (SCADTA), said to be the first commercially successful airline in the world, had operated in Colombia since 1919. Its planes shortened the trip from the mountain capital of Bogotá to coastal Barranquilla from weeks by riverboat to a three-hour flight, making Colombia much easier to govern. In 1931, Pan American World Airways—which had long sought to eliminate competitive German and Italian airlines in Latin America—bought control, although the managers and pilots continued to be Germans. SCADTA eventually became *Aerovías del Continente Americano ("AVIANCA")*, Colombia's national airline, but control was maintained by Pan Am. In May, 1940, Assistant Secretary of State Adolf Berle and U.S. Ambassador Spruille Braden put the heat on neighboring Colombia to eliminate the German pilots, a supposed threat to the Panama Canal. On June 10, 1940, under U.S. pressure, and against the wishes of the Colombian government, Pan Am fired all the Germans and replaced them with pilots from the U.S. When some of the fired pilots sought to return to Germany, the British government protested because, as Berle wrote in his diary, "these men will probably be used to bomb London," and if they remained in Colombia, they would be used to bomb the Panama Canal. Eventually, the pilots were interned in Canada.[42]

On August 10, 1940, the *New York Times* headlined a typically overheated story by Russell B. Porter, "Germans Maintain Losing Airline Inside Panama Canal Defense Zone." The "defense zone" by then extended beyond Colombia to the Andes, and this time the airline was the *Sociedad Ecuatoriana de Transportes Aéreos* (SEDTA) whose entire fleet consisted of two old, slow, German–built cargo planes.[43]

By the time Arias became president of Panama in October, 1940, the anti–German hysteria was a fact of life. In March, 1941, five months into Arnulfo's presidency, forty–eight German sailors on the merchant ship *Eisenach* scuttled their vessel* at Puntarenas, Costa Rica. The sailors were expelled from Costa Rica, and, making their way via Panama, where they could board a ship to Japan, they were arrested at Berle's behest, shipped to the U.S., and ended up in internment camps in Montana and South Dakota. This was one of the

---

* The *Eisenach* (Capt. Gerhard Loers Struck) reached Puntarenas Sept. 1, 1939. The same anti-Nazi frenzy afoot in Costa Rica led to rumors that, even after its radios had been stripped, the ship was broadcasting to Germany messages received from shore by signal light. On March 31, 1941, the *Eisenach* exploded and sank, but it was salvaged later and returned to cargo service. Roberto Le Franc Ureña, C.R. *Museo Nacional,* cit. "Long Scuttled Cargo Ship [the Italian *Fella*, scuttled same day, still on the bottom] Becomes Environmental Case," *A.M. Costa Rica,* May 11, 2012, online ed.

first instances of a non-belligerent country's detaining foreign nationals and shipping them to another for internment.[44] Neither Panama nor the United States was then at war with Germany.

In September, 1941—only two months after the July 7 Panamanian police massacre—President Roosevelt,

> determined to coax a reluctant public into a necessary war for a just cause, took to the airwaves to warn Americans that "Hitler's advance guards" are readying "footholds, bridgeheads in the New World. ... Conspiracy has followed conspiracy" in Latin America. ... German agents are at that very moment carrying out "intrigues...plots...machinations...sabotage." The most recent sign...is the discovery of secret air landing fields in Colombia, within easy range of the Panama Canal.[45]

Had not the Panamanian police reported, just a few weeks earlier, that Swiss settlers clearing brush just across the Costa Rican border from Piedra Candela were preparing a landing strip, and that a spring-cooled dairy shed, on an isolated farm three hundred miles from the Canal, was a clandestine radio station?

To be fair to Arnulfo, it must be said that only after he was deposed was the final decision taken to round up *all* the Germans, Italians and Japanese in the Republic of Panama, and the round-ups did not ratchet up to their full intensity until after the Japanese attack on Pearl Harbor. In the single week—eight days, to be precise—between Sunday, December 7, when Pearl Harbor was bombed, and Monday, December 15, 1941, the same police who had perpetrated the Cotito massacre in July, and who had overthrown Arnulfo on October 7, arrested a thousand people, most of the Axis nationals in the Republic. There were initial objections from Foreign Minister Octavio Fábrega: many of the Germans were naturalized Panamanians, or—like the German husband of Fábrega's own aunt—they had married into families with *palanca*.*,[46]

---

* "A lever," the Spanish slang term for political leverage.

By December 20, 1941, the State Department's desk officer for Central America was writing,

> I feel that it is wise to clear as many young Nazis [generally taken to mean all Germans] out of Central America as possible. ... While I do not think we should urge any government to deport Axis nationals [apparently, Assistant Secretary of State Adolf Berle and the Embassy in Panama disagreed], I see no harm in discreetly pushing the matter when an opening is given."[47]

In Panama, accustomed to the big stick since the days of Roosevelt the First, no such discretion would have been necessary. According to the U.S. Embassy,

> [t]he request to have these enemy aliens in the Republic of Panama detained and interned was made by the United States Government, because of reasons connected with the defense of the Panama Canal.[48]

The effect of the deportations on individual lives was devastating. Werner Julius Kappel was a German–speaking, Jewish refugee in Panama, 18 years old in 1940. In 1938, the Gestapo had forced him and his father, Fred Kappel, out of Germany. They made their way to Panama, where they found jobs driving buses. After Pearl Harbor, they were arrested and interned in a U.S. prison camp in Texas. In 1943, when certain "stateless" Jewish Germans (already deprived of their German citizenship by Nazi decree) were released from the camps, young Werner, now 21, was drafted and sent to fight in the Philippines, where he was wounded and spent six months in the hospital. When he applied for U.S. citizenship, his petition was at first denied because he—a prisoner forcefully transported under guard from Panama in U.S. custody—had entered the United States as an undocumented immigrant.[49]

> Of the 247 Germans deported to the United States from Panama from 1941 to 1945, approximately 150 were "cases" [for which there is detailed information. These] ...included twenty–one Nazi Party members and thirty

> Jewish refugees, five of whom had spent time in Buchenwald, Oranienburg, or other...camps. There was also a handful of "drunks," "cranks," and "beachcombers." ... On the other hand, thirty-seven out of fifty-eight of the members of the local Nazi organization were left behind in Panama.
>
> [P]rotecting the Canal was a vital goal...[but] the policy led to the internment of more Jewish refugees than Nazi Party members, while the majority of Nazis were left behind in Panama... .[50]

Folly marked the entire internment program. Germans in the United States were treated much more leniently, and because they were so numerous, or perhaps because their friends and relatives could vote, few were interned. Perhaps the temper of the times and the chaos that marked wartime "strategic policy" decisions in Panama, the worthless "intelligence" given credence by the authorities, and the mentality of U.S. bureaucrats, is summed up best by Max Paul Friedman. Chapter 2 of his *Nazis and Good Neighbors* opens with an anecdote from a moment perhaps a hundred days after the massacre at Cotito:

> Panama, November 1941. War looms ever closer to the Americas. The Canal Zone, under U.S. military jurisdiction, swarms with soldiers and construction workers in the wet tropical heat: laying mines at the entrance, stretching anti-sabotage nets across the locks and spillways, setting up anti-aircraft installations on all sides. Lieutenant Jules Dubois, chief of the Intelligence Branch of the U.S. Army's Panama Canal Department, sits at a table in the unassuming little restaurant run by German immigrant Wilhelm Heinemann. Dubois, a self-confident, future anti-communist crusader whose taste for the mixed metaphor will emerge in his memoirs, knows that Heinemann [had] arrived from Europe only two years before.
>
> "With their sights trained on Latin America, the Axis powers began to groom puppets and sympathetic groups

in every republic to seize the reigns *[sic]* of their governments' machinery," he will write after the war.⁵¹ It makes no difference that Heinemann is a Jewish refugee with a heart condition who fled Hitler in Germany, Franco in Spain, and Mussolini in Italy, before finally finding asylum in Central America. The U.S. government—even President Roosevelt himself—has often issued public declarations and private memoranda warning of the danger that Jewish refugees might serve as Nazi spies, and Dubois is a fervent believer.⁵²

The intelligence chief takes his job seriously. His handiwork leads to so many cases of German civilians interned as dangerous enemy aliens that post–war investigators will label him "the ubiquitous Dubois."⁵³ His memoirs reveal his assumptions:

"There were approximately three million Axis nationals residing in Latin America then, each of whom could have been made available to form part of a militant striking force capable of implementing the plans of the Axis at the appropriate time."⁵⁴ That this figure can be reached only by including every last Italian grandmother and Japanese toddler does not deter the newly minted intelligence agent from seeing evidence of a fifth column under every rock. Swallowing the dregs of his coffee, the lieutenant peers into the bottom of the cup and sees a twisted piece of straw in the shape of a numeral 4. Convinced it is a secret code signal, Dubois denounces Heinemann as a Nazi spy, and the refugee is arrested and interned in the United States.⁵⁵

It seems evident that the folly of this U.S.–imposed policy also led indirectly to the utterly pointless and utterly depraved annihilation of the Swiss at Cotito. Of the twenty–three colonists, there were seven German nationals: two of these were German citizens born and raised in Switzerland; one was Helmut Brauchle, a young son of the 1929 immigrants from Schramberg; and four were the German owner of the Cotito farm, his wife and two children, hosts of the

Swiss colony, who had left Germany in 1928. Of these seven German nationals, none of whom lived in or had any loyalties to Nazi Germany, four were killed and two seriously injured in the massacre. Eight others—non–Germans—were killed along with them, and five others injured.

AND SO IT CAME to pass during the first of Arnulfo's three truncated terms in office—and in the midst of this pushmi–pullyu game being played out among the President, his radical supporters, the conservative upper classes, the half–militarized regular police, Arias's personal secret police, the U.S. Army and U.S. intelligence agencies—that the settlement of Swiss and a few Germans at Cotito was annihilated in what can only be called a "police massacre."

It is possible, as is often alleged, that Arias explicitly ordered it, hoping to make a proper example of this infestation of German–speakers in Chiriquí who had repeatedly refused to report to David with three new photographs for yet another registration. It is also possible, though it seems unlikely, that he intended to employ mass murder as a means of demonstrating that new, fervently anti–Nazi zephyrs were wafting through the Palace of the Herons, a gesture meant to help him remain in office. It is even possible that Arias simply capitulated—with a shrug, a wink and a nod, or even an explicit but resigned *"¡Dále!"* ("Go for it!")—to the demands of the defiant police or the U.S. authorities. It seems clear, however, that *even if he knew about the massacre in advance,* Arias—unable to control the police, unable to resist the anti-Nazi fervor of the times—*would have been incapable of doing anything to prevent it.*

It is conceivable also that Arias, rather than having ordered or acceded to the massacre, was personally appalled by it, and that his private outrage after the slaughter prompted him to confront the rebellious police yet again. If so, he would have had to be discreet. The spin-doctors and the yellow press were already reporting the sordid incident as the necessary rescue of the Republic from a Nazi fifth-column insurrection in Chiriquí, put down by Captain Antonio Huff's valiant Third Battalion. The American embassy concurred. Once the massacre had occurred, simple fear—or call it political prudence, if you will—would have rendered Arias incapable—even if he were so inclined—of repudiating it publicly. Acting after the fact would only have hastened the progress of the coup developing against him. To the end of his days, Arias denied having ordered the shooting, but responsible or not, he became willy–nilly its apologist.

Although justified *ex post facto* by President Arias himself, reluctantly caught up in the anti–Nazi frenzy sweeping Panama, it appears the slaughter of the *Suizos* was simply the product of the sheer homicidal incompetence of the ill trained, frenzied, inebriated detachment dispatched to deal with those obstinate foreigners.

To make the leap from the possibility that Arias might have harbored vague aspirations, however irrational, of benefitting in future from an Axis victory, to a charge of his having directly ordered the brutal murder of women and children, men young and old, is more than the evidence supports. One may conclude that someone in authority *had* to have given a direct order, but in the ill trained and undisciplined Panamanian police force of 1941, some "cowboy" might just have fired a single shot that unleashed the slaughter. (The cowboy would have been Lucas Garcés.) If Sepp Niederberger,[*] a disinterested observer, is to be believed[†], even Huff, the commander of the detachment, was far from the line of fire, with his boots off, and was himself surprised by the violent fusillade. We do not know who gave the fatal order because, perhaps, in the end, nobody ever did.

In a country where freedom of information legislation was not passed until 2002, and where the only two fines ever imposed on any official for withholding public information were never collected,[56] secret files revealing the truth are unlikely ever to surface.

---

[*] Josef ("Sepp") Niederberger was a native of Lucerne who had immigrated in 1935. He, Josef Kaiser and Alfred Waser owned a farm later sold to Gustav Haug Sr. Niederberger worked on the construction of the first hospital in David, and in 1941 was working on railroad construction in Chiriquí when Huff sought him out and asked him to accompany the squad to Cotito as interpreter. Intv. with widow, Cerro Punta, 2014. *See also* pp. 142, 216, *infra*.

[†] *See* Mixed Commission report, ¶ 17, p. 142, *infra*; and Haug's report, p. 217, *infra*.

BY SEPTEMBER, 1941, less than two months after the massacre, U.S. Ambassador Edwin C. Wilson was reporting rumors of a *golpe*, "'reliable information' that Arias's attempt to curb" the powers of the police "was making [them] restless." On the morning of October 7, Arias "suddenly left for Cuba, ostensibly for medical reasons, actually to spend a few days in Havana with his mistress." Once Ambassador Wilson signaled to the opposition that the U.S. would take no action to thwart a coup, it took place immediately, on October 9.[57] The Supreme Court ruled that since the Assembly had not, as the 1941 Constitution required, authorized his absence from the country, Arias had forfeited the presidency. The U.S. ambassador invited Ricardo Adolfo De la Guardia, until then Arnulfo's Minister of Government and Justice, to take over, and Arias was gone.[58] He would be back.

| COTITO AN ISSUE IN 1984: GOOFY POLITICS IN A SHAM ELECTION

CHAPTER VI OF *Cotito* is an excursion into the bizarre byway of the military's trumped-up 1982 historical fabrication, *Holocausto en Panamá,* and its use in the election of 1984. The Author explains the origins of Hassán's book—the one I was reading at the lunch counter—an attempt, forty-one years after the massacre, to exploit what was already a dreadful episode in Panamanian history. Perhaps I should clarify my reservations, mentioned earlier, about Chapter VI.

In 1977, Jimmy Carter and Omar Torrijos were seeking U.S. Senate ratification for the treaty they had signed, transferring the Canal and reverting the Canal Zone to *de facto*—as opposed to the traditional, sorta, kinda *de jure*—sovereignty of Panama. When it came to ratification, General Torrijos had to deal with his "tin–pot dictator" image, but the existence under military rule of a puppet civilian presidency and Torrijos's promise of future "free" elections were sufficient, at least for the time being, to mollify U.S. senators reluctant to entrust the Canal to a larcenous military dictator.

Torrijos died in a plane crash in 1981, four years after he and Jimmy Carter had signed the treaty whose provisions were to be phased in until final transfer of the Canal at the end of 1999. Torrijos was succeeded by his protégé Manuel Antonio Noriega, and by 1982, the military's image abroad had hardly improved. With seventeen years still to go before the Canal was to be handed over to Panama—seventeen years in which anything could happen—it was evident that the election scheduled for 1984 was still necessary window dressing. Yet another stooge nominated by the "Democratic Revolutionary Party," a stand—in for the Army, would be added to the list of puppet presidents headed by Demetrio Lakas (1969–78), Aristides Royo (1978–82), Ricardo De la Espriella (1982–84) and Jorge Illueca (five months in 1984).

Noriega's military apparatus knew that Arnulfo Arias, at 81, thrice elected and thrice deposed by the armed forces, was waiting in the wings for yet another run at a fourth presidential term. They knew also that—despite his three previous ousters from the presidency, his 1964 electoral loss to Marco Aurelio Robles, his age, unpredictability, reputation for racism and the incoherence of his program—the old *Caudillo* stood a good chance of winning. If he did, the Army would then find themselves between Scylla and Charybdis: Noreiga's gang could allow Arias to take office and watch him substitute his own autocracy for the military dictatorship, his own rackets for theirs, jeopardizing their own profits from the drug trade and business corruption. Alternatively, they could cancel the election or depose a victorious Arias for a fourth and final time, preserving their own power and their own rackets, but endangering the scheduled transfer of the Canal to Panama. Neither prospect was appealing.

Some few of the military clique apparently believed they could substantially diminish the threat of an Arnulfo Arias victory in 1984 by painting the old gadfly as a Nazi who had ordered the murder of (fictitious) innocent Jews at Cotito and Palo Alto. According to Dr. Cuestas, knowledgeable observers of the political scene believed Hassán wrote *Holocausto en Panamá* on assignment for his military cronies in an effort to draw—

> the attention of the influential Jewish community of the United States—solid pillar of the economic strength of the Superpower—to convince them subtly that it would be preferable if the elections in Panama were won by the

military—accustomed to running the country with a strong hand—and not the agèd and divisive populist leader who had sadistically exterminated the innocent children of Israel in the mountains of Chiriquí.[59]

Of course, the clichéd reference to American Jews "as the solid pillar of the economic strength of the Superpower" might be considered gratuitous. Just how many rich members of any ethnic group it takes to make it a "significant pillar" of economic power in a country as large as the United States is a matter for debate. There are infinitely more industrial magnates, billionaires, bankers, media barons, politicians and persons of political influence from other backgrounds than there are Jews in any of these categories in the United States, or in Panama, for that matter. Certainly in the United States, the evangelical Christian right is more effective in politics than is any particular faction of the Jewish community (divided among many). Somehow, however, even at this late date, it is the economic influence of some Jews that seems to generate near–reflexive comment demonstrating yet again how deeply runs—even among some enlightened intellectuals—the strain of xenophobia and ethnic stereotype in Panama and elsewhere, frequent avowals of devotion to supra-racial egalitarianism notwithstanding.

It is, moreover, hard to believe that anybody but ex–*comandante* Aristides Hassán, late of the traffic bureau, might seriously have believed that stirring up old rumors and distortions about the massacre of 1941 might be a useful ploy for attracting Jewish–American support for Noriega's front–man. Such reasoning among the military would have presupposed that, during the run–up to the 1984 non–election, influential members of the U.S. Jewish community—

    a. Were even aware that the election of yet another lapdog president would be taking place in Panama in 1984; *and*

    b. being aware of it, they somehow cared about the outcome of such an election; *and*

    c. being aware of it, and caring about its outcome, these American Jews would be likely to support the candidacy of Arnulfo Arias, *unless* they could be persuaded that Arias was a Nazi responsible for massacres of Jews in Panama; *and*

d. being aware of the imminent election, caring about it, and being persuaded that Arias was a Nazi who had killed innocent Jews in Chiriquí, *only then* could they be persuaded to redirect their support to the Panamanian military's stand–in candidate, Nicolás Ardito Barletta; *and*

e. that knowing there was an election, caring about it, being persuaded that Arias was a Nazi, and being disposed therefore to support Barletta,

they could then be induced to expend significant amounts of their own capital—or some of their abundant political capital in lobbying the United States government—to support the election of Barletta.

Such a fantasy would have been beyond delusional. By 1982, only old Panama hands in the U.S. would have even vague recollections of the name Arnulfo Arias! Those who did remember him would remember also that, ever since World War II and the Roosevelt administration, Arias had been viewed in the U.S., and by many in Panama, as an admirer of the *Führer*; that the U.S. had applauded, even authorized, his overthrow each time it had occurred; and that the "Nazi" label had stuck. In particular, it would have been especially absurd for anybody to be in the least concerned with inducing American Jews to reject his candidacy. They could not have cared less about an election in Panama, even if some infinitesimal number had, for whatever reason, a peripheral interest in Isthmian politics. It is unlikely that even those few might have supported Arnulfo Arias—a renegade *mestizo* radical—over Nicolás Ardito Barletta–a respectable conservative economist who favored his mother's Italian surname over his father's Ardito. American Jews were unlikely to have contributed to either candidacy.

The only conceivably rational reason for the Panamanian military to seek American Jewish support for Ardito Barletta's candidacy would have been to enlist largely illusory Jewish influence in persuading the American *government* to support Noriega's front man, but that would have been preachin' to the choir. In the conservative, Reagan–Republican United States of 1984, Arias was still viewed by officialdom as the mentally unstable, erratic, octogenarian populist that he was. He lacked a meaningful program, and his election could only lead to more political chaos in Panama. For the Reagan administration, the military represented order, and Arias represented the threat of instability. For the U.S., more unrest in Panama was not an alluring prospect.

The political consultants advising the Ardito Barletta campaign in 1984 were the same team of hired guns who had elected Jimmy Carter to the White House in 1976 and had managed to shepherd the Canal treaty through the U.S. Senate in 1977. They knew the Panamanian régime had an unsavory reputation in the United States, but they also knew that an unsavory reputation was irrelevant. Panama's military dictatorship already enjoyed implicit U.S. support. Even the liberal Jimmy Carter had found General Torrijos a suitable partner. United States policy in El Salvador and Nicaragua in those days made it clear how comfortable the United States could be in cozying up to the far right and the *traficantes*. Nobody had to teach Torrijos or his successor Noriega how little it took to remain in favor with the United States military, the CIA and the DEA. It was not a matter of trust; it was a matter of utility. John Dinges had it right when he wrote that in the months leading up to the election of 1984,

> [f]or someone in Noriega's subordinate position *vis à vis* the United States, establishing trust was not so important as establishing usefulness; he had learned that the locus of his own power was the favors he was asked to perform. Over the...months and years, he would find ways to be helpful in Central America. He would make the right noises about the war on drugs. He would pick a presidential candidate [Ardito Barletta] whose qualifications could have been written up in Washington (as some observers claim they were). Manuel Noriega had had a long relationship with the United States; he was confident he would do just enough, when the time came, to keep his North American friends happy—and looking the other way.[60]

The military knew from long experience that they could count on the United States to accept whatever election result Noriega decided to proclaim, as long as he went through the motions of a "free" election. In 1984, it would have mattered but little what Panamanian Jews thought about Arias and not at all what American Jews might have thought about him, if they thought about him at all. The U.S. government was never going to support Arnulfo Arias, and the close ties that had existed for decades between the U.S. government and the Panamanian military had no particular Jewish dimension.

Most printed copies of Hassán's book disappeared right after publication in 1982, but it was given huge play in 1984, serialized in the daily press and given over-heated dramatic readings on the radio, which would indicate that the intended audience was Panamanian; Jews in Scarsdale do not read *Crítica*. To the extent that the Panamanian military attached any importance at all to the publication of Hassán's incoherent, fraudulent and Jew–obsessed book, they probably saw it as a means of exerting some minor influence on the Panamanian public at large, including, to be sure, the small, moderately influential, community of Panamanian Jews. The target audience for an anti–Arias crusade in Panama would logically have been far wider than the Jewish community: the congregants of the prestigious *Cristo Rey** synagogue had known about Arias's Nazi sympathies and xenophobia for forty years, and would have required little persuasion to make them mistrust Arnulfo Arias. If there had been a massacre of Jews at Cotito or Boquete, they would already have known about it.

Oh, yes, a few Panamanian Jews might well have figured among the Arias campaign's wealthier supporters, simply because they feared Arias less than they feared Noriega and his anointed candidate. Not so naïve as Barletta, who genuinely believed that if elected he could control the military and clean up the government from the inside, some Jews would simply have supported whatever opposition to Noriega was available. In this, they would have differed not a whit from other supporters of Arias, the old *Caudillo*.

"Arias did not offer a concrete program to counter the technocratic promises of Barletta. His message was a powerful indictment

---

* "Christ the King" [!] synagogue, popularly so–called because of its former location near the Roman Catholic church of that name.

of the government's decades of corruption and a promise that his régime would sweep aside the evildoers."[61] In short, Arias represented whatever his mercurial *Panameñismo* was at that particular moment, and his populist appeal for the masses was undiminished. Barletta was an apologist for naked military oppression, a professional technocrat who had come of age serving Torrijos, and who had somehow achieved international stature as an economist. He was prepared to serve as puppet president for what was then one of the most corrupt régimes in the Latin America of the time, no mean distinction. (Panama has now slipped back into a sort of business-as-usual level of civilian corruption.)

Barletta's campaign flacks managed to get even CNN to report the incoherent tale concocted in *Holocaust in Panama*, but, if the military really believed they could engineer Arnulfo's defeat by manipulating the Jewish community in the U.S., it would have been one of their more irrational notions. Of such notions, however, they held many, and if they did so delude themselves, they certainly should have chosen a hack more capable than Aristides Hassán to execute the assignment. Hassán's book would not have persuaded any thinking person about anything, and neither the serialization of the book in the newspapers nor the readings on the radio did much to save the election from Arias. Despite the frenzied effort, he won fair and square by a modest margin...only to have victory awarded to "*Fraud*ito" Barletta—as he was thenceforth called—by a grossly manipulated vote count. When Arias's supporters protested, the military opened fire (as his backers had done in 1938). *Plus ça change...*

In retrospect, Panamanians talk about their valiant opposition to the military dictatorship that lasted for twenty-one years. In fact, of some three million Panamanians, only a handful—journalists, a limited number of politicians and lawyers, and a scattering of quixotic *guerrilleros* in Chiriquí—did very much to overthrow it, beyond banging on their *pailas* (soup kettles) and waving white handkerchiefs in the odd demonstration. Once the dictatorship was toppled by the invasion of an outsider, but few Panamanian public officials, whatever their party affiliations, did much to eliminate the corruption and governmental incompetence that plague this country.

If there was a tragedy in 1984, it was not so much a matter of who won. It was that once again a fraud–riddled, comic–opera election had come down to a choice between an octogenarian demagogue of uncertain mental stability, whose simplistic slogan–politics promised little for Panama, and (what is called in New York politics) a "suit," an outwardly presentable character sufficiently vain to believe he could have made a difference under Noriega. Given its advantages, Panama might have become the Switzerland of Latin America. Panama's tragedy is that for the foreseeable future, it seems unlikely that probity, capability, wisdom or inspirational leadership will mark any but a very small proportion of the various candidates for public office, let alone the all–powerful presidency.

UNFORTUNATELY, HOWEVER, although Hassán's distortion of the Cotito incident and his invention of a "holocaust" did not prove in themselves influential in the election of 1984, the serializations in the daily press did have a lasting effect. For many readers—as in my case until just before I began this writing—Hassán's book was their only source of information about the legendary Cotito massacre. The widely propagated myths linger even today among those who absorb such "facts" by casual osmosis. Only recently, yet another fellow immigrant insisted to me, as others have, that there was a massacre of Jews just outside Boquete in 1941, a belief based on sheer rumor (as his Spanish is not good enough for him to have read Hassán's deranged fantasies).

THE FIRST FIVE chapters of Dr. Cuestas's book deal with the Cotito massacre and its aftermath (to differentiate them from Chapter VI, which deals only with Hassán's attempt at obfuscation forty years later). In those five chapters, the reader will meet Arias's appointee Fernando Gómez Ayau and an assortment of other politicians and military careerists who continued along the path toward turning Panama's almost amateur police force into a military machine. Later, President José ("Chichi": "Baby Face") Remón, elected in 1952 and gunned down at the race track in January, 1955, took giant steps along that road; Boris Martínez and Torrijos took the final steps; and Noriega brought the whole thing crashing down, at least for now. When Jorge Kam Ríos wrote in his 1993 prologue that *Cotito* is a tale of "yesterday for today," he anticipated that the euphoria of 1989–90 over the disbanding of the army and the restoration of civilian government could be short lived, or that the process would be at best incomplete. The fact is that there remains the threat of militarism, which perennially flourishes more vigorously than the subservient judiciary and irresponsible executive that should control it. Seventy years after the slaughter of innocents at Cotito, Betty Brannan Jaén of *La Prensa*, commenting on the 2010 police shooting (happily less lethal) of other innocents in Bocas del Toro, observed:

> [T]he current [Martinelli] administration—like so many administrations—refuses to understand that there is a crucial difference between a police force and the military. Hence, our police (and civilian officials) continue to use military titles, render each other a military salute, wear military uniforms, submit to the command of [former] military officers and take their training in military schools such as the [U.S.–run] School of the Americas. And that is why they respond to civilian protests as if they were at war, endowed with the unlimited right—or from their perspective, even further, the duty—to use all the weapons available to ensure their victory in the battle of the day, even if they lose the war insofar as maintaining the confidence of the citizenry in their government.*

---

* Betty Brannan Jaén, *"No más perdigones de plomo"* ["No more lead shot"], *La Prensa,* Aug. 8, 2010, p. 15A, col 1. In this incident, "the Government acknowledged two fatalities, but the special commission [appointed by Pres. Ricardo Martinelli, and which was calling for exhumations,] mentions four, and the ombudsman *[Defensoría del Pueblo]* seven." José Otero and Rafael Luna, *"Muertes quedarían impunes"* ["Deaths would go unpunished"], *ibid.,* Nov. 3, 2010, online ed.

In his inaugural address on July 1, 2014, *Arnulfista* Pres. Juan Carlos Varela admonished the police—ostensibly civilian—on civil rights. The new president had perhaps noticed that the inaugural color guard marched not in dress–blue police uniforms, but in camouflage battle fatigues, carrying rifles

Continued→

FOREWORD

IF THE PRESENT book corrects a few mistaken beliefs about what happened in 1941, then it will have accomplished Dr. Cuestas's purpose. My purpose in translating and expanding it is to seek the wider audience his book deserves, and to provide some of the additional information that might allow a foreigner to approach an understanding of what happened at Cotito and why.

There are, here in Panama, as everywhere, always dedicated and capable people, such as the Author, who labor to engender in Panamanian public life a spirit of open inquiry, of support for human rights, of toleration and civic responsibility. This book is a part of that labor.

—D.M.F.

«EL ALTOZANO»
MAGUEY DE VOLCÁN, CHIRIQUÍ
JULY, 2013

| EDITORIAL NOTE

In the translation, I have followed the text as literally as I could, only altering word order where English syntax differs from Spanish, with several minor exceptions:

- I have combined related sentences into a hugely reduced number of paragraphs. Where I found the sequence of the author's exposition confusing, I have relocated certain entire sentences, identifying these with small beginning (→) and ending (←) arrows.
- Where the word "(sic)" appears thus, in roman type and parentheses, it was inserted by the Author; if in brackets and italicized "*[sic]*," it was inserted by me. I have revised the Author's footnotes and bibliography to comply more nearly with standard U.S. citation forms.
- The words *commune, colony* and *settlement* are all translations of the Author's *colonia*.
- Taking a cue from other writers in English, I have—with this apology, but convinced that it is the most practical solution to an insoluble editing problem—used "American" for both *norteamericano/a* and

---

← *Continued from prev. page.*

with bayonets fixed. As *La Prensa* observed, the uniforms might have been confused with those of any national army, though Panama theoretically has none. *Id.*, Election Supp., July 2, 2014, p. 1, col. 5.

- *estadounidense,* either of which sounds fine in Spanish but is impossibly awkward in English. "North Americans" would include Canadians and Mexicans, who have their own troubles. I have often evaded the issue by substituting "U.S." as an adjective.
- I have capitalized the Spanish words *alemanes, arnulfistas, chiricanos, gringos, nica, panameñistas, panameñismo, suizos* and *yanquis* when used in an English context, though in Spanish it is not standard to do so.
- Many given names were unnecessarily "translated" to Spanish, and many names were simply misspelled in government records or press accounts. I have used the following spellings, carefully reviewed to determine the names individuals actually used: **Albert Baumann Ehrman Gonzenbach** Gustav Schaper Senn Troetsch Häusle Klara Klärli **Lehner** Loni Margarethe Müller Senn Sophie Wachter **Waser Werner Wehrli Zulauf.**
- I have used the old-fashioned *née* to clarify some women's names.

| PREFACE TO THE REVISED ENGLISH EDITION

Any 100,000-word text translated, edited, researched, largely re-written, typeset, laid out, proofread, indexed and published by a single septuagenarian will contain errors of form and content, and the first edition of this book is no exception. As far as I know, most of the errors (including a few misidentifications of individuals in the photo captions, corrected by Werner Senn) were minor, the only real factual whopper being a careless reference to the Arias brothers as sons of the Chiriquí working class, when in fact they were sons of the upper middle class from Coclé (a correction for which I am indebted to Sr. Ernesto Weigandt). This second edition is an attempt to correct errors of form and style, but it differs little in essential content from its predecessor, except that the meticulous correction by Mrs. Jacqueline Finch has made all the difference in the details.

D.M.F.

«EL ALTOZANO»
APRIL, 2015

Notes to *Editor's Foreword*

[1] Cit. Walter LaFeber, *The Panama Canal: The Crisis in Historical Perspective* (1st ed., 1978), p. 76.
[2] Max Paul Friedman, *Nazis and Good Neighbors* (2003), p. 266 n. 39.
[3] *Id.*, p. 2.
[4] *Id.*, p. 9.
[5] Aristides Iván Hassán R., *Holocausto en Panamá* (1982).
[6] *Id.*, p. 19.
[7] *Id.*, pp. 27-28.
[8] *Id.*, p. 78. Eng. ed. (1987), pp. 56-7. The quotations are the Editor's translations from the Spanish ed., as the English edition is often hard to understand; a typical sentence: "He made another signed to Ehrman, who came immediately, saying, please order your excellency." P. 58.
[9] *Id.*, p. 78.
[10] *Id.*, p. 23. Eng. ed., p. 20.
[11] *Id.*, pp. 25-6.
[12] *Ibid.*
[13] *Id.*, pp. 193 *ff.*
[14] *Id.*, pp. 169-80.
[15] *Id.*, pp. 237-240 (misnumbered.) Eng. Ed., p. 178.
[16] *Id.*, p. 78.
[17] Trudi [Gertrude Häusle] Worrell, *"Die Brücke am Chiriquí Viejo: Bericht einer Auswanderung nach Panama"* (1993).
[18] Morf family papers; photocopies courtesy Elfriede Morf and Rosario Laws de Schmieder.
[19] Albert Morf Sr., corresp. with mother & sister, *ibid.* (1938).
[20] Friedman, p. 18.
[21] *Ibid.*
[22] Koster and Sánchez Borbón, *In the Time of the Tyrants* (1990), pp. 60-61.
[23] John Gunther, "World Crisis and the Good Neighbor Policy in Panama, 1936-41," pp. 147, 152 (March 13, 1941), q. LaFeber, p. 95.
[24] 1923, per Koster & Sánchez, p.59; 1926, per LaFeber, p.63
[25] *Id.*, p. 59
[26] LaFeber, p. 93.
[27] *Id.*, p. 82.
[28] *Ibid.*
[29] *Ibid.*
[30] Koster and Sánchez Borbón, p. 60.
[31] LaFeber, *ibid.*

[32] U.S. Dept. of State, Mil. Intel. Div., Memorandum, in U.S. National Archives, (Oct. 7, 1940), cit. LaFeber, p. 93.

[33] Hitler to Arias, Oct. 18, 1940, *Archivos Nacionales*, courtesy Thomas L. Pearcy. Not too much should be made of a *pro forma* diplomatic letter. See image, p. 175, *infra*.

[34] Abbot, *The Panama Canal: An Illustrated Historical Narrative* (1922), pp. 233-36, cit. *ibid.*, p. 79.

[35] *Id.*, p. 91.

[36] Public Law 72/19[41]. Robert C. Harding II, *Military Foundations of Panamanian Politics* (2001), p. 34, cit. Dimas Arturo López, *Las fuerzas armadas de la República de Panamá* (2001).

[37] Thomas L. Pearcy, *We Answer Only to God: Politics and the Military in Panama, 1903-1947* (1998), pp.79-80.

[38] Stimson *Diaries*, v. XXXII, p. 94 (Jan. 9, 1941), cit. LaFeber, p. 95

[39] Friedman, p. 82, citing other sources.

[40] *Id.*, p. 55.

[41] *Id.*, p. 148, citing archival sources.

[42] *Id.*, p. 107, citing Berle's diary Oct. 12, 1940.

[43] *Id.*, p. 56, citing *N.Y. Times* and writings of Spruille Braden, U.S. Ambassador to Colombia and later Cuba.

[44] *Id.*, p. 107.

[45] *Id.*, p. 1, citing Roosevelt's collected *Fireside Chats* (1992).

[46] *Id.*, pp. 107-8.

[47] Q. *id.*, p. 109.

[48] Q. *id.*, p. 108, cit. State Dept. records, Natl. Archives.

[49] *Id.*, p. ix, citing intvs. with Kappel and his file in the Natl. Archives.

[50] *Id.*, p. 110-11.

[51] Dubois, *Danger Over Panama* (1964), p. 53, cit. Friedman, p. 47.

[52] Friedman, *ibid*.

[53] Lengthy citations omitted.

[54] Dubois, p. 57, cit. Friedman, *ibid*.

[55] Lengthy citations to wartime files and studies in U.S. National Archives omitted.

[56] Yahir Leis Alvarado, "*Defensoría No Cobra Multas Por Violar Ley*", *La Prensa*, Jul. 4, 2013, online edition.

[57] LaFeber, p. 97. Citations omitted.

[58] Koster and Sánchez Borbón, p. 61.

[59] See Chapter VI, Section 2, p. 206 *infra*.

[60] John Dinges, *Our Man in Panama* (1990), p. 164.

[61] *Id.*, p. 170.

Cotito

SCHMIEDER FAMILY PHOTO
The Cotito farm. *ca.* 1940

AUTHOR'S INTRODUCTION
[TO THE 1993 SPANISH EDITION]

AT ABOUT 6:00 AM on the morning of Monday, July 7, 1941, two detachments of National Police, composed of forty–five policemen and senior officers under the command of Captain Antonio Huff, chief of the Third Battalion[1] [garrisoned in] Chiriquí, attacked the colony of Swiss–German farmers settled in the region of Cotito, in the jurisdiction of the district of Bugaba.[2]

After a brief but ferocious attack, of the twenty–three colonists, ten lay dead and ten wounded in the colony's main house. A few hours later, two of the most gravely wounded, young Karl Schmieder Jr. and Klara Werren, bled to death as they and the other wounded were carried [on improvised stretchers and borrowed horses] to the town of Volcán.

The colonists were accused of intransigence for having refused to go down to David [capital of the province of Chiriquí] to register with the Alien Affairs section of the National Police. They were [later] accused of possessing an arsenal of weapons including machine guns, of broadcasting from a clandestine radio station, and of having constructed an aircraft landing strip on their property. Finally, they were accused of being members of a Nazi fifth column operating in Latin America during the war years.

They were also alleged to have fired the first shot on the day of the bloody incident, against the police officers who had then responded appropriately. This version of events, recorded in the official record over the objection of only a few dissident voices that were never heeded, was never debated, and in the end, the judges who examined the conduct of the perpetrators of the massacre were persuaded [that this version was true], granting the [police] final exoneration.

→The Swiss immigrants were not undocumented aliens. They came from a neutral, traditionally peaceful country, where the delirious theories of Hitlerian National Socialism did not resonate. President Arosemena's executive order [granting them the right of permanent residence] already reposed in the files of the Alien Affairs section when, in mid-1941, the captain commanding the Third Police Battalion in Chiriquí was directed to serve [what was essentially an administrative subpœna] on the colonists, requiring them to report to David for inspection of their documents, an inspection which had already been carried out by the police themselves scarcely a year earlier.*←[†]

Fifty years later, it is our desire to reconstruct this case, in order to give voice to those who never were able to tell the truth about this lamentable episode in the history of Panama.

—*C.H.C.G.*

PANAMA, R.P.
1993

---

* Former police officer Efraín González relates that in mid-1940, he and Officer Lucas Garcés, traveled through all the villages of the highlands inspecting the passports of European foreigners residing in these areas. González intv. with Author, David, Mar. 5, 1993.

† [Symbols →← explained on p. lxxv, *supra*.]

Notes to Author's Introduction

[1] [The police units in the various provinces were called *secciones* in 1941, but "section" sounds odd in this context; police and fire units are often called "battalions," in later years a favorite term of the military in Panama; hence, I translate *sección* as "battalion."]

[2] [A *distrito*, functionally equivalent to a U.S. county, is the principal subdivision of a Panamanian province, and includes one or more *corregimientos*, or townships, the largest of which is the *cabecera*, or county seat. The government of the *distrito* is the *municipio;* the chief executive is the *alcalde* ("mayor"), formerly appointed by the provincial governor, now elected. At the time of these events, Volcán, Cotito, Santa Clara, Río Sereno and Piedra Candela were all included in the *distrito* of Bugaba, whose *cabecera* is La Concepción. (Río Sereno is now the *cabecera* of a new *distrito*, Renacimiento, which includes Piedra Candela and Santa Clara.)

[The executive officer of each *corregimiento* was in the past the *corregidor* (pron. co-ray-hee-DOR, not kregguh-DAWR as in the war movies), a magistrate vested with the judicial authority of a justice of the peace and limited executive authority. The title evolved not (as is commonly believed) from the verb *corregir*—"to correct," as a judge might do—but evolved rather from the title of the Spanish *co-regidor*, a "co-ruler" dispatched by the Crown to supervise local officials in the colonies. The *corregidor* continues to exercise limited authority over local police detachments in ordering arrests, execution of judgments, etc., but the police force is national, with the chain of command extending through the provincial *cuarteles* ("headquarters") to general police headquarters in Panama City.

[The judicial decisions of the *corregidor* are still appealable to the *alcalde* of the district, an executive-branch official, and then to the provincial governor; judicial independence of the executive branch is a still-evolving concept in Panama's Iberian tradition. This fusion of judicial and executive authority in local government gave rise to the somewhat archaic name of the *Ministry of "Government and Justice,"* to which in 1941 the police, the appointed provincial *gobernadores*, district *alcaldes*, township *corregidores* and the *comisarios* in the hamlets were all subordinate, and which will be frequently encountered in this book. The Ministry's functions were akin to those of the ministry of the "interior" in most European countries.

[In our day, the executive function in each township is exercised by another hybrid, the *representante*, originally a member of the 505-member, rubber-stamp *Cámara de Representantes de Corregimiento* ("House" or

"Chamber" of Township Representatives") created by dictator Omar Torrijos as a malleable alternative for circumventing the national legislative Assembly. The *Cámara* has for all practical purposes ceased to function, and the *representante* is no longer a putative legislator, but is rather a kind of mayor in each township. Depending on the personality of the *representante* and local politics, the *junta communal* or town council, supposed to function as a local legislative body, is often a powerless appendage.

[To its own great detriment, Panama has never distinguished between a civilian police force and a military establishment; the same "public force" under different names has always exercised both functions. The colonists' advance scout, Albert Morf, was surprised to learn, as he wrote to his mother on Nov. 5, 1938, that "There is no military service here, as Panama has no Army, although the Republic is twice as large as Switzerland." He was voicing the conventional wisdom, but the distinction between the national police force and a politicized military has never been strictly demarcated in Panama.]

FOTO FLATAU

David, capital of the province of Chiriquí, *ca.* 1941.

I | A SWISS RELIGIOUS COMMUNE

1 | SWITZERLAND DURING THE NINETEEN-THIRTIES

AT THE END OF the nineteen–thirties, the economy of Switzerland, like that of almost all the countries of Europe, was in dire straits. The great conflagration brought considerable instability to Switzerland. National unity was at the breaking point, as the French– and German–speaking sectors of the population favored, respectively, France and Germany, the powers opposed in the conflict.

→Problems that had originated during the First World War had grown worse after the war ended.← Four years of military mobilization and modernization of the Swiss armed forces produced a wartime economy occasioning grave privations for the civilian population. Unemployment increased alarmingly and necessities, especially foodstuffs, grew scarce. With less than ten percent of its land dedicated to farming—given the mountainous topography of the country that made intensive agriculture difficult—Switzerland was not self–sufficient in food: it had to import wheat and other cereals, although it did provide for its own needs with respect to dairy products and fruit.

As 1930 approached, approximately twenty–two percent of the population depended on agriculture,[1] but in those years the prices of farm products fell precipitously, and industrial exports were reduced to a minimum, which increased unemployment and exacerbated the condition of the population. Although, in comparison with other countries in Europe,[2] socio-economic levels remained high, Swiss farmers contemplated the future with trepidation. In the agricultural cantons of Bern, Vaud, Zürich and the Aargau, many peasant families faced the specter of hunger and cold.

By the eve of the Second World War, the Swiss had recovered their unity, as Nazism found few friends in the country, but because of its strategic location, the situation became much more complicated. National–Socialist Germany and Fascist Italy shared borders with the Helvetian state. Only the Swiss tradition of neutrality, their humanitarian activity and their determined will to repel any outside invasion of their soil,[*] saved them from the horrendous conflagration of the war.

It was in no way strange, therefore, that in 1938 some families considered leaving their homeland in search of new opportunities, despite the fact that in making the attempt, they would forfeit the right to return. This was the fate of the Swiss farmers who came, from Vairano in Switzerland to live in the highlands of Chiriquí, in an isolated place called Cotito.[†]

2 | THE FOUNDING OF THE COMMUNE

JUST HOW IS not known, but slowly, around 1936, a group of Swiss–German families, almost all of peasant origin,[‡] were organizing an agricultural commune that they had established at Vaira-

---

[*] [Not to mention their "neutral" banking system and the diplomatic services that the Swiss, as "neutrals," provided the Germans abroad, both of which served many purposes useful to the Nazis.]

[†] [A *coto* is a fenced pasture (or, in some places, a hunting preserve). *Cotito* is merely the diminutive.]

[‡] [In fact, they were *not* mostly of peasant origin, but were rather a mix of town dwellers with various professions and trades. *See* p. xl, *infra*.]

no, a locality situated between Brissago and Locarno, on the shores of Lake Maggiore, in the canton of Ticino,[*] near the Italian border.

They were a cohesive group, united by profound religious convictions and by the strict observance of a severe regimen for communal living. They practiced the economic communism of primitive Christian groups: they shared their goods and the fruits of their labor were used to meet their needs. They were industrious, peaceful, hospitable, and projected a profound sense of human solidarity.

In the religious realm, the colonists were in correspondence with the Peace Mission Movement, founded on the opposite side of the Atlantic in New York by the African–American Father Divine, a former Baptist preacher whose teachings they followed. Nevertheless, they read all kinds of mystical books, especially those relating to the ancient oriental masters.

The commune had formed around the person of Karl Lehner, fifty years of age and a native of the small town of Lower Helfenschwil, and who, before moving to Vairano, had lived for a long time in Zürich. He [in the view of a sympathetic former follower]—

> was not a boss, but was rather a guide, not a [great] lord who imposed his will, no. He preached the word of God, well and profoundly, and especially Father Divine, practical living, and said again and again that there should be no improprieties like—to say it straight out—love affairs.
>
> So the ladies apart, the gents apart. And to be completely consecrated to God. To eat no meat, and above all, as the Bible teaches, no pork. We did consume milk and cheese and all the vegetables.[†]

---

[*] [This canton, in the predominantly Italian region of southern Switzerland, is usually known in English by its Italian name, *Ticino,* but in the German spoken by the members of the commune, it was known as *Tessin.*]

[†] Werner Robert Müller, intv. with Author, Panama City, May 8, 1992. [Müller had spent his childhood with his parents in Lehner's group. His

Continued→

In 1938, at least twenty persons constituted the group under the leadership of Lehner. There were five families: the Morfs, the Werrens, the Müllers, the Rieser–Wehrlis and the Häusles [(sister and brother)]. There were also [three] single people: Anna Siedler, Heinrich Ott, as well as Lehner himself, who had no family.

- Albert Morf, 37, native of Gossau, then a small industrial center of about eight thousand inhabitants, situated on the railway from Zürich to Rorschach. He was married to Elfriede, a young woman also from Gossau, and they were the parents of Albert Jr., [Elfriede ("Friede")], Walter and [Leonora ("Loni")] Morf.

- Gottfried Werren, born in 1879 at Zweisimmen, a small, mountainous locality of 2,400 inhabitants, situated at 3,100 meters altitude in the Simmental range of the Bernese Alps. He was married to Klara, also from Zweisimmen, and was the father of Klärli, a 16–year–old of exceptional beauty, and Cornelia, 13.

- Werner Müller, 34 years old, born at Trimbach, a mountainous locality in the Swiss Jura near the French border;[3] married to Sophie Baumann, 33, a native of Zürich. They were the parents of Werner Robert, [called "Böps",] 8 years old.

- Paul Häusle, a young German national of 19, born at St. Gallen in Switzerland, the son of Franz Häusle[, an architect,] and Gertrude Kraner. He was accompanied by his sister Gertrude ("Trudi"), 22.

- Viola ["Vio"] Rieser–Wehrli, 30, a native of Herrliberg,[4] Zürich, separated from her husband Georg, and mother of

---

← *Continued from prev. page.*
own and others' testimony makes it clear that the sexual segregation was theoretical, not actual, and did not apply to Lehner and several women.]

the little Virgilio, [three] months old [when he died in murky circumstances].*

- Of the origins of Anna Siedler and Heinrich Ott, we know only that Ott was 58, was born in a place called Seen, probably a small mountain village.[5]

What most of the colonists had in common was their origin in small mountain areas with deep-rooted traditions of agriculture and handicrafts. The colonists knew not only how to cultivate the land, to raise cattle, to make dairy products and to preserve fruit; they had also learned to be skilled carpenters, to work iron, and to construct their own tools and dwellings. In other words, the commune was practically self-sufficient; they had very little need for

---

* [Viola Wehrli in later years told her family that it was her husband Georg Rieser who had been drawn to the Lehner group and had introduced her to it. He later left the group, she said, and they were divorced before the departure for Panama. (Ed.'s intv., Erica Witzig–Fassler, dtr. of Viola Wehrli and her second husband, Volcán Feb. 2015.) Vio Wehrli's status as the mother of the infant Virgilio Rieser (whom she had named for the ship on which the colony intended to sail to Panama) was one of the most complex issues in the history of the colony, and, according to contemporary reports, Virgilio was the first of three children to disappear during its existence in Switzerland and Panama. According to a Swiss diplomat's report, Viola Wehrli was—
 born Feb. 4, 1908 at Kilchberg (near Zürich)...was married to Georges [*i.e.,* Georg, the German form] Rieser of Affeltrangen (Thurgovia), but the marriage was dissolved Sept. 12, 1938, at Locarno. They had a son, Virgilio Rieser, born Aug. 21, 1938, at St. Nazaro, who died Dec. 1, 1938, in the latter locality. It appears that Mme Rieser was at that time a member of the Lehner group, which, in 1938, was living at San Navaro before emigrating to Panama. Apparently, the infant Virgilio Rieser died a few days before the group embarked for Panama and Lehner failed to report the death of the infant to the appropriate authorities. A. Gonzenbach, Swiss *chargé d'affaires,* Caracas, to Swiss Civil Status Service, Nov. 12, 1943. Transl. from French. *See also,* Viola Wehrli's deposition, Appendix B, p. 223, *infra.*
[Trude Haüsle Worrell "testified for Vio's [later] children at their probate hearing in Switzerland that the aforementioned baby had indeed died in Switzerland and never made it to Panama." Yvonne Worrell Pover, dtr. of Trudi Häusle Worrell, e-mail to Editor, Aug. 30, 2011.]

contact with the neighboring towns in order to supply their needs, →[and] they isolated themselves from strangers.← They were not, [however], an [entirely] closed group. They were hospitable and open with everyone, albeit severe in the strict observance of their religious belief and rules of practical living. They were a "different" group, and this caused more than a few problems.

3 | THE CULT OF FATHER DIVINE

HOW DID THIS small community, settled in the mountains of Ticino, come to identify with all the teachings of Father Divine, to the extent that even today, some sixty years later, some of the survivors[*] continue to practice his teachings?[†] To answer this question, we need to know more about this figure.

---

[*] [When this was written, only Roberto Müller appeared to have observed any of the colony's practices.]

[†] [Father Divine had at least some small following in Switzerland before and after World War II, as the following report from *Time* magazine's issue of Oct. 14, 1946, would confirm.

[Religion: Swiss Heaven

["I spared Switzerland from war and famine because I am there."
[—Father Divine.

[As usual, the little Father needed to be translated. He meant his spiritual body, not his own plump, proper person. And in Divine lingo, spiritual body included the 2,000 white "angels" who live in Swiss "heavens" and believe Father's word that he is God.

[Last week in Zurich some 80 angels, mostly female, flocked to a heaven (in a *"restaurant sans alcool"*), to hear a German translation of Father Divine's latest "office talk." Reader Alfred Riesen, Father's governor in Switzerland, kept asking: "Aren"t you glad?" Many angels wept for joy. "We thank thee, Father," they sang. "Oh, how wonderful is our Father Divine. ... We belong to him with every atom of our body and soul."

[Most of the angels were shabby, tired and obviously unhappy—a sort of bespattered mudguard of the lower middle class. Their beliefs were probably best expressed by Joseph Jacob Greutmann, 57-year-old pastry cook, onetime hypnotist, who founded the first Swiss heaven. Says Greutmann:

Continued→

It is not known with certainty in what year the preacher George Baker was born. Some say 1864,[6] 1877,[7] or 1878.[8] Others give the year as 1880.[9] Baker was a charismatic religious leader, a man of color who began preaching in the South of the United States around 1900. He soon abandoned the Baptist denomination and moved to Sayville, N.Y., where he founded the Peace Mission Movement. In 1900 he took the name Major J. Devine, and later, in 1919, the name of "Father Divine," as he was known until his death in 1965. His message contained a mixture of primitive mysticism and elements of the spiritualist and Pentecostal movements. The salient characteristics were:

1. A ministry centered on the person of Father Divine, whom the faithful—called "angels"—considered a god incarnate.
2. Communal living, cooperative work, conveyance of the ownership of all material possessions to the Divine, who provided food and lodging gratis or at low cost to the faithful, and they, in turn, reposed an unconditional faith in his miraculous powers.
3. Vows of strict morality, celibacy and charity. The members were invited to repent of their sins, and every transgression they committed was denounced before the congregation.
4. Respect for racial equality.[10]

← *Continued from prev. page.*
["We worship Father Divine because he is the second incarnation of God. ... We are all white but we think there should be no difference between human races. ... It is just a symbol to mankind that God chose the body of a Negro when He came to earth this time. It is another symbol that the black Mrs. Divine vanished and rose again, but as a young white girl."
[The reporter's concentration on race reflects attitudes of the time. The epigraph of the article would appear not to apply to the Swiss "angels" who, having emigrated to Panama, were not "spared," but rather had been murdered five years earlier. The Ed. is indebted to Dr^a. B. R. Thayer of Panama City for locating online and forwarding the article quoted.]

PEACE MISSION MOVEMENT
Penninah, the first Mother Divine.

Followers were invited to live in houses called "heavens," and to contribute to the work of the Movement. The "heavens," according to Father Divine, were characterized by the separation of the sexes and the union of all the races in community, resulting in multicultural communal life. He also taught that there would come a moment in which all the races would be totally integrated, that the *New Day* (the Movement's newspaper) was the bible, that all would be forgiven by the Father, and that heaven was to be found on earth.[11]

His first "heaven" was founded in Sayville, but there soon existed 178 of them across the country, most in New York and Philadelphia. The number of angels also grew, rising to approximately five hundred thousand. The circulation of the *New Day* rose and it was to be found in the most unlikely locations. Father Divine was purported to draw no salary, but he surely had free access to a fortune above a million–and–a–half [uninflated, pre–war] dollars, which he used generously to aid businessmen of color, some of whom, in turn, when they had achieved success, returned substantial profits to the Movement to finance its activities. The Divine maintained a luxurious lifestyle, which attracted criticism and more than a few problems. Accused of cor-

PEACE MISSION MOVEMENT
Father Divine and his second wife Edna Rose, who he said was Penninah's reincarnation.

ruption, he was obliged to leave Harlem, in New York City, and move to Philadelphia. →In 1946, upon the death of his first wife Penninah, he married Edna Rose Richings, a white follower 21 years of age, who became the new "Mother Divine" and was supposed to have remained a virgin.←

The secret of Father Divine's success was the devotion of his quite competent followers, recalls [the Panamanian lawyer] Jorge Fábrega Ponce, who was contacted back in the nineteen–sixties and retained by the disciples of Father Divine to incorporate the movement in Panama, which he did to the satisfaction of the demanding emissaries.[12]

Father Divine's movement arose during the so–called post–Reconstruction period, when, because of their extreme poverty and social marginalization, messiahs arose everywhere, offering a response to the anguished problem of the black population. →It is easy to understand how in those difficult years, the thousands of homeless who filled the streets of cities in the United States looked with favor on the establishment of these terrestrial "heavens"; and how this favorable view extended beyond the confines of the United States.←

During the Depression of the nineteen–thirties, the Peace Mission Movement conducted a campaign on behalf of the black minority of Los Angeles that increased the Movement's popularity. The teachings of Father Divine were expounded then in the *New [Day]*, a publication in which he preached opposition to the entrenched practices of segregation in that American metropolis. The Movement began a new newspaper, *The Spoken Word,* which continued the proselytizing work begun fifteen years earlier. →It was probably then that the Swiss of Vairano came in contact with the Movement. The contact possibly occurred through the reading of the *New Day* or *The Spoken Word,* whose distribution was entrusted to the followers of the Divine, intent on supporting a Movement in a time of rapid growth.←

In reality, the circumstances of the Swiss colonists were not so different from those of the thousands of paupers produced by the Depression in the agricultural southern United States. The religious figure Karl Lehner, perhaps mentally an atavistic Calvinist for whom the totality of human activities was to be submitted to religious control, identified fully with a movement that placed the rules of Christian communal living above any secular authority. In addition, he advocated charity and racial equality in a world divided by so many barriers and proclaimed that the goal of the commune was the birth of human liberty.

The Swiss leader achieved the foundation—around the teachings of Father Divine and his own—of a new terrestrial "heaven" in the mountains of Vairano, although in this particular heaven he was the undisputed leader. In the predominantly Catholic canton of Ticino, the "different" members of the Vairano commune, with their thick beards, their rough sandals and their women dressed as men, would not have an easy time of it. Karl Lehner, Müller and the others would constantly be visited by the police.

PHOTO BEATRICE KÜNZ FOR *NEUE ZÜRCHER ZEITUNG*, COURTESY WERNER C. SENN

In 1994, Werner Robert ("Böps") Müller—or Roberto Miller, as he was known later in life—was photographed for the Swiss newspaper *Neue Zürcher Zeitung*. His July, 1941, childhood photograph may be seen on page 167, *infra*. His resemblance to his father Werner, killed in the massacre, is striking. *See* photo, p. 98, *infra*.

4 | THE COMMUNE'S PROBLEMS

FOR EXPOSITION OF the following information, we have relied on the testimony of Werner Robert Müller, the only survivor of Cotito whom we were able to interview,[*] and on one of the letters ad-

---

[*] Werner Robert Müller, intv. with Author, Panama City, May 8, 1992. [Robert Müller served as a principal source for the Author, and for Peter Gaupp, who wrote an extensive article about the massacre for the *Neue Zürcher Zeitung* in 1994. The Editor cautions the reader that Sophie and Robert Müller may not have been entirely reliable witnesses, particularly with respect to privations suffered later, financial matters and matters of inheritance following the dissolution of the colony.

[The Author, a lawyer analyzing a historical case record, does not describe Roberto Miller (as he was known in Volcán), in any detail. Roberto and his mother, Sophie, *née* Baumann (later Wachter), lived the rest of their lives in Chiriquí. In later life, Roberto continued to observe some of the idiosyncratic practices of Lehner's colony. He wore his hair and beard uncut, and when he was not barefoot, he wore old, unlaced shoes. He drove a battered old truck, collecting scrap metal and other salvage; in one anecdote, having been told not to remove some steel rails he had "found" on a neighbor's farm, he is said to have replied "things belong not to those who have them, but those who need them." Those who did not know him well referred to him as *"Roberto el Loco."* He was said to have been a rational conversationalist, as his interviews with the Author and Gaupp also demonstrate, although—perhaps because he had spoken a mixture of German, Swiss-German dialect and Spanish as a child, or perhaps because of some impediment—his Spanish was said to be somewhat difficult to understand. He did have one salient idiosyncrasy, however: he was forever untying dogs or setting loose other caged or leashed animals he found in town, to the natural consternation of their owners. It was generally believed that this practice was a a result of his having learned in the colony of the obligation of humans to protect animals. Felipe Serrano Pandiella, intv. with Ed., Volcán, 2010.

[According to both Gustav Haug (the Swiss who emigrated just after the colony did but later grew disenchanted and set up on his own) and Albert Schmieder (who was, along with Müller one of the colony's few children), Robert, then known as Böps, was severely abused as a child by Lehner, with the consent or even participation of the parents themselves. Schmieder believes Müller's confinement phobia stemmed from his having repeatedly been shut up at night in an attic, bound to a plank with leather straps, a punishment Schmieder says he did not actually witness, although he frequently saw the apparatus in the attic and, he says, "everyone knew that it was for punishing Böps."

Continued→

dressed by Gustav Haug Sr. to the Swiss Consul in Panama, and which is now held in the archives of the Helvetian legation in our country.[13]

According to Müller, there then existed very strange regulations in Ticino, such as that which prohibited farmers from consuming the entirety of their own produce, obliging them to offer it on the market, and also prohibiting the barter of farm products. Similarly, farmers were obliged to purchase on the market products for their own use.

There were also regulations in force that established production quotas and fixed prices in order to avoid disequilibria between supply and demand. It was obvious that the members of a practically self-sufficient commune could hardly adapt themselves easily to fit the mold of these strictures, meaning that friction with local authorities and the neighbors must have been frequent. There were at least two incidents that contributed to the colonists' determination to emigrate. The first was the incident of the frogs, and the second the affair of the chestnuts.

THE COLONISTS WERE strict vegetarians. They were permitted to eat only root vegetables, [certain] fresh vegetables,[*] fruits and grains. They could also consume dairy products such as cheese and butter.

← *Continued from prev. page.*

[Schmieder says Sophie was one of the earliest devotees of Lehner's proselytizing and the one who was most submissive to the cult leader. Schmieder, intv. with Ed., Aug. 2011. Müller himself told Gaupp, the Swiss journalist, that his mother had been "intimate" with Lehner. Sophie ended her days in the care of the local Pinedo family with a small stipend from the Swiss government. Gaupp, *"Massaker in Cotito,"* (1994). *See also* Gustav Haug, "My Experience with the 'Molch' Colony" (July 1941), which appears in full in a new German-to-English transl. by Barbara Traber from a copy in the Swiss archives in Bern, in Appendix A, pp. 179 *ff, infra.*

[*Molch,* German for "salamander," was the followers' nickname for Lehner; *see* p. 36 *infra.*]

* [*verduras, hortalizas*: In Panama, *verduras* refers to root vegetables such as *yuca* ("manioc"), *ñame, otoe,* carrots and others, such as squash and *chayote,* etc., generally boiled in soup, while *legumbres* and *hortalizas* are more general terms for vegetables.]

CHAPTER I | A SWISS RELIGIOUS COMMUNE

Their beliefs forbade shedding the blood of animals. Hence, it was natural that animals found a refuge on their property in Vairano. Among these were frogs, considered a delicacy for some Swiss, [French] and Italian communities, which prepare the hind legs in different ways. There was an abundance of frogs in the commune, and one night, outsiders sneaked onto the property for the purpose of capturing hundreds of frogs, from which they took only the hind legs, discarding the rest on the spot.

This episode had grave repercussions. Aside from the trespass on their property, it constituted a grave offense against the religious belief of the colonists. Their protests to the authorities in Locarno, in whose jurisdiction Vairano lay, proved useless.

The other incident was that of the chestnuts. According to Müller's version, unlike the Swiss–Germans, the Swiss–Italians did not customarily gather the chestnuts abundant on the conifers in the region.[*] The colonists secured the permission of a neighbor to enter on his property for the purpose of gathering the abundant chestnuts there. The neighbor assented and granted them permission, but other neighbors accused them of trespassing on private property.

> But the neighbors said, "Look, they are trespassing," and went to make a complaint to the magistrate of the place, the *bund*. Then they went to arrest my Papa and the head of the colony, Mr. Lehner, who they said were trespassing, and with all this going on, the owner said he had given them the chestnuts, but they were not allowed to keep them.[†]

It was then, affirms Müller, that the possibility of emigration to the mountains of Panama arose, and then that the colonists determined to exercise that option.

---

[*] [Chestnut trees are not conifers.]

[†] Müller. [I translate *corregidor* as "magistrate." The *bund* would not have been a magistrate, but perhaps Müller, retelling for the Author anecdotes he had heard from his father before he was 10, confuses his father's reference to some town council or other collective authority.]

In 1938, Gustav Haug was living at Rovin, also in the canton of Ticino, where he owned and operated a *pension*. In the middle of that year, he remembers, he received a visit from Werner Müller and Albert Morf, who, after informing him that the colonists were thinking about emigrating to Panama, asked for information about the province of Chiriquí and about Haug's German friend Karl Schmieder, who had emigrated sometime previously, settling in the mountains of that Panamanian province.

Two days later, Haug and his family traveled to Vairano, where they met Lehner. Lehner impressed them profoundly, and told them that he had read Schmieder's name in a book entitled *Tropical Homeland: Panama–Mexico* by the Swiss author Werner Zimmermann [1893–1982.*] After making [further] inquiries about

---

* [Zimmermann, a teacher and social reformer, was founder of the Swiss *Freiwirtschaftsbund* ("Free Economic Union"), known as the "F.F.F." for its slogan, *Freiwirtschaft durch Freiland und Freigeld* ("Economic freedom through free land and free money"). The group advocated the nationalization of farmland and low interest rates, ideas developed by the reformer Silvio Gesell (1862-1930).

[In 1928, three German followers—Anton Hils and Karl Schmieder from Lauterbach and Josef Kohler from Schramberg, adjoining small towns in the Black Forest of Southwestern Germany—emigrated to Panama and settled in the Cotito area as pioneers in the jungle (though Kohler soon returned to Germany). In 1929, Alfred Brauchle, Fritz Schaper and their families followed Hils and Schmieder to Cotito. Zimmermann had met them when speaking to the Schramberg group headed by Brauchle. That year, Zimmermann made a trip to Central America, among the principal motives for which was a desire to locate the Cotito pioneers. He reported on what he found in the book he published in Switzerland in 1930.

[Brauchle had been a worker in the Hamburg–American Clock factory, the principal industry of Schramberg. Zimmermann reported in his book that when he visited Panama, Brauchle told him, "You know how it was in Germany, in the Black Forest. With 30 Reichsmarks [a week, (1928 value, approx. US $7.15) at a time when skilled workers in the US were earning $30–35 for a six-day week], I had to support my wife and two children, and make payments on the 2,500-Reichsmark [about US $600] mortgage, at ten percent interest, on my little house. And the pressure on a factory worker was ever greater. The worst was that there was nothing ahead, no way we could ever in our lifetimes work ourselves out from under this situation." According to Zimmermann, Brauchle said, "We picked ourselves up and acted: it was either that or go under."

Continued→

the colonists, whom he considered honest people, Haug recommended that before making a final decision they send an emissary to Panama to study local conditions. Haug then wrote to Schmieder, informing him of the colonists' plans and asked him to help them.[14]

5 | KARL SCHMIEDER'S FARM

KARL SCHMIEDER, A German born at Schramberg, his wife Margarethe and his fellow Germans Anton and Mari[e] Hils, Friedrich and Martha Schaper, and Alfred and Lydia Brauchle, and the children of the three families, had arrived in the highlands of Chiriquí in 1928[−29.*].[15]

← *Continued from prev. page.*
[Lydia Brauchle told the visiting Zimmermann, " 'Oh, those dumb Schrambergers.' What she meant was that most people believe that they can only live there, where 'there are factories. And the most beautiful of all is the golden freedom. Here you don't hear any factory whistles. ... Naturally you don't get your weekly pay, but here there are no problems, or very few.' " Translated and abridged from Carsten Kohlmann, article in the *Schwarzwälder Bote* ["Black Forest Messenger"] and *Schwäbischer Zeitung,* ["Swabian Newspaper"], Aug. 10, 2002, from e-mail version sent by Kohlmann to the Schaper family, Nov. 12, 2002.
[Within ten years, Frau Brauchle's husband would die in an enemy–alien internment camp in the United States, one of her sons (who had joined the Swiss colony at Cotito) would be murdered in the massacre, and another son would spend seven long years in U.S. internment and working his way back to Panama. In the end, the Brauchles' farm would pass to the Hilses in return for the care they gave *Frau* Lydia. Werner C. Senn, intv. with Ed., 2011. In her later years, Lydia Brauchle lived in Volcán with the Schapers, with whom she and her family had emigrated in 1929.]
* ["As at the end of the German Weimar Republic [1919−33], the economy was ever−worsening, and with the worldwide economic crisis and the onset of mass unemployment, Alfred Brauchle, Anton Hils, Josef Kohler, Fritz Schaper and Karl Schmieder saw no future in their homeland and begin to consider emigration." The Schmieders, Anton Hils, and Josef Kohler sailed on April 21, 1928, on the *S.S. Orinoco*, from Hamburg to Panama. On the advice of the consul there, they sought out a German (probably Richard Neumann, who was farming at Macho de Monte), who had lived in the area for a long time and who generously put at their disposal rent−free a thousand hectares of land at an altitude of 1,000 m. The settlers built a house in the remote area and with the onset of the dry season (which would have been shortly after their arrival), they cleared land

Continued→

The Germans settled at Cotito, several hours on horseback from [El] Hato [del] Volcán[*], and there pursued farming and stock raising. Pioneers in a practically virgin area, they built their houses of the precious hardwoods growing in the mountains, which reminded them of the Black Forest of Germany from which they had come. They found the area ideal for their agricultural pursuits because of the fertility of the soils and the temperate climate favorable for raising livestock.[16] Schmieder had about 100 hectares [≈220 acres] along the Cotito River, a tributary of the Chiriquí Viejo, with lowlands suitable for cultivation surrounded by wooded mountains of medium altitude [the area is generally at approximately 1,500 m, ≈5,000 ft, above sea level]. The German immigrant raised corn, bananas, coffee, vegetables and fruit, and had a sizeable herd of cattle and horses. Schmieder did not have fee–simple title to the farm at Cotito, but like most Panamanian farmers, he had *derechos posesorios,* [possessory or "homesteader's rights" rights, legally recognized in Panama; such properties may be inherited and sold. There is a procedure for "titling" the *derechos posesorios*.].

← *Continued from prev. page.*
by burning and put in their crops. With their meager capital (Hils had about $100, Schmieder about $400) they bought seven cows, seven horses and two hundred chickens. Having positive reports from the first group, a second group followed a year later. Alfred and Lydia Brauchle and their family, and Fritz and Martha Schaper (who was Karl Schmieder's sister), arriving in Panama on Sept. 3, 1929. On Nov. 1 the latter group reached Volcán where the Schmieders, Hilses, and Kohler were already settled and had prepared a temporary *rancho* (thatched hut) for them to live in. Kohler returned to Germany when his fiancée refused to emigrate. Kohlmann, ibid.]

* [An *hato* is a herd or flock; in the Americas it can mean a cattle ranch. Volcán refers to the Volcán Barú, at over 11,000 ft, the highest point in Panama, on whose slopes the town stands at about 1,400 m, 4,650 ft., altitude. The township is now called simply, and officially, *Volcán*.]

CHAPTER 1 | A SWISS RELIGIOUS COMMUNE

SCHMIEDER FAMILY PHOTO
Margarethe ("Gretel") Schmieder, sons Karl Jr. and Albert ("Benni"), on the Cotito Farm in 1938, before the Swiss joined them. Gretel recalled these years as the "happiest" of her marriage. Karl Sr. (not pictured) and Jr. both died in the massacre three years later.

→His farm was bordered on the north and west by those of his countrymen.← →Fritz and Martha Schaper bordered on the North. Their property was the one that reached farthest up the slope of the central ridge of mountains. To the [east] lived Anton and Mari[e] Hils and their three children. To the south of the Hilses were Alfred and Lydia Brauchle and their three adult sons, Alfred Jr., Erwin and Helmut.← Having corresponded with the Swiss commune from the middle of the nineteen-thirties, [Schmieder] at some point must definitely have come to share their religious beliefs and rules for living. →[A] year after the Swiss had [arrived in Panama and] begun working [the 500-hectare tract the government had granted them[*]] at Piedra Candela,[*] where they had built a camp

---
* [See p. 26 *infra*.]

and were raising corn,[17] Lehner's group would relocate to Schmieder's farm.← Schmieder and his family were incorporated into the collective. The decision would not sit well with [Schmieder's] sister and neighbor Martha [married to Fritz Schaper], or with Gustav Haug, who [later] wrote from Switzerland to express his apprehensions about his friend's decision.† According to the [dubious] statement of Werner Robert Müller, Schmieder, unable to pay off a loan from another sister living in the United States and on the verge of losing the property, had offered to sell out to the Swiss.[18] However, this version seems unlikely, not only because it is uncorroborated, but also because most of the sources consulted confirm that the Schmieders had [freely] granted their hospitality to the settlers. [Müller's version was probably colored by his and his mother's lifelong belief that the rest of the settlers had been cheated out of some claimed equity when Schmieder's widow Margarethe and her second husband, Gustav Haug sold the farm.]

Another factor motivating the colonists at Vairano to emigrate from Switzerland to the Republic of Panama was that Panama had adopted legislation favorable to the immigration of farmers coming to settle under-populated areas and to develop the practically non-existent agriculture there.[19] In fact, under the presidential administration [1932–36] of Dr. Harmodio Arias Madrid, executive order № 3 (Jan. 17, 1933) was issued; article 5 exempted those

---

← *Continued from prev. page.*

* [Literally, "flame stone," presumably from deposits of flint-like stone useful for striking a fire.]

† Gustav Haug Sr. [The correspondence referred to is intriguing because even today, an airmail letter from Europe can take two weeks or more to thread its way through the Panamanian mails to Volcán, and in the 1930's the town was much more isolated than it is now. Correspondence took months in each direction; in 1941, Albert Morf wrote his family, "Your letter of Nov. 14, 1940, was received here in early March, 1941." Albert Morf to family, Mar. 30, 1941. Werner C. Senn, now living in Volcán, and whose father, Hans August Sr., was the first postmaster, relates that in the post office, German and English were the commonly heard languages, Panamanians being, then as now, unaccustomed to using the cumbersome mails. Intv. with O. Iván Flores and David Dell, Volcán, 2009.]

SCHMIEDER FAMILY PAPERS, COURTESY ALBERT & ROSARIO SCHMIEDER

Identification page from the German passport of Karl August (b. Mar. 28, 1905) and Margarethe Luise (b. Aug. 21, 1895) Schmieder, issued at Lauterbach on February 11, 1928. The passport bears a visa for Panama issued by the consul general at Hamburg on February 18, 1928, and, having arrived in Panama City, the couple registered at the German consulate on May 21.

The passport expired on February 7, 1933, soon after the Nazis had taken control of Germany, and does not indicate a renewal. Eight years later, in 1941, the settlers were ordered to report to David for verification of their status. As Germans with expired passports, they might have been, like the Brauchles, subject to deportation and internment in the U.S.

Along with numerous other identification documents, the passport was confiscated by the police after the massacre. It turned up half a century later in the files of the Civil Registry, where the surviving son Albert, born in Panama, had gone to transact routine business.

immigrants and their families who undertook to live in the interior of the Republic and pursue agricultural activities from posting the otherwise–required repatriation bond, provided they possessed sufficient resources to support themselves for at least a year.* The executive order also charged consular officials with the obligation to secure publicity in favor of the country and to provide immigrants with "full information so that they can fully understand our institutions and our natural resources with potential for the pursuit of their activities and developing the various resources of our national economy."[20] [As the German historian Holger M. Meding[21] relates, the general goal of planned immigration was to benefit from the expertise of the Europeans and what were believed to be their superior genes, while limiting the "in–creeping" of undesirables from the Canal Zone, especially the thousands of West Indians who had been brought there by the United States.

> [T]he European was seen as the desirable immigrant who, by means of his example and his superior knowledge, would contribute to the general welfare. ... The (often clearly stated) objective of Panamanian immigration policy was not merely economic and social; it also included *"el mejoramiento etnológico del país"* ["the ethnic improvement of the country."]†

---

* [This legislation remained in force until the mid–1990's, long after many parts of Chiriquí had become, if anything, over–populated, deforested and intensively farmed. It has since been repealed.]

† ["This objective of the Government of Panama met with the approval of the Canal Zone [authorities]. Several reports from the O[ffice of] N[aval] I[ntelligence] cited with approval the works of Gustave Le Bon, characterizing the Latin American races, together with the observation that an increase of 'Nordic elements' would have the consequence of higher economic development, together with an indication that in South and Central America, the 'evolution of a better basic racial stock through immigration' was to be desired." Meding's note, citing Panamanian Min. For. Rel., 1926 MEMORIA, at xciv, and U.S. Office of Naval Intelligence, "Memorandum for the Director," January 19/20, 1927, U.S. Natl. Archives, Rec. Grp. 38, file C9b, doc. 18,685.]

[The Government finally settled its remaining Germans at Boquete in Chiriquí,[22] where the climate was more favorable, and where some of them encountered long–term success with coffee plantations and orchards.

[The government's efforts were not fated to be crowned with success. Early on, in 1905, a Russian colony in Chiriquí failed,[23] and an attempt to bring Austrians into the country remained unsuccessful; at the end of 1924, forty–to–fifty Germans from the Rhineland came to Panama, invited by the Porras administration. However, they faced rejection from the rural population.[*] The government then supported their resettlement in the area of Capira, with land grants and startup funds. Mutual commitments remained unfulfilled, however, due to adverse natural conditions.

[...

[In the nineteen–thirties there was contact with the Swiss government promoting the settlement of Helvetian farmers in Panama.[24]]

6 | AN EMISSARY TO PANAMA

[GUSTAV HAUG, THE Swiss who had previously visited Chiriquí, was consulted by the colonists and "recommended that—if they had thought through everything carefully—they should send a man to Panama to have a first–hand look at conditions and to make the

---

* [" 'A local Ku Klux Klan directed against aliens of all sorts could be easily organized and would be extremely popular. In particular, Panamanians are nearly as intolerant as Americans,' shouted the Star & Herald." Meding's note, citing [U.S. Army Corps of Engineers,] Headquarters Panama Canal Dept., "Summary of Intelligence" № 7, Dec. 16, 1924, U.S. Natl. Archives, Rec. Grp. 165, file 255–H–27. "After failing to provide sufficient settlement land near Capira, the Government settled the remaining Germans in Boquete." *Id.* "Panama" in Thomas Adam, Ed., *Germany and the Americas* (2005) 863 at 864–5.]

necessary arrangements with the Government."*] The colonists decided to send as their envoy Albert Morf Sr., [then 38 years of age] who soon journeyed to Panama, charged with the mission of obtaining a group immigrants' visa, not only for the members of the commune, but also for several other persons interested in making the trip as well: Gustav Haug, his wife Elise and children Liselotte, Alfred and Gustav Jr., as well as Verena Zulauf.

[Morf, whose letters to his mother and sister in Switzerland show he was of a deeply religious disposition and a fervent believer in the leadership of Karl Lehner, described his three-week voyage to Panama, via Bermuda, Nassau, Havana and Jamaica. [In a letter sent from David on November 5, 1938, he relates that at Havana most of the European passengers had disembarked, to be replaced by a "different segment of humanity," mostly *"Mischlinge und Neger"*—"of mixed race and Negroes"—with whom he says he could communicate well because they spoke English; in addition to

POSTCARD, PHOTO FLATAU. COURTESY WERNER C. SENN

The post office, late 1940's, at the northeast corner of the intersection of the Concepción-Sereno Highway and the Volcán-Cerro Punta road, now the center of the town of Volcán. Help for the wounded was summoned from here in July, 1941.

---

* [See Haug's report in Appendix A, p. 181, *infra*.]

CHAPTER 1 | A SWISS RELIGIOUS COMMUNE

CANAL ZONE GOVT. (?) PHOTO. COURTESY DOÑA ROMELIA VDA. DE HILS
See caption overleaf.

twenty-five Chinese traveling across the Isthmus to take ship on the Pacific coast for their homeland.] Morf arrived in Panama [on September 29,*] 1938. Because of some question about his documents, immigration officials ordered him ashore at Colón and sent him to Panama City, where he found a friendlier official reception. [As still happens so often, one of the officials, upon learning that Morf's goal was to settle in the highlands of Chiriquí, told the would-be immigrant he would like the area, that the official himself had *"dort oben ein Ferienhäuschen,"* "a vacation cottage up there."25]

→At the time, Dr. Juan Demóstenes Arosemena was the president of the Republic [elected in 1936] and *Don* Leopoldo Arosemena was the Secretary [a title later changed to Minister] of Government and Justice.← Morf communicated to the Secretary

---

* [The Author says "early November," but *see* Morf to mother and sister, Nov. 5, 1938.]

23

←PHOTO PREVIOUS PAGE
Correspondence between German pioneer Karl Schmieder and the members of the commune in Switzerland would have passed through the Volcán post office, here shown in 1948. Previously, it had been located in the postmaster's home, and it remained a gathering place for German and Swiss settlers. Just visible on the farther table is the Morse code telegraph receiver, still in use in 1948. The wooden telephone with its crank-operated bell generator was still common in rural areas of Panamá as late as the 1960's.

The first postmaster, Hans August Senn, was a Swiss from Winterthur who had come to Panama in 1930 with a wife and two sons, after a stint in Sumatra with Goodyear Rubber. Hans August Jr. (left), was the telegrapher. The telephone operator (right) was Sra. Esther ("Maya") Bósquez. She later opened a *fonda*, or simple restaurant, in Volcán.

When the Swiss colonists first arrived at Volcán, they stayed on the Senn family farm before journeying on to Cotito. According to Hans August's younger brother Werner, still a resident of Volcán in 2015, the wounded could be seen from the post office as they were brought out on horseback, accompanied by police. In 1941, it was the postmaster, Hans August Sr., who contacted the Swiss Franciscan Sisters in David and arranged for them to send help. Eventually, the wounded were taken in old Ford trucks, one of them owned by Kurt Hermerling of Bambito, on the six-hour journey to La Concepción, and from there by train to the hospital in David.

---

his desire to reside in the province of Chiriquí in the capacity of farmer, and, at the same time, requested permission for his compatriots to travel to Panama for the purpose of establishing an agricultural colony in the area of Volcán.

[Morf's mission was successful.] →The colonists could come to the country. They were not members of prohibited ethnic groups,* and they fully met all the requirements.← →They only needed someone to guarantee the obligations they would assume *vis à vis*

---

* Art. 17 [of Pres. J.D. Arosemena's executive order № 3 (Jan. 17, 1933)] prohibited the immigration of Chinese, Lebanese, Palestinians, Syrians, Turks and Negroes whose native language was not Spanish. ["Turks" in Panama referred to any resident of the former Ottoman Empire, including many Jews who emigrated from the Near East with Ottoman passports, and their descendants. Note also that the word "Palestinians" did not refer exclusively to Muslims, as it has since partition in 1948 of the former British mandate. The "Negroes whose native language was not Spanish" were the West Indians whom the U.S. had brought to Panama as laborers.

the country that would receive them, and soon they would find one.←

[Morf left Panama City after a few days and journeyed to Chiriquí, where local German and Swiss immigrants and Panamanians at various institutions were helpful in introducing him to officials. He made the arduous journey to visit Karl Schmieder at Cotito, and remained two weeks. Returning to David, he received a letter on November 1, informing him that the colony would be sailing from Europe on December 13. As he could not complete the process for obtaining their immigration papers until November 7, he visited the farm of the Troetsch family at Camarón, near Santa Marta. Alexander Troetsch would later serve as the settlers' financial guarantor. Morf sent details of the agriculture and stock-raising he had observed. He noted that two crops of potatoes were possible annually, that cattle could be kept out of doors year-round, requiring only salt in addition to their pasturage, explaining also that blatanen are a kind of banana that taste delicious when roasted, and a papaja is a kind of melon that grows on trees.[26]]

7 | A GROUP IMMIGRANT VISA

ON NOVEMBER 23, 1938, President Juan Demóstenes Arosemena issued executive order № 542, granting the petitioner [Albert Morf] leave "to remain indefinitely in the territory of the Republic to engage in agricultural pursuits, and "to bring to the national territory, for the purpose of engaging in agriculture in the interior of the Republic, the following persons of Swiss nationality:

- "[Albert's wife] Elfriede MORF [and their daughter, also named Elfriede, but known as] "Friedy"; Albert Morf, Jr.; Walter [Otto] Morf, Leonora ["Loni"] Morf;
- "Gottfried WERREN, Klara Werren, [and daughters Klärli and] Cornelia Werren);
- "Karl LEHNER.
- "Werner MÜLLER, Sophie Müller, Werner Robert Müller;
- "Anna SIEDLER;
- "Viola RIESER, Virgilio Rieser;

- "Paul HAUESLE (sic), [Trude] Hauesle (sic); [sister and brother]
- "Gustav HAUG, Elise Haug, Liselotte Haug, Gustav Haug Jr., Alfred Haug;
- "Heinrich OTT; and
- "Verena ZULAU[F]."

→Arosemena accepted the personal guarantee offered by R. Alejandro Troetsch for the sum of 1,800 balboas [B/.1.00 = U.S. $1.00] and authorized the Consul General of Panama at Zürich to exempt the issuance of the respective visas from the repatriation deposit.[27]←

8 | THE JOURNEY TO PANAMA

→ NOT ALL OF THOSE authorized to emigrate made the trip. Anna Siedler[*] never did, nor did Verena [Zulauf].← [Gustav Haug emigrated a few months after the colonists with his son Gustav Jr., but wife Elise and children Liselotte and Alfred are not known to have traveled to Panama.[28] [Mysteriously, Vio Wehrli's son Virgilio Rieser died several days before the scheduled sailing.[†]]

---

[*] [Gustav Haug, in the report in Appendix A, *infra*, indicates she may have died under emotional stress. *See* p. 217.]

[†] [The death of the Rieser infant figured later in accusations of infanticide leveled against Lehner by Gustav Haug and others. *Cf.:* "I report to you, Herr Consul, that one of the dead children was the child of Viola Rieser–Wehrli, buried eight days before the departure from Europe..." Gustav Haug to Juan Blau, Swiss hon. consul in Panama, q. Peter Gaupp, "Massacre at Cotito," Apr. 24, 1994. Transl. from German by Barbara Traber. According to Rosario Laws de Schmieder and Erica Witzig-Fassler, the second husband of Viola Wehrli (who had married Meinhard Fassler after the massacre and lived several years in Puerto Armuelles before the couple returned to Switzerland) did not learn until after her death many years later of the existence of the earlier child Virgilio or the circumstances of his death. Intv. with Ed., Aug., 2011, Volcán. Confirmed by Erica Witzig-Fassler, intv. with Ed., Feb. 2015.]

CHAPTER I | A SWISS RELIGIOUS COMMUNE

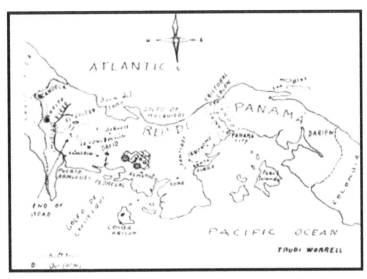

COURTESY BARBARA TRABER
See caption overleaf.

→Paul Häusle, a German citizen [who was born and raised in Switzerland and belonged to the Swiss commune], had been obliged to renew his passport at the German consulate in Lugano on September 28, 1938. The consul, one Rausch, renewed the document, valid for departure from [Switzerland within three months,] no later than December 31, 1938. Several days later, on October 1, the same official issued a German passport for Häusle's sister Gertrude ("Trudi"). *←

---

* Passport, with no photograph, of Paul Häusle. Germany file. Archives, Min. For. Rel. See *also* Declaration of Kinship of Gertrude Häusle *(loc. cit.)*. [The photo later appeared among those removed from passports and distributed to the press by the government as part of the propaganda effort to justify the massacre after the fact, and which ultimately landed in Hassán's *Holocausto en Panamá*. After Paul died, Trudi petitioned for return of his passport and her own, held by the Min. Govt. & Justice. *See* p. 172 *infra.*]

←*MAP, PREV. PAGE*

Frontispiece to *Die Brücke am Chiriquí Viejo* [*"The Bridge on the River Chiriquí Viejo"*], the light-hearted memoir of the positive side of life at Cotito, written in English by Gertrude Häusle, but published only in German translation in Switzerland. Trudi's younger brother Paul was the first victim in 1941, and she was herself wounded by a bullet in the back. Later, she married Ray Worrell, lived in the U.S., and had three children. Half a century after the journey, she included this map of the journey in her book. The arrow indicating "end of road" points to the town of Volcán, not otherwise identified. "Our farms" are indicated with location points at Cotito and Candela.

At the beginning of December, the Vairano colonists mobilized to obtain the visas that would permit them to travel to Panama. As for the Consul General of Panama at Zürich, he entered the visas in the passports of the emigrants, valid for them to "travel to the Republic of Panama and remain in the country, exempt from fees in accordance with section 11, subsection 34, clause *f*, of the Consular Tariff."

The travelers arranged passage with the Italian Transatlantic Company to sail from Genoa on the *Virgilio,* scheduled to land at Colón [the Atlantic terminus of the Panama Canal] on December 31. On December 10, 1938, they left Bellinzona. Haug accompanied the train as far as Chiasso, where he bade them farewell; Lehner pressed him to join the colony if he decided to emigrate to Panama and even promised him two hives of bees if he were to do so. [Haug would follow six months later with son Gustav Jr., apparently leaving the rest of his family behind.] On December 12, the *Virgilio* sailed from Genoa and after an uneventful, nineteen–day crossing dropped anchor at Cristóbal [the port of Colón*] on the scheduled date.† The following day, the birth of their new life coinciding with the birth of the year 1939, they set out by land for the westernmost

---

* [Cristóbal Colón is the full name in Spanish of the man known in English as Christopher Columbus.]

† [Trudi Häusle remembered that when loudspeakers blared out the notice that "disembarkation will be delayed about an hour as a result of some new customs regulations," the Swiss emigrants "noticed a wave of fear and anxiety grip the many Jewish refugees" aboard. *Die Brücke*, p. 21."]

province of Panama, [more than] five hundred kilometers [300 miles] distant, [mostly on unpaved roads].

After many hours' travel [tightly packed in a rusting *chiva*], they arrived at David, where they were received by Prof. Sebastián Gilberto Ríos, an outstanding Panamanian educator who had pursued university studies in Germany [and Switzerland]. They were housed at the former La Primavera elementary school, [later] the provincial office of the IPHE [*Instituto Panameño de Habilitación Especial*, the Special Training Agency of Panama], where the children had prepared a cultural evening in their honor. They spent several days in the school building, before setting out for Volcán [about 30 KM west, 30 KM north of, as well as 1,600 m (or 4,500 ft) higher than, the provincial capital]. Having arrived in the highlands they stayed on the farm of [postmaster Hans August Senn Sr.[29]] until they were able to travel[.]

→Upon granting the immigration visa, President Arosemena had put at the colonists' disposal about 500 hectares [1,100 acres] of vacant land at Piedra Candela, on the border with Costa Rica, for them to bring into production.← To arrive at Cotito [where Schmieder's farm was located] and from there to Piedra Candela must have required a long journey on horseback that would take many hours. Leaving El Hato del Volcán they had to follow the route to Barriles and Fila de Caisán[*] and from there turn north, to

---

* [(The spelling *Caizán* is now standard.) Via the Volcán–Caizán route mentioned in the text, the distance from Volcán to Barriles Creek is just over 6 KM (3½ MI). (The Creek, a tributary of the Chiriquí Viejo, was named for aboriginal, barrel–shaped, stone artifacts discovered in the area. For a review in English of the anthropological and geological history of the this part of Chiriquí, see Olga Linares *et al.*, "Prehistoric Agriculture in Tropical Highlands," *Science* (Jan. 17, 1975), available at www.jstor.org/stable/1739731.) Where travelers once forded the Barriles Creek, there is now a small concrete bridge. The Río Chiriquí Viejo was nearly uncrossable until the *Suizos* built their wooden bridge on the route branching north from the Volcán–Caizán road to Cotito and Santa Clara. The distance from Volcán to Fila de Caizán is just short of 30 KM (18 MI).

[In 1939, the present direct route to Cotito, the modern, 40–KM (25–MI), asphalt Volcán–Río Sereno highway, did not exist, although there were tentative plans to make this the route of the Pan–American Highway, only completed after W.W. II, when it was decided to follow the coastal

Continued→

cross the torrential Chiriquí Viejo River, whose dangerous waters had claimed more than one life. →[Upon arrival at] Candela, [they] finally erected a camp on the very border.←

→After a year of hard work at Piedra Candela, the Swiss settlers decided, in mid–1940, to move down to Karl Schmieder's farm. It is not entirely clear, but it appears that Schmieder, his wife Margarethe and his sons Karl, 10, and Albert, 8, although the "natives" of the area, agreed to submit to the leadership of Lehner and put all their possessions at the disposal of the new settlers.←[*]

9 | COTITO IN 1939

→[THE SWISS IMMIGRANTS who did not belong to the commune,] Gustav Haug Sr. and Jr., made the trip in July, 1939 [about six months after the members of the commune,]. They lived briefly with the colonists at Cotito, but later left to set up on their own at [nearby] Santa Clara.←

← *Continued from prev. page.*
route. Trudi Häusle (*see* p. lxxii, n. 17, *supra*) describes the approach of the crews building the gravel road from Volcán to Río Sereno as a harbinger of encroaching civilization little welcomed by the colonists.

[Running for most of its length parallel to, and north of, the older Caizán road (paved in 1994), is the modern two–lane asphalt road. At the western edge of Volcán, a steel bridge crosses the River Chiriquí Viejo, still impressive though much reduced in force by diversion of water and the construction of small hydroelectric dams. From there, the winding modern road runs about 16 KM (10 MI) westward—through dairy and coffee country—to Cotito, where it now passes the front gates of what were the Brauchles', Hilses', Schapers' and Schmieders' farms. The Schapers, the Sicilias (owners of the Schmieder farm) and others still grow coffee and raise dairy cattle in the area, but in no sense could Cotito be considered a "town" or "village." The journey from Volcán to Cotito, once about four hours on horseback, now takes 20 minutes by car, somewhat longer on the frequent buses. From Cotito, the road continues west to Santa Clara—where it crosses the Río Colorado—and an unpaved road branches northward to follow the border to Piedra Candela. From Santa Clara, the modern road descends to Río Sereno, where a steep, rutted, unpaved street marks the Panama–Costa Rica border.]

* [Margarethe's consent was very reluctant, according to her son and daughter–in–law, Albert and Rosario Laws de Schmieder.]

At the beginning of 1939, Cotito was practically what the German immigrants Schmieder, Brauchle, Schaper and Hils had made of this beautiful region of Chiriquí. These pioneers, we are told by Prof. Héctor Staff [in his 1988 history], endured many difficulties in reaching this place. They had left Germany [a decade after] the end of the first World War, assailed by hunger and political persecution. The pioneers, their wives and children, arrived in 1928, except for [Schaper and] Brauchle, who made the journey in the following year, and their first contacts were with Prof. Richard Neumann, who then had a farm in the area of Macho de Monte,[*] near La Concepción. Alois [later called "Luis"] Hartmann, another German[-speaking immigrant from Moravia[†]] who had arrived in Volcán in 1912, provided great assis-

NIEDERBERGER FAMILY PHOTO

European immigrant hunter (Alfred Waser?) and *macho de monte*, late 1930's.

---

* [*Macho de Monte* ("tough guy of the brush land"), local name for a species of tapir, and the nickname of one of the more feared battalions of the defunct Panamanian *Fuerzas de Defensa* under the military dictatorship).

† [According to one family account, Alois Hartmann's (1891–1970) paternal surname was *Strassele*. A native of Moravia, then a province of the Austro–Hungarian empire, now part of the Czech Republic, he emigrated first to the United States, then to Panama. There, finding his name was considered unpronounceable, he adopted the surname of his mother, Cresenz *Hartmann*, and his given name *Alois* evolved into *Luis*. He was interned as an Austrian national during most of World War I, first on Taboga Island, then in an internment camp in the U.S. When the Austro–Hungarian empire was dismantled in 1918, he became a national of the new Czechoslovakia. When that was annexed to Germany in 1938, he became a German national. After World War II, Czechoslovakia became a Soviet Socialist Republic. Hartmann returned to Panama after his World War I internment, and lived there until his death; he is buried on a hill overlooking the family coffee estate at Santa Clara. Ratibor ("Tibo") Hartmann, Jr., (grandson of Alois), intv. with Ed., Volcán, Aug. 16, 2010. Biographical information from intv. of Ratibor Sr. ("Chicho") and Ziska Hartmann, sons of Alois, with O. Ivan Flores and David Dell.]

tance to the German families when they arrived to settle the area on the banks of the Cotito River.

These first German immigrants endured many difficulties in arriving at Cotito. They lacked precise coordinates for the area; there were no access roads. Venomous animals, wild beasts and the vegetation made the area impassable; and the rivers were much more torrential. Their seed and domestic provisions were carried largely on their backs, as there were no tracks for pack animals. That is how the first residents of Cotito became established.[30]

A decade later, Cotito continued to be practically isolated. There was no true access road joining this region to the town of [El] Hato [del] Volcán. They were separated by four hours on horseback on narrow trails. The torrential waters of the Chiriquí Viejo continued to represent a danger for the peasants who ventured to transport their produce by lurching through the waters of the ford that crossed the river. The waters of the Río Colorado and those of the Cotito itself, with stronger currents than now, rose dangerously during the rainy season [March or April until it peaks in November]. →We must imagine the difficulties the new Swiss arrivals must have confronted, traveling with children and all their belongings, including heavy equipment such as bellows, anvils, hammers, saws and machines for processing milk. We must understand these circumstances in order to comprehend why the settlers were reluctant to embark as a group on the return trip to David that in the end was demanded of them.←

SCHMIEDER FAMILY PHOTO
The Schmieder family home at Schramberg.

CHAPTER I | A SWISS RELIGIOUS COMMUNE

GEGEN PHOTO, WIKIPEDIA

Schramberg, in the German Black Forest, from which Schmieder and other settlers emigrated to Chiriquí in 1928-29, as it appeared in 1950. The resemblance of the terrain to the highlands of Chiriquí is striking.

10 | THE GERMAN NEIGHBORS

THE EARLIER GERMAN pioneers, the Schapers, Hilses and Brauchles, viewed their new neighbors with a certain reserve. Martha Schaper, *née* Schmieder, disapproved of her brother Karl's having practically given away the product of many years of hard work. Nor did the other [German] settlers share the strange customs of the [Swiss], and rumors about Lehner's behavior respecting his cruel treatment of his followers, and his alleged abuse of the women, especially the younger ones, created a climate of mistrust about the person of the head of the colony. None of the German families, although good neighbors among themselves, practiced communal

HILS FAMILY PHOTO, COURTESY DOÑA ROMELIA VDA. DE HILS

Mrs. Lydia Albert Brauchle, a widow by the time of this riverside outing in the late 1940's, had come to Panamá in 1929 with her husband Alfred, who was interned as a German national four days after Pearl Harbor and died in a U.S. prison camp. Their son Helmut joined the colony and was murdered in the massacre.

The little girl is Gertrudis Hils, daughter of the German neighbors, in 2015 still living in David.

ownership of property, nor did they observe such austere rules for living.

Nevertheless, the life of the colonists attracted Helmut, at 28 the youngest of the Brauchles, who soon decided to join Lehner's group, unaware that the decision would cost him his life on July 7, 1941. His namesake Helmut Hils, the young son of Anton, in 1941 a youth of 16, relates: "Those two people [Schmieder and Helmut Brauchle] were won over by those people: they seemed to like it. They joined that group."[31]

HELMUT BRAUCHLE, THE young son of robust physique (as [Robert] Müller also recalls[32]) was, like his father [and Karl Schmieder], a native of Schramberg in the German Black Forest, and had arrived at Cotito as an adolescent. He died when he was struck down by the police detachment under the command of Captain Antonio Huff. Although neither Helmut Brauchle's father Alfred Sr. nor his elder brothers Alfred Jr. and Erwin shared his fate in this tragic incident, they did not fare much better elsewhere. [Six months after the massacre at Cotito where Helmut was killed, four days after the Japanese attack on Pearl Harbor] and a few days after war be

CHAPTER 1 | A SWISS RELIGIOUS COMMUNE

SCHMIEDER FAMILY PHOTO

The *Bienenhaus,* or apiary, on Schmieder's Cotito farm.

"This year," wrote Albert Morf on March 30, 1941, to his mother in Switzerland, "we have already produced 600 lbs. of honey. Two years ago, we had two hives in our bee house; now there are almost 30. The bees reproduce so rapidly here, this year we have established 18 new hives. ...The forest provides all that is needed for our life.

"You can see that the faith and knowledge of our friend Molch have been proven, and that we are much better off than we deserve. More and more it is revealed with what grace he bears a heavy load; it is he who is the most abject in his humility and consistency everywhere; he is our wonderful example.

"He is the one who brings Jesus closer. So you can be without concern for us, because we are in the care of the best leadership there is, which is open to all who have the faith and trust entirely to Jesus Christ, the father spirit, creator of all who is always willing to help us to and to shield us...

"So my beloved, take this to heart; it could well be the last letter to you; you are indeed the only ones with whom I was still in touch. You will easily recognize the reason, because we do not go to the post office when we are in our new home [the farms at Candela and in Costa Rica]. Be strong and of good cheer, we will all meet again, though not in this dress...." Morf to Mother and sister, March 30, 1941, Morf family papers.

Ninety-nine days after the letter was written, Albert Morf, his wife and one of his sons, Molch and eight others were dead.

35

tween Germany and Panama was declared, they were arrested and turned over to the custody of the United States War Department in [what was then] the Canal Zone. Alfred Sr. and his son Erwin were deported and placed in an internment camp located in Kenedy, Texas. The older son Alfred Jr., married to Panamanian citizen Zoila Miranda and father of two young children born in Panama, remained for a time in Panama. His [subsequent] arrest, which occurred at La Concepción, aroused the indignation of the local populace, who considered him an industrious and responsible husband and father, and his wife a highly esteemed teacher.

Almost two years later, in August, 1943, the wife and mother of the Brauchles, the 60–year–old Lydia, *née* Albert, begged the Minister of Government and Justice, Camilo De la Guardia, Jr., to intercede with the U.S. military authorities to request the release of her husband Alfred Sr. and her son Erwin, or at least the latter. The beleaguered woman explained her difficult situation:

> They were interned on December 11, 1941, and I do not know the reason. We immigrated as farmers with the permission of the Panamanian Government in the year 1929, and since that time we have lived in the mountains. According to my conscience, our conduct was always proper, complying always with the law of the country. I heard from various people that the internment of my husband and my son was the result of a mistake or a false accusation. I am 60 years of age and I am unable to work, because I am often ill. I therefore request that Your Excellency review this matter [to determine if it is] possible that both of them, or at least my son Erwin, be released. He was only 17 years old when he entered Panama[;] hence he has spent most of his life in this country, never being involved in politics, because that is not his nature.[33]

As usual, war produced bad results for innocent victims. Mrs. Brauchle received a response on September 25, 1943. Major W. L.

Bristol of the War Department's General Headquarters for the Panama Canal dispatched a note to Captain Alejandro De la Guardia, chief of the Alien Affairs section of the National Police, replying that said office "considered the return of Alfred Brauchle or Erwin Brauchle to the Republic of Panama inadvisable." He added that "Mrs. Brauchle has been given every opportunity to accompany her husband and son to the United States." He suggested that if Mrs. Brauchle were so disposed, "she could still be reunited with them in the United States."*

Alfred Brauchle died during his captivity in the Texas internment camp and his son Erwin returned to Panama on June 29, 1947, two years after the end of the war. He had been deprived of liberty for nearly seven years merely because he had been [born] a German citizen.

11 | THE ORGANIZATION OF THE COLONY

SOON AFTER TAKING up residence on the farm at Cotito, the Swiss–German colonists resumed the regimen of communal living that they had so zealously practiced in Vairano. Industrious to the core, they made considerable improvements to the farm. The first thing they did was enlarge the main

PASSPORT PHOTO (?)
Karl Lehner, "Molch" to his followers, the leader of the colony.

---

* [Meaning, of course that at the age of 60, ill, and already having lost her youngest son to a police massacre of the sect he had joined, she was "entirely free" to abandon the family farm in Panama—where they had come as economic refugees and where they had labored for 14 years—and to travel 500 KM by truck, boat and train to Colón. From there she could sail to New Orleans and then take the train to Texas in order to join her husband and another son in the "family" prison camp at Crystal City, Texas.] Maj. W. L. Bristol to Alejandro De la Guardia, Sept. 25, 1943. (Germany file, Archives, Min. For. Rel.)

PASSPORT PHOTO (?)
Heinrich Ott, the master builder.

dwelling house to make space for the twenty reclining chairs [used as sleeping cots] they had themselves made from from the precious hardwoods in the area. Near the main house, they built or improved three outbuildings they equipped as a kitchen, storeroom and apiary. In the space intended as a storeroom, they outfitted three shops: a smithy, a carpentry shop and a mechanical shop. They had brought from Switzerland, as indicated earlier, a cream–separating machine that they used to produce the famous "Cotito cheeses" and some carpentry and iron–working tools. They set out to improve seventy hectares [≈150 acres] of pasture for raising cattle and horses. In addition, they had several hectares of wooded mountains rich in hardwood trees that they used for construction of homes and equipment. In mid–1941, the colony was possessed of almost a hundred head of cattle and several horses, as well as a chicken house.[34] Property was held in common. Robert Müller remembers that everything belonged to all, and no one had private ownership of anything. Those who planted tomatoes, milked or raised potatoes did so for all. The same held true for those who repaired furniture or made shoes.[35]

CHAPTER I | A SWISS RELIGIOUS COMMUNE

COURTESY WERNER C. SENN

Felling timber, clearing land with axes and human labor. At left Josef ("Sepp") Niederberger, a Swiss carpenter and builder who lived in the area and was taken to Cotito by the police as an interpreter and witness. At right, Niederberger's friend Alfred Waser, named receiver of the colony's property after the massacre.

Gustav Haug and his son lived briefly with the colony before departing for the Santa Clara area. Haug describes in detail the daily activities of the Cotito colonists. They began work very early, at approximately 5:15 AM, and continued until 1:30 or 2:00 PM. There was a break for breakfast at 8:00 AM. Toward the end of the workday, lunch was eaten. The afternoon was devoted to different activities such as sewing, putting tools in order, or reading in the small library. At 6:30 PM, milk, tea or fruit was served. At about 9:00 the community retired to sleep on the [reclining chairs] that were hung [when not in use] from the walls of the main house.

39

They dressed simply: all the men had long beards and, curiously, within the confines of the colony, they went about barefoot. At mealtimes, they sat at table around the figure of Lehner, whom they nicknamed Molch (German for "salamander"),[36] and who distributed the bread, food and drink without the use of knives. Milk and tea were served in *totumas* [dried gourds]. They consumed quantities of milk, cheese, bees' honey, corn, beans, green beans, root vegetables and every kind of local fruit such as pineapples and bananas. They boiled their beans green with sugar, which they also used in quantity. They were forbidden to eat meat of any kind, or to season their food with salt or spices. They did not eat onions, garlic or raw vegetables. With respect to the latter, they said that it was harmful to eat vegetables such as cabbages, turnips or radishes that had not yet completed their life cycle, as opposed to grains such as dried beans or corn.

DIE BRÜCKE

Trudi Häusle sketched a similar timber-felling scene from memory 50 years later.

In reality, the colonists gave up almost everything, relying only upon the indispensable. Haug remembers that firewood, and even matches, were carefully husbanded, and split logs to

DIE BRÜCKE

Once felled, massive trunks required sawing into planks, a huge job when done by hand. Sketched here by Trudi Häusle Worrell, perhaps after a photograph or a journal sketch (?).

heat the fireplace had to be requested from the elderly Gottfried Werren.³⁷

Karl Lehner was the undisputed *jefe*. The only photograph we have of him shows a man of penetrating but not severe visage, endowed with a large head of hair and the thick, white beard of a biblical prophet. Müller says he "knew about medicine, the human body, and he was an astronomer of the stars."³⁸ Others saw him differently. They saw a stubborn man, fanatical about his religious ideas, who, because of his radical positions would lead the colonists inexorably to the tragic incident of July 7, 1941. According to a newspaper account of the time:

SCHMIEDER FAMILY PHOTO
The bridge under construction.

> The disgraceful incident at Cotito was due solely to the absurdities of the head of the colony with regard to the practice of their religion, which did not recognize any worldly authority not emanating from God in Whom they place their faith.³⁹

Gustav Haug gives a similar negative version of Lehner. He considered him a cruel man who, in the guise of a kindly spiritual guide, repressed the members of his colony and abused his authority. He notes that there were rumors of Lehner's improper conduct and that there was talk of a hushed–up abortion in the colony, although he notes that when he confronted Lehner with this charge, the latter denied it categorically, and invited him to conduct an exhaustive investigation of the rumors directly with the members of the colony.40,*

Werner Müller [the father of Robert] was a skilled mechanic and Heinrich Ott was the master builder. The latter, [approaching 60 years of age,] with a long, graying beard, had been the principal force on the construction of the bridge the colonists raised across the Río Chiriquí Viejo and on which Gustav Haug and his son had

SCHMIEDER FAMILY PHOTO
One of 3 known photographs of the bridge, here shown near completion. The temporary wooden columns were replaced with sturdy concrete columns built on rocks in the river.

---

* ["The fact is that during the lifetime of the colony, Lehner had affairs with three women...and they are no longer alive." Walter Morf to Swiss journalist Peter Gaupp (offering corrections to Gaupp's 1994 article in the *Neue Zürcher Zeitung*), Apr. 28, 1996.

[One of the other two women was, presumably, Sophie Müller (despite the presence in the colony of her husband Werner), as confirmed by her son Robert and the recollections of the Schmieder family. The second was Klärli Werren, who appears to have had a miscarriage and two children by Lehner, none of whom survived. The identity of the third woman, if such there was, remains a source of speculation and debate.]

also worked.

It was a very bad road. The bridge built by the colony helped all the communities in the area because there had been no bridge. [Before the bridge was built,] people crossed on a cable with a sack of rice on their shoulder, and it couldn't take the weight and they fell in the water. It was a bridge 66 meters [220 ft] long, and the police passed over it when they went to murder the colonists.[41]

In addition to their work on the pastures and forests at Cotito, the colonists also grew corn, pineapples and *yuca* in the Piedra Candela area, where they had tried to plant corn in low–lying areas. This was the place that in 1937 had became famous all over Panama because of the rumored existence of a hoard of gold bars. When nothing was found, the site was put at the disposal of the colonists for agricultural production.[42]

There are indications that the Swiss also had access to land located on Costa Rican soil. The colonists crossed the nearby border regularly to tend to their [corn*] fields there. In fact, near the Río Negro in Costa Rica, a few kilometers in a straight line

This shed, with stalks of bananas stored under the eaves, was called the *Bananenhaus*. Trudi Worrell describes it as a place for quiet conversation in the afternoons. Shown (?): Karl Jr., Sophie Müller, Gretel Schmieder.

---

* [The Author refers to *arroz*, "rice," which is not productive at this altitude, but Albert Schmieder remembers clearly that this land was planted in corn. The sacks of rice mentioned in connection with the river–crossing would have been imports into the area for consumption.]

opposite the border crossing at Piedra Candela, there exists a place still called *Fila de los Suizos,* "Swiss Ridge." There is no doubt that this was the place where the colonists went after the June 24, 1941, visit of Captain Huff and several of his men to serve a government order. The order required them to go to David to register in person with the Alien Affairs section of the police. On that occasion, the Costa Rican authorities turned them back to Panamanian territory without incident. [43] [The massacre occurred two weeks later.]

12 | RELATIONS WITH THE PANAMANIAN NEIGHBORS

HOW DID PANAMANIANS look upon the members of the Cotito colony? The statements [the Author has] been able to gather of persons who visited inside the colony and who had a close relationship with the colonists concur in that they were peaceful and hospitable people with charitable habits. Federico Sagel De Santiago, who became the Governor of Chiriquí in the mid–nineteen–fifties, traveled through much of the Cotito area.

> I was in the Swiss colony many times. They were people who practiced a very strange religion. They were forbidden to shed blood. As soon as you got there, they would say, "Sir, stay for lunch, we will kill a chicken, but you do the killing." They would not kill it. I [was invited for lunch] but I had to kill the chicken. The people hunted snakes because they had cattle—they lived from making cheese and dairy products; they made a famous cheese they called "Cotito cheese"—and clearing their pastures they caught enormous vipers. Then they caught them alive, they threw them in a sack and went to dump them over on the other side of the Chiriquí Viejo River so they would not have to kill them.
> They were inoffensive people, very kind![44]

Efraín González Fuentes, who served during many years as an officer with the National Police in the area of Río Sereno, where he still lives, recalls that on many occasions he was received hospitably by the colonists. In 1940, as he was traveling through the highlands area accompanied by officer Lucas Garcés, checking the passports of foreign farmers who had immigrated to these areas, he arrived once again at Cotito:

> We were two days in Cotito. We ate there and slept there and we paid nothing, because they were charitable. They did favors for every traveler who passed through there. They had built a bridge at their own expense and they did not deny passage to anyone. They were very good.[45]

Aurelio Manuel Serracín, a fellow officer of González's also from Río Sereno, recalls that the peasants of those areas used to go to the colony to sell corn and beans and the colonists would hire them to help with their agriculture and stock–raising.[46] Wilhelm Probst, a German married to a Panamanian, who lived for many years in Chiriquí and who was arrested for protesting against the slaughter of the Swiss, dedicated a chapter of his unpublished book, *Vida y lucha de un hombre solitario ["Life and Struggle of a Solitary Man"]* to these peaceful people:

> When I was working in David, I also met the members of this religious sect who lived deep in the jungle, at a distance of three days travel on horseback from David, near the border with Costa Rica. These people often invited me to visit them.
>
> ...
>
> I found a colony of about 30 people including women and children. The men had long beards and went around barefoot. They worked in common, ate the same food, did not touch meat. They never killed an animal, not even a poisonous snake. They had created big meadows in the jungle. They had a lot of cattle from which they produced milk, butter and cheese, as well as corn, vegetables and fruit, which were their main foods. They worked only in the mornings. They said that they

were not put on this earth to get rich, only to possess what they needed for their subsistence.

...

We were two days in Cotito. We ate there and slept there

They grew a lot of fruit, especially pineapple plantations, and when they were ripe they gave off a delicious aroma. This attracted possums, mostly at night, because it was their favorite food. To protect the animals, they put out wooden traps in which they could catch them without harming them; then in the morning some of the men would go to the fields with sacks and put the animals in the sacks and carry them far off, more than a kilometer on the other side of the river, where they would again set them free. They knew that after a time, the animals would return.[*]

These poor men had, in the few years they lived there, changed the jungle into a paradise and they didn't concern themselves with the outside world; they only wanted to live in peace, quiet and harmony.[†]

Others had a different image of the colonists at Cotito. The Chiriquí correspondent for *Panamá–América* gave this version, after the fact:

Here in David, we have spoken with numerous persons from diverse social strata, and although all have declared to us the intransigence of the colonists with respect to their religion and way of life, in their dealings with them they found them neither surly, unsociable,

---

[*] [Albert Schmieder recalls that metal legbands used for chickens were fixed on the possums' legs to identify those that returned.}

[†] Wilhelm Probst, "Capítulo XXIV: Masacre de religiosos." In *Vida y lucha de un hombre solitario* Unpub. ms. (lent by Probst's son Josef to the Author), pp. 146–7. [Probst, who was a German native, wrote a somewhat stilted Spanish, but the translator did not attempt to reproduce the occasionally odd syntax.]

malicious nor withdrawn.[*] There was one thing: they put God above all authority and everything mundane, and this stubbornness had *a fortiori* to provoke strong reactions ... .⁴⁷

In reality, the bearded Swiss were seen everywhere, never with a provocative attitude. Godofredo Gómez Araúz recalls having seen them on the Austrian Luis Martinz's farm ["Carinthia"] in Cerro Punta, animatedly peddling their renowned cheeses.⁴⁸ Despite the language barrier, since Karl Schmieder had to serve as their interpreter and during the early years only the Werrens spoke some Spanish, the colonists continued to demonstrate their hospitable character to everyone who approached Cotito.

Perhaps Helmut Hils best explained the apparent contradiction. Asked whether the colonists were very rigid, he said, "Not so much. They just didn't want to mix with people."⁴⁹

Notes to Chapter I

¹ R.A.C. Parker, *"Europa entre las dos guerras: tendencias económicas y sociales"* ["Europe Between the Two Wars: Economic and Social Trends"], In *El Siglo XX: Europa 1918-1945* (12th ed., 1971), p. 114.

² Two extremes: while in Switzerland the rate of mortality for infants under the age of one year was 50 per 1,000, in Yugoslavia it was 159. The illiteracy rate for persons over ten years of age was 0.5 percent; in Yugoslavia, it was 31 percent. *Ibid.*

³ [Probably the village of that name near Olten in the canton of Soluthurn, not in the mountainous Jura region.]

⁴ [Spelled *Hilelberg* in the Spanish edition; probably an error.]

⁵ [Seen, not far from Zürich, is now part of the city of Winterthur.]

⁶ *12,000 minibiografías.* (2ⁿᵈ ed., 1986), p. 208.

⁷ *Encyclopædia Britannica,* __ᵗʰ ed., v. __, p. 943, consulted online.

⁸ [*World Book Encyclopedia?*] (Grolier Electronic Publishing), consulted online.

---

*[hoscos, huraños, díscolos o retraídos]

[9] *Travel World Book*, p. 243, consulted online.

[10] *Encyclopedia Americana* (1989 ed.) v. 9, p. 196, *sub nom.* Divine, Father. [Back-transl. from the Author's Spanish rendering.]

[11] *Encyclopædia Britannica*, [v. __, p. __.]

[12] Jorge Fábrega Ponce, intv. with Author, Bambito (Chir.), July 10, 1992.

[13] [The letter referred to by the Author is the report described on pp.11-12 n.*, *supra*.]

[14] *Id.*

[15] *See also* Lydia Brauchle (*née* Albert) to Camilo De la Guardia, Minister Govt. & Justice, May 5, 1943 (Germany file. Archives, Min. For. Rel.).

[16] Héctor H. Staff, *"Cotito: Historia y sucesos"* ["*Cotito: History and Events*"] in *La Voz del Barú y otros aspectos de radiodifusión y soberanía* ["*The Voice of the Barú and Other Facets of Radio Broadcasting and Sovereignty*"] (1988), p. 99.

[17] Elizabeth Haug, granddaughter of Gustav, intv. with Author, David (Chir.), April 9, 1992.

[18] Müller.

[19] Decree № 3, Jan. 17, 1933. In Guillermo Andreve (comp.), Decretos y Resoluciones Vigentes. Tomo 1: 1904-1939 (Min. Govt. & Justice, n.d.), at 145 *et seq.*

[20] *Id.*, Art. 3.

[21] [Meding (See pp. xliv-xlv n.† *supra*.)]

[22] ["Panama and the Canal Zone" in British Foreign Office, 1924 Annual Report, at 19, cit. Meding, p. 280.]

[23] ["[British Consul, later Amb., Sir Claude] Mallet to [For. Sect. Sir Edward] Grey, Sept. 16, 1912, United Kingdom, Public Records Office. Foreign Office 371.1420." Meding's note.]

[24] [Meding, pp. 278–82.]

[25] Morf, *ibid.*

[26] *Ibid.*

[27] A copy of the order reposes in the Sophie Müller file (Min. Govt. & Justice, Directorate of Immigration and Naturalization.)

[28] [Albert Schmieder, intv. with Ed., August, 2011, Volcán.]

[29] [Werner C. Senn, intv. with Ed. 2012. (See p. 20, n.†, *supra*.)]

[30] Staff, p. 99.

[31] Helmut Hils, intv. with Author, Volcán, Apr. 18, 1992.

[32] Müller.

[33] Lydia Albert Brauchle to Camilo De la Guardia (*See* p. 17, n. 19, *supra*.)

[34] County Judge, District of Bugaba, Report: "Inventory, Appraisal and Interim Disposition of Assets left by Karl Lehner and others, dec'd (Oct. 8, 1941." (Germany file. Archives Min. For. Rel.)

[35] *Id.*

[36] [Why Lehner was known as "Molch" (salamander) is not known. Perhaps—mere speculation—the allusion is to the mythological beast that lived in fire, immune to its effects, in some legends living without sustenance other than the energy derived from the flames.]

[37] Haug.

[38] Müller.

[39] *See Panamá-América*, July 8, 1941, q. Jorge Conte Porras, *Requiem por la Revolución* (1990), p. 193.

[40] Haug.

[41] *Id.*

[42] *See* V.D. Ocaña, *"Las barras de oro de Piedra Candela,"* in *Lotería* magazine № 280 (Jun. 1979), pp. 51-60.

[43] *Estrella de Panamá*, Jul. 10, 1941, p. 1.

[44] Federico Sagel De Santiago, intv. with Author, Panama City, Sept. 21, 1988.

[45] Efraín González, intv. with Author, David, Mar. 5, 1993.

[46] Aurelio Manuel Serracín, intv. with Author, Rio Sereno (Chir.), Jan. 21. 1993.

[47] *Panamá-América*, July 8, 1941.

[48] Godofredo Gómez Araúz, intv. with Author, Paso Ancho (Volcán, Chiriquí), Apr. 18, 1992.

[49] Hils.

NIEDERBERGER FAMILY PHOTO

Banana harvest, Chiriquí, late 1930's; Swiss neighbors of the colony: (L-R) Alfred Waser, Josef Niederberger, Gustav Haug Sr.

II | THE YEAR 1941 IN PANAMA

1 | THE PRESIDENCY OF ARNULFO ARIAS MADRID: 1940-41

THE YEAR 1941 began in Panama with a new Constitution and the presidency of a 30-year-old man whose personal imprint, for good or for evil, would influence the history of the Republic for half a century. Dr. Arnulfo Arias Madrid had been sworn in as president a few months before the end of the previous year, on October 1, 1940. He thus began the first of his three presidential terms, none of which he was permitted to complete; the last of the three was abruptly interrupted by the military coup of October 11, 1968. [His fourth election victory was overturned by the notoriously fraudulent vote count in 1984.]

Like his elder brother Harmodio, he had emerged as a protagonist in national political life as one of those who perpetrated the *Acción Comunal* coup of January 2, 1931. Harmodio was [soon after] seated in the presidential chair for the 1932–36 term. He was succeeded by Juan Demóstenes Arosemena, the administration candidate who had been Harmodio Arias's minister of foreign relations, and whom, according to some historians, the outgoing president had imposed as his successor.[1]

Arnulfo Arias Madrid, physician by profession, [trained in the United States], occupied important government posts during the administrations of Harmodio Arias and Juan Demóstenes Arosemena. Under his elder brother, he had headed the Ministry of [Health and Public Works], where he developed social welfare policies. President Arosemena appointed him envoy extraordinary and minister plenipotentiary to the government of France.

On December 16, 1939, President Arosemena died suddenly. Two days later, Samuel Augusto Boyd, then ambassador to the United States, was installed on an interim basis as Minister of the Presidency *Chargé* [*i.e.*, "acting president"]. It was Boyd who presided over the most traumatic electoral period in the history of the Republic. His open support of Arnulfo Arias Madrid and the repression unleashed against the forces of the opposition [during the presidential campaign] carried the administration's candidate to the presidency as an unopposed candidate.

Arnulfo Arias Madrid [still in France three months after the Nazis had occupied Paris on June 14, 1940] →was nominated [*in absentia*], on October 23, as the candidate of the National Revolutionary Party of Panama for the 1940–44 presidential term.← [He] returned to Panama on December 19,* and, accepting the presidential nomination in a memorable speech on Plaza Cinco de Mayo, he sketched the principles of the *Panameñista* ["Panamanianist"] doctrine that would guide his future administration.

> *Panameñismo*, political thought characterized by a message of strong nationalist content, advocated a welfare state *["estado social"]* that would intervene in those productive activities where private capital [showed itself to be] evasive or timorous.[2]

---

* Conte Porras writes (p. 174) that Dr. Arias arrived in Panama on Dec. 19, although he notes (p. 180) that it was on the 21st that he made his famous speech. [The Nazis had invaded France in June, 1940. By July, the Germans were bombing Britain and the British the cities of Germany. Arias had thus remained in Europe a year-and-a-half after war erupted, and in France three months after the French government collapsed and the Nazis had occupied the capital.]

The *Panameñismo* message, however, allowed a glimpse of the authoritarian personality of its leader.

> Here in Panama, there must exist, germinate and develop only one creed, a single doctrine, a single mandate: Our *Panameñismo*.³

Having won the 1940 election, he proclaimed in his inaugural address the links of *Panameñismo* with the January 2, 1931, political platform of *Acción Comunal*, which had had a nationalist character[*] and [had called] for the reform of public institutions. In the address, he stressed the necessity for creating an "Executive Branch in which the president would be endowed with sufficient powers to realize, energetically and promptly, this comprehensive renovation of public institutions." Arnulfo denounced dramatically the problem of racial minorities,⁴,[†] and accused the English–speaking West Indian

---

* [Among the simplistic principles for proper conduct enumerated in the *Panameñismo* platform were: "(1) Teach your children to love the country. (2) Teach your children to respect the flag. (3) Speak correct Castilian Spanish. (4) Address foreigners in Spanish. (5) Ask for Panamanian currency and count in balboas. (6) Do not make purchases in stores that advertise in English. (7) Do not make purchases in stores that do not employ Panamanians." Isidro Beluche M., *Acción Comunal: Surgimiento y estucturación del nacionalismo panameño [Emergence and Structuring of Panamanian Nationalism]* (1981), and Conte Porras, *Arnulfo Arias Madrid* (1980), cit. and transl. Pearcy, *Only to God*, pp. 61–2.

[Point (3) anticipated the "English Only" movement popular in the US in the early XXIst century. After his election, Arias did order the issuance of paper currency in balboas (point [5]) but it inspired little acceptance and its existence was short lived. Given Arnulfo's racial criteria for defining Panamanian nationality, points (6) and (7) are eerily reminiscent of the Nazi boycott of "non-Aryan" retail establishments after the *Kristallnacht*.]

† [Note that the "problem of racial minorities" was *not* the discrimination they suffered, but rather the "problem" they posed for the "rest" of the country. In a report to Washington on Arias's inaugural address, the U.S. Embassy staff—reasonably, though, it should be remembered, not entirely, reliable—noted that "Arias...rejected 'as biologically without justification the "demagogic concept" that "all men are born free and equal," then "referred to the desirability of improving the nation's racial strain by [selective] immigration and criticized the entrance of large numbers of [N]egroes.'" Walter LaFeber, *The Panama Canal: The Crisis in Historical Perspective* (1978), p. 94. Once president, Arias "adopted racial policies that damaged many. Chi-

Continued→

population of being a foreign body encysted within the Panamanian community.[5] Many of these objectives were fixed in the Panamanian Constitution that took effect [early in Arnulfo's first term] on January 2, 1941, and in more than a hundred social–policy statutes passed in the brief period of a single year by the National Assembly[*] dominated by the governing party and which—it is admitted by all—modernized the Panamanian state.

It is not our task in the present work to pass judgment on the twelve months of the Arnulfo Arias administration of 1940, which would require a more extensive study than the present one. We wish to emphasize, nevertheless, the circumstances that allowed Arnulfo Arias to arrive at the presidency of the Republic and the authoritarian means employed during his administration, principally through the militarization of the National Police, because this will allow us to understand the broad context of the tragic episode at Cotito. The years 1940–41 were not only years of institutional renovation; they were also a period of intolerance, of political persecution, of armed uprisings and police repression, and the Swiss–German colonists who settled in this remote region of the province of Chiriquí were caught up, unbeknownst even to them, in this spiral.

2 | ARNULFO ARIAS, UNOPPOSED CANDIDATE

AS HAS BEEN noted, Arnulfo Arias Madrid was named the National Revolutionary Party's candidate for the Presidency of the Republic on October 23, 1940. This presidential nomination of the party then in power was ratified a few days later by the Conservative Party (October 29), the National Liberal Party (November 4), the Democratic

---

← *Continued from prev. page.*
nese, Jewish and East Indian storekeepers were baited and forced to sell cheap to Arnulfo's favorites. ... [F]orty thousand Panamanians of West Indian descent were menaced with loss of Panamanian citizenship." Richard M. Koster and Guillermo Sánchez Borbón, *In the Time of the Tyrants: Panama: 1968–1990* (1990), p. 61.]

* [Then as now, Panama's unicameral national legislature.]

Liberal Party (November 11) and the United Liberal Party (November 23).

The opposition Popular Front—consisting of the Doctrinal Liberal, the Renewal Liberal and Socialist parties—nominated Dr. Ricardo J. Alfaro. Dr. Alfaro, like Francisco Arias Paredes and Demetrio Porras, had opposed the ruling–party candidate Juan Demóstenes Arosemena in 1935. Dr. Alfaro, living in Washington, then had to return to Panama in January, 1940, to begin the electoral campaign. According to Julio E. Linares, Alfaro returned on January 19,[6] though Jorge Conte Porras states that he returned on the 24th.[7] Both agree that his partisan supporters received him at the railroad station[*] opposite the Plaza Cinco de Mayo, and accompanied him the length of Avenida Central to a rally in Santa Ana Park. Once they had arrived at this popular spot for the exercise of Panamanian democracy, Francisco Arias Paredes, Demetrio A. Porras and Sergio Gonzales Ruiz addressed the rally. But at the instant that Dr. Ricardo J. Alfaro[, Arias's opponent,] mounted the platform in the Santa Ana Park pavilion, he was greeted by a hail of stones, and as if by the art of magic, a contingent of National Police cavalry appeared from the streets facing the park, firing into the air, until they had completely dispersed the popular demonstration supporting Alfaro's candidacy.[8] Dr. Alfaro protested the show of force to the National Election Board, the provincial governor, and the mayor of Panama City.[9] The complaints fell on the deaf ears of the acting president, Samuel Augusto Boyd, who continued to support the administration's candidate, Arnulfo Arias Madrid.

In the absence of adequate guarantees for a genuinely democratic electoral process, Alfaro withdrew his candidacy and Arnulfo Arias ran unopposed for the presidential chair.[10] Ironically, the same truncheons and rifles of the National Police that in 1940 had

---

* [Travelers from the Eastern seaboard and Europe usually disembarked at Colón and took the train, whose Pacific terminus was the old station on Plaza Cinco de Mayo, in the heart of the city. (The station later became the Museum of Anthropology.) When trans–isthmian rail service resumed in the 1990's, the Pacific terminus was the station near Canal headquarters in Balboa, in the former Canal Zone; trains no longer come into the city proper.]

cleared the way for the presidential candidacy of Arnulfo Arias would drive him from office a year later, before completion of the first of his three separate presidential terms.

3 | THE ARMED UPRISINGS

THE OPPOSITION HAD no alternative but to resort to the extreme: the use of force. On May 26, 1940, a group of supporters of socialist leader Demetrio Porras took up arms in the town of La Laguna, in the district of San Carlos, producing a confrontation with the National Police that left a toll of three dead policemen. The government reaction was immediate. The National Police were ordered to proceed to the arrest of numerous opposition leaders, and Francisco Arias Paredes, head of the Renewal Liberal Party, accused of financing the uprising, as well as Diógenes de la Rosa and Felipe O. Pérez, were arrested.

During subsequent months, other guerilla outbreaks, ruthlessly repressed by police forces, occurred at Chame and La Chorrera. On January 20, 1941, an armed group attacked the La Chorrera police station. In a carefully planned action, telegraph and telephone communication lines were cut, and then the police were fired upon from a truck carrying arms and ammunition, resulting in the wounding of policemen Isidro Rodríguez and Barolo Pérez. After a heavy exchange of fire, the police managed to capture Moisés Cedeño Bermúdez, Pablo Boza, Pedro J. De Icaza, Marcos Sucre and Ernesto Testa. Subsequent investigation led to the identification of Domingo H. Turner and Félix Oller, among others, as participants in the uprising. Francisco Arias Paredes, Manuel Antonio Bernal, Adriano Brown, Manuel Garrido, Humberto Ortega Valdés, Arturo Recuero and Victoriano Soto were arrested on suspicion.[11]

In addition to these actions motivated by party loyalties were others whose motivation was less apparent, but which were repressed with equal vigor by the National Police, as in the case of the Nicaraguans[*] who rose in arms in the Gariché mountains of Chi-

---

[*] [Presumably banana pickers abandoned in Chiriquí. *See* p. 68, *infra.*]

riquí. This was not reported by those involved in the first year of the *Arnulfista* presidency, nor does it appear in the judicial records of the period. The only mention of it is a minimal news report in the national press during the first days of January, 1941, insufficient for us to determine with any certainty whether the Nicaraguans who confronted the police did so as an attack on established constitutional authority or because of other circumstances, such as those resulting from their being illegal, undocumented aliens—a status they had in common with hundreds of Central Americans in Chiriquí and a thorny problem for Panamanian governments from the nineteen-twenties on—a problem they tried to resolve with a strong hand.

What is certain is that toward the end of 1940, Guillermo Araña, Nicolás Estrada, Luis González, Hernán Gutiérrez, Carlos Alberto Martínez, Luis Alberto Mena, Francisco Morales, Francisco Moretti, José Ángel Sánchez, Pablo E. Rivera, Enrique Somarriva and Jesús Soto Araica, all figured among the Nicaraguans who confronted the police on the heights above the Gariché River [in Chiriquí]. In the skirmish, one policeman and one of the foreigners were killed, but the police force was able to stifle the movement and arrest all those who had risen in arms. The investigations were begun by the judge of the Second Superior Tribunal of the First [Appellate] Judicial District,[*] but he remanded it to the criminal division of the Circuit

---

* [In Panama, minor criminal and civil matters are heard by *corregidores* (*see* p. xlv, n. 2, *supra*) subordinate to the Ministry of Govt. & Justice, or in municipal courts in each administrative district. Cases above a certain threshold of gravity are tried in the Circuit Courts in each province, where judges are designated First Civil Judge, Second Civil Judge, First Criminal Judge, etc. The government is represented by the circuit *fiscal* or prosecutor, a member of the *Ministerio Público*, subordinate to the Prosecutor General. To what extent, if any, the Prosecutor General and the lower-court prosecutors can act independently of the president and his executive-branch administration is always a source of political conflict.

[The circuits are grouped in appellate "districts," where the Superior Tribunals of Justice hear appeals, and, in certain matters, exercise original jurisdiction. At the time of these events, the Chiriquí Circuit was part of the First Judicial District.

[Appeal from the superior tribunals is to the Supreme Court of Justice, which has various *salas* or chambers with specialized jurisdictions.

Continued→

Court in Chiriquí, believing that it was an offense subject to the jurisdiction of the circuit judge. The same reasoning was followed by the investigating judges of the Superior Tribunal handling criminal charges against Francisco Arias Paredes, Gilberto Brid, Julio Ramos, Demetrio Porras and others involved with the [earlier] La Laguna incident.[12]

4 | THE MILITARIZATION OF THE NATIONAL POLICE

IT MIGHT HAVE been predicted that President Arnulfo Arias and his Minister of Government and Justice, Ricardo Adolfo De la Guardia, reacting to these constant public disorders, would focus their attention, as President Juan Demóstenes Arosemena had done, on use of the National Corps of Police to control the militant opposition. In one of his first decisions in 1941, Arias began to set in motion the conversion of the police into a genuinely military institution. It was not the first time that administrations rooted in *Acción Comunal* had tried to transform the only armed force in the country into an army. Arnulfo's brother Harmodio, reacting to the militant social protests led by Demetrio Porras's socialists during the rent strike of 1932, [when West Indians no longer supported *Acción Comunal*], and the ongoing conspiracies of Francisco Arias Paredes, had planned to transform the Panamanian Public Force into one or more units empowered to exercise police and army functions, in order to "support the Government in the maintenance of public order...when this maintenance [should be] necessary," and for the "national defense against external dangers." Harmodio's Minister of Government and Justice, Galileo Solís, sponsored the creation and organization of official agencies charged with acting as organs of the Public Forces.[*],[13] In addition, during the administration of Juan Demóste-

---

← *Continued from prev. page.*

[Readers familiar with the U.S. judiciary should bear in mind that in Panama, district courts are *superior* to circuit courts, the opposite of the U.S. federal system.]

* [For years, various governments had tried to control and professionalize the military. "Panama's leaders [during the Depression] instituted a series of

Continued→

nes Arosemena, Public Law Nº 39 (Nov. 24, 1938), was passed, providing for the organization of a military academy.[14] But these projects were not put into practice, and the National Police were not, at that time, converted into an army.

Arnulfo Arias made another attempt to militarize the police at the beginning of 1941, under a carefully designed plan that was only frustrated completely when he was removed from power on October 9 of that year. First, the institution would be reorganized along strictly military lines, for which purpose he could rely on the services of an expert foreign advisor, Guatemalan Lieutenant Colonel Fernando Gómez Ayau, who, with the title of [Instructor] General[*] of the Police, reported directly to the President of the Republic. Once having achieved this goal, legislation would be

Lt. Col. Fernando Gómez Ayau, ca. 1941.

← *Continued from prev. page.*
measures aimed at making the...police...a more formidable obstacle to would-be opponents. ... [T]hey built new...facilities...; they also began to place large groups of their own armed supporters within the ranks of the police, to neutralize any dissension within the police force. ... [E]fforts...to modernize Panama's police greatly enhanced its capacity to function in a military manner,...developed the officer corps professionally, and engendered a profound sense of camaraderies among its officers, inducing an 'acute awareness among the officers of their messianic vocation.' ... The '*esprit de corps* among police officers,' and 'technological advances...in armaments, increased the police's institutional autonomy and made it an increasingly difficult organization for civilians to control." Pearcy, *Only to God* (*See* p. lvi n. 37 *supra*), p. 8, q. Mario Esteban Carranza, *Fuerzas armadas y estados de excepción en América Latina* (1978).]

* [The Spanish text refers to an *Inspector* General, but other sources indicate the title was *Instructor* General, a post that had existed at the highest levels of the police department at various times since Independence. As in the case of Gómez Ayau, who previously had the same title in the Guatemalan Army, the Instructor General was a foreign expert brought in as *de facto*

Continued→

passed, initially in the form of presidential executive orders, and subsequently by means of an organic law converting the police force into an army.[*]

On this point, we disagree with several who single out José Antonio Remón Cantera [the police colonel who became president after a coup in 1951, rather than Arnulfo Arias] as the "architect of the militarization" of the only armed force in the country.[15] In reality, as of 1941, Remón Cantera, in spite of being one of the few career military men in the police, [after being restored to the force by Arnulfo Arias,] had ascended merely to the rank of captain, and was still posted to the province of Chiriquí.[†] It is Arnulfo Arias, with his plans for militarization, who set Remón Cantera, the future colonel and president of the Republic, on this road [and it was Remón who, in

---

← Continued from prev. page.
commander, in an effort to reorganize and modernize the police, and to secure its loyalty to the incumbent president. In 1903, Panama's first president, Manuel Amador Guerrero, hired New York City police official Samuel B. David to "provide Panama's newly organized National Police with 'adequate scientific instruction.' " In 1909, President José Domingo De Obaldía hired U.S. Army Major Wallis B. Clark as Instructor General. From 1917 until 1927, A.R. Valdés of the Washington, D.C. police was Instructor General of the police. Pearcy, pp. 44, 46, cit. U.S. govt. reports in the Natl. Archives.]

* [Arias hired Gómez Ayau with the acquiescence of the notorious Guatemalan dictator (1931–44), Gen. Jorge Ubico y Castañeda (1878–1946). Like Arias, Ubico, something of an admirer of Hitler and Mussolini, was first elected without opposition and was intent on administrative modernization and public works, albeit at the cost of a militarized police state and harsh treatment of dissenters. Infamous also for supporting the ruthless employment practices of foreign coffee planters and the United Fruit Company, and for using so-called vagrancy laws to extract forced labor from the rural population, Ubico was overthrown by a popular uprising in 1944. Lt. Col. Gómez Ayau was a product of Ubico's army and brutal military dictatorship.]

† According to *La Estrella,* Capt. José Antonio Remón, who had commanded the Third Battalion in Chiriquí for more than a month, was transferred to central police headquarters in Panama City as senior captain. *Estrella de Panamá,* Jan. 28, 1941. ["Chichi" ("Babyface") Remón served as national commander of the police under Harmodio Arias, was later fired and then rehired by Arnulfo Arias. He was promoted to colonel, became commander again, and was a virtual military dictator behind puppet presidents 1948–52. He was elected president himself in 1952. Remón was a principal agent of the 1941 and 1951 coups that ousted Arnulfo Arias.]

turn] in one of the ironies of fate, would violently overthrow Arnulfo Arias on May 10, 1951, putting an end to Arias's second presidency.

5 | THE MILITARY REORGANIZATION OF GÓMEZ AYAU

AT THE BEGINNING of 1941, Lieutenant Colonel Fernando Gómez Ayau, with his impressive record of service in the Guatemalan army, held the post of [Instructor] General of the Police Department in that Central American country. The Panamanian government had requested his services from its Guatemalan counterpart as early as December, 1940, and on January 3, 1941, President Jorge Ubico granted the Panamanian request.[16]

The military advisor was initially retained for a period of six months, subject to renewal, at a starting salary of B/.400 per month. Among his assigned tasks were the drafting of a new organic law for the National Corps of Police and the design and establishment of a school for police and military training.[17] His primary task, however, was to carry out the reorganization of the Corps of Police, for which purpose he was awarded the post of [Instructor] General [until then held by Third Chief Abel Quintero.]. →Lt. Col. Gómez Ayau, despite being a member of a foreign military force, became the virtual commander of the Corps of Police, [and the immediate superior of] the Third Chief, Major Quintero, since in that period there appears no mention of a First or Second Chief.*←

The Guatemalan military man arrived in Panama on January 12, 1941, and soon began work on the restructuring of the National Po-

---

* General Order of the Day № 149, July 15, 1941. [I translate *Patria* as "Fatherland," and *Benemérito* as "Most Worthy." The latter is an honorific awarded to institutions, such as the police and fire departments, that remains a part of their official titles. Gómez Ayau's belief that a coup was impending seems evident. The Editor finds it difficult to pass over without comment that the motto calling for "Loyalty to the Chief of State"—as opposed to the Constitution or the Republic—; the phrase "soldiers of the Fatherland," and the call for obedience to, and "causing others to respect at all times" "the orders of the Executive Authority" (meaning *El Presidente,* a/k/a *El Hombre,* a/k/a *El Caudillo*); are redolent of the oath of loyalty to the person of the *Führer* required in Germany at that time in history.]

lice, which then consisted of about two thousand police officers and senior officials.[18] One of his first measures was the rotation of the officer corps. His first reassignments, affecting the length and breadth of the Republic, took place at the end of January, 1941.

- Captain Oscar Ocaña, who had been the head of the First Battalion, in Panama City, was transferred to command of the presidential bodyguard.
- Captain Antonio Huff was designated supervising captain of street patrols in the City of Panama.
- Captain Carlos Enrique Tejada was assigned to the garrison in the Model Jail.
- Lieutenant Saturnino Flores was temporarily put in command of the Third Battalion in Chiriquí.
- →Captain José Antonio Remón Cantera, a 1931 graduate of the Military Academy of Mexico, was transferred from the Third Battalion, in Chiriquí, to the First Battalion, in Panama City, as senior captain assigned to central headquarters.←

Gómez Ayau planned to utilize Remón's military knowledge to organize the most important police command center in the country. →This convinces us that Remón's military career benefitted from President Arnulfo Arias's reorganizational plans, and that it was then, [in 1941,] that the militarization of Panama began the upward spiral that would end dramatically on December 20, 1989, with the sanguinary U.S. invasion.← It does not therefore seem to us that, as Renato Pereira asserts, it was President Harmodio Arias who had [years earlier] named Remón chief of central police headquarters, nor does it appear that from then on, Captain Remón "dedicated himself entirely to the military model of organization, in particular, the selection and training of officers."[19] If Remón had joined the National Police in 1931 with the rank of captain, as this author asserts[20]—and if he had had this important mission entrusted to him by [President Harmodio Arias]—it seems improbable that so many years later, he would still have been posted to the interior of the Republic at the same rank.

The members of the police force were subjected to intensive military instruction throughout the Republic, and [Instructor] General

Gómez Ayau began to impose severe disciplinary penalties on police officers who failed to attend.[21]

On June 27, 1941, the Minister of Government and Justice, Ricardo Adolfo De la Guardia, informed Gómez Ayau of the decision to put the personnel of what was then the General Superintendence of the Police into uniform, and to award the Superintendent and subordinate officers military ranks and military authority for the exercise of their functions. Thus it was that General Superintendent Nicolás Valderrama was awarded the rank of lieutenant colonel; his assistant Tomás Herrera L. and secretary José del Carmen Castro were named captains.[22]

In General Order N° 267 (Aug. 29, 1941, [after the massacre at - Cotito]), Minister De la Guardia accepted the resignation of the Third Chief and Instructor General of the Police, Major Abel Quintero, named *attaché* to the Panamanian legation in Cuba. In reality, Quintero was to be sent abroad in order to attend the Cuban Military Aviation School, a result of direct intervention by Gómez Ayau, as may be seen from the farewell speech given upon his departure.[23]

In the same General Order of the Day, all individuals attached to or employed by the National Police were ordered to wear the uniforms corresponding to the ranks assigned them, and the commander of each post was directed to instruct the personnel under his command to obey the order of General Quarters, that is, the command requiring the strictest order and that all police officers fall in with full equipment.[24] The system of reserves and barracks alert was strengthened, and severe penalties of arrest were established for their violation. All sentries on duty at all the posts of the institution were ordered to keep bayonets fixed twenty–four hours a day.[25] A machine gun section was organized and required to be on alert and in regulation uniform even during military reviews, such as the one given at General Headquarters to commemorate the first anniversary of the inauguration of Dr. Arias Madrid as the First Magistrate of the Nation.[26]

It was Gómez Ayau who signed the general orders of the day and who imposed iron military discipline, providing for thirty–day sentences to the stockade for abandoning one's post without adequate cause while on guard duty, or endangering the state of readiness by consuming alcohol, twenty days for failing to obey the order of a superior officer, fifteen days for failing to attend regulation military training, ten days for endangering the state of readiness, eight for addressing a colleague in an improper manner, five for failing to carry the regulation military pay book, and dismissal for drunkenness or provoking an individual to fight.

The severity of military discipline imposed by Gómez Ayau was the cause of dissatisfaction in the public forces, according to Gil Blas Tejeira. This well known journalist, biographer of Minister Ricardo Adolfo de la Guardia (a *golpista* who participated in the coup), says that the military goose–stepper[*] dressed all of his troops in picturesque uniforms, treated officers contemptuously, and that this treatment, which might have produced good results in the Guatemala of Ubico, was not so successful in Panama where the forms of interaction were different.[27]

Tejeira takes Gómez Ayau to task for failing to recognize the authority of Minister De la Guardia and for obeying only the orders directly issued by President Arnulfo Arias. I note, however, that this does not appear reflected in the general orders signed by the Guatemalan advisor. We have seen that Minister De la Guardia himself communicated to Gómez Ayau the decision to uniform the personnel of the General Superintendence of the Police. Moreover, a general order of the day at the beginning of October, 1941—several days before the overthrow of Arnulfo Arias—transcribed a communiqué, drafted by Minister De la Guardia, that was published in the pro–government *La Tribuna* of September 26[. The communiqué gave the] official response to a September 24 *Panamá–América* article under the headline, "In many cases the Police act irrationally and thoughtlessly."[†]

---

[*] [*"Chapín,"* in Spain, literally a "clog" (shoe), implying an excessive devotion to military discipline and pomp.]

[†] [*de manera alocada e irreflexible (sic)*] General Order of the Day N⁰ ____, Oct. 2, 1941. [The Author inserts the (sic) because the word *irreflexible,* which I translate as *thoughtlessly,* is not standard Spanish, but seems to mean "unreflectingly."]

We think that Gómez Ayau reported directly to President Arias (we have only to remember the motto he proposed for the Corps), but not that he failed to respect the hierarchy, unless Tejeira believes that De la Guardia was the commander–in–chief of the Public Forces. In addition, De la Guardia also participated, as head of the ministry involved, in the militarization of the National Police before and after October 9, 1941.

This process took a major step forward on April 14, 1941, when Executive Order № 64, awarding military ranks, was issued. Noting that for many years, in addition to performing their particular policing duties, the National Police had also performed an "essentially military" function as guarantors of the independence of the Nation, President Arias and his Minister De la Guardia conferred the rank of "Major of the Army of the Republic" on Police Major Abel Quintero and on Police Captain Oscar Ocaña. Similarly, they awarded the rank of Captain of the Army of the Republic to Police Captains Rogelio Alba Jr., José A. Remón, Francisco Aued H., Carlos Enrique Tejada J., Bolivar Vallarino and Antonio Huff. Arias and the minister proceeded in the same way to name nineteen lieutenants and thirty–five second lieutenants of police.[28] Four days later, President Arias and Minister De la Guardia signed an order conferring the rank of Lieutenant Colonel of the Army on Olmedo Fábrega, the President's military *aide–de–camp*.[29]

→On July 15, 1941, [a week after the massacre and three months before Arias was deposed by the police, his appointee Gómez Ayau was] on the eve of departure for Guatemala. The [Instructor] General drafted a message to the commanders, officers, non–commissioned and rank–and–file officers of the National Police, in which he describes his mission and his special relationship with the President of the Republic. He explains that he came to Panama by "special mandate" of President Arias Madrid, in order to offer his police and military knowledge in the reorganization of the National Corps of Police. He said that if he had met with some success in his effort, it was undoubtedly because of the "magnificent military spirit" shown by all. He recommended in an exaggerated manner that "as soldiers of the Fatherland" the primary duty of all was to obey and to cause others to respect at all times the orders of the Executive

Authority and that he was confident that every member of the Corps would know how to honor the motto of the Most Worthy Corps, "Loyalty to the Chief of State.".*←

After Ricardo Adolfo De la Guardia seized power, following the 1941 overthrow of Arnulfo Arias, as Minister *Chargé* of the Executive Branch [*i.e.*, acting president] the process of militarization continued apace or broadened in scope. The new chief executive awarded the rank of colonel to Rogelio Fábrega and named him First Chief of the National Police. Reviewing the general orders of the day for the months of October and November, 1941, we find that police officers were continuing to be sentenced to terms in the stockade for failing to report for regulation military training.

In 1953, President Colonel José Antonio Remón Cantera would transform the National Police into a militarized National Guard. In 1983, Public Law № 20 would convert the Guard to the Defense Forces as a virtual army, with policing, criminal investigation and even administrative functions such as immigration and the issuance of passports.[†]

---

* General Order of the Day № 149, July 15, 1941. [I translate *Patria* as "Fatherland," and *Benemérito* as "Most Worthy." The latter is an honorific awarded to institutions, such as the police and fire departments, that remains a part of their official titles. Gómez Ayau's belief that a coup was impending seems evident. The Editor finds it difficult to pass over without comment that the motto calling for "Loyalty to the Chief of State"—as opposed to the Constitution or the Republic—; the phrase "soldiers of the Fatherland," and the call for obedience to, and "causing others to respect at all times" "the orders of the Executive Authority" (meaning *El Presidente*, a/k/a *El Hombre*, a/k/a *El Caudillo*); are redolent of the oath of loyalty to the person of the *Führer* required in Germany at that time in history.]

† [From Independence (1903) onward, Panama's single public force, known as the National Police, was gradually more militarized until 1953, when it was renamed the National Guard by Pres. Remón. It incorporated both civilian police and military functions, though Panamanians were still proudly declaring in the 1960's that like Costa Rica, they had no army because they had no need of one. "The Guard developed directly out of the police, and the police now [1978] form part of the Guard." LaFeber (*see* n. 4, p. 48, *supra*), p. 114n.

[The public force continued to be known as the *Guardia Nacional* until soon after Noriega's assumption of power in August, 1983. Noriega, by "expanding, reorganizing and 'professionalizing' the military and reincarnating

Continued→

6 | THE NATIONAL POLICE IN CHIRIQUÍ

IN MID-1941, THE Third Battalion of the National Police headquartered in Chiriquí consisted of about two hundred men.[30] Their chief was Captain Antonio Huff, recently transferred from Central Headquarters, where he had been in charge of street patrol in Panama City. The senior officers of the Third Battalion were Second Lieutenants Ernesto Ruiloba, Primitivo Rivera and Luis Ardila.

At that time, the police barracks were situated in the so-called *El Peligro* ["Danger"] neighborhood, now called Barrio Bolívar, on the square opposite the Cathedral of San José, specifically in the building now occupied by the health center for that section of the city of David. There were also detachments posted to the principal district towns of the province, and one in the village of Cañas Gordas in the area of the Costa Rican border.

The rank-and-file troops in Chiriquí, as in other rural areas of the country, were little affected by military discipline, as is shown by the impressive number of sanctions imposed on policemen serving in the province. In the general orders of the day for the months of May, June, July and August, 1941, of the two hundred individuals serving there, disciplinary sanctions of from five to sixty days in the stockade were reported for nearly a fifth, that is, about thirty-nine police officers, and in numerous instances there were orders of sus-

---

← *Continued from prev. page.*
the National Guard as the more elevated National Defense Forces of Panama [*Fuerzas de Defensa, FF.DD.* in Spanish, PDF in English], was able to please both the United States, which was financing the upgrading, and his officers, who reveled in the rapid promotions and prestige." John Dinges, *Our Man in Panama* (1990), p. 10.

[After the U.S. invasion in 1989, the "Defense Forces" were promptly disbanded and the National Police reestablished, sparking a fierce debate over which former military figures should be permitted to continue in the guise of civilian police. To what extent the police use military forms and methods, and to what extent they are commanded by former officers of Noriega's PDF, continue to be thorny issues in Panamanian politics. See, *e.g.*, the comments of *La Prensa* correspondent Betty Brannan Jaén, p. lxx, *supra. See also* Ricardo Arias Calderón, *Democracia sin ejército: la experiencia de Panamá* (2001).]

pension or final dismissal from service. Leaving one's post, failure to attend civilian and military training, sleeping on duty, failure to obey the orders of superiors, disrespect, negligence in guarding prisoners, but most of all a proclivity for the consumption of alcohol and provoking mayhem were the most common disciplinary failings reported. Thus, for example—

- officer J. D., badge Nº 1223, for leaving his post to go to a beer garden in David, thirty days' arrest;
- officer I. G. S., badge Nº 1224, for drunkenness while in uniform, provoking fights, threatening use of a firearm, dismissal from the force and transfer to the custody of the civilian authorities;
- officer V. M., badge Nº 1030, for neglect of duty, arguing with a fellow officer and consumption of alcohol while in uniform and on duty, dismissal;
- officer A. H., badge Nº 1192, for starting a fight with a fellow policeman while patrolling a dance, and for subsequently offering the Deputy Chief of the La Concepción detachment $B/.$ 5.00 [a week's wages for a common laborer] to reduce the punishment, dismissal;
- officer M. A., badge Nº 1389, "for making a spectacle of himself by walking the streets of David in a state of complete intoxication and showing his police officer's badge as a member of the Corps of Police while drunk," dismissal;
- officer T. S., badge Nº 1306, "for failure to respect superior officers and exceeding his authority on duty, and for being completely drunk," dismissal;
- officer G. C., badge Nº 1449, for appearing at the Puerto Armuelles police station in a state of complete intoxication with a prisoner in custody, three months' suspension; and finally,
- officers H. C., badge Nº 1411, and E. A., badge Nº 1415, for threatening the state of readiness by consuming liquor, thirty days' arrest.[31]

These were some of the men under the command of Antonio Huff, who himself, some witnesses of the period recall, was a very "arbitrary and aggressive official."[32] The police chief, of German ancestry, was born in 1911. He was a tall man of a Caucasian type; he had lost an eye—it was said a woman had thrown acid on him in a fight—and he filled the vacant socket with a glass one; he was considered abrupt and showed no trace of diplomacy.

Germán Alfaro, who knew him well, recalls that at the famous trial for the assassination of President Remón, Huff was put in charge of conducting the defendants charged with the murder to the courtroom of the Second Superior Tribunal of Justice in Panama City, and returning them to the Model Jail. In the wee hours at the end of the last day of the trial, after the jury had acquitted Rubén Miró[*] and the other defendants, two ladies who were members of the jury, Imelda Sagel and Teresita Castillo, asked Huff to arrange for transportation to their homes, and he in reply launched an aggressive verbal tirade against them.[33]

Huff's character involved him in a number of problems with local authorities during his sojourn in Chiriquí. A sharp confrontation several months later that almost turned physical, between Huff and Circuit Prosecutor Abel Gómez Araúz,[34] the prosecutor investigating the Cotito episode and who wanted to interrogate the arrogant police captain, is still remembered.[35]

Nevertheless, it should be recalled that Huff's assignment in Chiriquí was not an easy one. Apart from the inefficiency of his subordinates, the commander of the Third Battalion lacked sufficient

---

[*] [Elected in 1952, Police Col. and Pres. José Remón was assassinated Jan. 2, 1955, at the racetrack now known as the *Hipódromo Presidente Remón*. No one was convicted of the crime but the consensus among historians is that the assassination was the work of thugs working for "Lucky" Luciano—the U.S. mobster then trying to take over the drug trade moving through Panama—and of Miró, a lawyer and nephew of Harmodio Arias. Remón was succeeded by 2nd V.P. Ricardo Arias (a member of the oligarchical family of that name, no relation to, but a political ally of, Harmodio and Arnulfo Arias). *See* Larry LaRae Pippin, *The Remón Era* (1964). Miró was acquitted, and was himself assassinated in 1969, presumably by the G–2 military intelligence unit under Torrijos.]

personnel to carry out his work and lacked even adequate police stations to meet the growing policing needs of an area as spread-out as Chiriquí. As late as October, 1942, the only police battalions in the interior of the Republic that had modern stations were those in La Chorrera and Río Hato. The remaining towns, including David, third largest city in the country, had buildings that were "unhealthy, dank and without comforts."36

One of the worst problems facing Huff was the immigration situation resulting from the activities of the Chiriquí Land Company on the banana plantations in the area of the district of Barú [Puerto Armuelles]. This multinational firm [local subsidiary of United Fruit, creator of the "banana republics"] hired hundreds of Central Americans on a temporary basis, mainly Nicaraguans and Hondurans, to harvest the fruit, but the company did not fulfill its obligation to return them at the end of their contracts to their countries of origin. These people remained on Panamanian soil, without legal documents authorizing their permanent residence, working at starvation wages.[*] The immigration problem became a grave social problem and there were frequent bloody incidents that the police were incapable of preventing. Many of these aliens were deported, but they returned to this country, and upon being arrested had to be held in the jails while their cases were processed, causing a drain on public funds.

Huff, despite the limitations of personnel and facilities, must have done an efficient job in this area, as the report of the First Chief of the National Police indicated that the Alien Affairs section, creat-

---

* [Banana company manager Mark Trafton Jr., in a memoir *ca.* 1982, describing the situation in 1928, when a plantation operation he was supervising was halted for lack of labor, wrote: "The...*Chiricanos*...were cowboys and had no desire to work in the sweltering rainforest, so the Company had to import labor from Nicaragua...[as] 'axe and shovel' men. ... [A] boatload of *Nicas* arrived, about 200 real tough but hard-working men who were anxious to work for the relatively high wages in a new banana division as compared to the poverty-stricken situation in their country." The "relatively high" wages, were however, apparently insufficient to attract Panamanian labor. Mark Trafton Jr., "Introduction to Panama," unpub. memoir, *ca.* 1982.]

ed in 1937, during the brief time it had been operating, maintained rather complete tracking of the foreign residents in the national territory and in transit, and could be categorized without reservation as extraordinarily effective[37]

The report of the First Chief, Colonel Rogelio Fábrega, covering the biennium 1939–41, emphasized that the Alien Affairs section had the capacity to supply complete information on the foreign residents in the country, including their present locations, but even so, he recommended that, for improved performance, branches be established on the borders with the neighboring republics of Colombia and Costa Rica "since the number of clandestine immigrants who enter through these areas is enormous."[38]

7 | RELIGIOUS INTOLERANCE: THE CASE OF THE SEVENTH-DAY ADVENTISTS

THE *ARNULFISTA* ADMINISTRATION showed itself to be intolerant not only of opposition politicians, against whom it employed a militarized police force, but strangely, it also used these repressive forces against some minority religions. In an unprecedented episode that occurred in San Andrés, in the district of Bugaba, a month before the tragic incident at Cotito, the police, on the direct order of Minister De la Guardia, banned Seventh–day Adventist services in Chiriquí and arrested various followers of this religious sect. On June 7, 1941, while several people were gathered at the residence of Mr. Teófilo Quiroz for Adventist services, the police broke into the house and arrested all those present, except for the women. Those arrested, all members of the West Caribbean Corporation of the Seventh–day Adventists, were taken to La Concepción and put in the custody of the mayor of the district.

It appears that on May 19, Mr. Reynaldo Mattinson, a representative of the Adventist sect, had been warned by the mayor of David, Alejandro González Revilla, that he should suspend religious services. The mayor informed him that the order came from [Provincial] Governor Rafael Terán Albarracín, and upon making inquiries of the governor, Mattinson was informed that the original order had been issued by the Minister of Government and Justice himself.

On May 24, Mattinson communicated with Minister De la Guardia informing him that the West Caribbean Corporation had been incorporated since 1923 and that since then had acted in strict compliance with the law. He received no reply whatever.

A few days later, the Adventists were released, but on June 12, the mayor of Bugaba fined Mr. Quiroz ten balboas [US $10, a month's wages for a common laborer] for having permitted these persons to conduct their services in his house, in violation of the order of the *corregidor* of San Andrés who had ordered the closing of the Adventist church in the township.[*]

Since the order banning the religious services had come from the Minister of Government and Justice, the representatives of the Adventists were induced to file suit against [Minister] Ricardo Adolfo De la Guardia in the Supreme Court of Justice, seeking a Writ of Constitutional Guarantee to nullify the order for violating Article 38 of the newly passed *Panameñista* Constitution. →The case became a national issue. The *Panamá–América,* then an opposition newspaper, followed the proceedings, reporting on them in three successive issues.[†]←

What motivated this religious persecution, unprecedented in the province of Chiriquí and possibly in the entire Republic? It is not easy to find a categorical answer. The only indication that we have we take from a conversation with José Ehrman, who at the time held the position of under–secretary of Treasury and Finance in the Arnulfo Arias administration. According to Ehrman, a citizen had

---

[*] [For a brief explanation of the functions of the governor, *alcaldes* and *corregidores* mentioned, their mixed judicial and executive functions, and their relationship to the Min. of Govt. & Justice, *see* p. lxxxiii, n. 2 , *supra.*]

[†] *Panamá–América*, June 12, 14, 17, 1941. [*Panamá–América* is part of a newspaper chain then owned by its founder, ex–Pres. Harmodio Arias, brother of Arnulfo. The Author says it was "then an opposition newspaper" because Harmodio at that time was feuding with his younger brother over Arnulfo's radical policies and attempts to gain control of the paper. During the next few months, "Harmodio, in one of his typical political schemes, plotted to have the [U.S.] embassy act as front–man in bringing down Arnulfo." LaFeber (*see* p. 48, n. 4, *supra*), pp. 94–5. The U.S. government, eager to see the "pro–Nazi" Arias gone, indicated in advance it would not act to oppose a coup. *Id.,* p. 97.]

lodged a complaint against a religious sect (the Adventists?) that was carrying out religious activities in the streets of Chitré. The local parish priest complained to the Minister of Government and Justice, who, in order to prohibit the activities, requested the authorization of President Arias to undertake a census of the various religious groups.[39]

A similar version is offered by Harmodio Miranda, who asserts that at the end of the nineteen–thirties, there was a proliferation of religious sects and "naturist" settlements in Chiriquí, which at that time was not so demanding in its requirements for the entry of foreigners.[*] During the first *Arnulfista* administration, President Arias wanted to put things in order, something he began, but which he could not finish.[40] These small incidents may provide the key to understanding the events at Cotito. The government knew that in the mountains of Chiriquí there existed a sect that many believed was composed of religious fanatics. In addition, they were "Germans," and on the eve of Panama's entry into the Second World War, controls [seemed even more] justified.

All these antecedents paved the way for the drama at Cotito. An authoritarian police chief, an undisciplined police force given to alcohol abuse, governmental intolerance, the religious fanaticism of the colonists, and the rumors, initiated by no one knows whom, that these Swiss people were armed and dangerous Nazi agents; all these combined to determine the fatal outcome of the morning of July 7, 1941.

Notes to Chapter II

---

* [It should be noted that the district of Bugaba is, in the present day, home to numerous Protestant Christian denominations, "naturist" (referring to health and nutrition, not nudism) groups, a Muslim mosque located near the Costa Rican border (in the district of Barú, where many Middle Eastern immigrants are in trade), all of which seem to operate freely under the protection of the current Constitution, which makes Roman Catholicism the national religion of Panama, but guarantees the free exercise of others. The Adventists, discussed here, have several thriving congregations in the district of Bugaba and operate large primary and secondary schools in both Bugaba and in the provincial capital of David.]

[1] Conte Porras (*See* p. 37, n. 39 *supra*), p. 172.

[2] Arnulfo Arias, *"Discurso pronunciado en su llegada a la Ciudad de Panamá"*

[3] Conte Porras, p. 174.

[4] The Inaugural Address is reprinted in Ricaurte Soler, *El Pensamiento político en los siglos XIX y XX* ["*Political Thought in the 19th and 20th Centuries*"], v. 6 (1988), pp. 367-77.

[5] Conte Porras, pp. 181-2.

[6] Julio E. Linares, *Enrique Linares en la historia política de Panamá, 1969-1949.* (1989), p. 368.

[7] Conte Porras, p. 176.

[8] *Ibid.*

[9] *Ibid.*

[10] [See also LaFeber, p. 93.]

[11] Decision, Sup. Trib., 1st Judicial District. 1941 REGISTRO JUDICIAL at 168. (Jan. 1941.)

[12] *Estrella de Panamá*, January 10, 1941.

[13] Conte Porras, pp. 163-4.

[14] GACETA OFICIAL, № 7,917 (Nov. 2, 1938).

[15] Renato Pereira, *Panamá, fuerzas armadas y política* [*Panama, Armed Forces and Politics*] (1979), p. 13.

[16] *Estrella de Panamá*, Jan. 14, 1941.

[17] *Cristóbal Rodríguez, Sect. Gen. of the Pres. of the Rep., to Raúl De Roux, Minister For. Rel., Dec. 17, 1940.* (Guatemala file. Archives, Min. For. Rel.)

[18] Communiqué, Min. of Govt. & Justice. In *La Tribuna*, Sept. 26, 1941.

[19] Pereira, p. 13.

[20] *Ibid.*

[21] General Orders of the Day, May-July, 1941, *passim*. (Archives, National Police).

[22] General Order of the Day № 142, June 7, 1941, p. 4.

[23] *Ibid.*

[24] *Ibid.*

[25] General Order of the Day № ___, June 13, 1941.

[26] General Order of the Day № ___, Sept. 30, 1941, p. 4.

[27] Gil Blas Tejeira, *Biografía de Ricardo Adolfo De la Guardia: Página de la historia panameña* (1971), p. 37.

[28] Executive Order № 164, Apr. 14, 1941. Min. Govt. & Justice, 1940-42 MEMORIA, at 591-2.

[29] Executive Order № 72, Apr. 18, 1941, *Ibid*.

[30] General Order of the Day № 130, June 23, 1941, p. 3. The number is deduced from the new numbering of police badges that was to take effect on June 26.

[31] General Orders of the Day, May 9 and 19, June 18, June 17 and 24, Aug. 23 and 30, 1941.

[32] *[arbitrario y atropellador]* Harmodio Miranda, intv. with Author, Panama City, Apr. 21, 1992.

[33] Germán Alfaro, conversation with Author, Panama City, Nov. 9, 1992.

[34] [Grandfather of the author.]

[35] Julio Gómez Araúz, conversation with Author, Dec. 24, 1991.

[36] Report of the First Chief of the National Police, Col. Rogelio Fábrega. In Min. Govt. & Justice, 1943 MEMORIA, at 1,216.

[37] *Id.*, at 1,211.

[38] *Id.*, at 1,213.

[39] José Ehrman, conversation with Author, Panama City, Apr 4, 1991.

[40] Miranda.

SCHMIEDER FAMILY PHOTO
The Schmieders' farmstead, late 1930's

III | THE SLAUGHTER AT COTITO

1 | THE IMMEDIATE ANTECEDENTS

IN SEPTEMBER, 1939, just ten days after the outbreak of war in Europe, the Government of President Juan Demóstenes Arosemena ordered the renewed registration of all foreigners residing in the Republic and the exercise of greater vigilance over them. Executive Order Nº 55 (Sept. 11, 1939) obliged every alien residing in the Republic to "inform the Alien Affairs section of the National Police of the place where he had established or would establish his domicile of record." This information could be submitted either to the Director of Immigration in the Ministry of Government and Justice, to the Alien Affairs section of the National Police, or to the municipal administration of each district. If the resident alien was the head of a family, he could include in his declaration of domicile all his dependents living in the national territory. Each failure to comply with the directive would involve a fine of B/.5 for the first offense and B/.25 for each subsequent violation, to be imposed by the mayor of the respective district.¹

→There is evidence that the police had visited the colony for this purpose on various occasions before June, 1941.← →It seems to be a fact that the police on two occasions appeared at Cotito to serve notice on the Swiss that they must register with the Alien Affairs section at police headquarters in David. This is confirmed by Wilhelm

Probst [in his unpublished book], although he notes that the Swiss ignored the notices.

> A few months later, all the foreigners in Panama had to register as I mentioned earlier, it took three days on horseback to get to David. I lived twenty–five years in the jungle, not far from David; I know how I felt when once in awhile I had to go to David; you leave home reluctantly; you are always glad not to have to have anything to do with the city.
>
> That's how it was with those poor people; they were notified; they didn't pay any attention; they were notified again, also without result; then they sent a captain with fifty policemen to take this band of Nazis, as they were falsely accused of being, dead or alive.[2]←

We have seen[3] that in 1940, police officers Efraín González and Lucas Garcés had toured the Volcán region of Chiriquí inspecting the passports of the largely European foreigners, and that thus engaged the police officers had visited the Cotito colony several times. →Sophie Müller, giving evidence [later] to the investigating prosecutor, said that they had [1] first been visited by Sergeant Nicasio Saldaña and a subordinate named Luis Ponce. Later [2] it was Second Lieutenant Primitivo Rivera, accompanied by Saldaña and Ponce. Then it was the turn on June 20, 1941, of [3] the same Saldaña and police officer Aurelio Serracín, and finally, [4] Captain Huff himself had journeyed to Cotito on June 24, accompanied by other officials from the Third Police Battalion. Each time, the colonists were told they would have to go down to David.[4]←

2 | Captain Huff's Service of Notice

→[IN JUNE, 1941,] a few days after the arrest of the Adventists at San Andrés, the chief of the Third Police Battalion was ordered [by the high command in the capital] to direct all European residents in the highlands of the province [of Chiriquí] to come down to police headquarters in David for further immigration formalities. The Europeans were required to bring their personal data up to date, and to provide at least two recent photographs of each individual. [Like the

CHAPTER III | THE SLAUGHTER AT COTITO

order, issued a few weeks previously, directing the Adventists in David to suspend their religious services, the registration order] had come directly from the Ministry of Government and Justice.←

Given these circumstances, it is appropriate to ask why—

- If the mayor of the district of Bugaba [at La Concepción had been] authorized [since September, 1939] to enforce Executive Order № 55 in the Chiriquí highlands, why did this express order come [at that point, in early June, 1941,] directly from Panama City?

- If the heads of families could include their dependents in their declarations, why were all of the [settlers] required to go down [to the provincial capital], and

Capt. Antonio Huff, commander of the Chiriquí garrison, *ca.* 1941

- If the stated purpose was to carry out an exhaustive census of foreigners, why was this not carried out right in Cotito, where officers of the National Police had already been on more than one occasion?

We cannot answer these questions definitively; we can only conclude that the Panamanian government showed unusual interest[*]

---

* [The 1939 registration order of Pres. J.D. Arosemena appears to have been, until then, something of a dead letter. The Editor would argue that the explanation for the unusual interest in enforcement of the order might be found in the reaction of police commanders and cabinet ministers to pressures coming from the upper classes, who were in turn responding to pressures from the United States, the example of roundups of Axis nationals in

Continued→

in the Cotito colonists, only partially explicable by the earlier treatment of the Adventists and to some extent by the unfounded suspicion that the Swiss colonists were Nazi fifth columnists. →This uncommon interest included an element of hostility and even irrational fear of individuals known to be peaceful and hospitable.←

Upon receiving the order from his superiors, Huff telephoned Second Lieutenant Primitivo Rivera, chief of the detachment at Cañas Gordas [on the Costa Rican border], ordering him to go to Cotito to inform the colonists they would have to go down to David to renew their registration. Rivera, in turn, told [Sergeant] Nicasio Saldaña, badge Nº 92, and officer Aurelio Manuel Serracín, badge Nº 1033, to execute the order. Sergeant Saldaña and officer Serracín left Cañas Gordas for Cotito, where they arrived [on the third visit described by Sophie Müller] in the early hours of June 20, 1941. Regarding this contact between the police and the colonists the communiqué issued by the Ministry of Government and Justice gives the following official version:

> [H]aving arrived at said camp or settlement, the Panamanian officers informed the foreigners of the object of their visit, and were informed in reply that they were determined to obey no one; that neither the laws of Panama nor the President of the Republic mattered to them; that they would leave only of their own volition and could only be removed if they were dead; that their religion was that practiced in the United States by Father Divine, a Negro agitator with a known [*historial, i.e.,* criminal] record in the United States.
>
> The officers were informed by neighbors residing in the vicinity that the rebel colony was well supplied with firearms and ammunition, which is why the Panamanian officers, having inferior numbers and firepower, and

---

← *Continued from prev. page.*
the Canal Zone and elsewhere in Latin America, and the internment of foreigners at Camp Empire in Balboa. *See* pp. xvii *ff, supra.*]

having no instructions from their superiors, decided to return and report on their mission.[5]

[One writer, in a commemorative magazine article written more than twenty years after the fact, observes that—]

[a]t the time, reports were received at La Concepción indicating the Swiss nationals were engaged in suspicious activities, stating that they had stored large quantities of arms, and that their residences were surrounded by fortifications. Informed of these reports, the provincial authorities summoned them to appear for the appropriate formal interrogation. That was where the seed was sown for what would be one of the most terrible events in the memory of the people of Chiriquí.

It was only natural that the Swiss tillers of the soil would refuse to leave their camp, where they lived happily, struggling against the wildness of the mountains, the inclement climate and the bad roads; these dedicated farmers sealed their fate when their leader gave his categorical refusal to answer the summons of the zealous Panamanian officials.[6]

This version is unconvincing. We do not think rumors of the existence of arms in Swiss hands gave rise to the first visit of the police to Cotito [or] that neighbors reported the alleged arsenal to police during their visit. →To the contrary, one would deduce from the official communiqué← that these rumors of the colonists' having armed themselves—which would prove their undoing—arose only *after* the police officers had returned from the colony. It is logical to suppose that if the police authorities had [indeed] had reports, still unconfirmed, of an arsenal in the hands of the foreigners, they would have sent not just two solitary police officers, but, rather, a larger contingent to confront the colonists. In reality, [the reports do not appear to have existed before Saldaña and Serracín were sent to the colony, or more men would have been sent, and by their own testimony] it was not Saldaña and Serracín who informed Huff of the existence of a supposed arsenal; this version appeared *a posteriori* to justify the slaughter of July 7, 1941.

→Aurelio Manuel Serracín, whom the Author interviewed in early 1993, himself contradicted the last part of the communiqué. Serracín denies that the neighbors had informed him of an alleged arsenal in the hands of the colonists. To the contrary, he affirms that Saldaña and he were well received (entering the house as far as the dining room), although he does state that Lehner let them know in a very vehement manner that the colonists would not go down to David.[7]←

It is not only Serracín who denies the existence of the supposed arsenal in the hands of the Swiss; it is also denied by the then 16–year–old Helmut Hils, one of the neighbors who supposedly had reported it to the police.

> They had no weapons[;] that is a lie. The mistake they made was to barricade themselves in, so they could not

COURTEST DOÑA ROMELIA VDA. DE HILS

Helmut Hils, a teenager at the time of the massacre, had vivid memories of the colony and his friends there. Here he is shown, (2nd from left) with his German immigrant parents Anton (r.) and Marie Hils, brother Wilfredo (l.), and sister Gertrudis.

be taken out of there.[8]

Robert Müller also emphatically denies the colonists had weaponry in their possession, but he confirms that they had constructed a sort of [defensive] stockade. He also explains the reaction of the colonists' leader Karl Lehner.

> No, Sir, we did not have any weapons. Absolutely, we were opposed to all weapons in general. ...
>
> The truth is that the chief of the colony said: "I will not go down to David, but everyone is free to do so. I propose that if we have to provide documents, that we pay the expenses for them to come here, and that they inspect the documents right here," and Huff promised they would, that that is how it would be done, so everybody was happy, but the chief of the colony said: "No, they won't come, they will riddle us with bullets. Let us build a strong fence so they cannot take us prisoner," and the fence was built by Brauchle in four days of work, with big, thick posts of *mameicillo** that they cut...

Sophie Müller's testimony confirms the reason for Lehner's demurrer and simultaneous proposal that an official of the Alien Affairs section go to Cotito[. S]he testified that Lehner answered Second Lieutenant Rivera by saying that when the colonists had first traveled to Cotito [in early 1939], the government had promised it would leave them alone; that the government was well aware that the colonists wanted only the freedom to work far from civilization; and the government knew there were no bandits of any kind among the colonists. She added that because they were so many, they could not all have gone down to David and that in any event, they were willing to pay out two hundred balboas[†] "so they could send a des-

---

* Robert Müller (*See* p. 7, n.†, *supra*). [*Mameicillo* is a tropical hardwood much prized for fence posts because of its density and resistance to rot. The name comes from the supposed resemblance of the acorns, properly *bellotas*, to another fruit known as *mamey*.]

† [₿/.200 = US $200, a very large sum in the Chiriquí of 1941: more than six months' wages for a farm laborer and several months' wages for a police

Continued→

ignated agent to the colony for the purpose of conducting the corresponding registration, as an official had done the previous year."[9] The police did not accept the proposal.

Saldaña and Serracín's report (confirming that the colony represented no danger) would have hardly justified sending a contingent of police to Cotito, but it did result four days later, on June 24, in Captain Huff's traveling to Cotito himself, accompanied by Second Lieutenants Ardila and Rivera, Sergeant Rosendo Aguilar and police officer Faustino Montenegro.

According to the official communiqué, on this visit Huff first met with Karl Schmieder, who served as interpreter for the chief of the colony, Karl Lehner. Lehner had confined himself to stating that the colonists would not go down to David, that they would not show any papers or passports, since they did not recognize any government, and that "they were prepared to support their decision by force if necessary." According to the communiqué, this statement was not a bluff, since Huff and his subordinates, while negotiating with Schmieder and Lehner outside the palisade, saw about twenty colonists, men and women, armed with sharpened machetes, while "several individuals who appeared to be armed with rifles and machine guns, were monitoring them" from the upper part of the main building,[*] "ready to do away with them in one fell swoop..."

[In the official version,] Huff and his men, pistols in hand, warned the colonists that they should put aside their resistance, that the police had come not to make war, but rather to be conciliatory. The Swiss gave the same answer: that they were not prepared to obey Panamanian laws, that the only way they would leave was if their dead bodies were carried out, and that that was the unanimous decision of all, men, women and children.

← *Continued from prev. page.*
officer, or the value of 300 acres of improved pasture land or a herd of 20 dairy cows.]

* [Although the impression given is that of an imposing fortress, the "upper part of the main building" would have been a window in a low attic above the single story of a small wooden house.]

CHAPTER III | THE SLAUGHTER AT COTITO

Huff then managed to calm the situation and persuaded them to let the police inside the palisade, and even to go into the dining room, followed by four men who were still aggressive in demeanor, so the police chief warned Lehner that he should remove his [armed] guards, which the leader of the colony did.

In the dining room, the police were offered a glass of milk and Captain Huff tried to convince Lehner that they must obey the authorities, but, once again, he received the same reply: "that they would die before they would obey Panamanian laws."

In a tour of the colony's outbuildings, Lehner let them inspect a smithy, a carpentry shop and a perfectly equipped mechanical shop, but he barred the officers from entering a closed room where he said there were two sick women. Once outside the palisade, Huff observed on the top of a nearby hill that there was a kind of guard post or observation point that dominated all four cardinal directions, and asked for permission to inspect it, but he was told there were also sick women inside it. Huff later observed that the colonists had a large extension of land, with approximately eighty hectares in improved pastures, "in an area that was completely flat, excellent for a landing and takeoff field if the need should arise."[10]

3 | Supposed Nazi spies in Cotito

TAKING OUR LEAD from Huff's observations about the conformation of the land on which the colony was located, suitable for use as a landing strip, the only possible source for the defamatory charge that the Swiss were dangerous Nazis, disseminated throughout the province, was the police. Not only was it claimed that the colonists possessed weaponry and an airstrip, it was also claimed that they operated a radio station for sending clandestine broadcasts to Germany.[*] Federico Sagel De Santiago well remembers the rumor that would be disproven only after it was too late:

---

* [At no point does anyone seem to have wondered what on earth the German government might have expected to find by spying on a few isolated farmers in a remote, heavily forested region of Panama, 500 KM from the Canal or, if an airstrip had existed in a cow pasture, to what use it might have been put.]

They were accused of being spies. The Swiss had made a concrete cooler in a creek. I do not know the system;[*] they gathered the water and this cooled it down in there; and this served for them like a refrigerator. Somebody invented the story that this was a radio station for broadcasting news to Germany.

So, based on that, they ordered them to take the people out of there and Captain Huff was in command of the detachment.[11]

The existence of a supposed radio transmitter was officially denied by the Costa Rican government, as may be gleaned from a laconic wire report of the Associated Press dated July 9, 1941, according to which "the government of Costa Rica has officially denied to the government of Panama that the Germans (sic) in the border area were operating a radio station."[12] What this means is that the San José [C.R.] government had not—as official Panamanian sources claimed—reported the existence of a radio station in the colony. The confusion was obvious. They were talking about Germans when most of the colonists were Swiss.

Efraín González noted [when interviewed] that on one occasion, when he, Sergeant Nicasio Saldaña and Corporal Faustino Montenegro were returning from David to Río Sereno, they stopped at the colony and spoke with Helmut Brauchle, who happily showed them a map of German advances on the Russian front, on which he had marked every military objective taken by the Germans with a red X.[13]

Whatever the truth of these assertions about the nationalist sentiments of the German Brauchle, it cannot be concluded that the Swiss colonists were agents of a Nazi fifth column, as González alleges.[†] →González also claims that the colonists hired Santiago

---

* [This appears to be what is called in the rural U.S. simply a "spring house," a storeroom for perishables built over a spring. Evaporation of the flowing water produces a cooling effect.]

† [Brauchle, a young religious zealot, without education, access to news reports or other knowledge of current events in Europe or even in Panama, perhaps had been taught that the Soviet Union of Josef Stalin was an atheist State that persecuted religious believers, which he considered a threat to liberty worse than the Germany his parents had chosen to leave (in 1929, be-

Continued→

Concepción Quintero to clear the brush on the site at Cotón in Costa Rica, where they intended to create [another] landing strip, but that when the Costa Rican authorities became aware of it, they sent a contingent of police to remove them from the area.← [Clearing brush, which of course may well have occurred, would have been for farming purposes, not for an airstrip, the reality of which was never demonstrated.]

Perhaps the definitive proof that the Swiss colonists had nothing to do with the Third *Reich* comes directly from German diplomats accredited in Panama. On July 8, 1941, the day after the massacre, the acting German *chargé d'affaires* in Panama, Hans von Winter, sent a cable[*] to his superiors in Berlin informing them of what had happened to this "sect of religious fanatics," composed almost entirely of Swiss citizens joined by the German Schmieder couple and one or two other German citizens who had had no contact with the German diplomatic mission since 1928 [five years before the Nazis rose to power in what Winter called "the Germany of today"].[14] This was not a report intended for Nazi propaganda; it was a confidential report sent by the German representative in Panama directly to the Ministry of Foreign Affairs in Berlin for its evaluation. The Swiss and German colonists at Cotito had nothing to do with the complicated history of spies and political intrigue, an image there was an attempt to create after the slaughter. Nevertheless, these false rumors and unfounded fears that the Swiss were armed would be significant factors in the events of July 7, 1941.

4 | ATTEMPTS TO AVOID TRAGEDY

ALTHOUGH HUFF'S TONE ON JUNE 24 was conciliatory, the Swiss colonists were still worried by the meeting with the chief of the

---

← *Continued from prev. page.*

fore the Nazis came to power) when he was 17. He would have been in large measure right about the Soviet Union. Where he might have obtained reports of German advances remains a mystery, as newspapers rarely reached remoter areas in those days, and the report of his situation map was probably a total fabrication after the fact.]

* [The text of Winter's cable may be read on p. 109, *infra*.]

Third Battalion. After Huff's visit, the colonists went over to Costa Rican soil, where they also had cultivated fields. The Associated Press wire report cited above said that several days before July 7, the Swiss, fearing that the government of Panama was about to expel them, had crossed the border to take refuge in Costa Rica, but their presence was detected by the authorities of the neighboring country, which ordered them to return to the territory of Panama. At that time, the Costa Rican government had adopted severe immigration regulations absolutely prohibiting the entry of Germans and Italians into the country.[15] The Swiss had no alternative but to return to Cotito and face the next inevitable visit of Huff and his men, who would undoubtedly be more numerous than on previous occasions.

Between June 24 and July 7, well informed people in David knew that preparations were being made for the incursion of a substantial contingent of police who would be sent up to Cotito to bring back the colonists by hook or by crook. Wilhelm Probst, who had spent three days in Cotito, became aware of the preparations through a lawyer whose name he does not mention. He suspected what could happen, and asked the attorney to intercede with Huff to obtain permission for him to accompany them, to serve as their interpreter, and in this manner assure that the Swiss would be brought in without anyone having suffered casualties. The lawyer interceded, but Huff paid him no attention. Several days later, the same lawyer informed Probst that the column of police had departed that morning and Probst later learned of the tragedy that his desperate efforts had been unable to avert.[16]

5 | A MILITARY OPERATION AGAINST UNARMED COLONISTS

TO SUBDUE THE colonists, Huff planned a typical military operation. At police headquarters in David, he mounted a column of about thirty officers and men armed with light automatic weapons and a few tear–gas guns. Second Lieutenants Ruiloba and Ardila carried machine guns.[17] He arranged with central police headquarters to have a reserve detachment of police on alert, ready to be airlifted to David if necessary.[18]

CHAPTER III | THE SLAUGHTER AT COTITO

According to his plan, the men he commanded directly would spend the night in Volcán or at Cotito itself, as the contingencies allowed, and they would be further reinforced by seventeen policemen stationed at [the border posts of] Cañas Gordas, Los Planes and Río Sereno. In other words, two columns of police, totaling about forty–five heavily armed men, would arrive at the colony at a given hour.[19] The primary column would advance from Volcán and the other, manned by police from the border, would block the way if the colonists attempted to escape to Costa Rica.

But Huff had done something else. →A day before the operation, Robert Müller relates, Captain Huff sent out his agents dressed as civilians.← As if planning for a battle in wartime, he sent the scouts to determine the supposed firepower of the "enemy." One of them was Probationary Officer Lucas Garcés, who was familiar to the colonists because they had granted him their hospitality several months previously. When they surrounded the settlement on the following day, the police officers would act as if they were travelling through the rural areas and, at a given moment, they would ask for a night's lodging at the camp. If they detected the presence of weapons, the police then would give a prearranged signal. If there were weapons, they would walk out slowly in order to avoid provoking a shootout, and if there were none, they were to raise their arms in a negative signal.

Huff's men arrived early on [Sunday morning,] July 6 and spent the day with the colonists. At lunchtime, Müller says, they refused to accept any food, which struck their hosts as peculiar. In addition, the weather was very fair. Normally, travelers asked for lodging when [they had arrived] in the evening [and the] hour was late, or when bad weather threatened, but on that day, before three o'clock in the afternoon—when they could [still] have gone [up] to Volcán without any difficulty—Garcés and his men asked to spend the night. The Swiss suspected that something odd was happening, but still they did not forego their usual hospitality, and Huff's agents spent the night in the settlement.

6 | JULY 7, 1941

DURING THE NIGHT, the police made their way up to the highlands in pursuit of their mission. To these men, who had not fully accepted the rigid military discipline imposed [since the beginning of the year, when he had begun his reorganization] by Gómez Ayau, the mission they had been ordered to carry out must have caused them some concern. They had also heard the rumors that trained Nazis were lying in wait for them at Cotito with an airstrip in the jungle and a dangerous arsenal that included machine guns, plus well-constructed fortifications overlooking the road where they would have to travel. Some believe that the police were drinking to fortify their courage. →In his acerbic, direct way, Helmut Hils corroborates that the police were inebriated when they confronted the Swiss at Cotito:

> That was murder, a few drunken cops, as usual never so brave as when they are full of booze and, like that time, fighting against defenseless people.[20]←

→WHERE DID THE POLICE who surrounded the Swiss camp spend the night? The answer is unclear.← [According to another account]—

> Visibly nervous, the police spent the night at La Concepción, drinking in the *cantina* of Mr. Félix Pittí. Aware of the news that the Swiss were heavily armed, the police drank all through the night that they passed camped out on Mr. Anton Hils's farm in Cotito, close to their objective.[*]

Others corroborate the fact that they were drunk, but differ in their versions of the circumstances:

> The frightened police mobilized after dark. ... They were drunk. In those days I bought cattle and hogs that I

---

[*] Gómez, *op. cit.*, p. 126. [This version appears to be garbled as to chronology; to have spent the night drinking at Pittí's *cantina* in La Concepción would have made it impossible to reach the colony at dawn on July 7.]

CHAPTER III | THE SLAUGHTER AT COTITO

shipped by boat to Panama, and I was around that area a lot.

You could go from Volcán to Cotito following the trail of *aguardiente* bottles and the *pachitas* that the police had dropped. They served as road markers, as a reference.[*]

Franklin Gómez affirms that they arrived at the home of [Anton] Hils and that his wife Marie, who was alone, "was very afraid for her safety. ... She heard the macabre comments that they, completely drunk, were making."[21]

→Robert Müller's version of what happened on July 7 is the following:← [He] indicates the police did not sleep at Hils's place, but rather on land owned by the colony, at a place called El Paraíso, where the Swiss had a *trapiche*.[22],[†] They left from there very early, when it was just beginning to get light, to perform their mission. In the early hours of Monday, July 7, hired man Agustín Beitía had started work very early in the corral where the milking was done. On occasion, the Swiss hired Beitía and other local peasants as milkers, since they needed considerable amounts of milk for their cheese-making operation. The horse trail that connected Cotito to Volcán via the southern route crossed through the corral. The gate also controlled access from the trail to the colony, and it was kept open during the day but closed at night.

---

[*] Sagel De Santiago. [*Aguardiente,* literally "firewater," is the slang term for *seco,* the cheap, raw liquor produced from sugar cane in Panama. The name in Colombia applies to a similar drink flavored with anise. A *pacha* or *pachita* is a half–pint bottle of *seco* sold in those days for a few cents and easily carried in a hip pocket.]

[†] [Traditional sugar cane press with wooden gears and rollers, turned by draft animals, although the colony probably did not actually own one, and no one but Robert Müller mentions "land owned by the colony at Paraíso."]

Lucas Garcés convalescing from gunshot wound on his cheek, in photo widely distributed by the Government.

After completely surrounding the camp, they sent a paper to the gate of the corral and a boy named Paul [Häusle] went out to get it.

Everybody yelled "Paul, no! Paul, come back! Don't take the paper!" but he would not pay attention to them, and he went to take the paper that the police handed him, and he was immediately struck by a bullet, and the police at the back must have thought that the Swiss had fired, and [the police opened] fire from the front and the back, and there was pandemonium and in the middle of it the Swiss died.[23]

BUT WHERE HAD that first shot come from? Who had fired the shot that caused the fatal confusion? According to the official version of the Ministry of Government and Justice, in order to try to reach an amicable understanding, Captain Huff had sent a written ultimatum to the chief of the colony with a deputation composed of Second Lieutenant Ernest Ruiloba, two police officers, and Garcés, the probationary officer, but when they got close "they were met with a heavy fusillade of gunfire that struck down Garcés, wounded in the face below one eye."[24]

Sophie Müller, who was about five meters from the police emissaries, stated that Huff ordered Lucas Garcés to deliver the note to Lehner. Paul Häusle received it and gave it to the leader of the colony, and he in turn passed it to Schmieder to read it [to him in German.] While the translator was reading the note, Garcés fired at Häusle "because he had a machete in his hand and Garcés told him to drop it and Häusle refused." Immediately after that, the police that surrounded the colony began firing at the settlers huddling in the house.[25]

FOLLOWING THE INCIDENT, the Panamanian government permitted a mixed German–Swiss commission to commence an investigation *in situ* that, when delivered to its respective governments, gave a version substantially similar to Müller's.

→The police had surrounded the living quarters. First, the column commanded by Huff arrived, and minutes later, the police from Río Sereno, under the command of Second Lieutenant Primitivo Rivera, were approaching southward from the nearby hills that lay to the north.← Captain Huff, who was about a hundred fifty meters from the firing line, sent a man to parlay, carrying a written ultimatum he had signed and addressed to Lehner, telling the latter the colonists had fifteen minutes to surrender or, if not, they would be "crushed." Lehner sent Paul Häusle, armed with a machete, toward the police officer who carried the ultimatum. The agent told Häusle to drop the weapon, but he refused. The officer then told him that if he took one more step, he would open fire; Häusle turned around, looked at Lehner, who shouted at him from the palisade that he should continue, and when he complied, the young man was struck by a bullet that threw him to the ground. Immediately, Huff's men opened fire.[26]

When they heard the shots, Aurelio Serracín and Efraín González recall that they were advancing toward the rear of the house; Rivera immediately ordered them to hit the ground and load their carbines. Efraín González remembers firing his weapon toward the house, although without his having seen anybody. Both confirm that the shooting at all four sides [of the house] lasted several minutes.[27]

In any case, the firepower of the police was lethal for the Swiss, most of whom were in the main house, some of them just getting out of bed. Müller states that the thickness of the planks prevented [self–inflicted, cross–fire] casualties among the police, who were firing high–caliber weapons from all directions toward the dwelling where older people and children were still sleeping.[28]

The official communiqué of the Ministry of Government and Justice gives a contradictory version. It does not explain how—

considering that the Swiss supposedly "had heavy weapons (including machine guns)..., the advantage of surprise, [and] had greeted the police with a blaze of heavy gunfire"—it was possible for the police to have suffered only a single casualty (Lucas Garcés).

The only survivor of Cotito we have been able to interview, Robert Müller, wounded at the age of 10, recalls his personal experience:

> When I got up and looked toward the fence, about twelve or fifteen meters away, a policeman was aiming right at me, and I did not [realize what he was doing], but my Papa had told me, "if somebody wants to photograph you, don't let them photograph you," and I, thinking he was photographing me, turned away, and when I turned away, he fired. He did not hit me in the middle. The shot went under my right arm and it burned me here in this part. It was one of those .30–.30 carbines.
>
> But at that moment, I only felt a cramp and I was able to run. We had another field on the other side, and when I saw that my Papa had fallen and the head of the colony also, I started running, to get away to the other field; it seemed I was running, but I wasn't running at all because they caught me right away. ...[29]

CHAPTER III | THE SLAUGHTER AT COTITO

> **Verzeichnis der beim Zwischenfall von Cotito getöteten Schweizerbürger.**
>
> In <u>Cotito</u> begraben:
>
> M o r f Albert, von Gossau (Zürich). Kopfschuss.
>
> M o r f Albert, (Sohn), von Gossau. Halsschuss.
>
> W e r r e n Clara (Tochter) von Zweisimmen (Bern).
> Beckenschuss.
>
> M o r f Frieda, von Gossau. Brustschuss.
>
> M ü l l e r Werner, von Trimbach (Solothurn). Halsschuss.
>
> O t t Heinrich, von Seen (Zürich). Lungenschuss.
>
> L e h n e r Karl, von Niederhelfenschwil (St. Gallen).
> Kopf- und Brustschüsse.
>
>
> In <u>Hato</u> begraben (auf dem Wege zum Spital gestorben):
>
> W e r r e n Clara (Mutter). Beckenschuss.
>
> ----------
>
> Die folgenden deutschen Staatsangehörigen wurden tötlich verwundet:
> S c h m i e d e r Karl, (Vater),
> S c h m i e d e r Karl, (Sohn),
> H ä u s l e Paul,
> B r a u c h l e Hellmuth.

SWISS ARCHIVES, BERN, COURTESY BARBARA TRABER

Undated casualty list indicating injuries and places of burial.

The attack from the front was so violent, only a few officers at the head of the column formed by the detachment of police from the border area fired any shots.

CLIPPING, SWISS ARCHIVES
Sole adult male survivor, Gottfried Werren, age *ca.* 62, wearing a leather work apron. Behind him with cast on arm is Paul Häusle, *ca.* 19. Picture must have been taken before the massacre, perhaps seized by police and given to the press. *La Tribuna*, July 12, 1941.

Huff immediately ordered a cease-fire and everything was calm. The commander of the detachment ordered Eleuterio Cubilla, Félix Escartín and Félix Beitía to climb over the palisade with fixed bayonets and to secure the open area inside. They did so, and when they opened the door of the main house they found Margarethe Schmieder, Viola Wehrli and the other women, who, despite being slightly wounded, confronted the police with swords,[*] but the captain ordered them to hold their fire and to try to subdue them physically. When the women continued to resist, the police chief ordered Adelo Miranda to throw some tear gas grenades inside, and yelled at the police to pull back. Miranda threw two grenades that choked the women and caused them to feel slightly faint.

Having subdued all resistance, Huff ordered his men to go into the house, and there the police found the elderly Gottfried Werren and two children [Albert Schmieder and Loni Morf] with their hands up.[†] Efraín González recalls that upon entering the

---

[*] [*espadas*, "swords" (machetes?)]

[†] [One of the two children was Albert Schmieder, whose recollection over the succeeding years was that "Somebody yelled for us to hit the floor. I was with my father and my brother. I was between them on the floor. Somebody said later that Gottfried Werren hid Loni and me, but that's not true. I was between my father and brother. Maybe Loni was with Gottfried." Karl Schmieder, Sr., and Karl Jr. were both mortally wounded. Gottfried Werren and Loni were, along with Albert, the only individuals who remained uninjured.]

house, he saw the walls spattered with brains and a lot of blood on the floor, and that a few days later Second Lieutenant Rivera ordered everything covered with lime.[30]

The [Czech] Alois ("Luis") Hartmann who lived nearby heard the shooting, arriving minutes after the slaughter and, confronted the police, shouting at them that they were cowards who had murdered these people like "pigs." Hearing this, Huff ordered him arrested, and the indignant neighbor was tied to a tree.[31]

Huff ordered Second Lieutenant Rivera to stay at the colony with his men and secure everything, while Huff took the wounded to the hospital in David. Arriving at Barriles, the police stopped at the home of Frank Wilfred Baker, a British subject, who had made his home in the area with his wife Melida Wilson. They asked the Bakers to lend them two horses to carry the wounded to Volcán, from where they would proceed by automobile to La Concepción and from there to David by train.

→They took the road from Barriles to Volcán,[*] carrying the wounded on improvised stretchers.← Melida Wilson Baker recalled that they lent them the horses and that a few hours later, when the animals were returned, they were completely covered with blood and had to be bathed in the creek.[32]

The wounded, including women and children, finally arrived at José Domingo De Obaldía Hospital in David.[†] The Morf orphans [Friedy, Walter and Loni] were sent to *Nuestra Señora de los Ángeles* boarding school operated by Franciscan nuns. The elderly Gottfried Werren, the only survivor among the men, was jailed in David, subject to the disposition of Chiriquí Circuit Prosecutor Abel Gómez Araúz. With the exception of Karl Schmieder Jr. and Mrs. Werren,

---

[*] [The distance from Barriles to Volcán is only 6 KM (3½ MI), but Cotito would have been several hours on horseback from Barriles.]

[†] Dr. Bernardino González Ruiz, then medical director of the hospital, recalls that when he was informed that there had been deaths and that the wounded were being brought in, he remained on duty until they arrived, toward midnight. *See* Conte Porras (p. 37, n. 39, *supra*), p. 193.

who were buried in Volcán,* the Cotito victims were buried in a common grave, directly in front of the main house of the colony.

7 | THE RESULT OF THE POLICE ATTACK

THE TOLL TAKEN by the police attack commanded by Huff was twelve dead and eight wounded. Probationary Police Officer Lucas Garcés was shot in the face, almost certainly a shot fired by the police themselves. Of the twelve dead, five men and three women were Swiss citizens, and four, all male, were Germans. In addition to Garcés, there were eight wounded, four seriously.

PASSPORT PHOTO (?)
Elfriede Morf, *ca*. 1938

PASSPORT PHOTO (?)
Paul Häusle, *ca*. 1938

- →Paul Häusle bled to death in horrible pain. He had received a shot in the stomach and his agony was prolonged for several minutes. He was the first to be wounded and he died without having received medical attention.

---

* According to Helmut Hils, [Klara Werren and Karl Schmieder Jr.] are buried at a spot near the *Pensión* Volcán[, which no longer exists. The site, now occupied by a commercial building, is at the southeast corner of the intersection where *Calle 10ª Este* ("East Tenth St.," usu. called *la calle del Cementerio*, "Cemetery St.,") crosses the main street of Volcán. Ironically, north of the main street, this street was called *Calle del Matadero* ("Slaughterhouse St."). Like the *pensión*, the slaughterhouse is long gone.

[When one mentions the Cotito tragedy in Volcán, many people recall the burial of those who died as they were carried on horseback from Cotito to Volcán, *en route* to the railway station at La Concepción. Most vivid of the memories, and perhaps among the more reliable as to the site of the burials, is that of the late *Doña* Yolanda Rivera Mora, who lived across the road that is now the main street of Volcán. Her daughters Nieves and Morena say she often recalled seeing the arrival of the police and the wounded, and in particular the body of Klara Werren tied over a saddle, her long hair, which had become loose, hanging straight down "nearly to the ground."]

CHAPTER III | THE SLAUGHTER AT COTITO

- [Nine others—Karl Lehner, the leader of the sect; Albert and Elfriede Morf and their son Albert Jr.; Karl Schmieder Sr.; Heinrich Ott; Klärli Werren; Helmut Brauchle, and Werner Müller—were killed inside or near the house and buried, together with Paul Häusle, in the common grave.]

PASSPORT PHOTO (?)
Werner Müller,
ca. **1938**

- Karl Schmieder Jr., whose father was buried at Cotito, received a blast in the knees which fractured them completely. He bled to death on the road to Volcán.

- Klara Werren [whose daughter Klärli died in the house and was buried at Cotito] died on horseback without having received medical attention, cared for only by Agustín Beitía, the hired milker, who slaked her thirst with a little cool water. She was also buried in Volcán.

- The most critically wounded was Gertrude ("Trudi") Häusle [sister of Paul, killed by the first shot], who suffered a gunshot in the lumbar region that appeared to involve her spine; it was feared that she would die. [*]

- Sophie Müller, whose husband died in the house and whose son was wounded, had her left arm broken by a projectile.

- Sophie's son Werner Robert had been shot in the right arm by a bullet that first grazed his chest at a point opposite the heart.

---

* [Trudi Häusle recovered, married and raised a family in the United States. She told friends in later life and wrote in her book—which does not mention the massacre—that her recurring back pain was due to injuries sustained carrying heavy timbers for the bridge construction project.]

- Margarethe Schmieder was also in serious condition, wounded in the face and in the spine, and the bullet had remained embedded in her right lung.

- Cornelia Werren was wounded in the left hand, so severely that the fingers were amputated.

- Viola Wehrli and Friedy and Walter Morf, whose parents and brother were buried at Cotito, were wounded only slightly, but also had to be admitted into the hospital.

- Gottfried Werren was not wounded, but he was affected by the tear gas and was the first to be taken into custody by the police.

The condition of the wounded, especially the children, was aggravated by their refusal to eat anything, and because in their rebellious mood they removed the bandages covering their wounds. The language barrier also complicated things. Trudi Häusle, who spoke some Spanish, explained with difficulty to the personnel of the hospital that they belonged to a naturist [sic] religious sect who ate only fruit, vegetables and milk.[33] The wounded were then served vegetables and milk, as they had not eaten a single mouthful since the incident. Young Müller then began to recuperate. Fifty years later, he still recalls that it was Mr. Abilio Ledezma who persuaded them, not without difficulty, to eat.[34]

DETAIL, *PANAMÁ-AMÉRICA* PHOTO

Loni Morf, 1941

RATHER THAN ACCOMPLISHING their mission of securing and protecting the property of the colony, according to Officer Gonzales, the police under the command of Second Lieutenant Rivera did precisely the opposite:

CHAPTER III | THE SLAUGHTER AT COTITO

DEATH SQUAD: **police pose for a proud photograph. Original 1941 *Carteles* caption: "Part of the police detachment that intervened in the episode at Cotito."**

> Many items were lost. They had workshops where they did ironwork, where they made shoes, did carpentry and cured hides. They were looted. My conscience is clear and so is Pedro Peralta's...[35]

On October 8, exactly three months and one day after the serious event, the widow "Gretel" Schmieder recorded in the official inventory that while the survivors had been confined to the hospital, valuable goods and tools were lost, for which there was never a satisfactory explanation. As a crime scene, the entire colony should have been zealously guarded, not only to protect the colonists' assets, which was the responsibility of the police, but also to preserve the evidence for the inevitable criminal investigation that would necessarily follow. Even so, the house and other facilities were the object of indiscriminate looting, and the principal object of suspicion were the police from the border posts who had been assigned the responsibility for custody.

8 | THE COVER-UP WORK BEGINS

THE NATIONAL PRESS was no more sympathetic to the Cotito victims. All the newspapers of the day accepted the police version at face value, and went far beyond the contents of the official communiqué. In all of them, there was confusion about the identity of the Swiss, generally referred to as Germans. *La Estrella de Panamá* reported that "the Germans opened fire against [the police] while the officers were obliged to take refuge to escape from the projectiles."[36] The English edition, the *Star & Herald,* said that the rebellious attitude of the German colonists had been the cause of the problem and

The original caption in *Carteles* read "Two rifles, three revolvers and several machetes and axes seized by Panamanian police at the Hacienda Cotito." The machetes, axes and post-hole diggers are ordinary farm implements in use in the area to this day. The firearms are of doubtful provenance, probably weapons and ammunition planted by the police from among their own equipment.

that "8 wounded Nazis [had been admitted to] David Hospital."[37]

The communiqué of the Ministry of Government and Justice went beyond national borders. In August, 1941, with elaborate graphic display, the magazine *Carteles ["Playbills"]*, published in Havana, reported on the events at Cotito. The magazine published fifteen photographic views that could only have been provided by the Panamanian government. The photographs show Captain Antonio Huff [see p. 79. *supra*], as well as a part of the police detachment that participated in the incident posing for the camera [p.101, *supra*] in front of David police headquarters, and there is a photo [p. 92, *supra*] of Lucas Garcés convalescing in his hospital room from his face wound.

There are also identification photos of the deceased Paul Häusle, Karl Lehner, Albert Morf, Elfriede Morf, Werner Müller, Heinrich Ott and Klärli Werren, and a photo of Viola Wehrli, who was wounded. There is an obvious difference between these identification photos [removed from confiscated passports] and the ones taken of the survivors Gottfried Werren [p. 96, *supra*] and the orphaned Walter and [Leonora ("Loni")] Morf [p. 100, *supra*], taken in outdoor locations [This photo of Loni and that of Albert Schmieder on p. lxxxiv, *supra*, were taken from a *Panamá–América* photo published July 14, 1941]. We do not have the slightest doubt that these photographs were supplied to the news media by representatives of the Panamanian government. However, in our judgment, the most relevant photo is the one [p. 102, *supra*] we consider part of a well–executed cover–up of the crime, showing two rifles, three revolvers and several machetes and axes. The caption beneath the photo says the weapons were "seized by the Panamanian police at the Hacienda Cotito."[38]

HOW CAN THIS information be reconciled with the testimony of Sagel, Probst and Hils, who knew the colonists and praised their peaceful ways? With the supposed firepower and the surprise factor favoring the Swiss, how can the fact of a single police casualty [a minor face wound] be explained? Where were the rifles, machine guns and radio equipment that Huff supposedly had seen during his visit to the colony? We believe that in light of the fatal error committed by the police, which resulted in an unjustified use of force against the unarmed colonists, the national government tried to divert attention about the truth of what had occurred and created a smokescreen to turn the victims into perpetrators, although we should not fail to recognize that the fanaticism of the colonists was also determinative of the tragic outcome of July 7, 1941.

9 | THE OFFICIAL STORY

DURING THE MORNING of July 7, as soon as it became aware of what had happened at Cotito, the Government moved quickly to put out an official version of the facts. The Office of Press, Radio and Public Performances sent a communiqué signed by Minister De la Guardia himself to all the principal dailies in the country. In addition, it was reported that the Government was suppressing all subversive movement in the country and that the First Secretary of the Ministry of Government and Justice, *Don* Agustín Ferrari, would the following day travel by air to David "with the mission of opening a detailed investigation in to the events at Cotito, which he would be required to submit directly to the Chief Executive."[39]

The President of the Republic, Dr. Arnulfo Arias Madrid, arriving back in Panama City from Colón late that night, said that

> the Government will use all its available resources to prevent that new movements of the kind that inspired the one in Chiriquí arise in any sector of the Republic..., that the Government was prepared to be as energetic as necessary in securing the elimination of such movements based on fanaticism.[40]

We conclude from his words that this was not the first time the Government had suppressed a movement it considered fanatical. We are reminded of the incident involving the Adventists and one must ask whether the initiative for banning this religion in Chiriquí came from the President himself or whether he had merely acceded to the request of Minister De la Guardia, as José Ehrman, [a member of the Cabinet at the time,] alleges. In any event, it is clear that the government gave its version of the facts, an official story, and never wavered from it during the next twelve years, until the courts of justice finally closed the case.

First Secretary Ferrari did not stay long in Chiriquí, where he went with Colonel Gómez Ayau. He flew to David on July 8, and returned the following day. The newspapers speculated on the contents of Ferrari's report and said he was keeping it in strictest confidence, but that it would soon be made public.

In fact, on the afternoon of Ferrari's return, July 9, Minister De la Guardia gave a report to the National Assembly on the events at Cotito. The Minister told the deputies that a group of Europeans, by all appearances of Swiss origin, had been located in this area close to the Costa Rican border, although he did not discount the possibility (and this was emphasized by the pro–government newspapers) that there might be one or another individual of German nationality among the colonists.

The subject individuals had been unwilling to submit to Panamanian law, and on repeated occasions had refused to comply with the order of the authorities. According to the report, the authorities had demanded *"on an infinite number of occasions"* that they present their personal identification and immigration documents, without result. In view of the foregoing, the police captain assigned to Chiriquí had been directed to investigate and demand the colonists' papers. The Minister added that [Huff] had done as directed, and that the result had been the same as on other occasions, that the subjects refused to recognize his authority, responding that they "had their own government." The police had immediately consulted the authorities in Panama and were told to attempt persuasion, that violence should be avoided.

Unfortunately, [De la Guardia said,] upon their arrival at the colony, the police were received with gunfire and were obliged to defend themselves by returning the fire, resulting in the death of numerous colonists and the wounding of others, and that a police officer surnamed Garcés had been injured, and there was fear for his life. The Minister concluded by saying that calm now reigned in the area, and that the incident could be considered concluded.[41] De la Guardia's report virtually repeats the facts set forth in the official communiqué published the previous day, from which we conclude that Ferrari's trip to Chiriquí had not contributed any new elements, and that, because of haste, he had been unable to conduct an exhaustive investigation of the real events at Cotito.

Nonetheless, the two documents were contradictory. In the report to the Assembly, De la Guardia stated that the authorities had insisted *"on an infinite number of occasions"* that the colonists present their personal identification and immigration papers. It was only after their [repeated] refusal that Captain Huff of the police deployed in Chiriquí was ordered to initiate an investigation and demand the presentation of their papers. From the official communiqué, however, we conclude Huff's mission was not to demand presentation of the documents (which, as Efraín González and Sophie Müller testified, had in any case been examined on various occasions by the police), but rather to persuade [the colonists] that they must go down to David to register in person with the Alien Affairs section.

De la Guardia asserted that the authorities—he did not specify which—had insisted without success on various occasions that the colonists present their documents; nevertheless, in the official communiqué, signed by the Minister himself, it was reported that they had served an offical order originating in Panama City. These contradictions raise the question of the origin of the order that resulted in the extreme severity of the police intervention at Cotito.

→Huff had drafted and signed the text of the two ultimatums addressed to Lehner (only one of which reached the chief of the colony) but he did not specify which of his superiors had ordered the ultimatums. In fact, Huff began the first of them by stating in general terms that he was acting "by order of the government of Panama." During the investigation, it was reported that, after a telephone conversation with Major Quintero, Huff had received a coded telegram sent by him with instructions for police action. It was also said that [Instructor] General Gómez Ayau had given the instructions to Huff by telephone, but there was no evidence that written confirmation existed. ←

Was the ultimatum Huff sent to Lehner—

- authorized by his ultimate superior at the time, [Instructor] General Gómez Ayau? *or*
- Was it the Third Chief of Police, Major Abel Quintero? *or*

- Was the ultimatum ordered by Minister De la Guardia? *or*
- by President Arnulfo Arias himself?

In truth, this was never clarified during the course of the investigations, and was precisely one of the points on which the various courts repeatedly ordered additional testimony. Some indications indeed point to Arias himself as the originator of the order, although the investigation was also unable to determine if this was true. The evidence pointing to Arias includes his own statements to the press made on July 8, 1941, as well as a now famous telegram.

10 | A COMPROMISING TELEGRAM

ON JULY 12, 1941 the President sent a telegram to Captain Antonio Huff, chief of the Third Battalion of the National Police. The message Huff received relayed by the General Police Headquarters, read as follows:

REPUBLIC OF PANAMA
NATIONAL TELEGRAPHS

1GKDC 52 FCO 7:40 A.M.   PANAMA, JULY 12, 1941

CAPTAIN ANTONIO HUFF. DAVID.

CONGRATULATE YOU AND OTHER MEMBERS POLICE CORPS UNDER YOUR COMMAND FOR DETERMINED AND EFFICIENT MANNER PUT AN END REBELLION OF CERTAIN GROUP OF FOREIGN RESIDENTS IN COTITO REGION.

ARNULFO ARIAS,
PRESIDENT OF THE REPUBLIC

7:40 A.M.

The telegram received by the General Headquarters was reprinted in the "commendations" section of the General Order of the Day of July 14, 1941, "for the information of all members of this Institution."[42] In other words, the Chief Executive considered the peaceful colonists in the same category as the mutinous political opposition at La Laguna de San Carlos, at La Chorrera, or the Nicaraguans who rose up in arms at Gariché.[43] He accused them of rebellion, one of the most serious offenses against the internal security of the state, and he gave a substantial pat on the back to the National Police.

Years later, upon ordering the "amplification of the file," [a judicial order for additional evidence to be inserted in the record of an open case,] the Supreme Court of Justice ordered that Arias be deposed, so that he could explain the facts underlying the telegram and, specifically, clarify if—

> he had, before the fact, any telephone conversation with said captain in which he gave any order for the fulfillment of which he [subsequently] congratulated him, and if such conversation did not take place, what was the motive justifying his having congratulated Captain Huff in the terms in which he had.[44]

This deposition was never taken, nor was Arias able to give his version in the judicial investigation, which is why it cannot be confirmed whether he had personally authorized the ultimatum. Many years later, in a 1984 interview on this point with U.S. television journalist Peter Arnett, Arnulfo Arias declared that he had learned of the incident after the fact and that a captain "acting on his own account and initiative had killed various members of a religious community."[45]

This does not mean, however, that the President of the Republic was unhappy about the actions taken by the police at Cotito. Lawyer Peter Vidal Escobar, present at the airport in David during a conversation between Arias and Huff about the Cotito incident, overheard the President tell the police chief that "when killing was necessary, killing was done."[46] Politically speaking, in our opinion, Arnulfo Arias preferred to put a blanket of silence over the truth about Cotito, rather than endanger his special relationship with the National Police [which ousted him in a coup three months later].

Some of Dr. Arias's sympathizers considered his having sent the telegram to Huff a political error, rejecting the possibility of any responsibility on the part of the *Panameñista* leader for what is properly called an act of bloody violence.

> To me, Dr. Arias's error was sending the congratulatory telegram for what Huff had done. That was the bad thing. That was his mistake, because he did not have to send that telegram.[47]

Helmut Hils, recalling the neighbors' reaction to the events, declares that many at that time laid the blame on Arnulfo Arias, "but no, the *sinvergüenza* [shameless character] was Captain Huff, that guy with only one eye."[48] This aspect of the case will be discussed in more detail in Chapter VI.

11 | THE REACTION

THE BLOODY DOINGS at Cotito did not pass unnoticed outside Panama, and the incident went beyond the confines of a simple domestic, political episode, at least during the weeks immediately following it. The victims were Swiss and German, and that made it necessary for both countries to demand an exhaustive investigation to support future claims for financial damages, if appropriate.

| A CABLE TO BERLIN

THE DAY AFTER THE event, at 10:32 PM, the German *chargé d'affaires*, Hans von Winter, sent cable № 221 to Berlin reporting on what had occurred at Cotito:

> A SECT OF RELIGIOUS FANATICS *["SEKTE RELIGIOSER FANATIKER"]* COMPOSED ALMOST ENTIRELY OF SWISS CITIZENS WHO HOLD THEIR PROPERTY IN COMMON HAS BEEN LIVING FOR SOME TIME AT COTITO, NEAR DAVID. A GERMAN MARRIED COUPLE, THE SCHMIEDERS, AND ONE OTHER GERMAN CITIZEN HAD JOINED THIS GROUP. THE DAY BEFORE YESTERDAY, THE PANAMANIAN POLICE APPEARED BEFORE THE SETTLERS AND REQUESTED THAT THEY PRODUCE THEIR PAPERS FOR INSPECTION. AS THE MEMBERS OF THE SECT REFUSED BASED ON THEIR RELIGIOUS BELIEFS TO RECOGNIZE ANY GOVERNMENTAL AUTHORITY, THERE SOON AROSE A VIOLENT ARGUMENT AND FINALLY THERE WAS A SHOOTOUT, IN WHICH OF THE 23 PERSONS, 13 COLONISTS, INCLUDING THE GERMAN SCHMIEDER, WERE KILLED; AND 8 WOMEN AND CHILDREN, AMONG THEM FRAU SCHMIEDER, WERE SERIOUSLY INJURED.
>
> THE FACT THAT AS OF TODAY THE GOVERNMENT OF PANAMA HAS STILL NOT PUBLISHED ANY OFFICIAL COMMUNIQUÉ

LEADS TO THE CONCLUSION THAT THEY ARE EMBARRASSED BY THE SLAUGHTER OF THE INNOCENT RELIGIOUS,[*] BUT ON THE OTHER HAND THIS HAS GIVEN RISE TO RUMORS IMPLICATING ALLEGED GERMAN ESPIONAGE, CLANDESTINE ALLIANCES AND THE "FIFTH COLUMN." THERE IS NO TRUTH TO THESE RUMORS, WHICH WERE DISSEMINATED IN UNITED STATES BROADCASTS BEFORE THE NATIONAL PRESS PUBLISHED REPORTS WITHOUT OFFICIAL CONFIRMATION. SCHMIEDER HAD NOT REGISTERED WITH THE AMBASSADOR AT THE RESPECTIVE CONSULATE IN PANAMA SINCE THE YEAR 1928, AND ENTIRELY UNCONNECTED TO THE GERMANY OF TODAY. THE GERMAN GEORGE ELL, WHO MADE STATEMENTS CRITICAL OF THE POLICE METHODS, HAS BEEN ARRESTED. I SHALL CONTINUE REPORTS AFTER GATHERING INFORMATION WITH THE RESPECTIVE PANAMANIAN AGENCIES. SENT ALSO TO THE MINISTRY OF FOREIGN AFFAIRS, THE EMBASSY IN WASHINGTON AND THE LEGATION IN GUATEMALA.

WINTER[49]

The cable was received at 9:40 AM on July 9 in Berlin, and so far as we know, received no reply. According to the former German Ambassador to Panama, Dr. Götz von Böhmer, this is the only document relative to the incident at Cotito that is to be found in the archives of the Ministry of Foreign Relations of the Federal Republic of Germany.[50] From deliberate analysis of Winter's cable, we may deduce that the diplomat was relying on the official communiqué, although he did not hew strictly to its content or stick to the facts. The official communiqué was published in the daily papers on the morning of July 8, the day following the events; nevertheless, the German diplomat gives the impression that the incident had oc-

---

* [The sanctimony of this observation respecting religious minorities and other innocents, given what was occurring in Nazi Germany and the countries of Western and Eastern Europe already overrun by Hitler, is hard to believe. On June 22, two weeks and one day before the Cotito massacre by the Panamanian police, the Germans invaded the Soviet Union, beginning the bloodiest phase of the bloodiest war in history. German persecution of religious minorities such as the Jehovah's Witnesses, Catholic and Protestant clergy, not to mention the Jews, was notorious at the time.]

curred on July 6 ("the day before yesterday"), and states that the government, two days after the incident, had still not released its official version. In addition, he is mistaken about the number of dead, which was twelve, not thirteen.

The low level of diplomatic relations between Germany and Panama during this period of belligerence led to the incident's being moved off the front pages in the face of the priority given to the approaching war. Later, German interests in Panama would be represented by the Spanish Legation, with very unsatisfactory results.[51]

|The American Intelligence Reports

THE INTELLIGENCE SERVICES of the United States War Department operating in the Panama Canal Zone sent a series of reports on Cotito to the State Department. The first was sent on July 9, through the Fifteenth Naval District command, and was received in Washington on the 12th. It reported that a clash had occurred two days previously in the Volcán area of the Republic of Panama, near the border with Costa Rica, between the Panamanian National Police and a supposed Swiss–German colony. Detailed confirmation was unavailable, but it was known that nine men and three women from the group had died and that eight had been seriously wounded, while [the police] had suffered one casualty.[52]

Two days later, on July 11, the commander of the Fifteenth Naval District amplified the "strictly confidential" report and the State Department Division of Communications and Records received and filed it on the 19th. The latter report confirmed that two men, three women and one child had been wounded, that twelve "German" colonists had died, and that one policeman had been wounded as well, after the colonists had refused to surrender their passports and personal identity cards to Panamanian officials.

This settlement situated near Volcán, [the commander reported,] had been established three years previously and [the settlers were] "generally considered [a] hardworking, peaceful and religious sect." Although Panamanian officials alleged that the colonists had operated a radio station, they had been unable to locate it. The colony's lands were used for crops, but it was possible that they had cleared brush to create a landing strip. "At present there is not [sic] evidence that [the] colony engaged in subversive activities,"[53] but the police considered their refusal to show their papers sufficient justification for the attack. A Nazi leader [probably Wilhelm Probst, no Nazi!] in the interior had been jailed for criticizing the slaughter.[54]

A little less than a month later, on August 15, 1941, the State Department received another, more detailed report on the events at Cotito, this time directly from the Military Intelligence Division of the General Committee[*] of the War Department. The report, entitled "Massacre of Colonists in Cotito," was contained in a more comprehensive report on the internal affairs of the Republic of Panama and briefly amplified the information already known, although with a certain lack of precision. According to this summary, on July 8, 1941, "the Panamanian police massacred twelve of twenty–three Swiss and German religious colonists at Cotito, in the province of Chiriquí, situated about twenty miles south of the Costa Rican border."[†]

---

* [It is not clear to which agency of the War Department the Spanish text refers.]

† [The distance from Cotito to the border is about 10 MI, not 20, and Cotito is due east of the Costa Rican border, not "south." The Panama/Costa Rica border runs almost due north–south, and only a tiny coastal strip of Costa Rica lies north of any part of Panama. Although one would presume U.S. military authorities stationed in Panama would know this, the erroneous perception is common.]

CHAPTER III | THE SLAUGHTER AT COTITO

Three of the colonists, an elderly man of 82 [*sic:* Werren was 62] and two children, were unhurt. The remaining six women and two children were wounded by police fire, and four of them were still in serious condition in the hospital in David. The report noted that this serious matter would be covered in detail in a special report on "Alien Activities in the Republic of Panama." It concluded that the prevalent public opinion everywhere was that "this attack on these people was hardly justified and it has created indignation [in] all quarters."55 The report was signed by Lieutenant Colonel L. D. Carter of Army G–2.[*]

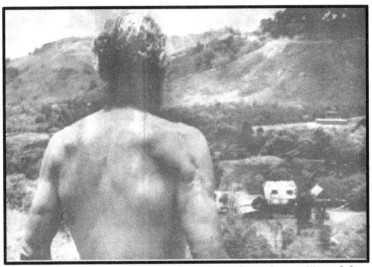

NEUE ZÜRCHER ZEITUNG PHOTO, COURTESY WERNER C. SENN

In 1994, Werner Robert Müller displayed his scars for the *Neue Zürcher Zeitung* photographer from Zurich. He posed on a hillside overlooking the site of the massacre, now the Sicilia family farm.

---

* ["G–2," the designation used by U.S. military intelligence unit has eerie overtones for Panamanian readers. The name was adopted under the Torrijos régime for the Panamanian military intelligence agency *cum* political secret police, after 1970 headed by Manuel Antonio Noriega. It was an instrument of repression under the dictatorship.]

Although this latter report accurately portrayed the situation with respect to the nationality, number and gender of the dead and wounded, and it especially clarified the point that only four, and not eight, of the wounded were in serious condition, it also was inaccurate on such basic points as the date of the event.

The report sent on July 11 appears to have been taken from the morning newspapers, especially the [English language] *Star & Herald*, of July 9. Both used the same expressions: "12 German colonists," "clash," "refusal." In addition, the *Star & Herald,* like the July 11 intelligence report, uses the word "Nazi." These coincidences lead us back to reflect on the Winter cable to Berlin. If the rumors of Nazi espionage activities in the mountains of Chiriquí originated, as the German diplomat alleges, in United States radio broadcasts before their publication in the Panamanian press, the source must be sought among the U.S. intelligence services in Panama. If it were not so, American intelligence would have confined itself to transcribing and transmitting to Washington the journalistic account of this clearly pro–U.S. newspaper. Curiously, the *Panamá–América* also headed its issue of July 8 with the following banner: "9 German [Men] and 3 German [Women] Die," although the official communiqué quoted in full in the same edition spoke of a colony formed of Germans and Swiss.

In any case, these meticulous observers of Panamanian internal affairs confirmed something already known in the Chiriquí highlands, namely that the Cotito colonists were peaceful and industrious people and that the violence against them was unjustified.

| THE PROTEST OF WILHELM PROBST

THERE WAS INDIGNATION among those who knew firsthand of the colonists' peaceful ways when they learned what had happened on the bloody morning of July 7. Alois Hartmann, who confronted the police and berated them for their action, was tied to a tree. Wilhelm Probst also suffered the rigor of the authorities for having dared to denounce publicly what he called "collective murder."

> After this mass murder, the police immediately prohibited talking about it, and since I was the only one they could take legal action against, because I had been up

there with those totally inoffensive people, obviously I did not keep my mouth shut, and I called the police captain and his people mass murderers. Three times they put me in jail, only because I took the liberty of telling the truth, [because I had] had the courage to contradict publicly their fairy tales and lies. The third time they wanted to shut me up forever, and they tried to take me to the island of criminals, Koiba (sic).[*]

But my wife put the best lawyer in David—who had known me for twenty–five years as an honest, peaceable, fearless man—in charge of my defense, and he contacted the President of the country, and as soon as he got his reply, they released me and did not bother me ther.[56],[†]

Probst's third confinement in jail appears in the judicial records of the period, because his wife Juanita B. Probst filed writs of *habeas corpus* on his behalf, one directed to Captain Huff and the other to the Minister of Government and Justice, De la Guardia.

Wilhelm Probst was then 46 years old. On the afternoon of July 20, at El Progreso, (in the district of Barú [Puerto Armuelles]), he made some comments to the manager of El Comisario[57] *cantina* about what had happened at Cotito. Sergeant Rosendo Aguilar, also present in the *cantina*, accused Probst of saying that what the government had ordered at Cotito was criminal, that those people were defenseless, that they had been killed like dogs, that the Swiss minister was investigating together with the German representative what had happened, and that the wounded police officer had been shot by the police themselves, so that they could say he was wounded by the colonists.[58]

---

* [From 1912 until recently, Panama maintained a notorious penal colony on the heavily forested island of Coiba off the Pacific Coast. It is now a nature reserve.]

† [A classic example of *palanca*, "leverage": government by influence. The attorney was not effective because he invoked legal authority or judicial intervention; he had sufficient leverage to call President Arias directly, and that did the trick.]

Sworn statements were also taken from Messrs. Arnoldo Hand, Bienvenido Alvarado and Severino Herrera, also present in the El Progreso *cantina*, on July 22, 1941.

Because of these statements Probst was arrested, jailed in David, subject to further order of the Superior Tribunal of Justice, where his wife had filed the *habeas corpus*. Within twenty–four hours, he was released "in the absence of complaining witnesses."[59] Nevertheless, he was arrested again, and again placed at the disposition of the Superior Tribunal. As for Minister De la Guardia, responding to the *habeas corpus* filed against him, he informed the Supreme Court that Probst was not in his custody, but that Probst was accused of "violation of the law for having formulated false and insolent accusations against Panamanian authorities."[60] As Probst explains, he was only released after the President himself, Arnulfo Arias Madrid, intervened.

| JOSÉ GUILLERMO BATALLA'S LETTER

DURING THAT PERIOD, journalist José Guillermo Batalla sent a strong letter to Juan Blau, the Swiss consul in Panama, criticizing him for having failed to represent the interests of his countrymen in a worthy manner. The letter, containing a full indictment against the Swiss official, deserves comment, not only because it shows the enormous disgust produced in some quarters of Panamanian society by the Cotito episode, but also because it is a document almost unknown among the Panamanian people. Batalla, by way of preamble, clarifies that he neither knows nor has even met the consul, who was, in turn, manager of the *Compañía Panameña de Productos Lácteos*,* so that the letter should not be ascribed to motives other than those that moved him to send it.

Batalla then refers to several of Consul Blau's statements published on July 10, 1941, in the *Panamá–América* regarding the painful events at Cotito in which "several peaceful countrymen of yours" lost their lives, and notes that four days after the event, the com-

---

* [A subsidiary of the Swiss Nestlé corporation. Seventy years after the events, Volcán residents of Swiss origin still criticize Blau's performance. *E.g.*, Werner C. Senn, intv. with Ed., Aug. 11, 2011.]

ments still engendered the same reaction, a reaction of "shock and disgust."

"The veiled criticism in the nature of bile" Blau, the representative of Switzerland in Panama, had "poured out on the still–warm, charred corpses[*] of your fellow countrymen," and the "readiness with which you prejudge and even approve the execution, which has all the appearances of a massacre," "appear illogical and irrational." Batalla reproves Blau for his "unheard of, inconceivable, inexcusable conduct" to the point of putting into doubt whether he was indeed a citizen of that "noble land of the perpetual snows." In the mournful emergency that all regretted, Blau's conduct had been imprudent and implied a disdain for the Swiss consular service, which had always been marked previously by "equanimity, competence and patriotism."

Batalla lamented that for those jealous of the good name of Panama, it was shameful that the Swiss consul had chosen this hospitable soil to sound the discordant note that had so disgusted the community and, at the same time, had been felt so painfully in the breast of the diplomatic and consular corps accredited to the Republic.

Batalla excoriated Blau for having—although it defied belief—"desired to ingratiate himself with the Executive Authority of this Nation and to protect the interests of the firm [Blau] represented, established among us by a contract whose approval had been the result of bellyfuls of firewater[†] and which continues daily to enrich itself more and more at the expense of Panamanian children."

The missive concludes by warning Blau that his attitude will not pass unnoticed and that the letter and the censure it contained was "posthumous compensation" for the consul's compatriots who were so "unjustifiably murdered in Cotito."[‡]

---

[*] *[los cadáveres todavía tibios de sus paisanos inmolados...]*

[†] *[hartazgos aguardentosos]*

[‡] Probst, p. 149. A copy of this letter was given to the Author by Josef Probst, son of Wilhelm. He says of the letter, "Still today, after so many years, I have a copy of the letter that some Panamanian citizens addressed to the Swiss consul, because among the murder victims there were also some Swiss people, and they said it was shameful for the entire community that

Continued→

Setting aside José Guillermo Batalla's perceptions, it fell to Juan Blau[, the Swiss consul in Panama,] and to Adolph Gonzenbach, the Swiss *chargé d'affaires* based in Venezuela, to undertake a prolonged battle to obtain from the Panamanian government compensation for the damages sustained by the colonists. These two officials and those who succeeded them in office tried in vain to obtain justice for the Cotito victims.

Notes to Chapter III

[1] *Decreto* № 155, Sept. 11, 1939, "adopting provisions related to the domicile of foreigners residing in the national territory." DECRETOS Y RESOLUCIONES VIGENTES (*see* n. 19, p. 21 *supra*), at 409-11.

[2] Probst (*see* p. 42,n. †, *supra*).

[3] *See* p. xlix, n.*, *supra*.

[4] Decision of Aug. 18, 1953, 2nd Sup. Tribunal, First Judicial District.

[5] Confirmed by the Min. Govt. & Justice in the official communiqué on the Cotito incident. In *Estrella de Panamá* and *Panamá-América* Tues., July 8, 1941.

[6] Franklin Gómez, "Los sucesos de Cotito." In commemorative magazine *Bugaba centenaria* (1963), p. 126.

[7] Aurelio Manuel Serracín, intv. with Author, Río Sereno, Jan. 21, 1993.

[8] Hils. (*See* p. 49, n. 31 *supra*.)

[9] Decision of Aug 18, 1953 (*See* p. 82, n. 4, *supra*.)

[10] Official communiqué (*See* p. 82, n. 5 *supra*).

[11] De Santiago (p. 40, n. 44 *supra*).

[12] Associated Press, July 9, 1941. In *Estrella de Panamá*, July 10, 1941.

[13] González (see p. 49 n.45, *supra*).

[14] Hans von Winter, acting *chargé d'affaires*, to German Min. For. Rel., cable № 221, July 8, 1941. (Bonn: Archives, Min. For. Rel., Fed. Rep. of Germany.) [Transl. from German to Spanish by Isabel Valsevicius and Juan

---

← *Continued from prev. page.*
the interests of these innocent, murdered citizens in the massacre had been so badly represented."

David Morgan Jr. The Ed's. English translation from the Spanish text may be seen on pp. 109, *supra*.]

[15] *Estrella de Panamá*, July 6, 1941.

[16] Probst, p. 147.

[17] González.

[18] *Estrella de Panamá*, July 8, 1941.

[19] Serracín and González recall that the agreed-upon hour was 6 AM.

[20] Hils.

[21] Gómez (see p. 84, n. 6, *supra*.)

[22] Müller.

[23] *Id.*

[24] Communiqué (*see* p. 58, n.18, *supra*).

[25] Decision, Aug. 18, 1953.

[26] Mixed German-Swiss Commission on the Events at Cotito, Report, July 17, 1941. (Archives, Swiss Embassy.)

[27] Serracín, González.

[28] Müller.

[29] *Id.*

[30] González.

[31] *Id.*

[32] Edward Baker Wilson, intv. with Author, Panama City, March 16, 1993.

[33] *Estrella de Panamá*, July 10, 1941.

[34] Müller.

[35] González.

[36] *Estrella de Panamá*, July 8, 1941.

[37] *Star & Herald*, July 9, 1941.

[38] The graphics of the magazine *Carteles* are reproduced in Hassán (see p. lxx, n. 5, *supra*), pp. 237-8.

[39] The *Estrella de Panamá* and the *Panamá-América* published it verbatim in their editions of July 8, 1941. The *Star & Herald* gave the complete version in English translation the following day.

[40] *Estrella de Panamá*, July 8, 1941.

[41] *Estrella de Panamá*, July 10, 1941.

[42] General Order of the Day № 148, July 14, 1941. (Archives, National Police.)

[43] *See* Chapter II, section 3, pp. 52 *ff, supra.*

[44] Decision of Aug. 18, 1953.

[45] Guillermo Sánchez Borbón, "Más," in *En pocas palabras: 1983-84* (anthology of daily newspaper columns from *La Prensa.*) (1992), p. 223.

[46] Rubén Núñez, conversation with Author, Ocú, Feb. 9, 1993.

[47] Miranda. *See* n. 32, p. 70, *supra.*

[48] Hils.

[49] Winter, Cable № 221 (n. 14, *supra*). [German words inserted by Author.]

[50] Böhmer to the Author, May 24, 1991.

[51] Oñós de Plandolit, acting Spanish *chargé*, to Ricardo Fábrega, Min. For. Rel., Dec. 31, 1941. In Min. For. Rel., 1941 MEMORIA at 44.

[52] Asuntos internos de Panamá: Dec. 29, 1940-Feb. 29, 1945. Microfilm roll 19, № 667. Office of Relations between Panama and the United States, University of Panama. [Back-transl. from the Author's Spanish rendering.]

[53] [Eng. in orig.]

[54] *Ibid.* [Rather than a Nazi spy, the jailed German was Wilhelm Probst, a fervent believer in due process and freedom of expression. *See* pp. 128*ff, infra.*]

[55] *Ibid.* [Quotation in Eng. in orig.]

[56] Probst (See p. 42, n. †, *supra.*), p. 49.

[57] [A *comisario* was a semi-official officer appointed in the tiniest communities by the *corregidor* of the township or the *alcalde* of the district, to serve as the representative of "Government and Justice."]

[58] July 1941 JUDICIAL REGISTER, at 25.

[59] *Id.*

[60] *Id.*

[He who does not desire to render justice cannot invoke the fact that he has observed the trappings of the law, because his fundamental attitude would make it evident that this was only an act of simulation.
[—A German criminal tribunal][1]

IV | A TWELVE-YEAR INVESTIGATION

1 | A CRIMINAL INVESTIGATION REPORT DISAPPEARS

THE FINAL RULING handed down by the judiciary regarding the events at Cotito was the Supreme Court's decision of October 20, 1953, modifying an earlier one and issuing a final judgment exonerating the defendants. This decision, written by [Justice*]Publio Vásquez, was not published in the JUDICIAL REGISTER because its "content" was considered of "no judicial importance."[2]←

---

* [In Panama, judges of the Superior Tribunals (intermediate appellate courts) and the Supreme Court are called *magistrados*. To avoid confusion with other officials called "magistrates" in this translation, the *magistrados* of the Supreme Court are called "justices," and those of the Superior Tribunals, "judges." As *municipios* in Panama are equivalent to U.S. (not British) counties, the *juez municipal* is called a county judge to avoid confusion with the *corregidor,* or "magistrate" in each township.

The full record,[3] identified as—

Proceedings to determine who, being one or more persons, is or are responsible for the criminal acts committed at Cotito, Province of Chiriquí, on July 7, 1941, in which various members of the National Corps of Police participated,

cannot be found in any official archive in the Republic of Panama. It is not in the judicial archives, nor in the National Archives where judicial files are required to be sent three years after they are closed.[4]

Some of those consulted about the possible whereabouts of the Cotito record suggest that it—together with thousands of other Panamanian documents in the files of the G–2[5] intelligence unit of the *Fuerzas de Defensa* on December 20, 1989—was seized by the invading troops of the United States and is in one of the ten thousand boxes of documents still under United States control.[6]

AUTHOR'S COLLECTION
The first prosecutor in the Cotito case, Abel Gómez Araúz.

This version has some logic, as will be explained in Chapter VI. The result is that it is difficult to make critical judgments about the criminal investigation that followed the event of July 7, 1941. Nevertheless, we have been able to reconstruct its most important elements from press reports of the time, still-unpublished diplomatic records, court files, police general orders of the day and the few isolated fragments of the actual record that we have been able to recover.

2 | PROSECUTOR GÓMEZ'S PRELIMINARY INVESTIGATION

AS SOON AS he learned of it, the prosecutor for the Judicial Circuit of Chiriquí, Abel Gómez Araúz[*] issued the order known as *cabeza de proceso,* [literally, "head of the proceedings," a document] opening [a criminal] investigation and ordering that the procedures established by the Judicial Code to establish the facts, [in this instance] the offense committed at Cotito, and to determine the criminal liability of those responsible for them, be conducted. On the same day, he took a sworn statement from Gottfried Werren, the only adult male survivor of the colony.

As *La Estrella de Panamá* reported, Werren "had repeatedly advised the head of the colony, Karl Lehner, that it would be better to obey national law and that they should avoid any conflict with the authorities, but Lehner did not want to listen, seemingly oblivious to reason, and although Werren implored him various times, Lehner continued to be stubborn. Werren added that Lehner finally threatened to expel him from the colony if he continued pressing these ideas, making it impossible for Werren to do anything [further], as in the colony the orders of the leader were the law."[7] Werren, like the rest of the colony's survivors in any condition to testify, denied that shots had been fired from inside the colony, and insisted that the colonists' resistance had been entirely passive.

Supplementing her father's declaration, the young Cornelia Werren, Gottfried's daughter, said that "she did not want to accuse anyone, that she could not find any peace, that she should be permitted to retract all her previous statements and she concluded by saying, as Christ had said on the cross, "Forgive them, Father, for they know not what they do."[8]

On July 9, Prosecutor Gómez went to Cotito together with Dr. Colindres of the José Domingo De Obaldía Hospital in David, and

---

* [Abel *Gómez Araúz,* the prosecutor in Chiriquí, is not to be confused with Fernando *Gómez Ayau,* the [Instructor] General of the National Police reporting to President Arias.]

with [Instructor] General Gómez Ayau, to continue the investigation. The task was disagreeable but essential to this type of criminal investigation. They had to exhume the bodies of the ten colonists buried in a common grave dug in front of the main house and, if possible, conduct autopsies on each. Dr. Colindres could not examine the ten interred corpses because of their advanced state of putrefaction, instead confining himself to an external inspection.

Efraín González recalls that when the group headed by Prosecutor Gómez, including the medical examiner and Captain Huff himself, arrived at Cotito, Huff ordered that the bodies be exhumed. Even the earth itself stank, but the police dug up the corpses. After they were taken out, Captain Huff said that it would be necessary for one of the neighbors acquainted with the victims to identify them.

Captain Huff assigned a detail of three policemen to go and find a German who lived nearby and bring him to make the identification; they went to get Anton Hils, [whose farm was adjacent to the east and] who identified them, weeping as he did it, giving the name of each one.[9]

After this procedure, which ended at about ten o'clock in the morning, the bodies were reburied in the common grave. Dr. Colindres performed his examinations only at Cotito, and he did not carry out any exhumation at Volcán, where the bodies of Karl Schmieder, Jr. and Mrs. Klara Werren were buried.

→The prosecutor was struck by the fact that the police commander had taken the surviving colonists into custody for "being complicit in the act of rebellion that occurred at Cotito," [while] having offered no further explanation about the conduct of his officers who had participated in the massacre.[10] ←

Returning to David, Prosecutor Gómez continued his investigation and summoned Captain Huff to appear for interrogation under oath, so that he could explain what had happened, and in particular give details of the origin and content of the two ultimatums he had sent to Lehner with Second Lieutenant Ruiloba. The prosecutor's summons angered Huff and was the cause of an immediate, serious confrontation between the two officials, ending in the dismissal of the prosecutor and the transfer of the police official to another post, as we shall see.

In addition, although Gómez Araúz and his group had traveled to Cotito on July 9, it was not until the 14th that the police produced the arms supposedly seized in the colony, and it was not until the 19th that the same arms were examined by the "experts" of the National Police, who were the principal objects of the criminal investigation. This significant aspect of the investigation also merits a separate comment.

3 | THE PROSECUTOR VS. THE CHIEF OF POLICE

CERTIFIED COPIES OF the ultimatums that Huff had drafted on July 5, 1941, and that he had sent with Second Lieutenant Ruiloba on the morning in question, [only one of] which was actually delivered to Lehner, eliciting no result,* were in the record of the investigation. The texts of both messages incriminated Huff, since they indicated that the captain in command was acting in obedience to orders from the Panamanian government to "crush" or "annihilate"[†] the colonists, although to the contrary, there was no indication in the record that such a prior order had been legally issued. Also, in a previous sworn statement, Huff had said that he acted in obedience "to orders issued by the high command of the National Corps of Police."11

The text of the first ultimatum read as follows:

REPUBLIC OF PANAMA
MINISTRY OF GOVERNMENT AND JUSTICE
NATIONAL CORPS OF POLICE—3RD BATTALION, CHIRIQUÍ
David, July 5, 1941
ULTIMATUM

Mr. Carlos Lehner, Chief of the Cotito Colony

---

* Only the first ultimatum could be delivered by Second Lieutenant Ruiloba.

† *[aplastar* and *aniquilar]*

Sir:

By order of the Panamanian government, I inform you that you will be allowed 15 minutes in which to surrender and give yourself up to the Authorities now present[;] once this term has elapsed, the Armed Force will crush you, for which I do not believe you will [want to] supply the motive, but rather [that you will] accept, separate the women and children, and prepare to suffer the consequences of your insubordination, and be advised that all resistance is useless, and that the weight of the law will be upon you [*Usted*, the singular pronoun, *i.e.*, individually], as the sole responsible individual.

If you wish to arrange a settlement, you must all leave the colony and follow the bearer.

Your obedient servant,
Commander of the Police

The text of the second ultimatum was the following:

REPUBLIC OF PANAMA
MINISTRY OF GOVERNMENT AND JUSTICE
NATIONAL CORPS OF POLICE—3RD BATTALION, CHIRIQUÍ

David, July 5, 1941

ULTIMATUM

Mr. Carlos Lehner, Chief of the Cotito Colony

Sir:

For the second time I urge you and the other members of the colony to surrender[;] if not, we will annihilate you and you will bear the sole responsibility. There is no reason to sacrifice so many lives. If you obey, nothing will happen if you yield. Avoid the spilling of blood.

Your obedient servant,
The Captain in Command

These documents written by Huff before the incident and his subsequent sworn statement appear to contradict his denial of having given the order to fire, although he does admit having ordered the cease–fire. On the other hand, the police officers who initially gave sworn statements—including Rosendo Aguilar, Félix Beitía, Daniel Corella, Guillermo Coronel, Carlos Polanco and Luis Ponce— said that although they had received strict orders not to fire unless first fired upon by the colonists—when that moment arrived, it was Huff himself who gave the order.

Prosecutor Gómez then decided to interrogate Huff to clarify these questions and to establish the truth about what had actually happened. If, as Huff alleged, he had acted in obedience to orders from the national government or the general command of the Police to "annihilate" or "crush" the colonists, it was also indispensable to clarify the respective responsibilities of Major Abel Quintero, then the Third Chief of the National Police; of [Instructor] General Gómez Ayau; of Minister [of Government and Justice] De la Guardia [to whom the police were subordinate]; and even that of President Arias. If [the Minister] were found responsible, the matter would come under the [original] jurisdiction of the Supreme Court of Justice; [if the President, under the jurisdiction] of the National Assembly, as the case might be.

Prosecutor Gómez summoned Captain Huff to his office, and forcefully instructed him to tell the truth. The indignant response was not long in coming, and a strong exchange of words between the two men ended with the matter inconclusively resolved.

4 | PROSECUTOR GÓMEZ IS REMOVED

THE CIRCUIT PROSECUTOR persisted in searching for the truth, but he only encountered obstacles among the upper echelons of the national government. Josefa Gómez de Cuestas, the daughter of the prosecutor [and mother of the Author], recalls that in those years she applied strong pressure on her father in an attempt to dissuade him from interrogating Huff.[12] In 1941, with Public Law Nº 15 (1941) in force, the office of the state prosecutor, [formerly considered an element of the judiciary,] had been subordinated to the executive branch. [Although the] authority of the [prosecutor general] over [local] prosecutorial personnel was clear, the appointment, dismissal, and the acceptance of resignations for the prosecutor general and the prosecutors in the circuit and appellate district courts, had to be approved by the president and by the minister of government and justice in executive orders.

If the [Arias administration] ordered the dismissal of Prosecutor Gómez, it would create the impression that it was attempting to keep Huff, boxed into a corner, from reaching the point where he would implicate higher officials in the administration itself. This might explain President Arias's telegram[*] to Huff just five days after the incident at Cotito, which I interpret as a message making it clear that Huff would not be left to confront the regular criminal justice system on his own.

On the other hand, Abel Gómez Araúz was no obscure provincial functionary who could easily be dumped. At the age of 46, Gómez had had a respectable political career. In 1922, he became a David city councilman. In 1928, he was elected principal deputy [to the National Legislative Assembly] for Chiriquí on the National Liberal Party ticket, but political intrigues resulted in his losing his seat; at the time, Gómez labeled the removal a *machetazo politico*[, a political hatchet job].[13] That same year, he was appointed alternate to the Second Judge of the Chiriquí Circuit Court. In 1930, in his capacity as first alternate, he served temporarily as acting governor of Chiriquí and in 1936, as an alternate legislator, he was finally able to occupy a seat[, again, temporarily,] in the National Assembly. He was a respected lawyer in the province, and was also esteemed in the National Liberal Party apparatus, where he had supported the candidacy of Arnulfo Arias in the 1940 elections.

Nevertheless, Gómez had to go, and Gómez went. By means of the political machinations that are the norm in this country, the Superior Tribunal of the First Judicial District, without having consulted him, appointed Abel Gómez Araúz the new Second Judge of the

---

[*] The text of the telegram may be read on p. 106, *supra*.

Chiriquí Circuit, and named lawyer Gonzalo Salazar to replace him as the circuit prosecutor. The formalities required the new Second Judge to present his resignation to his present superior, the prosecutor of the First District, Samuel Quintero. As soon as he received it, on August 4, 1941, Quintero accepted the resignation, immediately naming Salazar successor to Gómez Araúz.[14],[*]

Two days after the appointment of a new circuit prosecutor for Chiriquí, Captain Antonio Huff was transferred from the Third Battalion to the Second Battalion in Colón, and was replaced in Chiriquí by Captain Albano Palacios.[15] Several months later, Huff moved to Colón, then was named commander of the Model Jail[, the central penitentiary in Panama City], and from there, he was returned again to Colón.[16] Despite the existence of serious charges against him in the prosecutor's indictment, Huff was never suspended from service,

---

[*] [The political issue was *the extent to which the Ministerio Público,* the State Prosecutor's office, *could act independently* of the Minister of Govt. and Justice. The lines of authority here will confuse readers more familiar with U.S. practices than with the Panamanian system.

[The various functions of the U.S. Attorney General were then divided in Panama between two officials: the Minister of Govt. and Justice (a member of the President's cabinet) and the independent *Procurador General de la Nación,* who heads the *Ministerio Público*. Like the U.S. Attorney General, the Minister of Govt. & Justice serves at the pleasure of the president, but the *Procurador* is confirmed by the Assembly for a fixed term of ten years. Since presidents cannot be re-elected, the ten-year term of the *Procurador* overlaps with two or even three different presidencies, making the *Procurador* an independent "watchdog," permanently exercising a function that in the U.S. might be that of a "special prosecutor." The president can dismiss a minister, but the term of the *Procurador* is fixed, and dismissal would require impeachment proceedings in the Legislative Assembly.

[The *fiscal* in each Circuit is the equivalent of the U.S. Attorney in each Federal District, representing the Government in both criminal and civil matters. The *fiscal* for the Superior Tribunal in each appellate district is a subordinate of the *Procurador General* and the superior of the *fiscal*, in this case Abel Gómez Araúz, in each Circuit.

[During the brief Arias administration, Public Law Nº 15 (1941), made prosecutors for all practical purposes subject to the authority of the same member of the President's cabinet, the Minister of Govt. & Justice to whom the police reported. This limitation on the independence of the *Ministerio Público,* the prosecutor's office, made prosecution of the police at best problematic.]

much less arrested, not even after the fall of Arnulfo Arias on Oct. 9, 1941. Neither were Huff's subordinates inconvenienced. Second Lieutenant Luis Ardila was transferred from La Concepción to David, and later, he and Second Lieutenant Ernesto Ruiloba were sent to central headquarters in Panama City.[17]

[On August 29, Major Abel Quintero, the Third Chief of the National Police and Huff's immediate superior, was sent for training to Cuba with diplomatic status.] →As for [the [Instructor] General of Police,] Lieutenant Colonel Fernando Gómez Ayau, who might have been subject to indictment [if he had been found responsible of ordering the massacre, he] served out the first six months of his contract and returned undisturbed to Guatemala by air on July 16. He remained there for a month, resuming his duties in Panama on August 19, 1941.← Criminal charges would not be levied against Huff for the events at Cotito until 1951, when they were addressed [ten years after the fact] in one of the decisions of the Supreme Court of Justice handed down during the interminable course of these proceedings.

5 | THE COLONISTS' ALLEGED ARSENAL

→THE NEW CHIRIQUÍ circuit prosecutor, Gonzalo Salazar, [who replaced Gómez Araúz, "kicked upstairs" to a judgeship] on November 29, 1941, transmitted his investigative report, with all its deficiencies, to his superior, Samuel Quintero, prosecutor for the Superior Tribunal of the First Appellate District, responsible under the law for conducting homicide prosecutions. Quintero [just happened to be the] brother of Major Abel Quintero, who had been Acting Third Chief of the National Police.←

→Five months later, on April 21, 1942—without having carried out a reconstruction of the crime; without having interrogated a single one of the police officers who participated in the killing; without having clarified the origin of the orders allegedly received by Huff, the unanswered technical questions about the weapons or the trajectory of the bullet that wounded Garcés—Prosecutor Quintero filed[*] his conclusions with the Superior Tribunal.←

[As a criminal lawyer retained by the Swiss consulate to review the report later concluded in a memorandum, the most significant aspect of Salazar's report was that,] after the events at Cotito, the police had reported finding numerous weapons on the premises of the colony. National press reports had indicated that the Swiss were in possession of two carbines, three revolvers, a large number of machetes, axes and knives, hundreds of rounds of live ammunition and empty shells for long–range weapons and revolvers. If this were true, it would support the Government's official version of events made public on the same day, July 8, claiming that the colonists had fired the first shot, wounding the probationary officer, Lucas Garcés.

Despite the evidentiary significance of this detail, it was not until July 14 (seven days after the fact) that the weapons had been turned over to Prosecutor Gómez Araúz.[†] The *Estrella de Panamá* confirms the delay, reporting in its July 12 issue that weapons and ammunition of the Swiss rebels had been sent to David, but did not indicate the date.

According to the newspaper, included were—

- two carbines, one of which was a Springfield.

In addition, there were
- thirty machetes (ten long and twenty short),
- four axes,
- three pitchforks,

---

[*] [Used in the English sense, to "file" charges, to *initiate* a lawsuit. In Spanish, *archivar,* literally "to file," has the opposite meaning. In English, a lawyer "files" a complaint to begin a lawsuit. In Spanish, the court will *"file"* a case, send to the archives, to dismiss the plaintiffs' complaint, to close the case, to terminate proceedings.]

[†] "Memorandum on the Events at Cotito occurring on July 7, 1941," p. 4. (Archives, Swiss Embassy.) This 6–pp. document, unsigned, contains a criminal lawyer's serious study of the investigative report [*Sumario*], and is addressed to the Swiss consulate in Panama. It may be consulted in the archives of the Swiss Embassy.

- two hoes, and
- eight axe heads.

A large number of projectiles for firearms were listed:
- fourteen .32–caliber and
- twenty-four .38–caliber revolver bullets, and
- eighteen Springfield carbine shells.

It also speaks of another—
- 179 carbine shells, make unknown.

Of the empty shells,
- six were from a .32–caliber revolver,
- five from a .38,
- three from a Springfield carbine, and
- two from another carbine, make unknown.[18]

It was not until July 18, six days later, that the weapons already sent to David were examined by two National Police functionaries, mechanic Eusebio Escarreola and armorer Alfonso Samudio, neither of whose technical qualifications is given in the report. The criminal lawyers who examined the report for their memorandum for the Swiss consulate seriously questioned it.

"The police experts reported that the Springfield carbine, serial N⁰ 279549, model 1899, had been fired recently, as "particles of powder were found."[19]

- First of all, there was no statement that the experts had carried out a chemical analysis of the interior of the barrel. The "recent" firing could refer to July 7 or some subsequent date. The report did not account for who had custody of the weapons after the police seized them, nor did it state whether the weapons had been fired during that period.

- With regard to the two Colt revolvers with four empty shells, the criminal lawyer for the Swiss embassy objected that there was no indication whether they had been fired "recently."

- The experts also examined another weapon, a rifle not further identified, agreeing that it was in "good condition," but failing to state whether it had been fired or not.
- They had examined yet another carbine, make not given, and determined that the weapon was inoperable.
- Referring to the examination the experts made of 2–300 cartridges of different types and calibers, the criminal lawyer observed that they were for the most part unfired.
- As a final detail, he recommended that an investigation be conducted with regard to the "1899" model Springfield carbine, since the American army had not put this weapon into service until 1906, while in 1899 it used the Krag rifle, externally similar to the Springfield.[20]

The German diplomatic mission, as well as the Swiss, questioned the analysis by the expert witnesses of the weapons allegedly confiscated from the colonists at Cotito. At the end of July, 1941, the German *chargé d'affaires* Hans von Winter had sent a lengthy note[21] to Berlin in which he laid out the results of the investigation carried out by a Mixed Commission—composed of the Swiss *chargé* Adolph Gonzenbach, Swiss Consul Juan Blau, and Erick Cerjack of the German Legation—based on their visit to Cotito. The document in German, a copy of which I have been able to consult at the Swiss Embassy in Panama, casts doubt on the police claim that the first shot had been fired by the entrenched Swiss colonists. Referring to the weapons, it asserts that the Commission was shown a Japanese shotgun, with no apparent brand name, broken and inoperable, and a Springfield carbine with no ammunition. The Colt revolver shown to the Mixed Commission evinced no signs of recent firing, and according to reports gathered from among the neighbors, the weapons did not belong to the colonists at Cotito.[22]

The search for the truth would have been facilitated if it had been possible to recover the bullet that wounded Garcés (or at least to determine the physical location of Ruiloba and Garcés himself when the shooting began), but, according to the criminal lawyer for the Swiss embassy, probationary Officer Garcés's face wound presented points of entry and exit, and no bullet was recovered. In any case, no detailed physical examination of the wound had been conducted to determine the type or caliber of the bullet, although Winter recognized that such an examination might not have yielded satisfactory results.[23]

Quintero included a motion for final judgment dismissing charges against all of the accused under the command of Huff. This was, however, only the beginning of a long and torturous journey down the judicial road.

6 | THE TORTUROUS PATH OF A CRIMINAL PROSECUTION

THE INVESTIGATIVE REPORT was formally submitted to the Presiding Judge of the Superior Tribunal for the First Judicial District, Dr. Ricardo A. Morales, on April 21, 1942. In a decision drafted by him on April 29, the Superior Tribunal declined jurisdiction. →Under Public Law 25 (1937), Art. 99, the Supreme Court of Justice [had] original jurisdiction over crimes and misdemeanors committed by the chief of the police.← For the presiding judge [of the Superior Tribunal] and his concurring colleagues, Enrique Díaz, Lorenzo Hincapié, Alejandro Tapia and Erasmo Méndez, Huff's claim—that he had acted in compliance with specific orders from the Acting Third Chief of the National Police—was sufficient to require that the case be remitted to [the Supreme Court.*]

Served with the decision, Prosecutor Quintero appealed, on the grounds that there was insufficient evidence to prove that his brother, Third Chief Major Abel Quintero[, Huff's immediate superior,] had given Huff a written order, and requested that [before the case

---

* [This decision was in a sense a responsible one. It must be remembered that Quintero, the investigating prosecutor requesting that the Superior Tribunal dismiss all charges against the police, was the brother of a the 3rd Chief, Huff's immediate superior at the time of the massacre, and a possible criminal defendant. The Tribunal deferred to the Supreme Court.]

were remitted to the Supreme Court] additional testimony be inserted in the record. The judges agreed that additional evidence was required on the following points, ordering the prosecutor to—

1. "effectuate the deposition of Lieutenant Colonel Gómez Ayau, who Captain Huff alleges was the Acting Commander and Police Instructor on the date of the incident acts in question.
2. "determine if the Instructor Ayau had issued written confirmation of the telephonic orders given to Captain Huff, and if so to insert authenticated copies into the record.
3. "insert into the record copies of the various telegraphic or written reports submitted by Captain Huff on the subject of the Cotito colonists.
4. "determine precisely the number and quality of the weapons seized by the police in the colony."[24]

The decision made no mention of the deficiencies detected [in the forensic examination of the weapons], and accepted as proven fact that the police had seized a number of weapons at the colony.

Prosecutor Quintero complied to the extent possible with the order to obtain additional evidence, and resubmitted the file to the tribunal on July 27, 1942, reiterating his petition for definitive acquittal of the members of the police force involved in the case. The file sat for more than three months at the tribunal before it acted on November 4, 1942, once again declining jurisdiction over the case in favor of the Supreme Court of Justice. This time, they justified their decision by declaring that the former Third Chief of the National Police, Major Abel Quintero, [though now serving as] *attaché* to Panama's embassy in Costa Rica, was still subject to the original jurisdiction of the Supreme Court, [just as he had been when he was the Third Chief].

Quintero appealed this decision also, and on December 17, 1942, the Superior Tribunal revoked its earlier decision and ordered that the file be reopened, this time so that the Ministry of Foreign Relations could certify Major Quintero's status as a diplomat.[25] The prosecutor objected yet again, filing an appeal with the Supreme Court of Justice.[*] The high court received the file, but, accepting a recommendation of the national prosecutor general, quashed the order reopening the investigative file for the nth time, and remanded the case to the First Judicial District where it was received on March 5, 1943.[26] Here the file sat for three more years, until Superior Tribunal Judge Luis A. Carrasco (who replaced Judge Ricardo A. Morales, recently moved up to the Supreme Court) submitted the draft of a decision on January 16, 1946.

[However, i]n a March, 1947, communication from Foreign Minister Ricardo J. Alfaro to the acting Swiss *chargé d'affaires* René Naville, the Minister said the matter was once again pending in the Supreme Court, awaiting decision.[27] The Supreme Court, in a decision by Justice Erasmo De la Guardia, then ordered that additional evidence be inserted in the record. In essence, the court required prosecutors to—

1. establish the exact location of Ruiloba and Garcés at the moment the [first] shot was fired, following which the police returned fire.
2. determine who delivered the ultimatum.

---

* [This legal situation will be confusing to readers familiar with the Anglo–American *adversarial* system. To clarify: the *fiscal* had determined that the police, including a high police official (3rd Chief) who happened to be his brother, were innocent of wrongdoing, and was seeking to have the Superior Tribunal dismiss the case. The Superior Tribunal invoked a technicality: the *fiscal*'s brother was, at the time of the massacre 3rd Chief, and soon after became a diplomat, in either post subject to the original jurisdiction of the Supreme Court. Hence, they declined to rule on the prosecutor's request for dismissal and bucked the case up to the Supreme Court. The Supreme Court in turn declined jurisdiction, and sent the case back to the Superior Tribunal for a decision on the merits. During all these proceedings, no defense was necessary, as the prosecutor himself was requesting exoneration of the police. In the Anglo–American system, the prosecutor himself could have declined to prosecute, and the courts would have dismissed the case, but in Panama the court had to authorize the dropping of charges. The courts up to this point would neither try the case on the evidence or dismiss the charges.]

3. establish beyond doubt who gave the order to open fire and whether this order was given immediately after the first shot.
4. investigate [the claims of] Captain Huff regarding the origin of the orders that led him to draft the ultimatums.
5. take the deposition of former President Arnulfo Arias on the antecedents of the telegram sent to Captain Huff.
6. determine the possible criminal liability of the colonists.
7. determine the legal status of the colonists, and the criminal liability of the police officers.
8. determine why only eight death certificates and the medical examiner's report on ten corpses had been included in the record, if twelve dead were reported.[28]

The order for additional evidence did not raise the technical questions about the weapons, and the supplementary evidence it did require was never fully provided. Although at the beginning of 1951, the new prosecutor for the First Superior Tribunal, José María Vásquez Díaz, had been transferred to Chiriquí, he could do practically nothing. A revolution had broken out in Costa Rica, giving rise to the military incursion into Panamanian territory, and Captain, now Major, Huff and most of the police officers involved at Cotito were assigned to patrolling the border.

Nevertheless, Supreme Court Justice De la Guardia directed the circuit prosecutor then serving to obtain the additional evidence, adding additional points: deciphering the coded telegram allegedly authorizing Huff to give the colonists an ultimatum; taking the depositions of the surviving colonists; carrying out a reconstruction of the crime; and something else which had not been done up to that time: taking sworn testimony from the police officers engaged in the bloody episode.

As on previous occasions, the circuit prosecutor failed to obtain the additional evidence, although he did take depositions from Rosendo Aguilar Sánchez, Rodolfo Alvarado, Félix Antonio Beitía, Daniel Corella, Maximiliano Corella, Guillermo Coronel, Antonio Huff, Carlos Polanco, Luis Ponce, Nicasio Saldaña and Gavino Serrano, all members of the National Police. He did the same with Margarethe[, the widow of Karl Schmieder, by then remarried to Gustav] Haug [Sr.,] and took the sworn statement of Sophie Müller.[29] Two more years would pass before the courts finally put an end to the interminable criminal appeals.

7 | SWISS-GERMAN RECRIMINATION

[WHILE THE OFFICIAL superficial investigation was stalled and the judicial proceedings dragged on interminably, with obviously intentional delays, the Swiss and German governments undertook equally ineffective diplomatic initiatives on behalf of the victims.] Scarcely two days after the incident at Cotito, the acting German *chargé d'affaires,* Hans von Winter, was summoned to a meeting in the office of the Minister of Foreign Relations, Raúl De Roux, to which the Minister of Government and Justice, Ricardo Adolfo De la Guardia, was also invited. The German diplomat was desirous of learning the names of the German citizens who died or were wounded at Cotito, and requested in addition that all possible information regarding the lamentable incident be supplied to him. He asked that Minister De la Guardia show him the passports of the Germans involved and, in addition, formally requested a copy of the communiqué sent the previous day to the domestic press.

A few days later, on July 16, Foreign Minister De Roux held a similar meeting, in which the acting Swiss *chargé d'affaires,* Adolph Gonzenbach (who had arrived from Caracas especially for this purpose), and the Minister of Government and Justice participated. Taking advantage of Gonzenbach's visit to Panama, the Government authorized a Mixed German–Swiss Commission to go to Cotito to conduct an onsite investigation and submit a report to their respective governments. It was agreed that the Commission would fly to Chiriquí on July 17.

| THE INVESTIGATION OF THE MIXED COMMISSION

THE MIXED COMMISSION, as we have noted, was made up of the Swiss *chargé* Adolph Gonzenbach, Swiss Consul Juan Blau and an official of the German Legation, Erick Cerjack. At Cotito, they interviewed the police officers who had taken part in the incident, interrogated the German and Swiss neighbors, and obtained access to the investigative file being put together by Prosecutor Gómez Araúz. They had diagrams drawn of the land and improvements of the colony, and carried out a detailed inventory of the colonists' possessions.

Where they encountered difficulties was with the survivors convalescing in the José Domingo de Obaldía Hospital. The women refused to give explanations or to comment on what had happened; the children were refusing food and taking off their bandages. Only after a strong reprimand did the Commission manage to overcome the passive resistance of these people and bring them to their senses. The fruits of the investigation were handled in the strictest confidence by both diplomatic missions. In the course of his meticulous efforts, Winter, the acting German *chargé d'affaires,* prepared a summary of the main results of the onsite inspection, which he sent in late July to Berlin. The most relevant points were these:

1. In November, 1929, the German families of Karl Schmieder and his wife Margarethe; Anton Hils, his wife Marie and two children; Fritz Schaper and his wife Martha [Karl Schmieder's sister]; and Alfred Brauchle, his wife Lydia and three children, took up residence in Cotito.
2. On land put at their disposal by the Government of Panama, these pioneers, during ten years of hard labor, transformed the jungle into cultivated fields and pastures and constructed their home[s].
3. Schmieder was the individual who achieved the greatest prosperity, since he had received financial assistance from a sister residing in the United States and therefore enjoyed superior resources.[*]

---

[*] [The allusion to a loan from Schmieder's sister was probably based on rumors—repeated over the course of many years—spread by Sophie Müller and her son Robert, but there is no evidence that such a loan ever existed.

Continued→

4. In the summer [*i.e.,* the *verano,* as used in Panama, or dry season, which corresponds with the *winter* in the northern hemisphere] of 1939, a Swiss colony led by Karl Lehner arrived in the area. The Swiss were members of a religious sect "whose goals were not fixed," and whose "ideas were a little cloudy." Lehner had had problems with Swiss authorities on repeated occasions, and finally decided to emigrate to Panama.

5. The colonists drew attention to themselves because at the time of their arrival they had long hair and beards. The women dressed like the men, in trousers and shirts and wore rough sandals.

6. The Government of Panama put five hundred hectares of uncultivated land in the area of Piedra Candela, three hours on horseback, more or less, from Cotito, at the disposition of the colonists. *En route* to this place, they stopped at the farm of Schmieder, who gave them lodging.[*]

7. Lehner, who doubtless had great powers of suggestion, convinced Schmieder to join the sect, and in a short time achieved dictatorial domination of these people, who called him "Molch" ["Salamander" in German]. Lehner also recruited Helmut, a son of the Brauchles.

8. Lehner's philosophy rejected all terrestrial authority, while he exercised strict, even cruel, domination over the members of the sect. He opposed rendering obedience to the laws of the country. He had no contact with the neighbors; he en-

---

← *Continued from prev. page.*
Sophie and Robert sought to demonstrate that Schmieder had been in financial straits, that the Swiss colonists had paid off all or part of the loan, and therefore should have received a greater share of the proceeds when the farm was sold after the massacre by Schmieder's widow and her second husband, Gustav Haug Sr.]

* [A garbled oversimplification of the story of how the settlers came to live at Cotito. After they had largely abandoned their efforts at Cotito in 1940, the Swiss accepted Schmieder's invitation to return permanently to Cotito.]

closed himself with his followers in hermetic isolation from the outside world; nevertheless, there were no further difficulties for many months, although the life style of the people was observed with mistrust by the authorities and the neighbors.

9. When a few months ago the Panamanian government ordered all foreigners resident in the Republic to register, Lehner refused categorically; the efforts of police delegations who went to Cotito on June 20 and 24 to inform them that they were required to go down to David, proved fruitless.
10. When Capitan Huff informed him the government had determined to use force to enforce the law, Lehner replied that his and his people's dead bodies would [have to be] carried out of the colony, that he possessed "weapons" stronger than those of the police, but he was referring to spiritual weapons.
11. The captain of police sent a report to Panama City and received the order to use all means at his disposal and to proceed rigorously against the colonists.
12. Lehner, after the last visit from the police, ordered that the main house be fenced with barbed wire and surrounded by oaken planks. He also ordered that a large quantity of victuals, especially, cheese, honey and dried plantains, be stored.
13. In the early hours of the morning of July 7, Captain Huff in command of two second lieutenants and twenty–eight police officers surrounded the farm; the oak palisade was still not finished. The colonists, seeing the police, took refuge in the house, prepared to resist.
14. Captain Huff, who was about 150 meters from the line of fire, sent a negotiator with an ultimatum addressed to Lehner and signed by the captain himself, allowing them 15 minutes to give themselves up or be "crushed."
15. Lehner sent Paul Häusle, who was armed with a machete, to receive the ultimatum brought by the police. The officer asked Häusle to drop the knife, which the colonist refused. The officer then threatened to open fire if he took one more

step. Häusle turned around, and looked at Lehner, who shouted at him that he should keep walking.
16. Häusle obeyed [Lehner] and in a few seconds fell to the ground, gravely wounded by a gunshot. Immediately thereafter, the police opened fire in the north–south and east–west directions. They probably used two automatic weapons and in a few minutes destroyed the entire colony.
17. The Swiss Joseph Niederberger[*] was with Huff. [He said] the captain put on the boots he had removed a few minutes earlier, and as he ran toward the house, the women came out of the house screaming that the police should murder them, too.
18. The chief of the detachment then ordered that tear gas be fired, and although the attack was unsuccessful because the wind blew it back on the police, they ended up wounding *Frau* Schmieder in the renal area. Finally, the police who were behind the house got over the fence and handcuffed the women, who continued to resist.
19. The result of this attack was 10 dead and 10 wounded, and only the girl Leoni *[sic]* Morf, the boy Albert Schmieder and the elderly Gottfried Werren were uninjured.[30, †]

In determining liability, the commissioners arrived at the conclusion that the police had gone [to Cotito] with the intention of killing [the colonists], as they did not bring with them any medical personnel or first–aid supplies, and they had to improvise the stretchers on which the injured were transported. They discounted the possibility that the colonists had fired weapons against the police and raised doubts about the arms supposedly belonging to the colonists that were confiscated. Nevertheless, they accepted that the members of the sect had armed themselves with machetes and knives, and

---
* [Niederberger was a Swiss citizen working in David at the time. *See* p. lxv, n.*, *supra*; p. 216, *infra*.]

† [The correct total was 12 dead, 8 wounded and 3 unharmed.]

that they had used them to fabricate a kind of lances with bamboo shafts, and that it seemed that some of these had actually been hurled at the police during the mismatched combat.[31] They also acknowledged that the colonists were determined to bar the police from entering the barricaded house, and that they resisted physically. Winter, analyzing the Commission report, found the conduct of the police unjustifiable.

For another thing, they had failed even to take advantage of the physical location of the farm. The house was in a depression, and could easily have been filled with tear gas fired from above. In particular, however, the commanding officer had permitted, by his un–military conduct, the badly trained and frightened police, unthinkingly and without reflection, to unloose a disastrous fusillade against these people.[32]

Karl Lehner, in the German diplomatic report, still bore major responsibility: he was the "moral culprit" for having sabotaged the several police requests made clearly and unequivocally to the leader of the colony, understandable in the times in which they were living. Winter added that the incredible influence of Lehner had extended even after his death to the women and children in the hospital in David, who were refusing food and removing their bandages.[33] For Winter, the logical conclusion was that his government should demand compensation for damages suffered by German citizens.[*]

---

 * [Again, as much as one might sympathize with Winter's conclusions about the damages suffered by German citizens at Cotito, the sanctimony should be evaluated in historical context. It must be remembered that Germany had occupied most of Europe and was inflicting the most dreadful suffering on millions of civilians as they constructed their lunatic vision of a German *Reich* that would, together with the Italians and Japanese—until it came time to turn on them as well—rule the known world. The United States and Panama were not yet in the war, but Europe and Asia were in flames. Poland, Holland, Belgium and France were occupied, Greece had been divided between the Germans and the Italians, both were fighting the British in North Africa, and the Germans had invaded the Soviet Union. Concentration camps, and later extermination camps, were constructed all over Europe. The SS and the German Army, with the acquiescence of a supine judiciary, committed mass murders daily, and this was still only 1941. German consulates in the U.S. had already been closed by Pres. Roosevelt. In Ger-

Continued→

German claims

ON JULY 26, 1941, the German *chargé d'affaires* Winter communicated with Foreign Minister De Roux, reiterating his request for the "official and original text" of the press communiqué, as promised in the meeting of July 9. In addition, he asked for details regarding the incident in which the Germans Karl Schmieder, Sr., and Paul Häusle, had died, and Margarethe Schmieder and Gertrude Häusle were wounded, "having sustained considerable injuries which will cause them prolonged, even permanent disability." Winter also requested a copy of the charges when filed against "the perpetrator(s)"[*] by the acting prosecutor and added, explicitly:

> I reserve the right, having received from Your Excellency the aforementioned official documents, to return to this subject for the purpose, if it is in this case appropriate, to clarify matters with respect to compensation for the damages suffered by the German citizens.[34]

Two days later, Foreign Minister De Roux sent a copy of Winter's request to Minister De la Guardia, asking him to advise him what Government and Justice wished to do in this matter.[35] Eleven days later, Minister De la Guardia answered De Roux, requesting that he advise Winter he could not provide a copy of the judicial file "because it was still an ongoing investigation."[36] With regard to possible compensation for the damages suffered by German citizens, and Winter's reservation of the right to raise the matter again if appropriate, Minister De la Guardia stated in advance what the Panamanian position would be if faced with damage claims for the incident at Cotito:

← *Continued from prev. page.*
man–occupied Europe, in short, the Cotito massacre would have been but a drop in an ocean of blood for the "Germany of today" that Winter so proudly served.]

* [*"el o los responsables"*...] Winter to Raúl de Roux, Min. For. Rel., Jul. 26, 1941. The letter is reproduced in facsimile by Hassán (p. xv, n. 5 *supra),* 5th and 6th unnumbered pp. following p. "242" (also misnumbered).

In that regard, I take the liberty of cautioning you that it would be difficult for the Government of Panama to contemplate the possibility of paying damages for the events at Cotito, in light of the fact that the police who participated in them found themselves obliged to open fire to repel the colonists' attack to which they were subjected.[37]

It appears inconsistent for Minister De la Guardia to have justified his refusal to provide a copy of the file on the basis that the case was still in the investigative phase, and yet, at the same time, without waiting for the results of the investigation, to have arrogated unto himself judicial functions beyond his authority, ruling out any possibility of compensation.

On August 28, 1941, Foreign Minister De Roux communicated to Winter the points made by De la Guardia [Minister of Government and Justice].[38] This was probably the last correspondence regarding the Cotito incident conducted directly between the Panamanian foreign minister and the German representative. The strained relations between Panama and Germany also produced an official complaint from Winter regarding the use of the word "Nazis" to refer to the Germans [in Chiriquí] in an article published in the *Weekly Information Bulletin for Embassies, Legations and Consulates*, published by the Ministry of Foreign Relations.[39] Less than a month later, on October 18, the Panamanian government declared Erick O. Cerjack, civil attaché of the German Legation, *persona non grata* for "having engaged in this country in activities contrary to the interests of the Republic and that [tended] to affect directly the security of the governments of the Americas in their plans for the defense of the continent."[40] On December 14, 1941, a week after the Japanese naval air attack on Pearl Harbor, the Republic of Panama declared that a state of war existed with Germany.

On January 14, 1942, the *chargé d'affaires ad interim* of Spain, Manuel Oñós de Plandolit, informed the Panamanian foreign ministry that the Spanish Legation would assume the protection of German interests in Panama.* The Spanish diplomat could do practically nothing with respect to the potential damage claim for the Germans killed and injured at Cotito. On February 16, 1943, Oñós de Plandolit, representing the German citizen Gertrude ("Trudi") Häusle, asked Foreign Minister Octavio Fábrega for the return of her passport and that of her deceased brother Paul, documents which had been held by the Alien Affairs and Immigration section of the Ministry of Government and Justice since 1941, as a result of which, according to Trudi, she was for all intents and purposes an undocumented alien and urgently needed to put her civil status in order.[41]

As usual, the foreign minister transmitted the request to the Minister of Government and Justice, by then Camilo De la Guardia Jr., who, a few days later, answered that his office had no problem in returning to M[iss] Häusle the passport belonging to her and, if mutilated in such a way that it could not be used by another person, that of her "late husband" (sic).[42] Trudi Häusle was able to recover both documents. Nothing further related to the German victims at Cotito can be found in the files of the Ministry of Foreign Relations.

| SWISS CLAIMS

[THE READER WILL recall that, a few days after the massacre, the Swiss *chargé d'affaires* Gonzenbach had met with Ministers De Roux and De la Guardia. A week later,] the Swiss diplomat, in a *note verbale* to the foreign minister, indicated that he had informed his Government in detail of the events and that he reserved the right to raise the subject again to establish a possible claim for damages, once the Federal Political Department at Bern had considered the matter. Gonzenbach, although critical of the "strange mentality of those colonists," affirmed that in his view "so sad an ending might

---

* Oñós de Plandolit to Fábrega (*See* n. 51, p. 123, *supra*). [The Spanish Caudillo Francisco Franco having been aided by Hitler in overthrowing the Republican Government of Spain in the Spanish Civil War, Spain remained sympathetic to the Nazis but, like Switzerland and Sweden, "neutral" during World War II; hence the "German Interests Section" in the Spanish embassy in Panama.]

have perhaps been avoided if the Police had adopted a more humanitarian attitude." In an attached note of the same date, he requested that an authenticated copy of the criminal charges brought by the prosecutor in Chiriquí be sent to the mailing address of the Swiss Legation in Caracas, Venezuela, for which he would reimburse the costs.[43] →On July 28, Minister De Roux sent the Swiss request to Minister De la Guardia.44← It was evident that the [Swiss] diplomat had adopted as his own the conclusions of the Mixed Commission of which he had been a member, attributing to the National Police the greatest responsibility for what had happened at Cotito.

Two years later, the situation had not changed in any way. On March 5, 1942, the Swiss *chargé* Gonzenbach, in a letter from Caracas, reiterated to the Minister of Foreign Relations, Octavio Fábrega, his request for a copy of the criminal charges in the Cotito case. Gonzenbach had returned to Panama in August, 1942, had met with Fábrega, but had had little success at that time with his very ordinary petition. Despite the excellent relations between Panama and Switzerland, since in 1941 the Swiss government had accepted the representation of the interests of Japan, Germany, Italy and occupied China, the Panamanian Government seemed to pay little attention to the Swiss request.45 Ricardo Adolfo De la Guardia, who already in 1941, as Minister of Government and Justice, had practically declared that no kind of compensation for the Cotito victims was appropriate, now occupied the Palace of the Herons [Panama's "White House"], having replaced Arnulfo Arias after the coup of October 9] as "Minister Invested with Executive Authority," [*i.e.,* acting president].

But Gonzenbach persisted. On June 29, 1943, again by airmail, he once again requested from Minister Fábrega a copy of the indictment; on this occasion he reiterated the desire of the Federal Political Department to be informed of the progress made in the judicial investigation of the matter at Cotito.46 On July 3, 1943, Octavio Fábrega transmitted the new Swiss request, without result. The Swiss delegation did not stand with folded arms in the face of the official silence. They retained the services of a criminal–law expert to analyze the file which, since the month of March, 1943, had been pending before the Superior Tribunal of the First Judicial District. The legal expert was to prepare a chronology of the proceedings in the protracted case and examine in depth how far the investigation itself had advanced. This was done, serving as a basis for the Swiss Legation to reiterate its requests at the beginning of 1946.

Four–and–a–half years after the slaughter, the protagonists had changed. The Minister of Foreign Relations was Dr. Ricardo J. Alfaro, and the Swiss *chargé d'affaires* was René Naville. Naville met with Alfaro on December 7, 1945, and after a long conversation, the foreign minister condemned the incident and promised to use his good offices to expedite this still–pending matter. On February 11, 1946, Naville sent Alfaro a memorandum from Caracas recapitulating the progress of the judicial proceedings since November 29, 1941, when Circuit Prosecutor Salazar had [initially] transmitted the file to Superior Prosecutor Quintero; Naville concluded by noting that [after four years] there had [still] been no decision in the case.

The Swiss Legation expressed explicit confidence in the cooperation of the competent Panamanian authorities, convinced that they would take steps to accelerate the resolution of the case, [and reserving] for later the decisions relative to any possible rights of the affected Swiss parties–in–interest, and the compensation they might attempt to recover.[47]

Minister Alfaro then requested all possible information from Carlos Sucre Calvo, then the Minister of Government and Justice, who in turn instructed Manuel Burgos, second secretary of the Ministry, to request a report from the Superior Tribunal. On February 27, 1946, Presiding Judge J. A. Pretelt of the Superior Tribunal, after describing the long course of the proceedings, informed the Minister of Government and Justice that the file had been pending before the court since March 5, 1943, and that since January 16, 1946, the draft of a decision had been before the judges of the court for their consideration.[48] Having received no further response to his repeated requests, on April 22, again from Caracas, Naville again requested that Alfaro make inquiries to determine the results of the intervention he had offered.[49] The remainder of 1946 passed without the Swiss Legation's having received any response.

On January 30, 1947, Naville traveled to Panama expressly to remind Alfaro about the information requested and to reiterate to him that the Swiss Government was desirous of finding a solution to this matter now pending for five years.[50]

Alfaro had, back in May, 1946, already requested that Sucre, the Minister of Government and Justice, send him any available information on the judicial proceedings, and repeated the request on the occasion of the visit of Naville to Panama.[51] Surprisingly, the foreign ministry's own bureaucracy appeared to have contributed to the painful delays of the Cotito *affaire*, because when Second Secretary Burgos at Government and Justice replied to Alfaro's latest note, he made it clear that on March 1, 1946, his office had sent to the foreign ministry an authenticated copy of Presiding Judge Pretelt's report, which it appeared Minister Alfaro had not received.[52]

In the meantime, the case had been submitted for the nth time to the Supreme Court and Burgos, indicating he had requested further information, informed Alfaro that he would send the information as soon as he received it from the Supreme Court. On March 3, 1947, Dr. Ricardo A. Morales, chief justice of the Supreme Court, informed the second secretary, Manuel Burgos, that the file was "awaiting conference relative to the observations made in [response to] the decision drafted by the justice responsible for drafting the decision."[53]

The Swiss delegation, so far as we know, never received an authenticated copy of the investigative report and could not file suit for damages for the eight Swiss fatalities and six Swiss wounded at Cotito. Nearly six years would go by before the Second Superior Tribunal would definitively close the file.

8 | A DELAYED ACQUITTAL

WITH PRACTICALLY THE same omissions that had marked the defective criminal *sumario* filed by Quintero, the Second Superior Tribunal of Justice decided the Cotito case, definitively dismissing charges against Rosendo Aguilar, Rodolfo Alvarado, Benedicto Aparicio, Luis Felipe Ardila, Félix Antonio Beitía, Juan Caballero, Rubén Darío Caballero, Pedro Antonio Cedeño, Rafael Cedeño, Víctor Cerrud, Daniel Corella, Maximiliano Corella, Guillermo Coronel, Secundino Chávez, Rafael De Gracia, José Félix Escartín, Alfonso Fuentes, Oliborio Gaitán, Fidel Gómez, Efraín González, Pastor González, Pedro Guerra, Roberto Guevara, Antonio Huff, Arcinio Lara, Antonio Ledezma, Adelo Miranda, Adriano Miranda, Mario Augusto Miranda Moreno, Faustino Montenegro, Florencio Moreno, Pedro Peralta, Héctor Pittí, Carlos Polanco, Luis Ponce, Jacob Quiel, Manuel Rivera, Primitivo Rivera, Ernesto Ruiloba, Nicasio Saldaña, Andrés Samudio, Aurelio Manuel Serracín, Bienvenido Serrano, Gavino Serrano, Bolívar Urriola and "Margarita" Schmieder de "Hug."[*] It also dismissed the prosecution against Lucas Garcés, charged with the death of Paul Häusle, because Garcés had died of pulmonary tuberculosis on March 22, 1949.

TWELVE YEARS WERE consumed as the Superior Tribunal and the Supreme Court mutually declined jurisdiction, passing the case back and forth between them. Neither of these bodies was concerned with the search for factual truth, and they accepted as given the official version that the colonists had opened fire when Huff's emissaries had approached. They completely ignored the fact that the superior strength of the police would have made the use of firearms unnecessary, and that tear gas would have been sufficient, given that, at worst, the Swiss were armed with rudimentary lances and knives. Beyond any doubt, the attitude of the colonists had contributed to the outcome, but all indications are that at no time did they come to fire weapons, nor did they initiate any assault on the police.

Nonetheless, the Superior Tribunal judges [ultimately] decided to absolve the officers of the National Police, laying on the Swiss the responsibility for their own deaths. In a [1953] opinion written by

---

* [It will be remembered that Margarethe Schmieder, having lost her husband and one son, and having suffered serious gunshot injuries, eventually married Gustav Haug, who had been associated with the colony but who had questioned Lehner's leadership and left to set up on his own at Santa Clara. Hence the Spanish form of her two married surnames "Schmieder de Haug," the *de* indicating that "H[a]ug" was her current married name.]

Judge Angel Vitelio De Gracia, the Second Superior Tribunal put the matter as follows:

> On the day in question, there was a series of circumstances involving the colonists of "Cotito" and the police force that created fear, by any light well founded, on the part of the authorities, causing them to be firmly convinced of the possibility of an armed attack of serious proportions. Factors of a psychological nature contributed to the creation of this mental state, which together with the acts that occurred, completely destroyed the last remaining shred of serenity and the patience of the police authorities.
>
> First, the highly defiant action of the colonists, in open and flagrant disobedience and insubordination, with all the elements of a challenge, that caused that attitude of fear, including even of an armed conflict, among those who were responsible for making decisions for all; later in the place where the acts occurred, the assault on LUCAS GARCÉS D., which was the classical drop of water that made the glass of patience run over, making it evident that it was no longer a matter of mere words but of action.
>
> In light of this picture, everything that might have occurred in the instant of disturbance can be attributed only to *the necessity of defending oneself or another from a grave and imminent danger threatening life or honor, when those threatened by the danger had not voluntarily caused it and could not have avoided it by any other means.* Penal Code, Art. 48.
>
> It is thus that the Tribunal views the unfortunate events in which exemplary public servants found themselves involved, and in which fanatical people lost their lives uselessly, for in a fatal instant they lost their faith in God and in Man, so that, driven mad by rancor, and out of control, they allowed themselves to be dragged by the vortex of passion into the chasms of pain.[54]

The decision of August 18, 1953, was also signed by Judges Darío González and Luis Carrasco. From a legal standpoint, the members of the court found that no crime had been committed, since the police officers were justified in their actions; they had acted in the face of a state of necessity that could not, as specified in the Penal Code, have been avoided by other means. For the judges, it was an incontrovertible fact that the colonists had fired, placing Huff's men in grave and imminent danger, and they so described it as a finding of fact in the decision. This decision, which was affirmed two months later by the Supreme Court of Justice, closed off definitively any possibility that justice would be done for the victims of Cotito.

[It is interesting to note that in 1953, Colonel Remón, who had overthrown Arnulfo Arias in 1951, was president of the Republic, actively engaged in militarizing the police whose latest coup had placed Remón in office. With the militarized police firmly in control of the government, at least until Remón was assassinated in January, 1955, it was unlikely that any verdict holding what amounted to a death squad at Cotito responsible for murder or manslaughter at Cotito would be forthcoming.]

Notes to Chapter IV

[1][German *Bundesgerichtshof [Federal Court]*, 10 ENTSCHEIDUNGEN IN STRAFSACHEN ["DECISIONS IN CRIMINAL MATTERS"], 295 at 301 (1957), q. Otto Kirchheimer, *Political Justice: The Use of Legal Procedure for Political Ends* (1961), p. 339.]

[2] 1953 REGISTRO JUDICIAL, at 476.

[3] [The *instrucción* of the *sumario* is the first step in the *proceso*, often translated as "trial," but *proceedings* is a more accurate term. Since the *sumario* combines elements of a criminal investigation, an indictment, a bill of particulars, a statement of charges, and, to the extent that it contains depositions and exhibits, the case file, these terms are used interchangeably in the translation, depending on the context. The *expediente*, the mass of documents accumulated in the course of the *proceso* and bound into books, starting with the prosecutor's *sumario*, is called here either the *case file* or the *trial record*.

CHAPTER IV | A TWELVE-YEAR INVESTIGATION

[The Germano-Roman legal system practiced in Latin America, and the Anglo-American common law system familiar to English-speaking readers, approach criminal cases very differently. In Panama, as in Western Europe and the rest of Latin America, *la instrucción del sumario* by the prosecutor is a process of investigation and accumulation of evidence, including sworn statements from witnesses, copies of exhibits, etc. To call this process in English "the instruction of the summary" would be to inflict incomprehensible gibberish on the reader, but understanding how the system works is crucial to understanding the Cotito case.

[Once an aggrieved party has lodged a formal complaint (*denuncia* or *querella*), prosecutors have less discretion than they do in Anglo-American law to decline a case they believe without merit; they are obliged to investigate and file the *sumario*, although in practical terms this creates insurmountable backlogs. The system does not, however, require prosecutors to make much of an effort to prosecute. A fair-minded prosecutor—or one who had reason to "take a dive"—would include in the *sumario* exculpatory evidence as well. The Cotito prosecution requested what might be called acquittal or dismissal (*sobreseimiento*).

[A *proceso* may or may not include the examination of witnesses in open court that is considered a *trial* in Anglo-American law. While there is a growing trend toward hearing witnesses in open court—inspired as much by *Perry Mason* and *Law and Order* as by any theoretical jurisprudence—in 1941, the interrogation of witnesses was a function of the prosecutor. Hence, the prosecutor is the primary finder of fact, and the judges reviewing officers in what is essentially an oversight process. In the Cotito case, once Abel Gómez Araúz had been "kicked upstairs" to a judgeship, the prosecutors were largely sympathetic to the police.

[It took a twelve-year *proceso* for the police (and Margarethe Schmieder, of all people!) to see the charges against them dismissed, as the prosecutor who filed the charges against them had himself requested, but none of them had what Anglo-American law would consider a trial *per se*. The defense would have been free to present exculpatory evidence from other witnesses, also in writing, but there was no cross-examination. Judges considering the written record called for additional interrogation of certain witnesses, but—if it was conducted at all—it was not conducted in the presence of judges, let alone a jury, sitting in open court. Accusers did not confront perpetrators face-to-face. Various judges along the way questioned the evidence given by the police and the government, but in the face of political pressure and the absence of an effective prosecution, they ended up endorsing the prosecutor's (!) request for dismissal of his own charges.

[Seventy years later, hand-picked juries now review the record in murder cases in Panama, but juries are not available to defendants in most cases. Once arrested, a defendant sits in jail for years awaiting prosecution, let alone trial. In fact, a defendant's Constitutional right to a trial or a complete *proceso* is only theoretical, not real; the vast majority of people in jail have not had, and never will have, a trial or *proceso* considering their guilt or innocence. Lately, there has been legislation passed providing for speedy trial in open court, but it remains more an aspiration than a practical reality. In March, 2013, Assembly committees were reviewing legislation that would create the post of justice of the peace in each township and require they have a modicum of legal knowledge, eliminating the *corregidores*. The current situation is the subject for another book by a different author.]

[4] JUDICIAL CODE, Art.183 (19).

[5] [See p. 126, n. *, *supra*, regarding the name of the military intelligence unit.]

[6] Juan Materno Vásquez, intv. with Author, May, 1991.

[7] *Estrella de Panamá*, July 18, 1941.

[8] *Id.*

[9] González.

[10] *Cf.* decision of 2nd Sup. Trib. (n. 4, p. 60 *supra*), at 7.

[11] Decision, Sup. Trib. of Justice, First [Appellate] Judicial District, May 6, 1942. In *Estrella de Panamá*, July 5, 1942.

[12] Josefa Gómez de Cuestas [daughter of prosecutor, mother of Author], conversation with Author, David, Nov. 5, 1992.

[13] Abel Gómez Araúz to Blanca Araúz de Gómez, telegram, Aug. 28, 1928. Personal files of the Author.

[14] Prosecutor's order "Accepting the resignation presented by Mr. Abel Gómez and naming as his successor Mr. Gonzalo Salazar." Ratified by Executive Order № 247, signed by President Arias and Minister of Govt. & Justice De la Guardia. GACETA OFICIAL № 8,591 (Aug. 26, 1941).

[15] General Order of the Day № 168, Aug. 6, 1941.

[16] *Id.*, №___, Oct. 17, 1941, p. 3; № ___, Oct. 23, 1941, p. 3.

[17] *Estrella de Panamá*, July 16, 1941, General Order of the Day № ___, Aug. 18, 1941, p. 3.

[18] *Estrella de Panamá*, July 12, 1941. With respect to the revolvers, the memorandum mentions only two Colts. *See Id.*, p. 5.

[19] Memorandum on the Events at Cotito, at 4.

[20] *Ibid.* This particular weapon does not appear on the list published by the *Estrella de Panamá*, July 12, 1941.

[21] Winter to Min. For. Rels., Note, July __, 1941. [Transl. to English from Spanish version of I. Valsevicius & J.D. Morgan Jr. (Archives, Min. For. Rel.)]

[22] *Id.*

[23] *Id.*

[24] Decision, May 6, 1942.

[25] XL JUDICIAL REGISTER (Dec. 17, 1942).

[26] *Rem'd* to Sup. Trib., 1st Judicial District, DEC. 1942, XL JUDICIAL REGISTER at 149 (Dec. 7, 1942).

[27] Ricardo J. Alfaro, Min. of For. Rel. to René Naville, acting Swiss *chargé d'affaires* at Caracas, communication D.P. № 578-B, Mar. 11, 1947.

[28] Decision, 2nd Sup. Trib. of Justice, Aug. 18, 1953, at 5-6.

[29] *Id.*, at 4-5.

[30] Winter, Note.

[31] *Id.*

[32] *Id.*

[33] *Id.*

[34] *Id.*

[35] De Roux to De la Guardia, Note DP-1,845, Aug. 8, 1941. (Germany file. Archives Min. For. Rel.)

[36] De la Guardia to De Roux, Aug. 19, 1941 (Germany file.)

[37] *Id.*

[38] De Roux to Winter, Aug. 28, 1941. (Germany file.)

[39] *[Boletín Semanal de Información para embajadas, legaciones y consulados.]* Winter was referring to the article entitled *"Panamá protesta ante Alemania."* ["Panama protests to Germany"], in which he considered that the word "Nazis" had been used disrespectfully to refer to the constructive work accomplished by the *Führer* of the German Reich. Winter to De Roux, Sept. 30, 1941. In Min. For. Rel., 1941 MEMORIA, p. 7.

[40] Executive Order № 117, Oct. 18, 1941. In *Id.*, p. 10.

[41] Oñós de Plandolit to Fábrega, Feb. 24, 1943. (Germany file.) Both this document and the report of the Mixed Commission indicate erroneously that Trudi was the wife of Paul Häusle, rather than his sister.

[42] Camilo de la Guardia Jr. to Fábrega, Feb. 24, 1943 (Germany file) repeating the erroneous reference to the late Paul Häusle as the "husband" of his sister Gertrude.

[43] [Gonzenbach to de Roux and *Note Verbale*, July 23, 1941, (Switzerland file, Archives Min. For. Rel. [?], reproduced in facsimile in Hassán, 8th and 9th pp. following p. 242, (also misnumbered).]

[44] De Roux to Camilo De la Guardia, Note № 1,743. July 28, 1941. (Switzerland file. Archives Min. For. Rel.)

[45] Ernesto Jaén Guardia, Panamanian Ambassador to the U.S., to Min. For. Rel., Dec. 17, 1941. In Min. For. Rel., 1941 MEMORIA 650.

[46] Gonzenbach to Fábrega, Note, Jun. 29, 1943. (Switzerland file.)

[47] Naville to Alfaro, Feb. 11, 1043. (*Ibid.*)

[48] J. A. Pretelt to Burgos, Feb. 27, 1946. (*Ibid.*)

[49] Naville to Alfaro, Apr. 22, 1946. (*Ibid.*)

[50] *Id.*, Jan. 30, 1947. (*Ibid.*)

[51] Alfaro to Sucre, Jan. 31, 1947. (*Ibid.*)

[52] Burgos to Alfaro, № 475, Feb. 22, 1947. (*Ibid.*)

[53] Morales, C.J. to Burgos, 2nd Sect., Min For. Rel., № 492, Mar. 3, 1947 (*Ibid.*)

[54] Decision, 2nd Sup. Tribunal, August 18, 1953. [Emphasis added.]

V | THE DISPOSITION OF THE COMMUNE'S PROPERTY

1 | THE SURVIVORS

AFTER WHAT HAD happened on July 7, the families that composed the colony disintegrated. Of the twenty–three colonists, eleven survived, almost all of them women and children.

- Gottfried Werren, 62, lost his wife Klara and his elder daughter, Klärli. He and his younger daughter Cornelia, 16, survived.

- Margarethe Schmieder, having lost her husband Karl and firstborn Karl Jr., had only her younger son Albert. [She later married Gustav Haug, Sr., the Swiss who had left the colony to farm at Santa Clara.]

- Sophie Baumann Müller lost her husband and Werner Robert his father, Werner Sr.

- The Morf children, Leonora ("Loni"), Walter and Elfriede ("Friedy") lost both their parents, Albert and Elfriede, [and their brother, Albert Jr.]

- Trudi Häusle, having lost her brother Paul, remained alone.

- Viola Wehrli, was the only colonist who did not lose a family member [in the massacre, although her son Virgilio had died under questionable circumstances just before the group sailed from Genoa.*]

Among the German neighbors of the colony, the Brauchle and Schaper families also suffered losses.

- Martha Schaper lost her brother Karl Schmieder [and nephew Karl Jr., but her sister–in–law Margarethe and nephew Albert survived].

- Alfred and Lydia Brauchle lost their son Helmut.

The question of the disposition of the colonists' property then arose. With the death of all the able–bodied men, there also arose the immediate problem of the management of the cropland, the cattle and the effects of the colonists, which had considerable value. The estate had suffered losses when valuable equipment was removed from the colony's premises while the survivors were convalescing in the hospital in David. In addition, the communal ownership practiced by the colonists, probably not recorded in writing, surely complicated the disposition of the various legacies. Urgent steps to secure these assets had to be taken, and this the Mixed Commission and the survivors themselves undertook.

2 | MEASURES TO SECURE THE ASSETS

| THE INTERVENTION OF THE MIXED COMMISSION

THE GERMAN–SWISS Mixed Commission went beyond compiling its detailed report on the incident of July 7 and the circumstances giving rise to it. They were also concerned with the future of the survivors. After they had discussed the matter with the Panamanian authorities, in particular with Minister De la Guardia, a provisional plan was adopted. "The Minister of Government and Justice assured

---

* [See her sworn statement, Appendix B, p. 194, *infra*.]

the diplomats that the Panamanian government would cooperate in the rebuilding of the farm and that it would assist in the probate of the property of each of the deceased."[1]

The women and children would return to the farm once they had recovered from their injuries. A Swiss citizen named Alfred Waser would take charge of the management of the farm, but all important decisions would be taken by a committee of neighbors including the Germans Brauchle, Schaper and Hils, and the Swiss Haug and Waser.[2] The loss of several head of cattle, personal items, tools, clothing and food—during the period when the police had custody of the property—was confirmed, and was [later] admitted by former police officers Aurelio Serracín and Efraín González, (although they denied any personal involvement). The Mixed Commission [then] took an inventory of whatever property could be located and arranged for the government to lift its order freezing the assets of the colony. It should be remembered, in this regard, that the seizure of the assets had occurred as part of the investigation of supposed acts of rebellion committed by the colonists, not an investigation of the multiple deaths caused by the police.

| THE ACTIONS OF THE SURVIVORS

AFTER LEAVING José Domingo De Obaldía Hospital, the survivors, headed by Gottfried Werren, petitioned the First Circuit Court of Chiriquí to take the necessary steps to secure and inventory the property left by the deceased colonists. In Panamanian law, this measure of a precautionary nature is considered a logical preliminary step in preparing for the disposition of any decedent's property. The judge of the First Circuit Court, Félix Abadía, directed the Bugaba County[*] Judge A. A. Herrera, to go to Cotito to inventory and secure the property. On October 18, 1941, Judge Herrera, accompanied by his clerk Noel Del Cid and the official appraisers designated to as-

---

[*] [*Juez municipal*. As "municipal" in English implies a township or city, and "district judge" could be confused with judges of the First (Appellate) Judicial District, "county judge," *i.e.*, for the *municipio* governing the *district* of Bugaba, seems the least confusing translation.]

sess the value of the property arrived at Cotito to fulfill their judicial assignment. There they found Gottfried Werren, Margarethe Schmieder, Sophie Müller, Viola Wehrli, Trudi Häusle and the minors Walter and Loni Morf, Werner Robert Müller and Albert Schmieder, who also participated in the procedure. Alfred Waser, the appointed temporary administrator, was also present.

Significantly, neither any of the German neighbors nor [the Swiss] Gustav Haug—who as members of the committee of neighbors were supposed to participate in any important decisions under the arrangement worked out by the Mixed Commission—were present. The procedure was required to be extremely detailed with respect to identifying the property and in establishing as precisely as possible its value, and it was required that the inventory and appraisal include, separately, the value of the land, the principal house and outbuildings, the cattle, and then the household effects, tools and other items. The procedure took all day, ending at about 6:00 PM.

- The untitled land, which the appraisers calculated at about fifty–six hectares, forty of them under cultivation as improved pasture, and the rest woods, were valued at $B\!/\!.760$ (at the rate of $B\!/\!.15$ per hectare [about U.S. $7 an acre] for the area under cultivation and $B\!/\!.10$ for unimproved land).

- The dwelling house, with its three outbuildings (kitchen, storeroom and apiary), all built of wood, were valued at $B\!/\!.300$.

- The animals included seventy head of cattle (mostly breeding stock, but including calves), two horses, a mare, five colts and thirty hens and chickens, valued at $B\!/\!.817.50$.

- Curiously, the appraisers, although they took a detailed inventory of the household goods and implements of labor, assigned no value to them.[3]

Judge Herrera ordered the farm, house and livestock turned over to the receiver, Alfred Waser. As for the household goods and implements of labor in the custody of Margarethe Schmieder, they were to continue in her care. Mrs. Schmieder, however, declared that certain valuable items of jewelry had disappeared:

- Three watches (a wristwatch and two pocket watches) of Swiss manufacture; [and] two rings engraved with the name Karl Schmieder.

In addition, they were missing—

- forty bed sheets of white fabric, four camel's hair blankets, six ordinary blankets, a brand-new length of cloth sufficient for a man's suit, a roll of ordinary canvas, fourteen pairs of new shoes brought from Switzerland, and two buckets of medium weight.

- From the tools were missing five planes for tongue-and-groove milling, six handsaws, three pairs of pliers, eight pairs of needle-nosed and awl-nosed pliers, four hammers, a saddle, three pack saddles, three saddle baskets, eight saddle covers [*tapasilla*], a new canvas [for] saddle covers, six meters in length, three augurs, two hundred pounds of honey, as well as other small items such as thread, scissors, etc.[4]

Mrs. Schmieder, who as representative of the colonists signed the inventory, valued the losses at ฿/. 15. The appraisal fixed the total value of the colony's goods at ฿/. 1,877.50, in 1941 a considerable sum that did not include the value of the assets at Piedra Candela and the personal property that had not been inventoried. It is also probable that the area of the farm was much larger than fifty-six hectares, if we consider that a few years later, in 1954, Francisco Sicilia obtained the rights to the Cotito farm from the government and registered the respective title, declaring that its area was 123.015 hectares [>260 acres].[5]

Although the inventory and appraisal was conducted, there is no evidence that the survivors filed for probate in the Chiriquí Circuit courts.

HÄUSLE-WORRELL FAMILY PHOTO, COURTESY YVONNE WORRELL POVER

WIDOW AND ORPHANS. In this late-July, 1941, photo, taken just weeks after the massacre, survivors housed at the Franciscan convent in David seem curiously relaxed, although young Robert seems to favor his right arm and shun footwear. Margarethe Schmieder, wounded in face, spine and lung, appears much recovered. Obviously, the nuns thought proper young ladies—perhaps to their relief—should not dress in rough men's work clothes. New haircuts for the boys are in evidence. Back row (*L-R*): Mother Superior Martina, Margarethe ("Gretel") Schmieder, Vio Wehrli, "Friedy" Morf, Sister Metarda, Walter Morf, Cornelia Werren, Trudi Häusle. Front Row: Robert Müller, Albert Schmieder, Loni Morf, Sister Regina. Sophie Müller whose son is present, does not appear in the picture.

3 | THE PROBLEMS OF INHERITANCE

AN EQUITABLE DISTRIBUTION of the property was called for, but the régime of communal ownership did not make it an easy task. Did the farm belong to the Swiss colonists, as Robert Müller [throughout the remainder of his life] asserted, because they had paid off

Schmieder's [alleged] debt [to a sister in the United States]?[*] If not, how was each colonist's contribution of capital and labor to the aggregate value of the property to be calculated? The practical difficulties of employing judicial procedures to untangle the property issues in a remote area such as Cotito, and possibly the absence of documents substantiating possible rights, led to postponement of the matter, with Mrs. Schmieder continuing as manager of the farm. Slowly the bonds of solidarity among the survivors began to unravel. The void left by a charismatic leader such as Lehner could not easily be filled, and the lack of leadership began to have serious effects, especially economic. Exterior factors also affected the process. Alfred Waser's inefficient stewardship and the marriage of Margarethe Schmieder to Gustav Haug, which involved the latter [a non–member of the commune] in the practical administration of the assets, accelerated the dissolution of the commune organized years before at Vairano.

| Alfred Waser's stewardship

THE FARM AND livestock were entrusted in October, 1941, to the management of Alfred Waser—who lived at Piedra Candela—as receiver. Nevertheless, according to Robert Müller, Waser, living far away from the colony and managing his own affairs, paid little attention to the colony's assets, being rather more interested in the young Elfriede Morf, but as the young woman did not return his interest, he left the colony for good and it is not known if he rendered an account of his management.[6] In such circumstances as these, Margarethe Schmieder had to reassume management of the farm. She was practically the only person who spoke Spanish, and legally appeared to be the natural heir to the assets of her late husband Karl, to whom the principal assets, *i.e.* the main house and the livestock,

---

* [Margarethe Schmieder lived out her years, remarried, on the street then known as *la Calle del Matadero ("Slaughterhouse Rd.")* in Volcán. She vigorously disputed the claim made by the Müllers that some putative debt of the Schmieders' had been paid by the colonists.]

had legally belonged. For another thing, the principles practiced by the followers of Father Divine began to be applied less rigorously.

The internal dissensions always came down to questions of money and the restrictions that now seemed intolerable. The women began to argue about the respective contributions of financial capital of their respective husbands, and they complained about the oppressive life they were living, which prohibited their going out or eating what they pleased. In addition, there were worries about the future of the children, who did not even attend school regularly, and who could not learn a trade in the practically abandoned colony itself.

SENN FAMILY PHOTO
An apparently troubled Sophie Müller (r) with Swiss neighbor Mrs. Brünnhilde Senn and daughter, Volcán, late 1940's.

The distribution of the assets, considerably augmented by the lease of land to the construction company building the Pan–American Highway,[*] seemed essential.

| THE RETURN OF GUSTAV HAUG

THIS DISPOSITION OF the property was not carried out by a civil judge who determined the rights of inheritance and gave legal sanction to the distribution. In practical terms, it fell to Gustav Haug [Sr.], the Swiss who had been interested in travelling to Panama to-

---

* [At the time, it was thought the Pan–American Highway would be built along the David–La Concepción–Volcán–Río Sereno highland route. The contractors leased land from the colonists at Cotito to construct one of their road camps. When construction was resumed after World War II, the highway was rerouted along the coastal route of the railroad from David, via La Concepción, to the border crossing at Paso Canoas. In the 1954 survey of the Cotito property, however, the road is still shown as *Carretera Interamericana*.]

gether with Lehner in 1938, and had been included in the group that applied for immigration visas. Gustav Haug Sr. and Jr. made the trip on their own in [July, 1939], but were expected, once established, to bring the rest of their family. Nevertheless, the family, for reasons unknown, was never reunited. What is certain is that, the Haugs [father and son] arrived at Cotito and joined the colonists who had preceded them. Robert Müller recalls that they arrived one afternoon of continuous rain, and, having identified themselves, said they belonged to the colony, and as all were welcome there, father and son were lodged in the house.

The unique rules for daily living soon raised strong disagreements between Gustav Haug and Karl Lehner. Müller asserts that Haug and his son began to transfer part of the colony's goods to a farm they had begun to work in the area of Santa Clara, a few kilometers to the west of Cotito.

HÄUSLE-WORRELL FAMILY PHOTO, COURTESY YVONNE WORRELL POVER

In 1945, survivor Trudi Häusle, by then married to Ray Russell Worrell, a U.S. citizen she had met in the Canal Zone, returned on a visit to Cotito. Here, Albert Schmieder, about 9, whose mother had remarried Gustav Haug, is shown with a traditional Panamanian harvesting basket called a *motete* (a smaller version, for harvesting coffee cherries, is called a *java*). The infant is Trudi Häusle Worrell's daughter Yvonne, about 5 months old.

He began to take all kinds of seed, part of the cattle, horses, bales of fodder, bananas, lumber, everything, to Santa Clara; he said that it was for his son and he did not attend our meetings.[7]

Lehner then admonished him severely, told him that in the colony everyone worked for the common good and not for anyone in particular, and that Haug did not want to help with anything or participate in the decisions of the colony. He told him that if he did not wish to belong

SENN FAMILY PHOTO

Robert Müller with one of the trucks he so expertly maintained, *ca.* 1950. In later years, he wore the full beard customary in the colony.

to the colony, he should keep what he already had at Santa Clara, but that he should not come back.

Haug then got angry, and went to spread rumors about the colony to the police and to other people in the area, and that, Müller relates, was the source of the conflict.[8],[*]

As for Haug, he asserts that he distanced himself from the colony little by little because he realized that behind the love and kindness that they showed to the outside world, there existed completely irrational conduct that, sooner or later, would carry them to a tragic end. The spiritual thought of Lehner, he asserts, was a mixture of yoga, Sufi, Rosacrucianism, [and] Christianity, but also included black magic and a lot of suggestion.[9]

> Four times I tried to enter into conversation with him and to help these people, to resolve questions that were unclear, but nobody paid attention to me and I refused for obvious reasons to go to the colony.
>
> For his people, "Molch" was Christ. There are no words to describe how nice this man could be, but, ¡ay!, if anybody criticized the ends this colony pursued, "I dare," he said, "to be [both] your Savior and Beelzebub in one single person." He filled his people with kindness, love and wisdom. He calmed them with words, but he also mistreated them physically and spiritually.[10]

Gustav Haug says that he was very sorry for the death of his countrymen, and in a letter to his friend Emil Faeh, he categorized as stupidity the news reports in the daily papers to the effect that the Cotito colonists were involved in espionage activities on behalf of the Nazis. Sometime after the incident, Haug and the Widow Schmieder [whose son Albert also survived] were joined in marriage, the Cotito farm was sold, and the survivors liquidated their interests. The Morf children, who lost both father and mother, were entrusted to foster

---

[*] [Again Müller, interviewed by the Author, impugns the honesty of other members of the colony.]

The survivors stayed in touch through the remainder of their lives, several having moved to the United States. Seated, *L-R*: Elfriede Morf Gilcrease and Trudi Häusle Worrell; standing, Albert Schmieder, Loni Morf Marshall, Walter Morf. 1990's photo. As this revised English edition was being prepared, only Albert Schmieder was still living.

homes. The little Loni remained in the care of the Franciscan sisters at the *Nuestra Señora de los Ángeles* boarding school in David. Her brother Walter was sent to live with Raymond Weil at Pedro Miguel in the Canal Zone. As for Elfriede, she traveled to the United States and lived in Oakland, [New Jersey]. Trudi Häusle obtained employment in the Canal Zone in Panama. Only Sophie Müller and her son Werner Müller refused to accept their share of the legacy.

4 | THE SALE OF THE COTITO FARM

AT THE BEGINNING of the nineteen–fifties, Margarethe Schmieder [Haug] and Gustav Haug decided to sell the Cotito farm, as they planned to move to El Hato del Volcán. Margarethe was approximately 50 years old, and Gustav Sr. must have been about the same age. "The Santa Clara farm would remain the property of Gustav Jr., who had married young Cornelia Werren." [The children of Gustav Haug Jr. and Cornelia Werren live in Volcán and David.]

Despite the construction of a branch of the old Pan–American Highway linking Volcán with the frontier post of Río Sereno, a rough gravel road that rescued the farm from decades of isolation, the Haug–Schmieders declined to continue working the farm, now devoted to the cultivation of coffee and fruit trees. →What happened to the colony's livestock is unknown.[*]← We have not been able to establish the exact date when Margarethe Schmieder sold her homestead rights to the farm to the Spanish farmer Francisco Sicilia García, a naturalized Panamanian citizen who then lived in La Concepción.

We have no record of the price of the sale, although we do know that when Sicilia decided to put his affairs in order at the beginning of 1955, completing the process for obtaining full title to the Cotito farm from the government,[11] he paid the government $B/.394$, declaring that the improvements included "seventy hectares, more or less, of pasture, approximately one hectare of bananas, one hectare of coffee, and a small orchard of fruit trees," valued at $B/.1,500$, which, added to the value of the land, gave a total value of $B/.1,894$.[12]

What is certain is that a share of the proceeds from the sale to Sicilia and the other income received was due to the survivors, although Margarethe Schmieder and her son Albert had the right to the largest percentage, since they were the heirs to the property of the late Karl Schmieder, which was the greatest portion of the total value. Gustav Haug, as the new *pater familias,* took charge of the distribution of the assets, which were not entirely in cash. Müller asserts that each of the survivors—except for his mother Sophie and him, as they had refused to accept anything—received $B/.80$ at the time the farm was sold. Haug also arranged for the Morf orphans to travel to the United States to continue their education and take up residence. Albert, the Schmieders' surviving son, [lived in Volcán

---

* [Although Albert Schmieder recalls that it was sold in a single lot. He also says Haug's report of his assistance to the Morf orphans in relocating to the United States was exaggerated.]

and Panama City before he] traveled to the United States, [where he served in the Army, lived in Chicago and eventually] California.[13] ["Vio" Wehrli married the Swiss immigrant Meinhard Fassler, and they lived for several years in Puerto Armuelles where he was employed by the banana plantation, and had two children. Later they returned to Switzerland. Trudi Häusle and Friedy Morf eventually married American servicemen and moved to the United States.]

5 | THE MÜLLERS' RESERVATIONS

ONLY THE MÜLLERS, mother and son, declined to accept the decisions of Gustav Haug and Margarethe Schmieder. Haug approached the Swiss consulate regarding medical care for Sophie, who had never completely recovered from the serious injuries she had sustained. Thought was also given to sending Werner Robert to Switzerland, but that did not come to fruition. The open confrontation between the Müllers and the Haug–Schmieders grew more acute when Sophie and Robert Müller left the colony to live in the home of Waser at Piedra Candela, where [Müller asserts] they suffered great privation. Müller recalls that they had to eat like animals, raw corn and *chayotes*[*] boiled in a tin can. They dreamed of the bananas, the milk and the cheeses they had enjoyed in the colony. His mother then married another Swiss named Emil Wachter, who also lived at Piedra Candela, and moved there permanently, while the child was sent back to Cotito. [Later,] Wachter went down to Cotito and told Robert that his mother wanted him with her at Piedra Candela, and the child responded that he would have to get the permission of Margarethe and Viola, but [he claimed] they refused and threatened to provide him with neither food nor clothing if he disobeyed.† And

---

* [The fruit of a vine in the summer–squash family, prolific and cheap in Panama.]

† [The travails of Sophie Baumann Müller Wachter, reported by the Swiss consul in May, 1945, to be living with one Meinrad Fassler (who later married Viola Wehrli), continued until her death, while relatives of her late husband Werner Müller in Switzerland tried unsuccessfully to arrange for the son's education. At one point the Swiss community in Chiriquí recommend-

Continued→

thus it was that wearing shorts and barefoot, Werner Robert Müller set out on foot to Piedra Candela.[14]

Sometime later, Sophie (Müller) Wachter, *née* Baumann, then living in Cerro Punta, sought the assistance of attorney Eduardo Morgan to enforce her rights in the courts, but all efforts, until she died in 1990, failed. The son, who still expresses his dissatisfaction, lays claim still to a portion of the land to keep bees, as his parents had done.

6 | COTITO TODAY

IN 1955, FRANCISCO Sicilia García obtained title to the Cotito farm. For many years, he engaged in the working of his agricultural property, making such improvements as the construction of various outbuildings including storerooms and workshops. The Schmieders' old wooden house was replaced by a new building of concrete block.

On June 30, 1973, Francisco Sicilia died, and the undivided interest in his farm, now valued at B/.9,920, passed to his heirs Rosario Brauchle *née* Sicilia, Pedro Antonio Sicilia Saldaña, Orfidio Sicilia Bouche and Raquel Sicilia Álvarez.[15] In 1978, Orfidio Sicilia Bouche bought out the two–thirds interest of the other heirs, becoming sole owner of the property.[16] Today, the Sicilia farm is a beautiful coffee plantation watered by the Cotito River, [adjacent to] the Volcán–Río Sereno highway, just west of the bridge over the Cotito River and immediately before the long, curved ascent leading to the village of Santa Clara.

← *Continued from prev. page.*
ed psychiatric hospitalization for Sophie, but she resisted. The portrayal in later years by Werner Robert of himself and his mother as victims of Gustav Haug and Margarethe, Haug's second wife and the widow of Karl Schmieder, appears to be greatly exaggerated. The reader is cautioned to consider carefully the likelihood of some of Robert Müller's specific allegations against individuals. There is also some ambiguity, resulting from multi-level translations and the Panamanian pronunciations given German surnames, between the names of Waser, who was appointed to oversee the colony's property, and Wachter, the Swiss whom Sophie Müller subsequently married.]

Opposite the house of Orfidio and Digna Sicilia [was] an area about four meters square surrounded by maguey cactus and *abeto* palms; just beneath a gourd palm may be found the common grave of the ten victims who lost their lives on the morning of July 7, 1941. These mortal remains once again lie in their original place, having been exhumed, in 1980,[*] for reasons of unutterable political appetite, in what was not so much an exhumation but rather bore all the signs of an inexpressible profanation [which would be repeated yet again in 1984 in an event apparently staged for a CNN reporter from the United States.

[D^{ra}. B.R. Thayer recalls that CNN then took certain osseous remains to the U.S. for forensic analysis, and reported that they were those of a young female.[17] Those remains from a grave in which lay six men, two boys, one middle-aged woman, and one young woman, were *a fortiori* those of Klärli Werren, whose death and burial were already recorded in Panamanian, Swiss and German records and the memories of survivors and neighbors. Even Klärli's sister Cornelia, then married to Gustav Haug Jr. and living in Volcán, could easily have been consulted, if Arnett had bothered to inquire. Instead, like so many others, he relied on the perfervid imaginings of Hassán.]

---

* [Hassán gives the date of this exhumation in his book *Holocausto en Panamá* as the day following "the last Thursday in October, 1980," which would have been October 31. For dating, *see* Hassán, pp. 10–11, as well as the statements of the mother and wife of the present owner of the gravesite, p. 170, *supra*. For his cynical re-staging of the exhumation for the benefit of a U.S. television reporter successfully hoodwinked by the Ardito Barletta campaign in 1984, *see* p. 177, *infra*.]

Notes to Chapter V

[1] *Ibid.*

[2] Winter, Note.

[3] Report of Inventory and Appraisal (Oct. 18, 1941; *see* p. 35 n.34, *supra*).

[4] *Id.*

[5] *See* Parcel 6,569, 649 Chiriquí Provincial Land Register 314.

[6] Müller (p. 4, n.*, *supra*).

[7] Müller.

[8] *Id.*

[9] Gustav Haug to Emil Faeh, Jun., 1941. (Transl. German to Spanish by Franz Hunkeler.)

[10] *Id.*

[11] Office of the Notary Public for the Chiriquí Circuit, Property Deed № 145 (March 18, 1955); recorded in the Civil Registry, July 22, 1955.

[12] *Id.*

[13] *See* page xxxi, *supra*.

[14] Müller.

[15] First Circuit Court for the Chiriquí Circuit, Civil Branch, № 276, July 19, 1974.

[16] Olga Bouche, intv. with Author, La Concepción (Chir.), Apr. 20, 1992, Digna de Sicilia, intv. with Author, Cotito (Chir.), Jan. 21, 1993.

[17] Intv. with Ed., date unrecorded.

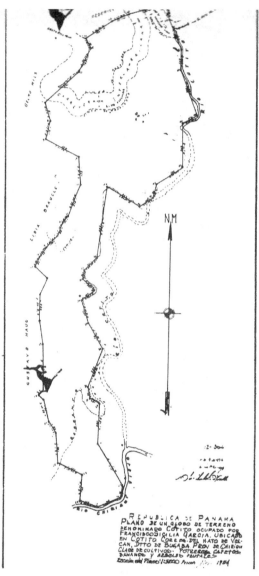

Surveyor's 1954 plat of the Cotito Farm, as recorded in the land registry by Francisco Siciia García in 1955. At lower right, the confluence of the ríos Cotito and Chiriquí Viejo. Adjoining property owners are shown (N-S) as "Gelmo" Hils, "Lidia Braucle" and "Gustavo" Haug.

First page of a formal letter in old German calligraphy on Adolf Hitler's personal letterhead, signed at "Berchtesgaden, Oct. 19, 1940," congratulating "Herr Präsident" Arnulfo Arias on his inauguration. The text of the letter, found in the national archives of Panama, is formulaic, expressing a desire for "even stronger" relations between the *Reich* and Panama. There is no hint of a personal relationship between the German chancellor and the new President.

PHOTO *HOLOCAUSTO EN PANAMÁ*, 1982
Pointless 1980 police exhumation of mass grave begins.

Gravesite as it appeared in 1993; at left Sicilia family home.
PHOTO BY THE AUTHOR

VI | 'HOLOCAUST' IN PANAMA, OR, A HOAX DISTORTING THE TRUTH

1 | THE ORIGINS OF A DECEPTIVE* BOOK

AFTER PROSECUTOR GÓMEZ ARAÚZ ordered the inhumation of the remains in the common grave [following the forensic examination of Dr. Colindres in 1941], nearly forty years would pass before the sepulcher of the Cotito victims was reopened by members of the same institution that had snatched away their lives.

As confirmed by Mrs. Olga Bouche and Mrs. Digna Sicilia, respectively mother and wife of Orfidio Sicilia [current owner of the Cotito property], in 1980 agents of the *Guardia Nacional* under the command of Aristides Hassán, appeared at Cotito dressed in civilian clothes and removed the osseous remains of the eight Swiss and two Germans who had died on July 7, 1941.[1] →At that time, Hassán was writing his book *Holocausto en Panamá,* much discussed in the elections of 1984.←

---

* [The Author's title for this chapter is *Origen de un libro institucional,* the word *institucional* referring to the military "institution." As the phrase "institutional book" would make no sense to the English reader, it is altered in the translation.]

They furtively extracted some dental gold from the skulls, then packed up everything and took off for parts unknown. Months later, other members of the military force returned with the bones and buried them once again, approximately half a meter [≈20 inches] from the original site, as the excavation had loosened the consistency of the soil that covered the common grave.

Why was this new form of violence inflicted once again on the colonists by agents of the Panamanian military forces? Having long reflected on the matter, we conclude that the Cotito Swiss were once again victimized, but this time because of political intrigues, of the boundless ambition for power of the military oligarchy that had usurped the direction of the State in 1968, and which in 1984 would attempt, through obscure electoral maneuvering, to secure legitimacy of the popular vote. In the prologue to his book, Hassán confirms the validity of this thesis. He recalls how the story of the massacre of certain Swiss people in Chiriquí had been related to him by his mother, and explains how the idea of recounting the episode in a book, which at one time he thought might be titled *Paper Bridge,* came to him. However, the truth is that what might have been a serious intellectual effort turned into a rude hoax distorting the historical truth. Everything came down to an institutional maneuver to discredit politically the man who had been president of Panama in 1941 [and again in 1951, and again briefly in 1968,] and who in 1984 would appear to be the most important opposition candidate: Arnulfo Arias Madrid. The plan was simple, but no less fantastic.

Around the framework of a genuine event, the crime against the colonists at Cotito, Hassán would weave the commission of other crimes that had never occurred, such as the supposed murder of two colonies of German Jews, one at Sierra de Palo Alto in Boquete and the other, in the region of Cotito itself.

The book [alleges that the] order for extermination had been given in person by Adolf Hitler, as part of an imaginary Nazi conspiracy in Latin America whose purpose was to exterminate Jewish communities that had managed, by putting distance between them, to evade Gestapo and SS persecution in Germany and the occupied countries. Hassán alleges that Arnulfo Arias was a Nazi agent and was willing to organize and execute a Jewish *Holocausto en Panamá*.

This idea, supposedly documented in Hassán's book and widely disseminated in the pro–government media in Panama, was intended to attract the attention of the influential U.S. Jewish community, strong pillar of the economic power of the Superpower, in order to convince them, subtly, that in Panama, it would be preferable if the elections were won by a military institution accustomed to running the country with a strong hand, not the elderly and disconcerting populist leader who, sadistically, had exterminated the innocent children of Israel in the mountains of Chiriquí. To accomplish this, it would be necessary for U.S. television networks to be willing to furnish reports showing, as graphically as possible, the clues to the alleged Jewish holocaust at Palo Alto and Cotito. Contact was made with the CNN network, which sent a television crew to Panama, directed by an experienced journalist.

From the beginning, the military clique ruling Panama was kept abreast of the project, because it was no secret that General Omar Torrijos Herrera was considered the "natural" candidate to squelch the re-election ambitions of Arias Madrid in 1984. Hassán confirms this when he says, in his prologue, that he was given a brief period of free time to write his book "thanks to a great boss and friend, who believed, as I did, in this odd history."[2] This "great boss and friend" in 1980 was none other than Omar Torrijos Herrera[; he] had not only authorized Hassán to produce this false version of Panamanian history[; he] also made available the means necessary for the author of *Holocausto* to organize a "well planned expedition" (as he called it) that would identify the sites where the imaginary German Jewish victims were killed and the places where they had been buried.[3]

Hassán asserts that on the last Thursday in October, 1980, [October 30, fittingly the day before Hallowe'en] at 3:30 AM, the expedition left from Chitré on a route that would take it [from] David [up to] Potrerillos, Boquete, [and] Palo Alto; [then back to] David, [from there west to] Bugaba [as La Concepción is commonly known], and finally [up to] Volcán and [west to] Cotito.

Despite the novelistic description that the author gives of his "efforts" to find the common grave of the "Jews" at Cotito, which he says was found by Julio César González "that afternoon, before nightfall," the truth is that Hassán and his men traveled to Cotito and, in front of the Sicilia home, began to dig up the grave of the Swiss colonists at a location known for forty years.

Anyone making an examination of the photographs published in Hassán's book, showing the excavation in the Sicilias' front yard, will immediately recognize the maguey cactuses and the *jícara* palm reverently planted over the grave by the surviving Cotito victims. That grave holds no remains of German–Jewish colonists, whom no one else had ever heard of. Apart from [the Moravian Czech Alois Hartmann's family,] the Schapers, Hilses, Brauchles, Schmieders and Lehner's colonists, no other community of German immigrants had ever settled at Cotito...or in Palo Alto, Boquete. But the historical truth had no importance for this hoax, which served the purposes of the electoral campaign of 1984; hence the strongest criticism that can be leveled against Hassán's book: it falsifies Panamanian history in order to serve subordinate interests.

2 | A FAILED ELECTORAL STRATEGY

HASSÁN'S BOOK WAS, according to the title page, published outside Panama [*i.e.*, in Bogotá] in 1982, but it was not until two years later that the Panamanian public began to be acquainted with it, and not just because it was offered for sale in the country's bookstores.* Starting in the first few months of 1984, the electoral campaign having begun, the pro–government dailies *El Matutino ["The Morning Paper"]* and *Crítica* began to treat the subject of the supposed massacre of Jews at Cotito and Palo Alto, as if these were historical facts that had occurred during the 1941 administration of Arnulfo Arias.

---

* Guillermo Sánchez Borbón, in his column *"En pocas palabras,"* ["In short..."], *La Prensa,* Apr. 18, 1984, states that the entire edition was seized by the National Guard, although a few copies circulated around the city. The daily *Crítica* reported, on Apr. 25, 1984, that the entire edition had been bought up by the Arias family.

Omar Torrijos had died on July 31, 1981, but the military plan to hold power remained in effect.

The government–backed ticket, composed of Nicolás Ardito Barletta, Eric Arturo Del Valle and Roderick Esquivel[, respectively the candidates for the first and second vice–presidencies,] was to face off against the octogenarian Arnulfo Arias Madrid, and Hassán's book was back on stage. On April 9, 1984, *El Matutino* published an unsigned, front–page article, stating that Dr. Esquivel was publicly challenging ex–president Arias to clarify the massacre at Cotito and Palo Alto that had occurred during his administration in 1941, and in which German children, women and elderly men had been murdered during the morning hours. Esquivel accused Luis [*i.e.*, Alois] Hartmann of having directly participated in the murder of German Jews. The author, without citing a specific source, wrote that—

> in the month of January, 1941, Dr Arnulfo Arias then being president, hired the services of Guatemalan Colonel Gómez Ayau to come to this country to "reorganize the national Police," [and] that in July of the same year, Gómez Ayau headed a group of mercenaries who attacked the Hebrew colonists while they slept at Sierra de Palo Alto at approximately 3:00 in the morning, raped the women and later threw them into a common grave.
>
> Later, they perpetrated another equally iniquitous slaughter at Cotito, where they killed the Swiss Carlos Schmieder and his wife Margarethe; Paul Häusle, Werner Müller, Heinrich Ott, Helmut Brauche (sic), Albert Mort (sic) and his son; massacred Klara Werren and her 18–year–old daughter, and wounded Sophie Müller in the left arm, Robert Müller, age 1 (sic), Corn (sic) Werren in the finger, and others who miraculously escaped uninjured because they hid and who were subsequently pursued by the Arias Government for racial and religious reasons.[4]

Reading just page 198 of Hassán's book [which recites virtually the same list of casualties] is enough to determine where the information in the *Matutino* article came from, although the writer of the article adds on his own that Arnulfo Arias had pursued the Swiss after the slaughter "for racial and religious reasons," which is completely false.

The campaign to discredit the opposition candidate for posterity began with this publication. During the days to follow, *El Matutino* and *Crítica*, always in unsigned articles, began to administer almost daily doses of content from Hassán's book. They gave it full play toward the end of April, reproducing the book's cover on their front pages, although, curiously, obscuring the name of the author. They affirmed that "various international organizations had commissioned the book [another falsehood] under the title *Holocausto en Panamá,* to [report] on the homegrown Nazi–Fascist crimes in Panama under the administration of Dr. Arnulfo Arias Madrid."[5]

It was also reported that the book was a best seller whose Spanish text had been translated into French, German, Hebrew and English, and that the original documentation that provided the basis for its reporting had been obtained from the secret societies to which the perpetrators of the massacre had and still belonged.[6]

Assertions such as these indicate, that, in addition to the imaginary facts narrated by Hassán and which we analyze below, the anonymous ["]journalists["] at *El Matutino* added other bits of historical disinformation such as the following:

1. During the [Oct. 1940–Oct. 1941] administration of Dr. Arnulfo Arias Madrid, [Supreme Court] Justice Vitelio De Gracia closed the case and suspended the investigation into the crime against the Swiss at Cotito.[7]
2. The Swiss government reserved the right to claim the corresponding compensation in the cases of dozens of German families of Jewish religion who lost their lives.[8]
3. The slaughter was perpetrated on the orders of the President of the Republic at the time, Arnulfo Arias, who fired Prosecu-

tor Salazar from Chiriquí when he interrogated Captain Huff.⁹
4. The platoon of men commanded by Gómez Ayau assassinated foreign colonists who had lived in the country for more than thirty years.¹⁰

As we have noted previously—

1. Judge Angel Vitelio De Gracia was the author of the majority opinion of the Second Superior Tribunal, which, on August 18, 1953, dismissed charges against Huff and the other officers of the National Police. In 1953, Arias was not the president of Panama and the investigations had been suspended many years previously.
2. It would have been absurd for the Swiss government to reserve the right to claim compensation for victims of German nationality.[*]
3. Prosecutor Gonzalo Salazar was not removed by Arnulfo Arias. After October 9, 1941, date of the first ouster of Arnulfo, Salazar remained in his post, and it was not he but Abel Gómez Araúz who had attempted to interrogate Captain Huff.
4. Finally, none of the German and Swiss colonists had, as of 1941, lived in the Cotito area for more than 30 years.

As if so much disinformation were still not enough, the American CNN network sent their reporter Peter Arnett to Panama. He was well known for his reportage of the Vietnam War and in 1992 had been in Baghdad during [the First] Gulf War ["Operation Desert Storm"]. None of this experience accounted for very much, as Arnett was profoundly ignorant of the history and realities of Panama, and

---

* [It was actually the German *chargé d'affaires* who had reserved that right, with respect to four German fatalities and two injured German women in a note of July 26, 1941, addressed to Foreign Minister De Roux. *See* p. 141, *supra*.]

had swallowed whole Hassán's historical fiction about a supposed Jewish *Holocausto en Panamá* in 1941.

On April 16, 1984, coincidentally with the *Matutino* and *Crítica* campaigns, CNN broadcast a report on the Panamanian elections, focused on the figure of the opposition candidate, Arnulfo Arias, and on his supposed Nazi past, for which Roosevelt had [allegedly] removed him from power in 1941. Categorizing Hassán's book as a trustworthy historical source, Arnett presented his U.S. television viewers with the mortal remains of some of the Cotito colonists, as if they were the supposed German–Jewish victims, and related as authentic historical truth Arnulfo's fog–shrouded conspiracies to carry out an extermination ordered in Berlin. [Arnett was taken to the grave at Cotito by Hassán and others in the spring of 1984, when the election campaign was in full swing. The 1980 profanation of the grave was restaged for him and others, and bones[*] were again removed, one of which he took back to the United States for analysis. All this Arnett reported as if it were a genuine revelation confirming that candidate Arnulfo Arias was a Nazi sympathizer who had ordered the massacre of "Jews" at Cotito.[11]]

If [Arnett] had had even minimal knowledge of the events of July 7, 1941, in particular, and the facts, in general; if he had known even a little of Panamanian political history; if he had learned that Arnulfo Arias, a candidate again in 1948, 1964 and 1968, was never accused of these atrocities even by his most vicious enemies—which should have led him to intuit that Hassán's version was a hoax— Arnett would have presented a different version. Perhaps he did realize it on his next broadcast, when he opted to interview Arnulfo Arias himself, so that he could give his version of events at Cotito, the ex–president replying then that the responsibility had been entirely Huff's.[12]

Also during this period, twenty–two Panamanian citizens of Jewish religion issued a press release in which they stated for the record that there were no indications or evidence in the archives of

---

* [The bones were probably those of Klärli Werren. *See* p. 172, *supra*.]

Jewish congregations and community organizations that there had ever occurred, in the history of the Republic, slaughter or genocide conducted against members of the Jewish religion of any nationality.[13]

However, although Arnulfo Arias cannot be accused of the supposed slaughter of German Jews at Palo Alto [and Cotito], there is no doubt that he approved of the conduct of Huff, and the National Police in general, with respect to the events of July 7, 1941.

In any case, the electoral strategy based on Hassán's book was a total failure, because Arnulfo Arias amply defeated official candidate Ardito Barletta in the ballot boxes, only to be barred by blatant electoral fraud from again taking office as president.

3 | SALVAGING HISTORICAL TRUTH

WE CONSIDER IT our ineluctable duty to rectify the historical inaccuracies contained in *Holocausto en Panamá*, although they have no

Alois Hartmann, from the Austro-Hungarian province of Moravia, arrived in Western Chiriquí in 1912, and among other German-speaking immigrants aided the *Suizos* when they arrived. His family reports that injuries to his hand, sustained when he was left tied to a tree by the police after the massacre, plagued him all his life.

direct relation to the events at Cotito. We do so with the greatest objectivity, out of respect for the Panamanians, who have a legitimate right to know their national history—free from distortions imposed by those with their own interests—and that is the purpose of this book.

We begin:

1. ON PAGE 2, Hassán reproduces a fragment that he attributes to President Arnulfo Arias's inauguration speech of October 1, 1940. Arnulfo [allegedly] said—

> Just as Panama has ceded its lands to the United States for the construction of a Canal, so it may also cede lands to the Germany of Adolf Hitler, so that they can build whatever they wish here and assist us against Imperialism.

Comparing this paragraph with the official text of the address that was published in 1940 and reprinted in 1988,[14] it cannot be

JOSEF NIEDERBERGER (?) PHOTO
Earliest known photograph of the mass grave at Cotito. It was desecrated twice by Hassán, in 1980 and in 1984. Date of photo unknown.

found, which is why it should be considered completely spurious.

2. PAGE 14: Hassán and his men did not excavate the remains of eighteen German Jews at Cotito and rebury them in the same place before traveling to Volcán. In reality, they exhumed the remains of ten Swiss–Germans, and transported [some of] them, presumably, to Panama City, where Arnett later included them in his reportage for CNN. Neither did they find a second common grave—[containing, supposedly, the remains of other] Swiss–German [victims]—because the only grave is the one at Cotito [and a smaller one at Volcán].

3. PAGE 14: Werner Robert Müller was not one year old at the time of the events at Cotito. Born in the year 1931, he would have been 10 years old.

4. PAGES 24–25: German – Jewish families did not settle at either Cotito or Palo Alto in the nineteen–twenties. The Cotito pioneers were [Alois Hartmann, who arrived in the area in 1912 and whose descendants still raise coffee at Santa Clara, and] the four German families of the Hilses, the Schapers, the Brauchles and the Schmieders, who arrived in the region in 1928 and '29. Ten years later, the Swiss colonists, followers of Karl Lehner, arrived. None was Jewish.

PHOTO BY THE EDITOR
The common grave as it appeared in 2013, adjacent to the home of the Sicilia family, who surrounded it with a railing and replaced the original maguey and palms with flowering shrubs.

5. PAGE 75: Antonio Huff was not a member of *Acción Comunal*. Exhaustive review of the names of the members who attended the organizational meeting of the society on August 19, 1923, the mem-

bers who attended the next twenty meetings, which is to say all the meetings held by the organization, and the names of all 342 members who took the membership oath, shows that the name of Antonio Huff appears nowhere.[15]

6. PAGE 75: Captain Antonio Huff was not transferred from David on September 14, 1941; [he was transferred August6] and he was never tried [or even suspended].

7. PAGE 82: The arrangements for contracting the services of Lieutenant Colonel Gómez Ayau did not begin on December 6, 1941, [the day before the Japanese attacked Pearl Harbor], but a year earlier, in December, 1940 [just after Arnulfo Arias took office].

8. PAGE 86: Arnulfo Arias was not inaugurated as President of the Republic on October 1, 1931, but on October 1, 1940. In addition, he was removed from power on October 9, 1941, so he could not have appointed Julio Briceño commander of the National Police on December 19, 1941.

9. PAGE 154: Frank (not *Franck*) Tedman, was not a German citizen, but a Canadian. He was born in Toronto and arrived at Boquete early in the century. He had previously been employed by the Interoceanic Canal Company.

10. Page 156: Neither Karl Schmieder nor his wife Margarethe nor their sons Karl and Albert were Berliners, nor did they move to Cotito in the nineteen–thirties. The Schmieders were natives of Schramberg, in the German Black Forest. [The couple moved to Cotito in 1928; their son Karl was born at Camarón, near Santa Marta, Chiriquí, in 1930, and their son Albert at La Concepción in 1932.]

11. PAGE 156: The Schmieder house was not located nearly an hour's journey from the supposed German–Jewish colony at Cotito. In fact, the Schmieder house was the home of the only agricultural settlement known in the area, that of Lehner and his followers.

12. PAGE 156: Josef Niederberger was not a German citizen, but Swiss. He was taken by Huff to Cotito to serve as a witness to the delivery of the two ultimatums previously drafted by Huff himself.

13. PAGE 194: The maiden name of Werner Müller's wife was not Sophie Lesner, but rather Sophie Baumann. After Müller's death, she changed her surname [again] when she married Emil Wachter,

also a Swiss national. Paul and Gertrude Häusle were not spouses, but siblings.

14. PAGE 197: Karl Schmieder did not fire an old shotgun, nor did Karl Jr., who was not 15 years of age, but 11. Probationary Officer Lucas Garcés did not hold the rank of sergeant. Heinrich Ott did not die in a granary, but in the main house where all the others were struck down.

15. PAGE 198: Robert Müller was not a year old, but 10; Walter Morf was not 16, but 15; Cornelia Werren was not 18, but 16. Similarly, Viola Reiser was 33, Margarethe Schmieder [46], not 40, Gottfried Werren was 62, not 50, and Gertrude Häusle was 25, not 30. Ten persons died at Cotito, and on the road to Volcán, two more perished. In addition, including Garcés there were nine wounded, not five.

SCHMIEDER FAMILY PHOTO
The Schapers, Martha (*née* Schmieder) and Fritz, at Santa Clara, *ca.* 1962. Martha's brother Karl died in the massacre.

16. Page 202: The colonists' grave was not dug far from the house, but immediately in front of it. Mrs. Klara Werren and her daughter were not buried together at Volcán. Mrs. Werren's daughter Klärli died instantly and was buried in the common grave. →Mrs. Werren died *en route* to Volcán, and was buried there, as was Karl Schmieder Jr.← The wounded were not taken by car to David, but rather were put on the train from La Concepción.

17. Page 208: It was not on October 7, 1941, that Arnulfo Arias traveled incognito to Cuba, but rather two days later, on the 9th, when he was thrown out of office.

18. Page 212: It is a false statement to allege that the lands of the Swiss–Germans and the putative German Jews of Cotito were given by Arnulfo Arias to Luis Hartmann as a gift, and that he, in turn, sold the Swiss–Germans' property to Aristides Abadía, who resold it to Andrés De Puy.

HARTMANN FAMILY PHOTO, COURTESY OSVALDO IVÁN FLORES

By the mid-1920's, Alois Hartmann had a substantial family. The current patriarch is Ratibor ("Chicho") Hartmann. He and his son Ratibor Jr. continue to raise coffee on one of the most environmentally conscious farms in the area, a noted bird sanctuary.

It is also untrue that Hartmann sold the land of the supposed German–Jewish colonists in part to Gustav Haug (not *Houg*), in part to Anton Hils, and in part to Federico Schaper (not *Shaffers*) "on the condition that they speak negatively about the Swiss–German colony." The only land involved in this whole story was Karl Schmieder's farm, where Lehner's colony settled, and which was later sold by Schmieder's widow to Francisco Sicilia, who perfected the title to it in 1955.

INCREDIBLY, DESPITE ALL its historical falsehoods, Hassán's book was the object of a ["]scientific["] study at the University of Panama. In a paper, *"Un caso de genocidio en Panamá"* ["A Case of Genocide in Panama,"] presented to the IVth Conference on Critical Criminology held at Havana in September, 1986, criminologist Marcela Márquez reprinted virtually entire pages of *Holocausto en Panamá,* accepting as fact the settlement of the two colonies of German Jews at Palo Alto and Cotito. The paper reviews the *Estrella de Panamá* report of July 9, 1941, [which she quotes] from the commemorative magazine *Bugaba centenaria* (1963) and the version in the book *La historia de Panama en sus textos* ["The History of Panama in the Original Text*s*"],[16] v. II: 1903–1968, which agree that the only victims were the Swiss–German colonists of Cotito. Together with these, which she categorizes as "relevant historical texts," she gives equal place to *Holocausto en Panamá,* the only publication asserting that Arnulfo Arias ordered the extermination of German–Jewish colonists at Palo Alto and Cotito.

Further on in the dogmatic study she makes of the Cotito genocide, she asserts that "race or religious belief" (in this case, the Jewish religion) was one of the characteristics of the victims, and she fully accepts Hassán's fantastic version about the motivation for the lamentable criminal act.[17]

This demonstrates how cautious social researchers must be before subscribing to documents that end up outside the bounds of scientific research.

Notes to Chapter VI

[1] Bouche de Sicilia (p. 168, n. 16 *supra*).
[2] Hassán (p. lxxii, n. 5 *supra*), p. 10.
[3] *Ibid.*
[4] *El Matutino*, Apr. 9, 1984, pp. 1, 9A.
[5] *Id.*, Apr. 30, 1984.
[6] *Id.*, Apr. 27, 1984.
[7] *Id.*, Apr. 10, 1984.
[8] *Ibid.*
[9] *Ibid.*
[10] *Ibid.*
[11] [Drª Berta Ramona Thayer, who was present along with Arnett at this staged re-exhumation in 1984, has described it for the Ed. in private communications, 2013.]
[12] Sánchez Borbón, pp. 222-3.
[13] *La Prensa*, May 3, 1984.
[14] Inaugural Address (p. 48, n.4 *supra*).
[15] Isidro Beluche Mora, *Acción Comunal: Surgimiento y estructura del nacionalismo panameño ["Acción Comunal: The Rise and Structure of Panamanian Nationalism"]* (1981), pp. 35, 46-7, 114-9.
[16] Marcela Márquez, "Un caso de genocidio en Panama." In *Cuadernos panameños de criminología ["Panamanian Studies in Criminal Law"]*, № __ (1986), pp. 33-35.
[17] *Id.*, p. 35.

| EPILOGUE

THE MOMENT FOR venturing a preliminary conclusion about the events recounted in this history having arrived, we believe it is true that the intransigence of the colonists was the determining factor in the tragic outcome of the events of July 7, 1941, although it is also true that the tragedy could have been avoided if, as the Swiss representative concluded, the police had acted more humanely.

To deny that Lehner's personality and his complete domination over the colonists were the key elements in the disgraceful event would be to deny reality; but it also must be said that there were excesses on the part of the National Police, because the colonists were unarmed and never represented a threat to the men under the command of Antonio Huff, much less to the national government.

If we emphasize that the colonists did no more than barricade themselves in a house that was easily penetrable on all four sides, that was situated in a depression and was easily dominated from the adjacent hills, and that they had only food and rudimentary tools inside with them, we can demonstrate that, rather than having aggressive intentions, they merely fell back on their determination to resist an order they considered unjust and which the government could have rescinded, permitting the colonists to register where they were, as they had previously requested.

It is the human factor, rarely comprehended in the logic of the actions taken by the State, reflecting the humiliation to which Lehner and Ott had been subjected in David, that is the possible explanation of their obstinate resistance to going down to provincial police headquarters. On the other hand, almost as the integrative element of the tragedy, is the equally rigid position of the government, intolerant and even hostile, to those who resisted in any manner.

Proof of this assertion may be found in the terms of the threatening ultimatums authorized by the government and the no lesser obstinacy of Huff, deaf to the mediation offered by Wilhelm Probst that could have avoided the cruel outcome. The excessive force used by the police, completely unjustified in light of the nonexistent, imaginary firepower of the colonists, left exposed a crime that would have to be covered up. Hence, the infamy of the official statements that converted the victims into the perpetrators, and the agony of the interminable judicial investigation, prompted by the intervention of the government that guided it toward the exoneration of the police and, up the chain of command, the superior officers who ordered the police action.

This desire on the part of the national government, the desire to justify the unjustifiable, prolonged a thorny issue that occupied our foreign ministry for years, and which virtually denied the survivors of Cotito fair compensation for their human and material losses. To this injustice was added the indescribable manipulation of the mortal remains of the victims in order to invent a supposed Jewish holocaust in Panama, all within the feckless electoral strategy that failed to prevent Arnulfo Arias Madrid from returning to another triumph at the polls, as he had in 1948 and 1968.

Who could have imagined what lay in store for the Vairano colonists when they boarded the train at Chiasso, beginning the journey that would carry them to the soil of Panama!

| APPENDICES*

A | MY EXPERIENCES WITH THE 'MOLCH' COLONY†

GUSTAV HAUG SR.
TRANSLATED FROM THE GERMAN BY BARBARA TRABER‡

Volcán, July 1941

ONE DAY IN THE EARLY summer of the year 1938, two "wild men" with long hair and long beards visited me at Rovio, in the canton of Ticino. These men—[Werner] Müller and [Albert] Morf

---

* The Appendices do not appear in the Spanish edition of *Cotito*; they were added by the Editor.

† Written by Haug a few days after the massacre; forwarded on September 12, 1941, by the Swiss *chargé d'affaires* at Caracas, Adolf Gonzenbach, to the "Political Department" (foreign ministry) in Bern. *Chargé* Gonzenbach was a member of the German–Swiss "Mixed Commission" that had investigated the massacre a few days after it occurred.

The existing typescript may have been the transcription of a handwritten report or an oral statement taken from Haug. The translator indicates Haug's German was unsophisticated, replete with errors of punctuation and orthography, indicating he may have typed it himself. It would have been pointless to introduce new errors into the English in an attempt to reproduce the effect of the original. Hence, this translation may read somewhat more fluently than the original. Swiss Embassy (Caracas) Archives, now in *Bundesarchiv*, Bern, file № E 2001 (D) 1000/1553, vol. 116, B.31.11.Pan.2. (In these Appendices, all notes were inserted by the Editor of this English edition.)

‡ With assistance from the Ed.

were their names—had learned from Werner Zimmermann, the author of the book *Tropenheimat, Panama–Mexiko ["Tropical Homeland: Panama–Mexico"]* that in 1935–36, I had visited the interior of Chiriquí, a province of Panama. [Werner] Müller and [Albert] Morf asked for information about the conditions there, as their commune, living at Vairano, [in the canton of] Ticino, intended to emigrate to that region. As the two made quite a favorable, honest impression, I happily provided this information and recommended that—if they had thought through everything carefully—they should send a man to Panama to have a first–hand look at conditions and to make the necessary arrangements with the Government. [They] could then take the decision to emigrate on their own account. I was prepared to provide information about Cotito, but they would have to make the [final] decision to emigrate on their own. The addresses of prominent individuals and of my friend Karl Schmieder at Cotito [that I provided] made it easier for the delegated Albert Morf to arrange their affairs in Panama.

In the course of October 1938, I received news from Müller that everything had gone well and the colony planned to travel in December. The Government of Panama had provided 500 hectares [>1,100 acres] of land and they intended to live alone, two days from the next settlement, etc. As I knew nothing about the principles of the Vairano colony and their endeavors, I stopped on a trip with my family to Brissago, in Locarno, to visit these "naturists."

In Vairano, I found them in a small, untidy house. "Molch"* as their "chief" called himself, entered the room accompanied by Sophie Müller and Vio Wehrli at his left and right. A strangely luminous, piercing glance from the eyes of this person awakened an uncomfortable feeling in me and left me with an impression of Rasputin. I asked, among other things, about the aims and the [purpose] of the colony. "We want to cultivate free men," was Molch's answer. In the [ensuing] free conversation, the initial bad impression vanished,

---

* "Salamander" in German. The full name of the leader of the colony was Karl Lehner. *See* p. 32, n. 36, *supra*.

but, all the same, these people seemed eccentric. They promised also to arrange my immigration visa at the same time, because due to the crisis in the hotel business that had already lasted many years, I had decided to emigrate and to change to agriculture. My acquaintance with the colony began with this short visit.

On approximately December 1, 1938, Molch suddenly came to see me in Rovio, again in the company of Sophie Müller and Vio Wehrli. Vio seemed quite disturbed and Sophie also looked mentally deranged. Molch explained to me that Vio had to rest for about a week as the packing before departure had been too strenuous for her. I understood that the separation must have caused much inner struggle for many of them. For me, it was the same. I had first intended to travel with this group, but at the last minute I hoped to be able to sell my property in Rovio to a Jewish Professor Wonke, and therefore postponed my departure.

Sophie Müller and Vio Wehrli were to remain as guests at my hotel in Rovio for eight days. Molch left us on the same day, carrying a rucksack.* Vio and Sophie were strikingly timid and withdrawn. It was impossible to get to know anything about the colony; everything was vague, religious, mystical, occult. On a Sunday, about December 10, 1938, the colonists traveled from Bellinzona to Chiasso, near Genoa. I accompanied Sophie and Vio to the train and traveled with them as far as Chiasso.

When I was standing at the railway station in Chiasso and looked at the cheerful adults and children, I said, "Now I have no fears for your future: with these healthy children, settling in the jungle makes sense." Müller said, "Oh, a[nother] very small child is still on the train." Molch promised to give me two hives of bees and any possible help when I followed to Santa Clara. So we parted company. The ship *Virgilio* took the group, [sailing] December 12, 1938 from Genoa to Cristóbal, [the port of] Colón.

---

* For details of this ominous visit, *see* Viola Wehrli's deposition, transcribed in Appendix B, p. 223, *infra*.

In January, I went to Horgen to meet Mr. H. Brunner, an architect from Oberrieden. Some people had gathered there as they wanted to see my photos of Panama, and now, for the first time, I met [other] people acquainted with the "Molch colony." I was hearing strange reports and so I pricked up my ears. One of the married couples—I have forgotten the name—had spent a few days with the colony in Ticino. When they learned that from then on their children would belong to Molch, that the linen and everything [else] was common property, that husband and wife were to be separated, etc., they had left. But Mrs. Bertha Wehrli from Kilchberg, the mother of Vio, whom I visited at the same time, told me things that were absolutely reassuring. The things Molch aimed at were difficult to understand, but the colony wanted only "the good." Mrs. Wehrli asked me if I had seen a "small child" at the departure of the commune [from the railroad station at Chiasso]. I had to reply in the negative, but I told her that somebody had mentioned at the railway station in Chiasso that a very small child was still on the train. Mrs. Wehrli confessed hesitantly that this was her daughter Vio's son.

The extremely negative reports about the Molch colony prompted me to get in touch with Künzli, [Panama's] honorary consul at Zürich. In a long discussion he confirmed that he had received similar bad news, but that in the end all reports of Müller and Morf had indicated the colony aimed only at "the good," and that the district attorney of the canton of Ticino had issued [a certificate of] *nulla osta,** *i.e.*, everything was in order. I explained then that I did not wish to aid a bad group and that I would regret it deeply if I were to find that this colony had abused my confidence and that of my friends in Panama. Consul Künzli could again reassure me. However, [I] wrote, all the same, to my friend Karl Schmieder and asked him to be careful, as I didn't want to send him "a gang of hoodlums." But the reports coming from Panama were only very positive ones.

---

* The decree of *nihil obstat* in Latin, or *nulla osta* in Italian—the language of the Ticino (or *Tessin*) region of Switzerland—is in Continental law a certification to the effect that there is no legal impediment to proceeding with some further transaction.

The colony was received in David by Dr. [Sebastián Gilberto] Ríos* or his representative; the schoolchildren sang and performed folk dances; for several days the schoolrooms were put at their disposal as lodgings, etc.

Then the colony started to build roads and a bridge 78 meters [260 ft.] long over the Chiriquí Viejo River. My friend Schmieder wrote me: "I shall never forget how unselfish these Swiss were in taking on this work," etc.

Things stood that way when I left Europe on July 25, 1939. Arriving in Panama, I found waiting at the Swiss consulate a letter from Karl Schmieder informing me that he had joined the "colony," and had given away his whole *finca*,† cattle and all, to the colony. My son [Gustav Jr.], my friend [Hans] Graf and I, travelling together, were more than surprised, and had premonitions about the worst. In an enclosure with the letter, Molch wrote that Schmieder's having joined the colony would not cause any inconvenience for us, and that he would give us any help Schmieder had already promised. We should just come, etc. But I was worried. How could this have happened? Schmieder, everywhere well known as an unrelenting, aggressive go–getter, handing over his *finca* to the colony? What was behind it? We had no choice but to continue on and examine what was happening on the spot.‡

---

* Dr. Ríos, a Panamanian who had studied in Germany and Switzerland and knew the language, received the group on its arrival in the provincial capital.

† Simply a "farm."

‡ In other versions, including that of Schmieder's surviving son Albert, interviewed many times for this book by the Editor, the elder Schmieder did not give the farm to the colony, but invited them to join his family on it. This would become a bone of contention with the surviving Müllers, Sophie and son Werner Robert, in the years following the massacre. Haug later married Schmieder's widow, Margarethe, they again took possession of the farm after the massacre, and sold it for less than two thousand dollars, which they shared with the other survivors who would accept the settlement.

Dr. [Federico] Ríos in Panama tried to reassure us and hoped for the best. He said that the colonists were already living on what they had planted. I had doubts, as only six months' time had elapsed since the arrival of the colony at Volcán. In David, we heard from [Alfred] Waser[, a Swiss who lived at Piedra Candela,] and [the Swiss carpenter Josef] Niederberger[, working in David,] that bad rumors about the colony had spread. Waser told us about Molch's affair with Klärli Werren: they slept alone in a *rancho* [in Panama, a simple palm–thatched hut], a small child was missing, people were hypnotized, etc. I said if the colony was such a good one it would survive; if not, it would disappear. The greatest source of outrage was the fact that Karl Schmieder's agèd parents had been ill treated and had gone back to Europe with only five hundred dollars.[*] This was a very bad omen for me, as I had started to like this old couple [on my earlier visit] and was looking forward to seeing them again. Now our paths had just

SCHMIEDER FAMILY PHOTO
(Standing) Margarethe ("Gretel") and Karl Schmieder, (front row) Karl's mother and stepfather, sons Albert ("Benni") and Karl Jr., on the Cotito farm. Haug was "outraged" by the treatment of the elders.

---

[*] The elder Schmieders intended to return to Switzerland via the United States. They were interned in the U.S. as enemy aliens. Rosario Laws de Schmieder, intv. with Ed.

crossed in Panama [City] without our knowing it.

IN VOLCÁN, THE rumors were even worse, everywhere only rejection and criticism of the worst kind for Molch's behavior. Among other things, it was said that more than 20 names had been on the immigration list (I think as many as thirty–two persons were listed) but of these only seventeen* had come. Again it was said that a small child was missing, etc., etc.

So Hans Graf, my son Gustav and I traveled one day through the jungle to Cotito. Let us go into the lion's den, I was thinking, and I wanted to settle everything at the location. It was pouring rain when we arrived at the colony. The reception was a very friendly and hearty one. We could sleep in a room above that of the chief, Lehner. Klärli Werren and Karl and Gretel Schmieder were with Lehner. We slept in the same small wooden house that later on was fortified and in which the colony met its sad end.

The members of the colony had a beaming, healthy look. The long hair and beards, the very simple clothes, the unshod feet, gave the impression of an old patriarchal family of the first century. The impression even increased when at dinner everybody sat around a table with Molch in the middle like Jesus at the Last Supper, breaking the bread—which was not cut with a knife† —serving food and drink. Bowls and cups made of coconut‡ served as containers for tea and milk. The food was unsalted but plentiful and good. It consisted mainly of milk, corn with honey, fine root vegetables, and pineapples, etc. The Molch doctrine frowned on meat and vegetables taken from living plants. Tubers,§ beans, all sorts of fruits that grew here were permitted, but not cabbage, carrots, lettuce, etc., as they had

---

* The correct number was 18.

† [A Jewish custom, apparently adopted by Lehner. The knife is seen as symbolic of the weaponry in Exodus 20:22 and Isaiah 2:4.]

‡ Coconuts do not grow in the area, and the shells would not serve for tableware. These must have been dried *totumas,* locally grown gourds widely used by local folk.

§ Manioc, known as *yuca* in Panama, and the tubers *ñame, ñampí* and *otoe* are staple foods. Morf, in his letters home, mentioned potatoes as well.

not completed their growing cycle before dying. A plant or fruit tree was not damaged at harvest. All condiments such as chives, onions, pepper or salt were firmly avoided, but a lot of sugar was used. Even green beans were cooked with sugar. For us, the "guests," chicken soup was often prepared, etc. Everything was made to make life in the colony comfortable for us.

On the morning of our arrival in the colony, I asked for a meeting with the chief to clarify our situation and the rumors and accusations we had heard. Present were Molch, Karl Schmieder and the three of us. My first question was about the missing child and the other people mentioned on the [immigration] list. Molch told us now, much to our amazement, that Vio Wehrli's child had died in her arms in Ticino, ten days before departure.[*] The cause was congestion of the lungs. As the colony was already exposed to serious hostility in Ticino, reporting the child's death to the police would have led to an investigation, and the whole emigration plan would have failed. Guided by his responsibility for the group, Lehner had failed to report the child's death and, on the Sunday [December 11, 1938,] when he had accompanied Sophie Müller and Vio Wehrli to my place in Rovio, he had carried the corpse in his rucksack and had buried it in a rocky creek bed. Now I understood Vio's timid behavior and sadness [at the time].

I could understand this distressing revelation but not approve it. [I was told that Werner] Müller, who had said at the Chiasso railway station that a very small child was still aboard the train, apparently had not known of its earlier death because in those days he was frequently absent, traveling by bicycle to Zürich to get the [visas] from Honorary Consul Künzli, etc. The other persons on the list [of emigrants] who were missing had [simply] not appeared. This clarified point 1 of my questions.

Then I asked about hypnotizing the members. Molch said someone who is under hypnosis acts like a puppet and does only what he

---

[*] *See also* Appendix B, p. 223, *infra,* the affidavit of Viola Wehrli regarding the death of her son before departure from Switzerland.

is told to do. This certainly was not the case with any of the members here. Of course, he was influencing people, but [only] in the same sense as Mussolini and Hitler had influenced people by their doctrines. But, his [own] work was *diametrically* opposed to everything existing, he said!

I asked about the reasons that had led to the breakup of the families and he said, "I was convinced that a good family was the nucleus for the foundation of any new state." Now Molch used sharp words and said in a loud and violent voice, "We can go anywhere beneath the great blue sky: show me a single family that isn't whorish, filthy and falling apart." None was to be found. Yes, he would like to make the acquaintance of any such that might be found.

I was surprised by his attitude and could not approve, but I continued with my questions. Was it true, as was said, that only Molch had the right to the women and girls? That the other men figured more or less as eunuchs in the colony? Lehner answered: "I can leave the colony for a few days if you wish; I will order the women and girls to give you clear and true answers to every possible question. You will not find a single one with whom I have had sexual relations; that's only the stupid gossip of people who cannot understand us."

Molch explained furthermore that they did not trade and lived only from their own work, that there existed no pressures at all, that the free will of everyone was respected, and that anybody who no longer liked the colony could leave him at any time. "We are living together as one family; our bond is free will, in and for everything."

This whole conversation ended with his assurance of as much help as possible for us at any time, with the offer for us to stay with the colony as guests until we had established our own home. For me the situation was clarified and we gladly accepted the hospitality. Subsequently, my son and I helped to harvest the corn, to build the bridge, etc. That was really a time of harmony and content in the colony. In the evenings, Molch read aloud; one of the most used works was *Leben und Lehren der Meister des fernen Ostens*,* also the writings of "Father Divine" and other religious books.

We started to work at 5:45 AM until about 1:30–2.00 PM. Breakfast was at 8 AM, lunch about 2 PM. The afternoon was free for specific tasks such as mending, repairing tools, reading or resting. At 6:30 PM tea, milk and fruit were served. After the reading or discussion, we went to bed at about 9 PM. We slept in reclining chairs, in a half-sitting posture. There was no [artificial] light except for reading. One did without as many things as possible, saving even matches, and the old man Gottfried Werren had to stoke the fire to keep the embers alive until morning. At this time, my friend Graf left me without a word in Volcán, taking all his luggage and the machines and tools.

In the meantime, in Europe the war had begun, and we wanted to await the reports from Switzerland to [decide whether we should] perhaps change our plans for settling at Santa Clara.

When the colony's corn was harvested, my son and I [then] helped the [German Brauchle] family in Santa Clara for ten days in harvesting theirs as well. Their son Helmut confessed that he was more and more drawn to Molch, with a power so compelling that he just had to go, that he could not stay at home any longer. I tried to press him not to join the colony yet, but to wait another year or two at least. I told him what people in Europe had said about the colony. In vain. One day, he left home with his small suitcase to join the colony. Bad moments followed. [Alfred] Brauchle Sr. went to the colony and asked why they had not given a horse to his son Erwin† for the delivery of goods. Molch said that he would gladly provide a horse for transporting the sick, etc., but not "to support trade," and he

---

* German translation (Zürich: Bollmann) of Baird T. Spalding (1872–1953), *Life and Teachings of the Masters of the Far East* (6 vols., 1924–19___).

† This seems to indicate that the Brauchles had asked for loan of a horse for Erwin, who did not join the colony, and that Lehner had refused. Alfred Brauchle Sr. and Erwin were interned as German nationals by Panama after the war broke out. Alfred died in an internment camp in Kenedy, Texas, and Erwin did not return to Panama until seven years later. *See* pp. 34 *ff, supra*.

would not provide any beast of burden for delivering butter and eggs, etc., to market.

They quarreled about this and pounded their fists on the table. Finally, the tempers calmed. Molch promised every possible help to Brauchle, and if he needed anything, he could just request it from the colony. They would care for him and his wife as long as they lived.* They had only to avoid commerce. Brauchle went home calmly and said he would think it over.

A few days before, I had gone to David together with Karl Schmieder and Albert Morf, and soon made a second trip. I wanted to get my *cédula*, the residence permit card. The others asked Governor [Federico] Sagel [De Santiago] about the cost of naturalization, etc. I [usually] carried my purse on my chest. I had [once] left it

SCHMIEDER FAMILY PHOTO

(Seated, rear L-R) Alfred Waser, Gretel and Karl Schmieder, Gustav Haug. *(Foreground)* Josef Niederberger, who accompanied the police to Cotito on the day of the massacre. *Ca.* 1941.

---

* Helmut Brauchle died in the Cotito massacre.

in the house for about three minutes when I went to the kitchen. Then I came back into the house, where Graf had remained. [On that occasion, m]y purse certainly had not been touched. I had also had this purse with me when I went to the Brauchles', then back to the colony, and I had entrusted it to Molch when I had had to go to David the second time. After my return, Molch returned my purse. When I counted the money, fifty dollars* was missing. I was shattered. Unfortunately, I had not counted the money before giving it to Molch and therefore I had no real proof. I complained about my loss, speaking first to Karl Schmieder, then to Molch. The latter immediately offered to pay the amount, as he wished not to have suspicion cast on the colony. I could not accept it, as any suspicion seemed to me absurd, although absolutely no other person in question seemed suspicious. Several days later, Molch hinted to me that according to astrological forecast, the thief must have been a woman, and quite bluntly, he mentioned Mrs. [Lydia] Brauchle. Later, when it was shown that this could not have been possible, suddenly [the suspect] became Hans Graf. But I knew quite well that Graf was a man of honor, and I did not like the astrological interpretation, which I thought was rubbish. Subsequently, these horoscopes would be the cause for strong suspicions in numerous instances.

I forced myself to carry on after these bad days and to reach my goal to become a free settler subject to my own will. Approximately at the same time there were rumors that Klärli Werren had been made pregnant by Alb[ert] Morf, Jr. The girl's condition did indeed show the imminent birth. I questioned Lehner, the chief of the colony, about this fact. To my astonishment, Molch confessed the following: "The child that will be born is my child. Of course, Albert Jr.[†] had relations with Klärli in Volcán in January, 1939, during my absence. But the child will be born in December, and therefore cannot be Albert's. You will see, a disaster is coming."

---

*[A large sum, the value of 5 dairy cows, more than 5 months' wages for a farm laborer, or 7 acres of land in the Chiriquí of 1940.]

[†] He would have been about 14 years old at the time.

Molch said that Klärli had already had a miscarriage before the journey and that her horoscope showed infallibly that she would now give birth to a child. If this child were not his, she [must have] had it from some street ruffian in Zürich. "But anyone who knows how many millions of souls in the universe were whimpering and weeping and wanted to be reincarnated, also what a girl suffers and what a release it is to be able to conceive." I was much astonished; so he had been lying previously when he told me: "I have no sexual relationships with our girls and women." Klärli was often weeping at that time, sitting outside all night or speaking to Molch in the house next door. No doubt, the disaster was approaching.

At this time, little Loni Morf scalded herself terribly with hot water. This child often cried at night. One evening, Molch threatened to take the child with a reclining chair into the jungle where no neighbors could hear anything, etc. He knew that he could not bear the little one's pain but only the mother, [Elfriede] who spoiled the child [with] this false maternal love, was to blame for the crying, etc. The Werren girl (K[lärli]), then 15,[*] said: "I would have thrown the child in a pot of hot water and covered it a long time ago." I was speechless when I heard so much coarseness from people who always spoke of life as being love, that one should not worship Christ but follow his example, etc.

When one day I said that I could not forget this incident and why "Koni"[†] *[sic]* had not been reprimanded for her remark, Sophie Müller answered: "You, Molch, have always said that you would heal us and free us from false maternal love." With this, the whole subject was dismissed. Mrs. Morf, the mother of the injured child, was suf-

---

[*] "Klärli Werren was three weeks short of being 18 years old when she had a stillbirth [Dec., 1939], and she was 19 years old when she had a child, five months [Feb. 1941] before the massacre." Morf to Gaupp (1993). *See* p. 33, n*, *supra*. According to immigration papers cited by the Author in Chapter I, Klärli Werren was 16 in 1938, which confirms Morf's estimates of her age, not Haug's insistence that she was a minor.

[†] The name *Koni* appears to be an unconscious conflation of *Klärli* (Werren), the name of the teenager who made the remark, and *Loni* (Morf), the little scalding victim.

fering terribly and when [Albert] Morf, the father, tried once to see after his ailing child, the attempt was viewed as mistrust of Molch's medical skills and strongly condemned.

One night there was a lot of noise. People were running around in the dark. Alb[ert] Morf went down on his knees before Molch and cried: "Molch, Molch, why has Friedy (Mrs. Morf) done this to you"? At dawn, Molch, who had [later] gone out, came back across the fields with Mrs. Morf on his arm. I asked Karl Schmieder, whose clothes were wet, what had happened. He told me Klärli had gone for a walk. I knew this was a lie and turned to Helmut Brauchle. He told me that Friedy Morf had tried to throw herself and Loni into the Río Chiriquí [Viejo] but was pulled out at the last moment. My presentiment had therefore been true.

Molch declared in the evening he would never again move a finger if anybody tried once more to throw away his life. The next day he said that he would sacrifice his life at any time for anybody, even the least among them, if it should be necessary. More and more I saw in Lehner the sadist who tortured people with diabolical satisfaction and then, in the face of a catastrophe, ironed out everything with love and kindness. "I dare to be redeemer and devil in person," was one of his sayings. "The whole universe is my footstool," he also used to say.

At this time, the boy "Böps" Müller was caught masturbating. Lehner ordered him strapped to a board each evening for several weeks so that he could not do this anymore. For a long time I had no knowledge of this torture, as Mrs. Müller had to sleep in the old henhouse away from the others, and many things were hidden from me.

All these incidents were driving me to leave the colony as soon as possible. In the beginning of December, I had to move to another building with my son. The birth and the foretold catastrophe were imminent. One evening Klärli screamed from labor pains, somebody was sent to the neighbors to ask if the midwife in Serra [Cerro] Punta had instruments necessary for a cæsarean section or forceps delivery. Then, in the deepest night, Helmut Brauchle had to go on horseback to the village of La Concepción, more than ten hours from the colony, to telephone from there for a doctor in David. Meanwhile we heard in the workshop below a constant hammering and grinding. Obviously instruments were being made!!

In the early morning, Albert Morf, Sr., was sent to meet the doctor and Helmut with the news that *everything was over* and his help was no longer necessary. In the morning after the birth, Lehner, then Karl and Gretel Schmieder,* were present. Oddly enough, Mrs. Klara Werren, mother of the pregnant girl, was not admitted. In the morning, Molch said that the child was now an angel, and how life had made everything turn out for the best, etc. Karl Schmieder said to me: "Gustav, you have no idea what a great doctor Molch is. Anyhow, you don't know yet who Molch really is." More and more, Molch would pass for a new Messiah, and he was accepted as such by the members of the colony. Whatever "He" did was right and never criticized. I wondered again and again how adults, men and women, could endure just about anything without speaking up about it.

Now I left the colony and stayed almost a year with the Brauchle family. Lehner, who had made a lot of promises to me with respect to help in developing my homestead, said on my last evening that he would never enter Santa Clara, for other people could then say: now he has his eyes on Haug. How did this fit together with the promised help? This help was limited to small things, although in view of the promise to help me I had waived the twenty–three dollars due me for goods I had delivered. Thanks to the collaboration with Brauchle, we made good progress [on Haug's own farm at Santa Clara]. Brau-

---

* "With regard to Klärli Werren's child, no one knows exactly how it died." Walter Morf to Gaupp (1993). *See* p. 33, n.* *supra*. Throughout his life, Morf downplayed negative reports about Lehner. *Cf., e.g.*, Ed.'s conversation with Ingrid Sicilia, Cotito 2015; conversation with Morf, ca. 1995. However, Haug confirms here that Margarethe Schmieder (whom he later married after she lost her husband Karl in the massacre) was present at the time of the birth. Margarethe confided to her son and daughter-in-law in later years that an abortion had been induced by Lehner, pressing down on the abdomen of the mother with a wooden plank. Rosario Laws de Schmieder, intv. with Ed., 2012.

chle's second son did not run away as Molch had predicted, the horoscopes were no longer accurate.

In the course of the year 1940, I again received alarming reports from Europe about the colony [at Vairano, before the emigration], *e.g.*, about a Mrs. Siedler from Männedorf on Lake Zürich. Her daughter had fallen into religious madness due to too much studying and had died; about the divorce of Vio Rieser–Wehrli, whose husband had become mentally deranged and had had to appear before the military court at Pfäffikon, in Zürich.

One day I heard also what Molch told his people about the inhabitants of other planets. On the moon, for example, lived men and women with a height of only 40–60 cm [16–24 inches]. The women had six small child–like fingers. One could sow and harvest within fourteen days, etc. The trees bore only the finest fruit. The wind shook loose the ripe fruit, which did not fall to the ground, but floated in the air due to the altered gravity of the atmosphere. There was also a winged goat that fed on fruit and returned every evening, with a full udder, to the kitchen, where it could milk itself into a kettle with its hooves. That is what Molch related. I thought at first these were meant as fairy tales, but the others said that Molch was able to see all this. He related similar abnormal fantasies about other planets. Even the greatest fantasy did not approach even the border of reality. In this sense, this man explained to his people the mysteries of his view of life and they believed everything. Similar was also his belief in the migration and development of the soul, in various spirits, etc. etc. Often he struck me as a man sunk deep in the Middle Ages, then he would suddenly use terms of nuclear or vibration [seismological?] research to explain his fantasies.

I had no doubts any more that Molch belonged to a certain class of mentally ill persons and feared the worst for the future. In addition, I recognized gradually how false he was to his best friend. The Troetsch family in [Camarón, near Santa Marta] who had once stood surety for the colonists upon their arrival and who had often visited them—oxen were exchanged for cows, radios and sewing machines—this Troetsch family was treated falsely. They had built a bridge over the river free of charge, an oven and a spring were repaired, a pump

APPENDIX A | GUSTAV HAUG'S REPORT

SCHMIEDER FAMILY PHOTO

A barefoot Karl Schmieder, front row, with sons Albert and Karl Jr., visiting the Brauchle family's log and bamboo cabin, Cotito *ca.* 1934. The Schmieders emigrated from Schramberg in 1928, the Brauchles in 1929.

Standing at right is Alfred Brauchle Jr. At left, identified on the reverse as a "Czech world-wanderer," appears to be Moravian neighbor Alois Hartmann. Seated (L-R) Helmut Brauchle, Mrs. Brauchle, son Erwin. Three of those pictured—Karl Sr. and Jr. and Helmut Brauchle—died in the massacre. Alfred Brauchle Sr. (not shown) and Jr. were interned as enemy aliens in Texas after Pearl Harbor, and the elder Brauchle died there.

installed for them, etc. etc. And [yet] in the colony I had to stand by and listen when it was said that nevertheless, this [Camarón] (referring to the big Troetsch farm) must perish. I heard it said also that the whole journey for me and my family to Panama would have been paid for if I had traveled with the colony. But I had never received such an offer.

After the birth at Cotito mentioned before, it was said that this was the last birth, and then in September 194[0], the girls and women were told it was better to raise small children than stray dogs. I could foresee what this would mean. At this time, suddenly an area eight hours from Cotito, in the jungle of Costa Rica, was fenced, roads were built and timber cut. Molch said once to me that in two or three years I could take over the whole *finca* in Cotito gratis, if only I did not oppose the colony. However, I did not count on this promise; I had been promised many things but only a few of the promises had been kept.

A fortnight later, Albert Morf told me on behalf of Molch that they no longer wanted any visits in the colony and that I was not to be allowed to enter it. Either that or I would have to decide to join the colony completely and forever. I answered Morf that I had to decline this obligation as I was sticking to my plans for settling on my own and would of course never enter the colony again. Morf said:

"You will see, the time will come when we shall have to defend the cause of Molch with our blood!"

I replied, "Yes, you must be able to do this when you become convinced that it is the good and the right thing." With this, I made a final break and the last ties to the colony were dissolved. The same demand was made of the Brauchle family, *i.e.*, to join the colony or to stay away. I was convinced that nobody would be able to observe any more what was happening inside the colony. And I believe that was what happened.

In the spring of 1941, some *Chiricanos* living at [Pata de Gallo, Costa Rica], said they had visited the Molch colony at Cotito, as the settlement there was known in Costa Rica. They had seen a very small child that had not died by this time,[*] as Molch had later said it had. He had been very friendly and nice, the people had planted a great deal, etc. Then I heard other rumors. Molch had locked Mrs. Schmieder up for four days until she gave herself to him.[†] I also

---

[*] Again according to Margarethe Schmieder, as related by her son and daughter-in-law (see previous note), the child in Costa Rica had also been strangled by Lehner because he could not stand its crying.

[†] Margarethe Schmieder—never a convinced devotee of Lehner's, and who had always opposed her husband Karl's decision to invite the colony to live on their farm at Cotito—denied to the end of her days that this particular incident, related by Haug as only a rumor, had ever taken place. She said that she had never been intimidated by Lehner and he would not have dared to approach her thusly.

heard that the colonists were refusing to go to David to have their pictures taken, in compliance with orders from the police in connection with a general inspection of foreigners. I knew now something was coming that Molch had been looking for. In recent weeks, he had been preaching: "I don't need any laws; I don't accept any government." And once they had [even] wanted to become [naturalized] Panamanians!

I tried to arrange a discussion about the smoldering problems but failed. I feared more and more an impending catastrophe. And everywhere the colony was known as the "Swiss colony." I wanted to try one final time to get in touch with Molch, because this name was being applied inaccurately to such a mad cause. Molch let me know that if I had something important to say I could write a letter. I refused. When later in David I had to give some explanations about the colony and again heard about their refusal to put their affairs in order, I tried once more to arrange a dialogue. I sent my son to the colony and Karl Schmieder told him boastfully: "We know what is coming and we know also what we have to do."

A few days later I met Albert Morf in the colony corral. I asked him:

"Albert, have you thought about people like Dr. Ríos, Mr. P[atiño], Mr. Troetsch, Governor Sagel, etc., all people who were prepared to help you at any time. Do you want to produce a stupid scandal because of three photos?"[*]

Morf said to me, "Gustav, you know that you can go to Molch at any time if you have something to say." His hair was disheveled like a madman's, he was rubbing his face and gesticulating. I drew Morf's attention to the fact that I was forbidden to enter the colony and that I respected this. However, my house was always open and a discussion would be very important for the colony but not for me. Then I went home. I heard from Waser [a Swiss neighbor], who visited the colony and received many gifts—a horse, saddle and saddle

---

[*] Referring to three new identification photos required for renewing residence permits.

blanket, shotguns, etc. etc.—that Molch had said: "We shall all be shot, you will see what will come now."

Not long before, it had been planned to build a shed over the corral, but now a totally different and incomprehensible measure was taken. They started to put a palisade of oaken planks around a wooden house and to build a buttress of stones and sand behind it; in other words, a sort of fortress of wooden stakes was constructed. They began to build an outer fence of barbed wire around the whole thing. Rainwater from the gutters was collected in empty steel drums; provisions such as cheese, honey, flour, rice were brought into this house.

I understood that Molch saw the end of his career coming, and that he now wanted to resign himself to martyrdom. His people still had no idea what was behind this man, they still believed in him as the new Messiah, and were wholly loyal and completely under his influence. Not one of them separated from this man or even made an attempt to refuse participating in the coming end. Molch foresaw from his horoscope that he would have a violent death and Karl Schmieder an unnatural one, etc. The people to whom had been told only a year previously that "the death of a person was only a failure" and unnecessary, these same persons suddenly were predestined by the stars to be shot. I often thought back to life in the colony. How many times had one or another of the women wept day and night, when Molch had tortured and harassed them in a very rough way and swore terribly, swearing at these gentle people, a complete devil, a devil in the truest sense of the word? And the next day from his mouth would issue only goodness and love, forgiveness and mercy. The same man, who once gave a two-year-old horse such a kick with his foot that it fell to the ground, who could gently carry away a bug, who did not want to kill a plant—what was going on inside this man? And where was the small child who had been born in Costa Rica as the people from Chiriquí had said? Here in the colony in Cotito, nobody had seen the baby. Whatever I had lived through with these people, I now viewed increasingly in a different light. It seemed to me that they lived under the wings of a madman, a sadist who needed victims and who was ruthlessly steering everything toward a terrible catastrophe. It must have given him the highest inner satisfaction to witness how all went to their deaths with "Him," believing in his divine mission. And so it came to be.

When, on Monday, July 7, 1941, at half-past six in the morning, I heard shots and gunfire from the river bend at Cotito, my son, who was at my side milking, said: "Papa, perhaps they are all dead already!" We both knew that for Molch, it was always a matter of "everything," and "everything" meant exclusively Molch's view of it. Never did he give way to anything and always maintained that his point of view was the right one and everybody submitted voluntarily to this unwritten law. "It is the slender silken thread of free will that keeps us together," Molch wrote once in a letter. Yes, indeed the free will of these people was only a hint of a slender silken thread. They thought they were bulletproof and immune to death like Father Divine, and believed themselves invulnerable to all weaponry. How many times had Molch told his people about Father Divine, who had been hanged, shot and drowned again and again and still existed! I had often tried to talk to Schmieder and Morf about these crazy illusions. All believed in this balderdash and I would only come to understand this later.

My neighbor Brauchle came over to me, pale. After we finished our essential chores, we go to the colony in Cotito, where we arrive approximately 1½ hours after the shooting. A sharp shot whistles past us when we are about two hundred fifty meters from the buildings. A concealed sentry has fired without giving a warning. We stop and soon a few policemen are running toward us. We ask what is happening. "All are dead or dying," says [Sergeant Saldaña]. Brauchle's son [Erwin?] falls to the ground unconscious when he is told his brother Helmut is among the dead. We are directed to the commanding officer. On the road, the wounded are lying in a long line of improvised stretchers. All women and girls.

I ask Elfriede Morf how this has happened.

"Because Jesus wanted it to," was her answer.

I said, "Jesus demands no murder and no slaughter."

"Oh yes, Jesus wanted this."

On the next stretcher lies Mrs. Werren; she is calling:

["]Gustav, come, I want to tell you something.["] But a policeman grabs me by the shoulder and shoves me toward the corral, where 30–40 policemen are busy with the horses and preparing the last stretchers. It is a mess. Everybody is screaming in confusion. Someone is yelling ["¡*Manos arriba!*"], "Hands up!" My companion raises my arms as I have not quite understood. Then I felt ropes around me and soon I was tied up and put against the fence. Behind me, a policeman stood with a drawn dagger or bayonet. I was searched for weapons. I smiled and said that I was here of my own free will and all this was unnecessary. Soon Brauchle and his son, who had recovered [from his momentary collapse], came over and they were tied up as well.

When the commanding officer of the detachment was summoned from the houses, he immediately freed us, as he knew us from our recent visit to David. He put his hand on his heart and assured us how sorry he was about all that had happened. But his emissary, who had approached the colony with the decree of the President,* had been immediately fired upon. Then [it was] "they" who had commenced firing. The women especially had been very aggressive. The agèd Gottfried Werren was sitting, tied up, on a pile of rocks. A voice was crying: "Children, think of Jesus." More wounded were lying on the grass between the corral and the buildings. Occasionally, one hears somebody groaning; they are almost unrecognizable, disheveled and smeared with blood. A glance to the "fortress" almost congealed our blood. Between the wall of the house and the palisade, the men lie dead. [Albert] Morf [Sr.] with his skull laid bare, [Helmut] Brauchle shot in the belly. Molch shot in the neck, temple and chest. Karl Schmieder, Werner Müller, Albert Morf Jr., the elderly [Heinrich] Ott, all shot. Also Mrs. Friedy Morf. Inside the building lies Klärli [Werren], Molch's lover, in her own blood. The smell of tear gas from the canisters that had been fired, which

---

* It was not a presidential decree, but rather an ultimatum issued by the commanding officer of the police detachment on the spot. *See* pp. 113 *ff*, *supra*.

the commanding officer said would have been of no value, is still in the air. We are shocked by the horrible catastrophe.

On a stretcher, Paul Häusle is stirring in his final convulsions. He would die shortly after our departure. As they are transported, Mrs. Werren and the young Karl Schmieder will die as well. Of the whole colony of twenty-three members, twelve were dead and eight seriously or slightly wounded. Only the elderly Gottfried Werren and two children, Loni Morf and "Albertli" Schmieder,* were were unharmed.

I left the place deeply shocked by the tragedy. The police troop, in a long file, left the valley that had once been so peaceful, taking all the machetes and alleged weapons with them. There was no first aid; only in Volcán would a doctor treat the wounded, who were then taken to the hospital in David.

Our Swiss compatriot Josef Niederberger from David† was with the police troop as interpreter [and observer], but when the firing started, he was far behind with the police commander. Therefore, there were many contradictory accounts of the exact course of the events that only an investigation would clarify, [and only] to a certain extent.

BECAUSE THE FIRST newspaper reports mentioned a Nazi coup, I would like to state here that within the colony no political activity was conducted, no newspaper reached this circle and Molch had said once, "If President Roosevelt will not accept the proposal of Father Divine *to buy* all the States in Central and South America to unite them with North America, the *devil Hitler* will conquer all these countries from Argentina. The German will make war on America with the ray that could be artificially fired, and only the aiming of

---

* Albert was called Albertli, the Swiss diminutive, by his mother, but his other childhood nickname was Benni, "because," he relates, "there were too many Alberts," including Albert Morf Sr. and Jr. Mrs. Brauchle's maiden name was also Albert, so her son Helmut, a member, would have been known legally in Panama as Helmut Brauchle Albert.

† Niederberger settled in Cerro Punta in the highlands, but he was living in David at the time of these events.

the ray was yet to have to have been worked out by the experts. But this could wait; wait only, wait!"

I WOULD NOT want to close this report without emphasizing that after the withdrawal of the police troop transporting the victims, a small guard remained. And now the colonists' neighbors had to watch as these officers of law and order were stealing whatever could be of use: cattle, saddles, suitcases, clothes and tools, everything vanished. The settlers had lived honestly* twelve [months] as neighbors, the police had never had occasion to interfere, and now there was this sight of absolute robbery by the guardians of the law.

Signed: *G. Haug*

Finca Cotito, late 1940's. STANDING L-R: Gretel and Gustav Haug, Lydia Brauchle, Gustav Haug Jr. holding son Gustali, Marie Hils.
SEATED: Albert Schmieder, Cornelia Haug *née* Werren, Gertrudis Hils.
Visible are the porch and glazed windows of new house.

COURTESY KIRSTEN SCHMIEDER

---
* The contrast between, on the one hand, Haug's descriptions of infanticide, fanaticism, theft (of the fifty dollars in his purse), deception, intrigue and false promises, and, on the other, his conclusion referring to the "honesty" of the settlers, is rather striking. One cannot rely too precisely on the details of a translation of a transcribed document written under great stress, but Haug was close to various members of the community; he would later marry Karl Schmieder's widow, and his son would marry Cornelia, a surviving daughter of the Werrens. Haug was no great admirer of Lehner, but his outrage at the looting of the property by the police and neighbors ostensibly appointed to safeguard it, is understandable.

B | DEPOSITION REGARDING INFANT VIRGILIO COLUMBIO RIESER, BORN SEPT. 21, 1938*

VIOLA WEHRLI
TRANSLATED FROM THE GERMAN BY BARBARA TRABER†

IN THE MOSCUMO GROUP in Vairano, [canton of] Ticino, Switzerland, Karl Lehner was the absolute *Führer* and chief accepted by everybody. With his eloquence and persuasive power he dominated everybody. He decided that the mothers had to hand their children over to him unconditionally. He raised them with the help of Mrs. Müller.

---

* The interrogation resulting in the deposition transcribed here was ordered by the Swiss Federal Department of Justice and Police, Bern, and conducted by the Consulate in Panama on March 28, 1945, nearly four years after the massacre. For reasons explained in a previous note, this translation may read somewhat more fluently than the original. (In the Appendices, all notes were inserted by the Editor.) Swiss Embassy (Caracas) Archives. (Now in *Bundesarchiv*, Bern, file № E 2001 (D) 1000/1553, vol. 116, B.31.11.Pan.2.).

† With assistance from the Ed.

This was also the case with my child, Virgilio Rieser. I was only allowed to see him for breast-feeding. On the afternoon of November 29, 1938, [when the infant was 3 months and 8 days old, and twelve days before the immigrants would board the train taking them to the port of Genoa, where they embarked for Panama], I saw Virgil for the last time alive. He was curiously calm but otherwise I noticed nothing special. In the evening I was told that he didn't need any nourishment. On December 1, in the early morning, Mrs. [Sophie] Müller brought him to me; she was agitated. The child opened his eyes once more, then never again.

COURTESY ERICA WITZIG-FASSLER
Viola Wehrli, *ca.* 1941

PASSPORT PHOTO (?)
Viola Wehrli, *ca.* 1938

Lehner ordered us to travel at once to Rovio [also in the] (canton of Ticino) where I would find peace for me and the very ill child. He accompanied Mrs. Müller and me to this place. On the journey he explained to me that the child was dead, and that he would take care of everything. In Rovio, he left Mrs. Müller and me waiting and returned after two hours. Then he accompanied us to the Pension Haug where we stayed until our departure for Panama. Later I found out that he had buried the child himself, but I don't know where. We were all under his influence—so much that we followed him into death without any protest or doubt, as the tragic end at Cotito shows. Whatever he said was revered as a revelation from the messenger sent by God.

Signed: *Viola Wehrli*

C | TRUDI HÄUSLE WORRELL'S COTITO MEMOIR, BRIDGE ON THE CHIRIQUÍ VIEJO*

ALTHOUGH TRUDI HÄUSLE Worrell's 1993 book *Die Brücke am Chiriquí Viejo* [*"Bridge on the Chiriquí Viejo"*] was a lighthearted memoir of her adventures in the Chiriquí wilderness, private notes† she wrote at the same time, and entrusted to friends, tell a very different story.

The unpublished English manuscript is lost. It was translated into German and published, both at her own expense, in Switzerland. Her omission of any mention of, or allusion to, the colony's tragic end, to its leader Karl Lehner, her brother's death, and to her own injuries and long, painful recovery, produced a certain amount of speculation among the few readers of the book who were acquainted with the realities of the Cotito story. What complex emotions had prompted her to write selectively for the public is unknown, but the private notes show her true recollections were vivid. "Oh, God!" she wrote in English in the notes.

> How I have tried to forget that day (now over fifty years ago) when our peaceful jungle paradise was shattered under a total massacre. An entire army charged from every direction with high-powered rifles. ... As I stood in-

---

* Like the Foreword, this Appendix was written by the Editor, and the Author of *Cotito* bears no responsibility for it.
† Trudi Häusle Worrell, personal statements (1993), forwarded (1994) to Elfriede Morf and her husband Robert Gilchrist "for [them] only to keep." This printing of the revised English edition has been edited to reflect the content of the newly found notes, photocopies supplied to the Editor, after the deaths of Trudi, Elfriede, and all the other survivors, by Albert and Rosario Schmieder.

side by one of the windows (no glass)...my brother stood on the outside below the window frame. Two of the police pointed their rifles straight at my brother Paul...as my brother held up a hand the police shot him right down without provocation...and immediately shot me. ... All about the same time, all hell broke loose, like war. ... I did not know that Elfriede's mother had been shot dead right behind me.

In her book, Trudi ascribes her lifelong discomfort to an injury suffered carrying heavy timbers for construction of the bridge, but she had been shot through the lung, under the left breast, and later in the hospital internal bleeding caused problems with her leg as well. At the time, her death was feared imminent. Though happily she was among the wounded who eventually recovered, the lifelong pain persisted. In the notes, she is angrily critical about the medical care administered in the Chiriquí hospital, but expresses immense gratitude for the Franciscan nuns and their care.

In the book, Trudi invented a gradual, peaceful dissolution of the community, attributing it largely to the unwelcome arrival of construction crews with heavy machinery preparing to open the road from Volcán to Río Sereno, in those days the proposed route of the Pan-American Highway. She describes her own departure as prompted by an opportunity to work as a waitress and general assistant in a "hunting lodge" located near Barriles, an hour or two from the colony on horseback. She did work there briefly after returning to Cotito from the hospital, and it was there that she met U.S. citizen Ray Russell Worrell. She eventually obtained employment in the Canal Zone, and, when she recovered her passport, was able to obtain clearance to marry Ray. They had three children in the United States, one of whom died in adolescence.[1]

In the book, Trudi was fairly direct in assessing the character of the various *dramatis personae,* but she invented fictitious given names, and in some cases surnames as well, for most of the members of the colony, probably out of a combination of respect for those then living who might have objected to her candid characterizations, and the hope that fictitious names might somehow attenuate the

ONOMASTIC TABLE:
NAMES USED IN *DIE BRÜCKE AM CHIRIQUÍ VIEJO*

Real Name	Fictitious Name
Helmut Brauchle	Never mentioned
Paul Häusle	Peter
Trudi Häusle	Trudi
Karl Lehner	Never mentioned
Albert Morf Sr.	Martin Amberg
Elfriede Morf (mother)	Vreni Amberg
Albert Morf Jr.	Arthur Amberg
Elfriede Morf (daughter)	Luise Amberg
Walter Morf	André Amberg
Loni Morf	Anneli Amberg
Werner Müller	Ruedi
Sophie Müller	Mathilda
Werner Robert (Böbs) Müller	Kurt
Heinrich Ott	Jörg Bürgi ("Heiri" in notes)
Karl Schmieder	Karl S.
Margarethe (Gretel) Schmieder	Margarethe (Gretel)
Karl Schmieder Jr	Lukas
Albert (Benni) Schmieder	Benni
Josef (Sepp) Niederberger	Sepp
Viola Wehrli	Theresa
Gottfried Werren	Philippe
Klara Werren	Elizabeth
Klara (Klärli) Werren	Magda
Cornelia Werren	Doris

effect of her more critical comments. It is not difficult for anyone familiar with the narrative to determine, based on abundant internal evidence, who is who in *Die Brücke*. For certain individuals such as the Germans Alexander Troetsch, Karl and "Gretel" Schmieder, who were not originally members of the Swiss commune, she used real names. The Author of Cotito was correct when he wrote that little is known about the origins of the colony, but *Die Brücke* gives at least some additional clues about how the colonists first came together.

FOLLOWING ARE INCOMPLETE summaries of Trudi Häusle Worrell's observations regarding individuals who belonged to the community, how they became involved in it, and a few related facts from other sources:

- **TRUDI HÄUSLE.** Of herself, Trudi writes that in 1938, her parents having died, she was living with her grandmother and under pressure from her uncle,* a sort of guardian, to open a dressmaking shop in Switzerland. It was her brother Paul, she said, who influenced her decision to join Lehner's group. She was at first skeptical and reluctant. A baptized Catholic, although not practicing her faith,[2] she wrote, "I was at a point in my life where I was disillusioned about most religions. But little by little at evening lecture discussions, I became less skeptical."[3]

BY NOVEMBER, 1938, she had moved from wintry Zürich to Vairano, in the canton of Ticino, in the warm south of the country, and was enthusiastically engaged in preparation for the adventure. She enjoyed the company of the other young people, though she had reservations about the religious nature of the group, and there was strong opposition to her participation in the emigration project from her family and a social worker from the *Gesellschaft für den Schutz junger Mädchen* (Society for the Protection of Young Women).[4] When the social worker appeared and sought to remove her from the group, she gleefully recalls, "Ruedi" (Werner Müller), "despite his religious principles," rolled up his sleeves and threatened mayhem, finally removing the social worker from the premises rather roughly.

Born February 5, 1916, Trudi was not quite 23 when on January 1, 1939, the group arrived in Panama, and she was 25 on July 7, 1941. Although she does not describe any of

---

* *See* his inquiry about her situation, reproduced on p. xvi, *supra*.

the tragic events in her book, and gives misleading data about her period of work at the hunting lodge, a letter from an official of the Swiss foreign affairs department named Feldschen to her uncle in Zürich, indicates that on December 24, 1941, she had recovered from gunshot wounds and was back at Cotito.[5]

- **PAUL HÄUSLE ("PETER").** Trudi describes her brother as "strong" and "fit," and not so skeptical as she. On a bicycle tour of southern Switzerland, he visited the Morfs, family friends living at Vairano, and became interested in the group they belonged to. Trudi recalled that he was "not yet 18" when he joined and urged her to do the same. When she objected that the other members might be too serious, he assured her that they had a sense of humor, and apparently, that was true, at least among many of the young people. Born January 11, 1919, Paul would have been 19 in 1938, and he was only 22 when he became the first to die at the hands of the police.

- **ALBERT MORF ("MARTIN AMBERG").** He was one of the earlier followers of Lehner, remained devoted, and it was through acquaintance with Morf, who had known their father, that Trudi and Paul Häusle encountered the group at Vairano. Several of his and Elfriede's children were born in the United States. Morf was a builder, and had constructed a "very modern" house in New York, where he had lived for several years with his family, designed by the late architect father of Trudi and Paul, hence the acquaintance that had led to Paul's visit. Their uncle, Trudi wrote, thought Morf "'was not the most responsible man...but as he is taking his family with him I presume* that he knows what he is doing.'"[6]

---

* *"Ich setze voraus..."*

On March 30, 1941, three months and seven days before he was killed, Albert Morf wrote to his mother and sister in Switzerland. An excerpt from the letter gives a clue to his fidelity to Lehner:

> Molch has been since Nov. 1940, in the jungle with some friends looking for passable routes through mountains so that we can find a new homesite. We now have, a day's journey from Cotito, which is already, as they say, at the end of the world, established a base. 5 hectares of forest is already cleared. ... So you need have no concern for us, because there we are in the care of the best guide, which is all part of having faith and trusting entirely to it. Jesus Christ, the Father Spirit has created all and always willing to help us, and to protect us, but we have set our mind free from all the worldly stuff and the desire for an intimate relation to Him that must grow ... So my dear loved ones, take this to heart; this will probably be the last letter to you; you are indeed the only ones with whom I have been still in touch. The reason you will easily recognize, as we do not go to the post office when we are in our new home. Be strong and joyful until we all meet again, if not in this dress.

...

The letter indicates that as late as November, 1940, the colonists still considered the sojourn with the Schmieders at Cotito a temporary measure, and at least some still intended to return eventually to Candela.

- **ELFRIEDE MORF ("LUISE AMBERG").** Trudi describes her as a young girl, petite, very feminine in appearance, with dark blue eyes and light brown hair she usually tied in a loose knot. Trudi had known her for years and was glad she would be present in the group. The two women are shown together in the photo on p. 168, *supra*.

- **HEINRICH OTT ("JÖRG BÜRGI," "HEIRI"** in the notes**).** Sixty years of age, Ott lived in the same village as Albert Morf. He was a quiet, friendly man, she recalls, with a full gray beard. He had been a carpenter and cabinet maker, and would later spearhead the bridge-building project. She says that at Vairano, Albert Morf frequently stopped to chat with Ott as he worked in his garden, and one day asked him, *"Warum kommst du nicht einfach mit?"* ("Why don't you just come along?") Within a week, she says, a for-sale sign appeared on Ott's house and it was quickly sold.[7]

- **WERNER MÜLLER ("RUEDI").** Trudi described him as strong and hard-working, possessed of many talents. "It was," however, "senseless to argue with him"—he always "knew better." It was best, she said, to let him have the last word. He and his family lived in the same neighborhood as the Morfs and their neighbor Heinrich Ott. By 1938, "Ruedi" (Werner Müller) had been separated from his wife for two years, but believing that "Mathilda" (Sophie Baumann Müller) was incapable of caring for their son "Kurt" (Werner Robert, or "Böps"), "they agreed to get back together in hopes of finding a better solution." He therefore agreed to join his wife and the group on the journey to Panama.[8]

- **SOPHIE MÜLLER ("MATHILDA").** Trudi says in her book, that she was "the first of the members of the group," which may safely be taken as an implication that she was the most devoted of Lehner's followers, a characterization that appears in many documents in the Swiss archives and in the memory of survivors. There is ample evidence in the record, not just from *Die Brücke*, that Sophie was a very troubled individual. Although Trudi expresses admiration for Werner Müller (and avoids mention of their son, except to refer to him as "Kurt") she reserves her most critical comments for Sophie, whom she dubs "Mathilda."

Trudi Häusle's antagonism to Sophie is barely contained. She describes her several times, the comments always unflattering: she admits that from a distance "Mathilda" appeared an attractive blonde woman, but up close, she says, her features were a trifle "too heavy,"* and "Mathilda's" mouth "reminded her of a rubber band stretched too tight." She dressed in rough, patched clothing that gave her the appearance of a clown; from behind, she had the appearance of a "hippo" or an "elephant." She describes her flatly as lazy, says she never did any work, and elsewhere writes that she spoke "unbearably" slowly. In her recollection of a world of very hard work, simple food, and material privation, Trudi writes that "Mathilda" spent her time under the shade of a tree meditating on what good things would be on the table for lunch. She wondered why the woman wanted to go into the bush, and says, sarcastically, perhaps "she had other talents."

Even Sophie's son indicated that she had been "intimate" with Lehner, despite the presence of her husband, and she married the Swiss Wachter shortly after Müller's death at Cotito.[9] In 1943, the Swiss foreign office wrote a relative, Herr Baumann-Hees in Zurich, that she suffered a "permanent nervous disorder" that made her hospitalization imperative.[10] An undated letter in Swiss archives from one "E. Schwendener" (d. 1945) which appears to have been dictated by Sophie, accuses Gustav Haug and his son of being "bitchy and obnoxious,"† Gustav Sr. of being a "Quisling" and supporter of Hitlerism.[11] On June 30, the Swiss chargé reported

---

* *"Groß..."*

† *"ganz gehässige, abscheuliche Subjekte..."*

that she was still living unconfined, and was cohabiting by this time with another Swiss, Meinhard Fassler, not with the husband Wachter. She herself wrote an insulting letter to consul Blau on July 7, 1943, signing herself "*Frau* Wachter," accusing Blau, the honorary Swiss consul, of dereliction. Trudi's remarks in *Die Brücke* indicate what were probably sentiments shared by others in the small community and their German and Swiss neighbors.[12]

- **GOTTFRIED WERREN ("PHILIPPE").** In the notes, Trudi says, "He was a very educated man and spoke five languages fluently." "Philippe," as she called him in *Die Brücke*, had been, like Gustav Haug, in the hotel business in southern Switzerland, moderately successful until he suffered a severe accident (in the private notes she refers to "strokes"), which left him mentally impaired, with his capacity reduced to that of a "four-year-old child," despite his "miraculous" physical recovery. If sent on an errand even a few doors away, she wrote, his wife Klara would hang a tag with his name and address around his neck in case he became disoriented.[13] In the event, Werren was the only adult male to survive the massacre.

- **KLARA WERREN ("ELIZABETH").** Fifteen years "bearing the double burden" of the hotel business, and a family that included her disabled husband and two adolescent daughters, had left Klara hoping for a less hectic life.[4]

- **KLÄRLI WERREN ("MAGDA").** A letter from Gustav Haug to the Swiss chargé, dated June 28, 1941, just nine days before the massacre, states that she had borne a child in December 1939, the birth unregistered with the civil authorities, and another daughter in 1941. Haug speculates whether Lehner might have impregnated her before she was 16,[14] but other evidence indicates that she was older.

Notes to Appendix C

[1] Psnl. comm. Barbara Traber, July, 2011, and Internet genealogical sources.
[2] Yvonne Worrell Pover, e-mail, 2011.
[3] Häusle (Worrell), *Die Brücke* (1994), p. 14.
[4] *Id.*, p. 9
[5] Feldschen to P. Häusle, Dec. 24, 1941. Swiss Archives.
[6] *Die Brücke*, pp. 10-11.
[7] *Id.*, p. 18.
[8] *Id.*, p. 19.
[9] Gonzenbach to Political Dept., Jun. 30, 1943.
[10] Foreign Office, to "Herrn Baumann-Rees," Zürich Apr. 9, 1943.
[11] Schwendener to Swiss embassy, Washington, D.C., n.d. Swiss Archives.
[12] *Die Brücke*, pp. 20, 137.
[13] *Id.*, pp. 17-18.
[14] *See* Haug to Blau, June 28, 1941. Swiss Archives.

BIBLIOGRAPHY

ARCHIVAL COLLECTIONS

Ministry of Foreign Relations, Panama City. (MFR)

Ministry of Government and Justice, Directorate of Migration and Naturalization, Panama City. (MGJ)

Ministry of Government and Justice, National Police, Panama City. (NP)

Embassy of Switzerland in the Republic of Panama, Panama City.

Second Superior Tribunal of Justice, First [Appellate] Judicial District, David, Chiriquí. (2^{d}ST)

Federal Republic of Germany, Ministry of Foreign Relations, Bonn.

[Swiss Federal Archives, Bern.]

University of Panama (UP), Office of Panamanian Relations with the United States, Panama City. (OPRUS)

University of Panama, Simón Bolivar Library, Hemeroteca [periodicals and documents collection], Panama City.

Ernesto J. Castillero Library, Hemeroteca [periodicals and documents collection], Panama City.

WORKS CITED

BOOKS AND ARTICLES[*]

Araúz Celestino, Andrés et al., eds., *La historia de Panamá en sus textos* [*The History of Panama in Its Original Texts*], Editorial Uni-

---

[*] Unless otherwise noted, for all works in this bibliography, place of publication is Panama City, Panama. Internet sources are cited by the Editor to the original works rather than to websites.

versitaria: '79. **Arias Madrid,** Arnulfo, "Discurso pronunciado en su llegada a la Ciudad de Panamá," Talleres Gráficos, n.d. "Inaugural Address," '40, in Ricaurte Soler, *El Pensamiento político en los siglos XIX y XX ["Political Thought in the 19th and 20th Centuries"]*, v. 6, Biblioteca de la Cultura Panameña, '88. **Beluche Mora,** Isidro, *Acción Comunal: surgimiento y estructura del nacionalismo panameño ["Acción Comunal: Emergence and structure of Panamanian Nationalism"]*, Editorial Cóndor, '81. **Conte Porras,** Jorge, *Requiem por la Revolución*, San José [C.R.], Litografía e Imprenta Lil, '90. **"Divine, Father,"** in *12,000 Minibiografías*, 2nd ed., México D.F.: Editorial América, '86. **Gómez,** Franklin, "Los sucesos de Cotito," in commemorative magazine *Bugaba centenaria*, '63. **Hassán,** Aristides Iván, *Holocausto en Panamá*, Bogotá: Canal Ramírez Antares, '82. **Linares,** Julio E., *Enrique Linares en la historia política de Panamá, 1969-1949*, San José [C.R.]: Litografía Lit, '89. **Márquez,** Marcela "Un caso de genocidio en Panama," in *Cuadernos panameños de criminología ("Panamanian Studies in Criminology")*, № __ ('86), U. of Panamá, Faculty of Law and Political Science. **Ocaña,** V. D. "Las barras de oro de Piedra Candela," in revista *Lotería* № 280 (Jun. '79). **Parker,** R.A.C., "Europa entre las dos guerras: tendencias económicas y sociales," in *El Siglo XX: Europa 1918-1945*, 12th ed., México D.F.: Siglo XXI Editores, '71. **Pereira,** Renato, *Panamá, fuerzas armadas y política*, Ediciones Nueva Universidad, '79. **Probst,** Wilhelm "Capítulo XXIV: Masacre de religiosos," in *Vida y lucha de un hombre solitario ["Life and Struggle of a Solitary Man"]*, Unpub, ms., n.d. **Sánchez Borbón,** Guillermo "Más" ["More"], in *En pocas palabras ["In short...."]*: (anthology of daily newspaper columns '83-84 from *La Prensa*), Editorial Chen, 1992. "En pocas palabras," *La Prensa*, Apr, 18, '84. **Staff,** Héctor H, "Cotito: Historia y sucesos," in *La Voz del Barú y otros aspectos de radiodifusión y soberanía ["The Voice of the Barú and Other Facets of Radio Broadcasting and Sovereignty"]* '88. **Tejeira,** Gil Blas, *Biografía de Ricardo Adolfo De la Guardia: Página de la historia panameña*, Impresora Panamá, 1971.

| INTERVIEWS AND CONVERSATIONS[*]

Alfaro, Germán, Nov. 9, '92; **Baker Wilson**, Edward, Mar. 16, '93; **Bouche**, Olga, La Concepción (Chir.), Apr. 20, '92; **De Santiago**, Federico Sagel, Sep. 21, '88. **Ehrman**, José, Apr. 4, '91; **Gómez de Cuestas**, Josefa, David, Nov. 5, '92. **González**, Efraín, David, Mar. 5, '93. **Gómez Araúz**, Godofredo, Paso Ancho (Volcán), Apr. 18, '92. **Gómez Araúz**, Julio, Dec. 24, '91. **Haug**, Elizabeth, David, Apr. 9, '92. **Ponce Fábrega**, Jorge, Bambito (Volcán), Jul. 10, '92. **González**, Efraín, David (Chir.), Mar. 5, '93. **Hils**, Helmut, Volcán, Apr. 18, '92. **Materno Vásquez**, Juan, May, '91. **Miranda**, Harmodio, Apr. 21, '92. **Müller**, Werner Robert, May 8, '92. **Núñez**, Rubén, Ocú, Feb. 9, '93. **Serracín**, Aurelio Manuel, Río Sereno (Chir.), Jan. 21, '93. **Sicilia**, Digna de, Cotito (Chir.), Jan. 21, '93.

| JUDICIAL DECISIONS AND ORDERS

Decision, 2ndST, 1st Dist., '41 REGISTRO JUDICIAL at 168 (Jan. '41). Decision, 1stST, 1st Dist., May 6, '42, in *Estrella de Panamá*, July 5, '42. Decision, 1stST, 1st Dist., Dec. '42 REGISTRO JUDICIAL at __ (Dec. 7, '42). Decision, 1st Circ. Ct. Chiriquí. (Germany file, MFR.) Decision, 2ndST, Aug. 18, '53, at 5-6, *aff'd* Supreme Court ('53). Decision, 1st Circ. Ct. Chir., Civil Branch, № 276 (July 19, '74).

| CORRESPONDENCE

Alfaro, Ricardo J., MFR to Sucre, MGJ, Jan. 31, '47. (Switzerland file.); to René Naville, acting Swiss *chargé d'aff.*, communication № D.P. 578-B, Mar. 11, '47 (Swiss Embassy). **Brauchle** (*née* Albert), Lydia to Camilo De la Guardia, Jr, MGJ, May 5, '43 (MFR). **Bristol**, Maj. W.L. to Alejandro De la Guardia, Sept. 25, '42. (Germany file MFR). **Burgos**, Manuel 2nd Sect., MGJ to Alfaro, MFR, Feb. 22, '47. (Switzerland file MFR). **De la Guardia**, Camilo Jr., MGJ to Fábrega, MFR, Feb. 24, '43 (Germany file MFR); to De Roux, MFR, Aug. 19, '41 (Germany file MFR). **De Roux**, Raúl MFR to Camilo De la Guar-

---

[*] Unless otherwise noted, place of intv. is Panama City.

dia, MGJ, № 1,743. Jul. 28, '41 (Switzerland file MFR); to De la Guardia, MGJ, № D.P. 1,845, Aug. 8, '41 (Germany file, MFR); to Winter, acting *chargé d'aff.*, German legation, Aug. 28, '41 (Germany file, MFR). **Gómez Araúz**, Abel to Blanca Araúz de Gómez, telegram, Aug. 28, '28 (Personal files of the Author). **Gonzenbach**, A., Swiss *chargé d'aff.*, to Fábrega, MFR, Note, Jun. 29, '43; to De Roux, Jul. 23, '41 (Switzerland file, MFR, repr. Hassán, q.v.). **Haug**, Gustav "Mis experiencias con la Colonia Molch." in Haug to Juan Blau, July '41 (archives, Swiss Embassy). **Jaén Guardia**, Ernesto, Pma. ambassador to U.S., to MFR, Dec. 17, '41 (MFR Memoria 1941). **Naville**, René, Swiss embassy to Alfaro, MFR, Feb. 11, '43, Apr. 22, '46. (Switzerland file MFR). **Oñós de Plandolit**, Manuel, acting Spanish *chargé d'aff.*, to Octavio Fábrega, MFR, Feb. 24, '43 (Germany file MFR); to Fábrega, MFR, Dec. 31, '41 in MFR MEMORIA '41. **Pretelt**, J. A., Presiding Mag. 2^dTS, to Burgos, MFR, "Note," Feb. '27, '46 (Switzerland file MFR). Rodríguez, Cristóbal Sec. Gen., Pres. Rep., to Raúl De Roux, MFR, Dec. 17, '40. (Guatemala file MFR); **Winter**, Hans von, acting German *chargé d'aff.* to De Roux, MFR, Sept. 30, '41 (MFR MEMORIA '41); to MFR, "Note" July __, '41 (archives, MFR); to De Roux, MFR, Jul. 26, '41; to German MFR, cable № 221, July 8, '41. (Transl. from German to Spanish I. Valsevicius & J.D. Morgan Jr.)

| GOVERNMENT DOCUMENTS

UP, OPRUS, "Asuntos internos de Panamá: Dec. 29, 1940-Feb. 29, 1945." Microfilm roll 19, № 667. MFR, '41 MEMORIA MGJ. NP, General Orders of the Day, May–Oct. '41. '40–'42 MEMORIA MGJ. GACETA OFICIAL № 7,917 (Dec. 2, '38). M("Depto.")GJ, DECRETOS Y RESOLUCIONES VIGENTES, v. 1: 1904-1939 (Guillermo Andreve, comp.) 1939; **National Judiciary**, REGISTRO JUDICIAL Jan. '41, Dec. '42, '43 passim. JUDICIAL CODE. **Hand**, Arnoldo, Bienvenido Alvarado and Severino Herrera, sworn statements, July '41 REGISTRO JUDICIAL, at 25 (July 22, '41); Property Deed № 145 (March 18, '55). Parcel 6,569, Notary Public's Office Chiri.Circ., recorded in 649 PROVINCIAL LAND REGISTER, at 314, July 22, '55). **Juez Municipal**, Bugaba, Report of Inventory, Appraisal and Interim Disposition of Assets left by Karl Lehner and others, dec'd (Oct. 8, '41).

| NEWSPAPERS

Crítica, Apr. 25, '84. *Estrella de Panama*, Jan. 14 '28, Jul. 6 8 10 12, '41; Jul. 5, '42. *El Matutino*, Apr. 9 10 27 30, '84. *The Star & Herald*, Jul. 9, '41. *Panamá-América* Jun 12 13 17, Jul. 8, '41. *La Prensa*, Apr. 18, '84. *La Tribuna*, Sep. 26, '41.

| CITED BY EDITOR

Arias Calderón, Ricardo, *Democracia sin ejército: la experiencia de Panamá* ["*Democracy with no Army: the Panamanian Experience*"], San José [C.R.]: Fundación Arias para la Paz y el Progreso Humano: Diálogo Centroamericano (2001). **Brannan Jaén,** Betty, "Nomás perdigones de plomo" ["No more lead buckshot"] In *La Prensa*, Aug. 8, '10. **Conte Porras**, Jorge, *Arnulfo Arias Madrid* (Litho Impresora Panamá,'80). **Dinges,** John, *Our Man in Panama* (New York: Random House, '90). **Dubois,** Jules, *Danger Over Panama* (Indianapolis: Bobbs-Merrill, '64) cit. by Friedman (*q.v.*). **Friedman,** Max Paul, *Nazis and Good Neighbors: The United States Campaign Against the Germans of Latin America in World War II* (N.Y.: Cambridge U.P., '03). **Gaupp,** Peter, "Massacre at Cotito," in *Neue Zürcher Zeitung*, Apr. 24, '94, *Wochenende* sec., transl. from German Barbara Traber. **Harding,** Robert C., II, *Military Foundations of Panamanian Politics* (New Brunswick: Transaction Pub., 2001). **Hartmann,** Ratibor Jr., intv. with Ed., Volcán, Aug. 16, 2010. **Häusle,** Trudi, *see* **Worrell.** **Heckadon Moreno,** Stanley, *De selvas a potreros: La colonización santeña en Panamá 1950-1980* ["*From jungles to pastures: The Settlement by Los Santos Natives in Panama 1950-80"]* (Exedra © '09). **Koster**, Richard M. and Guillermo **Sánchez Borbón,** *In the Time of the Tyrants: Panama: 1968-1990* (N.Y.: W. W: Norton, '90). **LaFeber,** Walter, *The Panama Canal: The Crisis in Historical Perspective* (New York: Oxford U. P., '78). **Le Franc Ureña,** Roberto, "Long Scuttled Cargo Ship Becomes Environmental Case" *A.M. Costa Rica* (May 11, '12) at www.amcostaricaarchives.com. **Linares,** Olga *et al.*, "Prehistoric Agriculture in Tropical Highlands," *Science* 187(n.s.):4,172 (Jan. 17, '75), pp. 137-45. **Meding,** Holger M., *Panama: Staat und Nation im Wandel ["State and Nation in Flux"],* 1903-1941 (*Lateinamerikanische Forschungen* [Latin American Studies] № 30, suppl. to *Jahrbuch für Geschichte von Staat, Wirtschaft und Gesellschaft Lateinamerikas ["Yearbook for Latin American State, Economic and Social History"],* Köln/Weimar/Wien: Böhlau, '02). *Id.,* "Panama" in Thomas Adam, ed., *Germany and the Americas,* (Sta. Barbara, CA: ABC-Clio '05). **Morf,** Albert Sr., corresp. with mother & sister '38 (Morf family papers, photocopies courtesy of Elfriede Morf Gilcrease and Albert Schmieder). **Morf,** Walter Otto, corresp. with Author, '96, and Gaupp (*q.v.),* '96, *loc. cit.* **Pearcy,** Thomas L., *We Answer Only to God: Politics and the Military in Panama, 1903-1947* (Albuquerque: U. N.M. P., '98). **Pippin,** Larry LaRae, *The Remón Era: An Analysis of a Decade of Events in Panama, 1947-1957* (Stanford CA: Stanford U.P., '64). **Scheips,** Paul J. "Lincoln and the Chiriquí colonization Project," *J. Negro Hist.* 37 ('52), pp. 418-53. **Senn,** Werner C., intv. with O. Iván Flores and David Dell, Volcán, '09; intvs. with Ed., '11-'15. **Sánchez Borbón,** Guillermo. See **Koster. Serrano Pandiagua,** Felipe, intv. with ed, Aug. 2010. **Schmieder,** Albert, intvs., Volcán (Chir)., '11-'15. **Schmieder,** Rosario Laws de, intvs. with Ed., Volcán, Dolega (Chir.), '11-'15. **Thayer F.,** Berta Ramona, intvs. Volcán, Pmá. '13. **Traber,** Barbara, e-mail corresp., Jul. '11. **Trafton,** Mark Jr., "Introduction to Panama," unpub. typescript (n.p.: *ca.* '82). **Witzig-Fassler,** Erica, intv., Volcán, '15. **Worrell,** Trudi [Gertrude Häusle], *"Die Brücke am Chiriquí Viejo: Bericht einer Auswanderung nach Panama"* ["*Bridge over the Chiriquí Viejo: Account of an Emigration to Panama"]* (Bern: Edition Erpf, '93), transl. (English to German) Barbara Traber. Worrell to Elfriede Morf and Robert Gilcrease, Sept. 9, '94; personal notes Apr. 16, June 24, '93.

|*Index*

Spanish names are alphabetized by *paternal* surname and *given* name. Page numbers in ***bold italic*** type refer to illustrations. Where entries contain inverted phrases (**Trespatines**, J. Candelario Nananina's complaint against~ 398; arrest of~ 399) the turned dash (~) indicates repetition of the guide word.

A

Abadía, Aristides 190
Abadía, Judge Félix (1st Circ. Ct.) 159
Abbot, William J. lii
Acción Comunal xlvi xlvi-xlvii liii lv 51 53 58 187
Adventists. *See* **Seventh-day Adventist Church**. *See also* **Mattinson**, Reynaldo.
Aguilar Sánchez, Sgt. Rosendo 84 115 127 137 149
Airlines. *See* SCADTA (airline); SEDTA (airline).
Alba, Capt. Rogelio Jr. 65
Alfaro, Germán 69
Alfaro, Pres. Ricardo J., as V.P. succeeds Florencio Arosemena xlvii; opposes Arnulfo 1940 xlviii, 55; as Min. For. Rel. (1945-7) 136 148-9
Alvarado, Bienvenido 116
Alvarado, Rodolfo (policeman) 137; exonerated 149
antillanos. *See* **West Indians** in Panama.

Aparicio, Benedicto (policeman) exonerated 149
Araña, Guillermo 57
Ardila, 2nd Lt. Luis Felipe 67 84 89 130; exonerated 149
Ardito Barletta, Nicolás lxviii*ff*; 1984 campaign lxix-lxxii 172n; election strategy 181 185
Arias Madrid, Pres. Arnulfo *xlv*; *Acción Comunal* xlvii; ambassador 52; appoints Gómez Ayau 61; background xviii xxxviii xlv-xlvii 51-3; bans Adventists 104; Constitution, replaces 54; Harmodio Arias (bro., *q.v.*), relationship with xlviii, opposes Arnulfo xviii xlviii lv; *Holocausto en Panamá*, in~ xxvii xxxi-xxxiii xxxvii*n* 178-9 180-6 194; immigration, views on xliv li; inaugurated 1940 52; internments lx; Jews and xxxvii 24n; loyalty oath demanded 65-6; Min. Commerce & Agric. xliv xlvii; Health & Pub. Works xlvii 52; Mussolini, Arnulfo admires~ xlvii xliii; police, militarization of~ 58*ff* 62; race, views on xliv xlviii-l lii-

liii 53n; releases Probst 116; religious persecution 71-2; Remón, influence on 60 62; resists U.S. pressures xliv-xlviii lii liii lv-lvi lxxi; social policies xlviii liii-lv; suppresses uprisings 56*ff* 104*ff*; succeeded in 1941 by R.A. De la Guardia 147; telegram to Huff 107; upper classes dislike lv; widow elected l*n*
deposed 1941 xviii li lvix 60n 130; ~ 1951 xviii xxi 60 152; ~ 1968 xxiv
elections 1936, ineligible for~ xlviii; ~ 1940 xlviii 52-55, Gómez Araúz supports 128, returns from Europe 52, unopposed 54-5; ~ 1948 194; ~ 1964 xxi lxvii 184; ~ 1968 xviii xxiv 194; ~ 1984 lxvii-lxxi 181 185
massacre Gómez Araúz investigates criminal liability 123; apologist for~ xlvi lxv 107-8 117 178, deposition ordered 107-8 138; responsibility for~ xxxviii xlv lxii 109, denies~ 4 108; initial statement re~ 104
Nazis, Arnulfo admires~ xlvii 53n; Hitler meets xlvii xlix; orders from Hitler xxxii-xxxiii 178;
See also Acción Comunal; CNN; exhumations; *Panameñismo.*
Arias Madrid, Pres. Harmodio xviii background xlvii l 52; *Acción Comunal and~* xlvi-xlviii 51; immigration policy 20; meets Roosevelt l*n*; opposes Arnulfo xviii xlv lii-liii, lv 72n; pres. 1932-36 xlvii-xlviii 51; police, militarization 58-61; publishing co. xxxvii 72n; race, views on~ l; Remón hired, fired 60 62; uncle of Miró 69n
Arias Paredes, Francisco 55-6 58
Arnett, Peter lxxii 108 172 179 183-4 187
Arnulfismo See Acción Comunal; Arias, Arnulfo, Panameñismo; National Revolutionary Party.
Arosemena, Leopoldo (Sect. Govt. & Justice) 23
Arosemena, Pres. Florencio xlvii
Arosemena, Pres. Juan Demóstenes appoints Arnulfo Arias ambassador to France 52; authorizes immigration lxxx 24-5 29; authorizes Military Inst. 59; bars Asian immigrants 24n; dies in office xlvii 52; elected 1936 xlviii; grants land at Candela 29; Min. For. Rel. under Harmodio Arias 51; police, militarization of~ 58; orders registration of foreigners 77 79n; succeeds Harmodio Arias 1936 51
arsenal, alleged. *See* **weapons**.
Assembly, National. *See* **Legislative Assembly.**
Aued H., Capt. Francisco 65
autopsy. *See* **exhumations**, coroner's.
Avenida de los Mártires, xxiv
AVIANCA. *See* SCADTA (airline).

B

Baker, Frank Wilfred 97
Baker, George. *See* **Divine**, Father.
Baker, Melida Wilson 97
Barletta. *See* **Ardito Barletta**, Nicolás.
Batalla, José Guillermo 116-8
Baumann, Sophie. *See* **Müller** (later Wachter), Sophie *née* Baumann.
beekeeping xl-xliii 28 **35** 40 141 161 171 197 201
Beitía, Agustín 91 99
Beitía, Félix Antonio (policeman) 96, 127, deposition 137, exonerated 149
Berle, Adolf (U.S. Asst. Sect. State) lix-lx
Bernal, Manuel Antonio 56
Blau, Juan (Swiss consul) criticized by Batalla 116-8; on Mixed Commission 133, 138; Sophie Müller writes 228
Boquete, alleged massacre near~ xxvi xxix xxxii-xxxiii lxxi 178; atmosphere xxxvii; German settlement near~ 21; *Holocausto en Panamá*, in~ xxvi xxix-xxxiii 178-9
Boyd, (Acting) Pres. Samuel Augusto xlviii 55
Boza, Pablo 56
Brauchle family 33-34 139 180 187 **211**; barred from colony 212; immigrates in 1929 15; Gustav Haug lives with 204 209
Brauchle, Alfred Sr. 14n 15n 17 31 34; background 14n-15n, confronts Lehner 204-5; dies in internment camp 15n 37; goes to colony after shooting

215; helps Haug 209; tied up by police 216
Brauchle, Alfred Jr. 34; arrested at La Concepción 34; tied up by police 216
Brauchle, Erwin 34; collapses after massacre 215-6; interned in U.S. 34-6
Brauchle, Helmut xli lxiv builds barricade 83; *Die Brücke*, in 223; Nazi "sympathies" 86-7; death of~ 99 158 216; joins colony 34 140 221; witnesses suicide attempt 208; summons doctor 208
Brauchle, Lydia *née* Albert 15n *34 218*; intv. Zimmermann 15n, writes to Min. Govt. & Justice 36; Lehner accuses of theft 206
Brauchle, Rosario Sicilia de 171
Brauchle, Zoila Miranda de 36
Brauer, Alfredo lviii
Brid, Gilberto 58
bridge (over Río Chiriquí Viejo) xliii *27-8 41-2* 43 199 203 210 222 226; modern bridge 29n
Bridge on the Chiriquí Viejo, The (book). See **Brücke am Chiriquí Viejo, Die**. See also **Häusle Worrell, Gertrude ("Trudi")**.
Bristol, Maj. W. L. 36
Brown, Adriano (policeman) 56
Brücke am Chiriquí Viejo, Die xxxvi frontispiece *27-8 40* 221*ff*; onomastic table 223. See also **Häusle Worrell**, Gertrude ("Trudi").
Bugaba centenaria (commemorative magazine) 191
Burgos, Manuel (2nd Sect., Min. Govt. & Justice) 148
buses. See **transportation**, public.

C

Caballero, Juan (policeman) exonerated 149
Caballero, Rubén Darío (policeman) exonerated 149
Camp Empire. See **enemy aliens**, internment of~.
Canal Zone xlv*in* xli 168 222; historiography ix; historical conflict xxiv xlvii xlviii*n ln* lv lxvi; internments in xix lvi-lvii 36 80n; wartime conditions lxii 111; racism in~ lii 20 21n; rr. station 55n. See also **enemy aliens**, internment of~
Candela. See **Piedra Candela**.
Capira, German settlement at~ xxix 21
Carrasco, Judge Luis A., (2nd Sup. Trib. 1st App. Dist.) 136, 152
Carteles (mag.) photo pub. in~ *102* 103
Carter, Lt. Col. L. D. 113. See also **G-2 (U.S.)**.
Carter, U.S. Pres. Jimmy lxvi lxix lxx
case file 109 126 139 142 148-9 151-3
Castillo, Teresita 69
Castro, Capt. José del Carmen 63
Cedeño Bermúdez, Moisés (policeman) 56
Cedeño, Pedro Antonio (policeman) exonerated 149
Cedeño, Rafael (policeman) exonerated 149
Cerrud, Víctor (policeman) exonerated 149
Chase National Bank xlix
Chávez, Secundino (policeman) exonerated 150
Chiriquí Land Co. immigration status of employees 70. See also **United Fruit Co.**
Chiriquí Viejo, Río *42-43* 16 29n 30 32 44 199 208. See also **bridge** (over Chiriquí Viejo); **Häusle Worrell**, Gertrude ("Trudi").
chivas. See **transportation, public**.
chombos. See **West Indians in Panama**.
Chorrera, La 70 107; police station attacked 56. See also **Arias Madrid, Arnulfo**: suppresses uprisings.
Circuit Courts 57n
Circuit Court, 1st (Chiriquí) 58 159
Circuit Court, 2nd (Chiriquí) 128
CNN television. See **Arnett**, Peter.
Colindres, Dr. (medical examiner) 123-4, 177
colonists agriculture 29 43; background xviii xli lxiv 3 10; character 3; arrival at David 29; casualties x lxxxi 103; dates xliii; decision to emigrate 14 20; diet xlii 12 100; dissension, internal~ xliii 196*ff*; German members

lxiv; *Holocausto en Panamá*, in~ xxix xxxi; infant deaths xxxviii 212; labor force xli; long-term survival xl-xli; move to Schmieder's farm xviii xl-xli xlii 14 30 199; Nazism, putative~ xx lxv 80 85 87; neighbors, relations with~ 32*ff* 44*ff*; police visit repeatedly 80-86; practices 37-39 105; religion 3 13 33 39-40 73-4; rescue possums, snakes xli 44-6; resistance to regulation lv 80 85 104-6; seek refuge in Costa Rica 43-4 86-88; visas 22 28; voyage to Panama 27*ff*; workforce xxxviii. *See also* colony, Vairano~; Piedra Candela; property; weapons.

colony, Vairano~ "chestnuts" incident 13; Father Divine, initial contact with~ 9; founding 2-5; "frogs" incident 13; Haug visits~ 16-17; members 5; police surveillance of~ 10; practices 3; teachings of Father Divine 3 7-9; trade restrictions on 12-13

Colorado, Río (Chiriquí) 30n 32

Comisario, El (cantina) 115

Communiqué, Ofc. of Press, Radio & Pub. Performances version of events 63 80-4 93-94 103 104-6; published in Carteles 102-3; Winter relies on 109-111 114; requested by Winter 138 144

Compañía Panameña de Productos Lácteos. See **Blau**, Juan (Swiss consul).

Concepción Quintero, Santiago 87

Conte Porras, Jorge 51n 49n 55 97n

Coolidge, U.S. Pres. Calvin, xix

Corella, Daniel, (policeman) 127 137; exonerated 149

Corella, Máximiliano (policeman) 137, exonerated 149

Coronel, Guillermo (policeman) 127 137 149

Costa Rica border runs N-S 112n; colonists' farm (Cotón) xliii 29 43-4 88 211-12; denies existence of transmitter 86; *Fila de los Suizos* 44; has no army 67n; opposes settlement of blacks in Chiriquí lin; incursion in Chiriquí 137; restricts German, Italian immigration 88; "landing strip" (Cotón) lx 87. *See also* **Colonists** Costa Rica, seek refuge in~; *Eisenach* (ship); **Concepción Quintero**, Santiago.

cotito defined 2n

Cotito, Río 32

Cotón (C.R.). *See* **Costa Rica**.

courts, org. of~ 57n, 129n

criminal justice system xxiv

Cuban Military Aviation School 63

Cubilla, Eleuterio (policeman) 96

Cuestas Gómez, Carlos H. ix-x xxxvi xxxviii-xxxix lxvii lxxiii lxxv 127

D

De Gracia, Angel Vitelio (Judge, 2nd Sup. Trib.) 151 182; *Holocausto en Panamá*, in~ 183

De Gracia, Rafael, (policeman) exonerated 150

De Icaza, Pedro J. 56

De la Guardia, Capt. Alejandro (chief, Alien *Aff* Sec.) 36. *See also* **police**: Alien Affairs section.

De la Guardia, Camilo Jr. (Min. Govt. & Justice) 36; Brauchle, Lydia writes to 36; returns passports 146

De la Guardia, Erasmo (Justice, Sup. Ct.) 136

De la Guardia, Acting Pres. Ricardo Adolfo; *Min. Govt. & Justice*: bans Adventist Church 71-2 104; compensation claims, denies 145 147; criminal liability investigated by Gómez Araúz 127; plan to rebuild Cotito farm 158-9; police, militarization of~ 63-66; Probst arrest 115-6; relationship to Gómez Ayau 63-4; responds to Swiss, German diplomats 138, 144 146-50; responsibility for massacre 107 127; report to Assembly on massacre 105-6; seizes power, coup 1941 lxii lxv; Tejeira biography of~ 64. *See also* **Communiqué**, Ofc. of Press, Radio, Pub. Performance; **Divine**, Father.

De la Rosa, Diógenes 56. *See also* **Arias Madrid**, Arnulfo: suppresses uprisings.

De Roux, Raúl (Min. For Rel.) deals with Germans, Swiss 138 144*ff* 183n
deforestation xlii-xliii
Del Cid, Noel (clerk, Bugaba Municipal Court) 159
Del Valle, Pres. Eric Arturo, v.p. candidate 1984 181
Dell, David xxxvi 18n 32n
Democratic Liberal Party 54
deportation. See enemy aliens, internment of.
Divine, Father *8* xxxv-xxxvi xlii 3 6-10 80 164 204 215; colonists followers of~ xxxix; De la Guardia calls "Negro agitator" 80
Divine, Penninah ("Mother") *8*. See also Richings, Edna Rose ("Mother Divine.")
Dubois, Lt. Jules lxii-lxiii. See also intelligence services, U.S.
Durán family xxxiii

E

Ehrman, José (Under-Sect. Ministry Fin. & Treas.) 73, 104
Eisenach (ship) scuttled in Costa Rica lix
Election 1984 xxxvi; importance to military and Treaty ratification lxvi*ff* 178 184; attempt to win Jewish vote lxviii*ff*; false charges in *El Matutino* 180-2; *Holocausto en Panamá*, use of~ lxvi*ff* 184; manipulation of vote 50; significance for U.S. 179. See also Arias Madrid, Pres. Arnulfo; Del Valle, Pres. Eric Arturo; Esquivel, Roderick.
Elections Board, Natl. (*Jurado Nacional de Elecciones*) 55
Ell, George 110
Elvira, La. See Boquete, German settlements near~.
enemy aliens, internment of~ xix-xx lix 31n *liv*; Camp Empire, C.Z. xix lviii 80n; statistics xix; threat illusory lxi-lxii; WW I xix. See also Brauchle, Alfred; Brauchle, Erwin; *Eisenach* (ship); Hartmann, Alois; Heinemann, Wilhelm; Kappel, Werner Julius & Fred; SCADTA (airline); SEDTA (airline).

Escartín, José Félix (policeman) scales palisade 96; exonerated 150
Esquivel, Roderick 181
Estrada, Nicolás 57. See also: Arias Madrid, Pres. Arnulfo: suppresses uprisings.
exhumations Bocas del Toro, in~ (2010) lxxiv; coroner's 124; Hassán's first (1980) xxvii *176* 177; Hassán's second (1984) xxvii xxxvi 172 187. See also Hassán R., Aristides Ivan; Arnett, Peter; grave, common~
expatriates. See immigrants.
expediente. See case file.

F

Fábrega Ponce, Jorge 9
Fábrega, Octavio (Min. For. Rel.) lx 146-7
Fábrega, Lt. Col. Olmedo 65
Fábrega, Rogelio (1st Chief) 66 71
Faeh, Emil 167
Fascists xlvii 2; Arnulfo admires xviii xlvii; *Holocausto en Panamá*, in~ 182. See also Mussolini, Benito.
Fassler, Meinrad 171 229
Federal Bureau of Investigation (FBI), U.S. xix
Ferrari, Agustín (1st Sec., Min. Govt. & Justice) mission to Chiriquí 104-6
FFF Movement 14n. See also Zimmermann, Werner.
Fifteenth Naval District, U.S. 111. See also Naval Intelligence, U.S. Ofc. of~.
"Fifth column." See Nazis; sabotage, threat of; enemy aliens, internment of~.
First World War. See World War I.
Flores, Lt. Saturnino 62
Flores Castillo, O. Iván vi xxxvi 18n
Franciscan nuns. See *Nuestra Señora de los Ángeles* School.
Free Economic Union. See FFF movement. See also Zimmermann, Werner.
Freiwirtschaftsbund (Free Economic Union). See FFF Movement.
Fuentes, Alfonso (policeman) exonerated 150

241

Fuerzas de Defensa 31n 67n; records seized 122. *See also* **police**.

G

G-2 (Panama) 69n 113n 122
G-2 (U.S.) 113
Gaitán, Oliborio (policeman) exonerated 150
Garcés, Lucas (probationary policeman) lxxxiin; charges dismissed 150-1; delivers ultimatum 92-7; died 1949 150; fires first shot 92 142; *Holocausto en Panamá,* in~ 189; Huff sends as scout 89; night before massacre 89-90; only police casualty *92* 93 94 98 103 105 189; shot by police 130-4; tours highlands 45 78
Gariché. *See* **Arias Madrid,** Pres. Arnulfo: suppresses uprisings.
Garrido, Manuel 56. *See also* **Arias Madrid,** Pres. Arnulfo: suppresses uprisings.
German immigrants. *See* **immigrants,** German.
Germany *33*; borders Switzerland 1-2; compensation claims 143-6 183; demands investigation 109; economy lxi lxiii14n; espionage pointless 86-7; *Holocausto en Panamá,* in~ xxviii-xxx xxxii 178 186; hypocrisy 110 144n; invades Soviet Union xxxii 110 143; Lehner's claims 217; Panama declares war on~ 145; racial, religious persecution xxxii-xxxiii lxi; relations with Panama xlix lx 111 145; represented by Spanish 146, by Swiss 147. *See also* **Hitler,** Adolf; **Mixed Commission; Winter,** Hans von.
Gómez Araúz, Prosecutor Abel *122* 129n; arrest of Werren 97; confronts Huff 69 183; *Holocausto en Panamá,* in~ 177; initiates investigation 123-5 131 129 153n; named Circuit Judge 128; removed from case 128-30 154n. *See also* **exhumations.**
Gómez Ayau, Lt. Col. Fernando (Instructor Gen. of Police) lxxiii *59*; appt. by Arias 181 188; deposition ordered 135; disciplinarian lv-lvi lxi 62-4 90; Gómez Araúz investigates criminal liability of~ 127; *Holocausto en Panamá,* in~ 183; Huff claims he ordered massacre 106 135; loyalty oath 66; *Matutino* calls "mercenary" 181; reorganization 59 61*ff* 181; Remón, and~ 62; title of Instructor Gen. 59-60n; succeeds Quintero as Instructor Gen. 61; travels to site of massacre 124; unindicted 135
Gómez, Fidel (policeman) exonerated 150
Gómez, Franklin 91
Gómez Araúz, Godofredo 49
Gómez de Cuestas, Josefa 127
Gonzales Ruiz, Sergio 54
González Revilla, *Alcalde* Alejandro 72
González Fuentes, Efraín (policeman) lxxviin 44 78 86 93 96 106
González, Julio César xxvin 180
González, Luis 57. *See also* **Arias Madrid,** Pres. Arnulfo: suppresses uprisings.
González, Pastor (policeman) exonerated 150
González Ruiz, Dr. Bernardino 97n
Gonzenbach, Adolph, Swiss *chargé* compensation claims 118 146-7; on death of Rieser infant 5n; forwards Haug report 195n; member of Mixed Commission 133 138 195n
grave alleged common~ at Palo Alto 179-80; common~ at **Cotito** xxxvi 99 172 *176 186 187*; CNN films 184; forensic examination 124; *Holocausto en Panamá,* in~ xxvii xxxii 172n 177-8 180 187 189; Volcán,~ at 98n 124 187 189. *See also* **Arnett,** Peter; **exhumations.**
Guerra, Pedro (policeman) exonerated 150
Guevara, Roberto (policeman) exonerated 150
Gunther, John xlvi
Gutiérrez, Hernán 57. *See also* **Arias Madrid,** Pres. Arnulfo: suppresses uprisings.

H

Hand, Arnoldo 116
Hartmann, Alois ("Luis") 31 97 114 *185* 187 *190 211*; Esquivel accuses

of murder 181; *Holocausto en Panamá*, in~ 187 190-1; interned World War I 31n; tied to tree 97 114 185
Hartmann, Cresenz 31n
Hassán R., Aristídes Iván (*Comandante*) author of *Holocausto* xxv-vii; military background xxiv-xxvi*n*; creates enduring myths lxxii; *Holocausto en Panamá* analyzed 177*ff*; invents "Jewish" settlements at Capira and Boquete xxix*ff*; invents massacre at Palo Alto (Boquete) xxxi lxvii 180-1; invents orders from Hitler xxxii-xxxii 178; Jews, obsession with~ xxxii-xxxiii; predicts killing of~ xxx; motivations xxxviii lxvi*ff* lxxi-ii 178; sources xxv-xxvii*n* xxiii; translations xxvii-xxix. *See also* **Arnett**, Peter; *Holocausto en Panamá*; exhumations.
hato defined 16n
Hato del Volcán, El. *See* Volcán.
Haug, Alfred 22 26
Haug, Elise 22 26
Haug, Gustav Jr. 22 26 39 43 165 *218*; marries, inherits Santa Clara farm 169
Haug, Gustav Sr. *49 205 218*; accompanies train to Chiasso 28; background 14; denies espionage charges 167; bridge, works on~ 43; describes child abuse 11n 26n; emigrates July 1939 26 28 165; executor *de facto* 19 140n 163-5 168*ff*; expresses doubts 19; leaves colony 212; Lehner, conflict with~ 41 165; meets~ 14; lives with colony 39; marries Margarethe Schmieder 140n 157 163; named to Committee 160-1; recommends emissary 21; report of~ 11-12 195*ff*; visa 22 26
Haug, Liselotte 22 26
Häusle family 26
Häusle Worrell, Gertrude ("Trudi") *162 168*; background 4; employed in Canal Zone 168; *Holocausto en Panamá*, in~ 189; joins Lehner's group 4 224; marries Ray Worrell 28 170; most critically wounded 99; present at inventory 160; renews passport 27; recalls voyage 28n; requests return of passports 27n 146; returns to Cotito 224-5; Swiss uncle's urgent inquiries xvi; testifies for Viola Wehrli 5n; translates in hospital 100; writes *Die Brücke am Chiriquí Viejo* xxxvi 28 99n 221*ff*
Häusle, Franz 4
Häusle, Paul *96 98;* background xli 4; bleeds to death 98; buried in common grave 99; citizenship xx; first victim xx 93; Garcés charges dismissed 150; German *chargé's* inquiries re~ 144; holding machete, shot by Garcés 93 141-2; *Holocausto en Panamá*, in~ 181 "mercenaries" blamed for death of~ 181; renews passport 27; sent to receive ultimatum 92-3 141
Heinemann, Wilhelm lxii-lxiii
Herrera, A.A., Bugaba County Judge 159
Herrera, Severino 116
Herrera L., Capt. Tomás 63
Hils family 16n 17 31 *82* 139; care for Lydia Brauchle 15n; *Holocausto en Panamá*, in~ 187
Hils, Anton background 15n; emigrates 1928 14n 15 16n; *Holocausto en Panamá*, in~ 191; identifies bodies 124; mistrustful of colony 33; named to Committee 159; police spend night on farm of~ 91
Hils, Helmut background xxxvi; says police were drunk 90; believes Arias not responsible 109; describes colonists 34 47; denies weapons charge 103; recalls burial site 98n
Hils, Gertrudis *34 218*
Hils, Marie de *82* 91 *218*
Hincapié, Judge Lorenzo (2nd Sup. Trib.) 134
Hitler, Adolf aids Franco lxiii 146n; admired by Arnulfo Arias xlvii-xlix; invades USSR xxxii; *Holocausto en Panamá*, in~ 178 186; "orders" massacre xxxiii 178; loyalty oath to 66n; racial views xlvix; refugees from~ xix-xx lxi; Roosevelt alleges threat to Latin America lx; Switzerland rejects lxxxvii; viewed by Lehner 203 217

Holocausto en Panamá vii **xxv** xxvii **176**; analyzed 177*ff*; English transl. xxxvii; motivation xxxvix xlii; 1984 election, in~ lxv*ff* 178-81 184; Jews targeted audience lxvii-lxxii 179; serialized lxxi; sources xxvii 180; translations claimed 182. *See also* **Hassán R.**, Aristides Iván; **Márquez**, Marcela.
Huff, Capt. (later Maj.) Antonio **79 101**; arrests Hartmann 97; Arias congratulates, later blames lxv 107-9 184-5; character 69-71; claim of superior orders, grave danger 106 125 127 134-5 137 152; claims colonists armed, planning airstrip 85 103; commands police detachment lxxxi 34 86; exonerated 130 141 150 183; Helmut Hils blames 109; *Holocausto en Panamá*, in~ 187-8; investigated by Gómez Araúz 124 127-8; massacre 92*ff* 124 141 193; named commander Third Battalion, Chiriquí 67; never charged 129-30; Niederberger places 150m away 142 217; offers to accept registration at Cotito 83; orders cease-fire 96; orders exhumation 124; plans attack on colony 89-90; poses for cameras 103; promoted to Capt. 65; refuses Probst offer 88 194; sends officers to colony 80; sends ultimatum with Garcés et al. 92 105-7 125; takes wounded to David 97; transferred by Gómez Ayau 62; transferred to Colón, Model Jail 129; visits colony 44 78 84ff 88 103 106

I

immigrants, English-speaking xxxvii
immigrants, German from Rhineland 21; from Schramberg lxiv 31; *Holocausto en Panamá*, in~ 180. *See also* **enemy aliens, internment of**; **Hassán R.**, Aristides Iván; **sabotage**, threat of; *surnames* **Brauchle Ell Häusle Heinemann Hils Huff Kappel Probst Schaper Schmieder Troetsch**.
immigration lii; clandestine 70; Costa Rica, to~ 88; Jewish xix xxvi-xxvii lii lxii lxx; Middle Eastern 73n; racial, religious exclusions li-lii 24; from Europe encouraged in Panama by Arias *et al.* xlivn xlv 18-21; foreigners ordered to report 77-8; *Holocausto en Panamá*, in~ 180; immigrants abandoned by banana plantations 70
intelligence services, U.S. xlix 20n 111*ff*. *See also* **Dubois, Jules**; **Fifteeenth Naval District**; **G-2 (U.S.)**, **Naval Intelligence, U.S. Ofc. of~**.
inventory. *See* **property inventory**.
Italian Transatlantic Co. 28
Italians. *See* **enemy aliens**, internment of; **Mussolini**, Benito.
Italy xlvii xlix xliii 2 147

J

Japanese. *See* **enemy aliens**, internment of~.
Jews Boquete area, in~ xxvi-xxvii xxix xxxi-xxxiii lxxiii 178 180; Cotito, at~ xxxi 178; economic influence 179; Hassán's obsession with~ xxxiii 178-9 187-8 190-1; immigration to Panama xix xxvi-xxvii lii lxii lxx; Jewish community statement 184-5; internment of~ lxii; massacre unrelated to xxxvi 187; political influence of~ lxvii-lxxii*ff*; press reports "massacre" of~ 179-182 184; reaction to *Holocausto en Panama (q.v.)*, lxviii*ff*; refugees xix 28n; treatment under Arnulfo Arias 24n. *See also* **Hassán R.**, Aristides Iván; **enemy aliens**, internment of~ lxii; *surnames* **Heinemann, Kappel**.
Jurado Nacional de Elecciones. *See* **Elections Board**, Natl.

K

Kappel, Fred and Werner Julius lxi-lxii
Kennedy, U.S. Pres. John F. xxiv
Kohler, Josef 14n 16n

L

Laguna de San Carlos, La. *See* **Arias Madrid**, Pres. Arnulfo: suppresses uprisings.
Lara, Arcinio (policeman) exonerated 150

Ledezma, Abilio 100
Ledezma, Antonio (policeman) exonerated 150
Legislative Assembly lxvi lxxxiiin 54 105-6 127-8 154n
Lehner, Karl xlii *37*; arrested in Switzerland 13; background xli 3-4 140; called "Molch" 12n 37; *Die Brücke*, not mentioned in~ 221; Haug's assessment of, conflict with 26n 41 150n 165-7 195*ff* 212 218n; Huff confronted 84-5; infanticide, child abuse, charges of~ xlin 5n 11n 41; killed in house 99; leadership of~ x xl-xli lvii 3 5n 9-10 14 40-1 140 143 163 193; *Holocausto en Panamá*, in~ 187 188; photo in *Carteles* 103; receives ultimatum 92 106 124-6 141-2; refuses to travel to David 82-4 123 141; Schmieder submits to~ 30, interprets for~ 92; women, treatment of~ 33 41-2 229
Linares, Julio E. 55
Linares, Olga 29n
Lincoln, U.S. Pres. Abraham xlin

M

Macho de Monte 15n 31; defined 31n
mameicillo 83
Márquez, Marcela 191
Martínez, Boris xxvin lxxiv
Martínez, Carlos Alberto 57
Martinz, Luis 47
Mattinson, Reynaldo 71-2. *See also* Seventh-Day Adventist Church.
Mena, Luis Alberto 57
Méndez, Erasmo, Judge, (2nd Sup. Trib., 1st App. Dist.) 134
military government xxiv xxvin xxxvii-xxxix xliv 178; *Acción Comunal* seeks to control~ 57-8; domestic opposition to~ limited (1968-89) lxxiii; elections under~ lxvi-lxxi 180-81; continuing tendencies lxxiv-lxxv; name change 67n; sponsor *Holocausto en Panamá* lxvi*ff*; US support for~ lxx-lxxii. *See also* **G-2 (Panama)**; **Arias Madrid**, Arnulfo; **Gómez Ayau**, Lt. Col. Fernando; **grave**, **common~ at Cotito**; **Noriega**, Manuel Antonio; **Remón**

Cantera, Pres. José Antonio; **Torrijos Herrera**, Omar.
Miller, Roberto. *See* **Müller**, Werner Robert.
Ministerio Público building xxiii; independence of~ 56 127
Miranda, Adelo (policeman) 96; exónerated 150
Miranda, Adriano (policeman) exonerated 150
Miranda, Harmodio 73
Miró, Rubén ix 69
Mixed Commission authorized to investigate 138; blames police 142-3; composition 138-9; findings 139*ff*; government responses to~ 144*ff*; Winter adopts findings of~138-9; Gonzenbach adopts findings of~ 147; recovery plan 158*ff*;
Montenegro, Cpl. Faustino (policeman) 84 86; exonerated 150
Morales, Francisco 57
Morales, Dr. Ricardo A., (Presiding Judge, 1st Sup. Trib. 1st App. Dist.; later Chief Justice, Sup. Ct.) 134 149; elevated to Sup. Ct. 136
Moreno, Augusto Miranda (policeman) exonerated 150
Moreno, Florencio (policeman) exonerated 150
Moretti, Francisco 57
Morf family 4 25; called "Amberg" in *Die Brücke* 223; orphans sent to *Nuestra Sra. de los Ángeles* 97; Paul Häusle visits 225; sent to meet m.d. 209
Morf, Albert Jr. 4 head injuries 216; *Holocausto en Panamá*, in~ 181; killed in house 99 216; photo in *Carteles* 103; rumored paternity 206
Morf, Albert Sr. acquainted with Häusles 225; appears agitated 213; background xl 4 225; contacts Haug 14 195-6; killed in house 99 216; Häusles' uncle mistrusts 225; loyalty to Lehner 22 198 215 225-6; obtains visas 23 25; photo in *Carteles* 103; travels to Panama 20-25 196, to David 205; suggests Ott join group 226-7; tells Haug visits unwelcome 212

Morf, Elfriede ("Friedy," daughter of Albert Sr. & Elfriede) xli 4 100 *162 168;* marries, moves to U.S. 170; says Jesus wanted massacre 215; sent to convent 97; Waser's attentions 163

Morf, Elfriede (wife of Albert Sr., mother of "Friedy") *98;* attempts suicide 208; killed in house 99 216; Lehner blames for Loni's pain 207

Morf, Leonora ("Loni") xli *100 162 168;* found in house with hands up 96; photo in *Carteles* 103; uninjured 142 217; scalding accident 207; sent to convent 97, to foster home 170, to US 170

Morf, Walter xxxiv xli *162 168;* chance encounter xxxiii-xxxv; injuries minor 100; present at inventory 160; defense of Lehner 209n; re Lehner's relationships 42n; sent to convent 97, to foster home 168, to US 169; *Holocausto en Panamá,* in~ 189

Morgan, Eduardo 171

Moscoso, Pres. Mireya li

Müller family 4 25

Müller, Roberto. See Müller, Werner Robert.

Müller (later Wachter), Sophie Baumann *164;* asserts Schmieders indebted to~ 139n 163n 199n; background 4; death of Rieser infant, and~ 197 202 219*ff; Die Brücke,* in~ 227*ff;* files suit 171; *Holocausto en Panamá,* in~ 181 188; injuries 99 181; marries Wachter 170 171n 188; massacre, describes 92-3; police visits, describes~ 78 106; "maternal love," considers~ false 207; present at inventory 160; privations at Wasser home 170; refuses legacy 168-70; relationship with Lehner 12n 42n; relationship with Fassler 170n

Müller, Werner xli *99;* background 4; contacts Haug 14 195-6; death of Rieser infant and~ 197 202; *Die Brücke, in* 223-4 227-8; *Holocausto en Panamá,* in~ 181; killed in house 99 157; loyalty to Lehner 198; photo in *Carteles* 103; skilled mechanic 42

Müller, Werner Robert ("Böps") xli 4 *10 113 162 166;* abused as child 11-12n 42n 208; asserts Schmieders in debt 19 139 162 199n; criticizes Waser stewardship 163; denies weapons charge 83; *Die Brücke,* in~ *227;* colony, describes~ 38; family seeks to aid 170; *Holocausto en Panamá,* in~ 181 189; hospitalized 99-100; Lehner, describes~ 41; massacre, describes~ 89-91 94; only survivor interviewed 11 94; practices in later life 6n 11n; present at inventory 160; privations at Waser home 170; refuses legacy 168-70 ;says Haug took property 165; Vairano colony, describes~ 10*ff*

Mussolini, Benito *("il Duce")* viewed by Lehner 203; as model for Arnulfo Arias lxviii. *See also* Fascists.

N

National City Bank xlix

National Revolutionary Party. *See Acción Comunal.*

Naval Intelligence, U.S. Ofc. of~ 20n

Naville, René, Acting Swiss chargé 136 148

Navy, U.S. *See* **Fifteenth Naval District; Naval Intelligence,** U.S. Ofc. of~.

Nazis Arnulfo admires liv; Arnulfo considered~ sympathizer xx l li lxi; colonists suspected 78 85 87 90 103 167; German legation offended by use of term 145; Latin America, in~ xx xlivn; little support in Switzerland 2; most in Pma. not deported lxii-lxiii. *See also* **Germany; Hitler, Adolf;** *Holocausto en Panamá;* **sabotage, World War II.**

Neumann, Prof. Richard 15n 31

Nicaraguans. US support for right-wing lxx; banana workers 70. *See also* Arias Madrid, Pres. Arnulfo: suppresses uprisings

Niederberger, Josef ("Sepp") *39 50* 200 *205; Holocausto en Panamá,* in~ 188; says Huff 150m away 142 217

Noriega, Gen. Manuel Antonio lxvii lxx lxxiv 67n 113n

Nuestra Señora de los Ángeles School 24 97 168 *162*
Núñez, Rubén 120n

O

Ocaña, Capt. Óscar 62 65
Oller, Félix 56
Oñós de Plandolit, Manuel (Spanish chargé) 146
Ortega Valdés, Humberto 56
Ott, Heinrich lxi 4-5 26 *38* 42 99 103 189 194 216 226

P

Palo Alto, Sierra de. See Boquete, alleged massacre near~.
Panameñismo xlin lxxii 52-3 72 108
Peralta, Pedro (policeman) 101; exonerated 150
Pereira, Renato 62
Pérez, Barolo (policeman) 56
Pérez, Felipe O. 56
Piedra Candela lxxxiin assets not inventoried 161; colonists leave xli 30; fictitious airstrip lx; farming at 19 29-30 43 140; granted by Pres. J.D. Arosemena 29 196; intention to return 226; name 17 18n; rumors of gold 43; Wachter lives at~ 170; Waser lives at~ 163 170 200
Pittí, Félix 90
Pittí, Héctor (policeman) exonerated 150
plaque, memorial *252*
Plaza Cinco de Mayo 52 55
Polanco, Carlos (policeman) 127 137; exonerated 150
Police
  Alien Affairs Section 71; colonists required to register lxxxi 44 71 78; US responds re Brauchles' internment 36-7
  National xvii xxi xxxix lxxiv; Arias's effort to control lxv lvi 54; Axis nationals, measures against~ lvii-lviii lxi lxv 34; becomes Natl. Guard 66; Bocas de Toro shooting lxxiv; discipline 66-69 73; illegal immigration 70-71; election 1939, in~ 55-6; facilities inadequate 70; Gómez Ayau as commander 61*ff*; opposition to Arnulfo Arias xviii-xx li lvi lxi lxiv-lxv; La Laguna at~ 56; militaristic tendencies lxxiv lxxvn lxxxiv*n*; military ranks conferred 62 64; militarization under Arnulfo Arias 54 58*ff* 63; Nicaraguans killed at Gariché 57; organization lxxxiii*n*; political repression at Chame, La Chorrera 56; Remón, rôle of~ 60 62 66; religious repression 71; U.S. commanders under Amador, De Obaldía 60n
  Third Battalion (Chiriquí) 67*ff* *101*; Arias praises~ xlvi 107-8; attacks colony lx lxiv lxxxi 34 92*ff* 112 136*ff* *142n*; authorization for massacre xlvi xlvi lxiv*n* lxv 106 126-7 141 147 152; commanded by Huff 67; communiqué, in~ 80-81 84-5 102 105; discipline 67-69; drunkenness before massacre 90*ff*; evacuate wounded 24*n* 97; depositions of~ 127; Garcés police casualty *92* 98 105 111 115 136; *Holocausto en Panamá*, in~ xxvi*n*; identify bodies 124; looting of property 101 159; motive for massacre lxv; personnel exonerated 1953 lxxxii; photos in *Carteles* 103; preparations for attack 88*ff* 91; reject mediation 84; report airstrip lx; strategic advantage 143 150; visit colony lxxxii*n* 44 71 78-80 84-5 106; victims 94 98 113.
  See also **exhumations; G-2** (Panama); **Gómez Ayau**, Fernando; **Hartmann**, Alois; **Herrera, L.,** Capt. Tomás; **Quintero**, Maj. Abel; **Probst**, Wilhelm; **Valderrama**, Nicolás; **ultimatums; weapons.**
Ponce, Luis (policeman) 78 127; exonerated 150
Popular Front (election 1940) 55
population xxiii
Porras, Demetrio 55 56 58
Porter, Russell B. lix
postal service xxxix 18n; post office, Volcán *22 23* 24 226. See also **Senn,** Hans August Sr., Jr.
Potrerillos Arriba. See **Boquete,** alleged masscre near~.

press coverage vii xxiii 60n 102 104 108 114 116 131 144 184 191. *See also* **Arnett,** Peter, *and names of newspapers.*
Pretelt, J. A. (Presiding Judge, 2nd Sup. Trib.) 148-9
Primavera School, *La* 29
Probst, Juanita B. 115
Probst, Wilhelm attempts mediation 88 194; called "Nazi" by U.S. 112; describes colonists 45-6 103; describes refusal to travel 77-8; evidence from 103; protests, jailed 45 114-6
property administrative committee, receiver appointed 159; appraisal 161; assets frozen 159; held in common 38 109 162; disposition of~ 157*ff* 164; Haug, of~ 168-9; *Juez Municipal* inventory 159; looting by police 100-1 158-61; sale of farm 168-70 *174*

Q

Quiel, Jacob (policeman) exonerated 150
Quintero, Maj. Abel (3rd Chief) 63 65; brother of prosecutor 130; diplomatic status 63 135; given military rank 65; responsibility for massacre 107 127 130 134; phone call with Huff 106; subordinate to Gómez Ayau 63
Quintero, Samuel (Prosecutor, Sup. Trib., 1st App. Dist.) accepts Gomez Araúz resignation 129; brother of police commander 130; investigative report 131 148; moves for dismissal 134; takes depositions 137
Quiróz, Teófilo. *See* **Seventh-Day Adventist Church.**

R

rabiblancos defined *ln*; detest Arias li; *Panameñistas* oppose liv-lvi
Ramos, Julio 58
Rausch, Panamanian consul at Zürich 27
Recuero, Arturo 56
"**Red Devils.**" *See* **transportation,** public

Remón Cantera, Pres. José Antonio ("Chichi") "architect of militarization" 60 62; creates *Guardia Nacional* 66; deposes Arias 1941, 1951 60; Gómez Ayau transfers to Panama City 61-2; given military rank 65; murdered 1952 lx lxxiii 69; promoted to Capt. 60; assassination trial 69
Renewal Liberal Party 56
Richings, Edna Rose ("Mother Divine") *8*
Rieser, Georg 4 5n
Rieser, Virgilio Columbio xli*n* 5; death of~ 26 158 219*ff*; named for ship 5n; visa 25
Rieser-Wehrli family 4-5
Rieser-Wehrli, Viola. *See* **Wehrli,** Viola.
Río. *See* **Cotito, Río; Chiriquí Viejo, Río; Colorado, Río** (Chiriquí).
Ríos, Dr. Sebastián Gilberto 29
Rivera, 2nd Lt. Primitivo (3rd Battalion) 67; confronts Lehner 83; visits colony 78 80 84; posted at Cañas Gordas 80 89; leads squad on n. side 93; exonerated 150; permits looting 100-1; transmits registration order 80; secures crime scene 97
Rivera, Manuel (policeman) exonerated 150
Rivera, Pablo E. 57
Robles, Pres. Marco Aurelio xxi; defeats Arnulfo Arias 1964 xxi lxxvii
Rodríguez, Isidro (policeman) 56
Roosevelt, U.S. Pres. Franklin D. Arias antagonizes~ lvii; closes German consulates 144n; dislikes Arnulfo Arias lvi-lvii lxvix; *Holocausto en Panamá*, in~ 184; meets Harmodio Arias xlix*n*; Lehner's view 217; on threat of sabotage lx lxiii
Roosevelt, U.S. Pres. Theodore lxi
Ruiloba, 2nd Lt. Ernesto (3rd Battalion) 67; exonerated 150; carries machine gun 88; delivers ultimatum with Garcés 92 124-5; location questioned 133 136; transferred to Pma. City 130

S

sabotage threat of~ illusory xix lx; influence on Panamanian politics xx lvi; vulnerability of Canal lxii; colonists viewed as threat 84 89*ff*
Sagel de Santiago, Gov. Federico 44 85-6 91n 103 205 213
Sagel, Imelda 69
Salazar, Gonzalo (Circ. Ct. prosecutor) 148; hands file up to Quintero (Sup. Trib. Prosecutor) 130-1; *Holocaustoen Panamá*, in~ 183; replaces Gómez Araúz 128-9
Saldaña, Sgt. Nicasio deposed 137; exonerated 150; tells Haug all are dying 215; visits colony 78 80 86; reports of~ fabricated 81-2 84
Samudio, Alfonso (police armorer) 132
Samudio, Andrés (policeman) exonerated 150
Sánchez, José Ángel 57
Santa Ana Park 55
SCADTA (airline) lix
Schaper family care for Lydia Brauchle 15n; emigrate to Panama 15-16 31 139; farm location 17
Schaper, Friedrich ("Fritz") 31 *189* emigrates 1928 15; *Holocausto en Panamá*, in~ 191; named to Committee 159
Schaper, Martha *née* Schmieder *189*; views colony with reserve 18 33; loses brother 158
Schmieder, Albert xxxiv xxxv xli 11n *17 162 165 168 200 211 218*; chance encounter xxxiv-xxxv; Müller, Morf inquire about 14; uninjured 142 217
Schmieder family xl *200 211* 31 144; contacts with German embassy 87 110; emigrate to Panama 15 139; *Holocausto en Panamá*, in~ 181 188
Schmieder, Karl Jr. *17 200 211*; buried at Volcán 97-8 124; *Holocausto en Panamá*, in~ 188-9; injured in knees, died on horseback lxxxi 81 95 97 99 217
Schmieder, Karl Sr. *19* 30 *200 205 211*; accompanies Haug, Morf to David 205; alleged indebtedness 18 139 163 199n; at Klärli's childbed 209; background xl 14-17 33; correspondence with Haug 15 23-24n 199; Cotito farm 16-17; death foretold by Lehner 214; Haug asks about Rieser infant 202, about stolen money 206, about Friedy's attempted suicide 208; *Holocausto en Panamá*, in~ 181 188-9; interprets for Lehner 47 84 92; invites colonists to Cotito farm 18 140; joins colony 30 33-4 140 199; killed in shooting 96n 109 144 216; legacy 169 171n 199; Morf visits 25; reverence for Lehner 209 213 215; shares Lehner's room 201; *Tropenheimat*, in~ 14; parents, treatment of~ 200
Schmieder, Margarethe ("Gretel") *17 19 162 200 205 218*; at Klärli's childbed 209; criminal charges dropped 1953 150; custodian of property 160-3; deposition of~ 138; found in house 96; *Holocausto en Panamá*, in~ 181 188-9; injured in shooting 100 109 142 144; loses husband and son 157; present at inventory 160; sale of farm 168-70; Lehner's advances 212; marries Haug 150n 163 167; reports theft of property 101 161; reluctant to join colony 30n 212; shares Lehner's room 201
Schmieder, Martha. *See* Schaper, Martha, *née* Schmieder
Schmieder, Rosario Laws (de) xlii
SEDTA (airline) lviii-lix
Senn, Brünhilde *164*
Senn, Hans August Jr. *23*. *See also* postal service: post office, Volcán.
Senn, Hans August Sr. 24n 29. *See also* postal service: post office, Volcán.
Senn, Werner C. 18n 24n
Serracín, Manuel Antonio xxvii*n*
Serracín, Aurelio Manuel (policeman) 45 78 80-2; approach from rear 93; confirms looting 159; denies reporting "arsenal" 81-2 84; exonerated 150
Serrano, Bienvenido (policeman) exonerated 150
Serrano Pandiella, Felipe 11n

249

Serrano, Gavino (policeman) 137-8; exonerated 150
Seventh-day Adventist Church 71-2
Sicilia, Digna de 172 177
Sicilia García, Francisco 161 169 171 174; farm of~ 180 191
Sicilia, Olga Bouche de 177
Sicilia Bouche, Orfidio 171-2 177
Sicilia Saldaña, Pedro Antonio 171
Sicilia Álvarez, Raquel 171
Sicilia de Brauchle, Rosario de 171
Siedler, Anna 4-5 25; declines to emigrate 26; dies in Switzerland 210
Sierra de Palo Alto. See Boquete.
Sittón family xxxiii
Socialist Party 55. See also Porras, Demetrio.
Solís, Galileo, Min. Govt. & Justice 58
Somarriva, Enrique 57
Soto Araica, Jesús 57
Soto, Victoriano 56
Spies, Nazi. See sabotage, threat of; enemy aliens, internment of; Germany; Colonists: considered Germans; "landing strip"; "radio transmitter" (spring house).
Spoken Word, The (pub.) See Divine, Father.
Staff, Prof. Héctor 31
Stimson, Henry L. (U.S. Sect. of War) lvii-lviii
Strassele, Alois. See Hartmann, Alois.
Sucre Calvo, Carlos, Min. Govt. & Justice 148-9
Sucre, Marcos 56
sumario. See case file.
Superior Tribunal of Justice, 2nd~ (1st App. Dist.) declines jurisdiction 1942 134 150; draft decision 1946 136 148; exonerates police 149-51 183; file closed permanently 1953 149; Min. For. Rel. states case still pending 1946 148; Min. Govt. & Justice requests report 148; Nicaraguans, killing of~ 58; Probst arrest 116; remits to Sup. Ct. 134 135 136n; Remón murder trial 69; reopens file 1942 135; Swiss order analysis of record 1943 147-8. See also courts, organization of.
Supreme Court of Justice xxiv xxxix 57n; Adventists 72; deposes Arias 1941 lxvi 108; draft decision 1946-47 136 149; 12-year delay 150; exonerates Huff 130; Holocausto en Panamá, in~ 182; final ruling 121 152; original jurisdiction 127 134 135; Probst 116; orders additional evidence 136-7; remands to Sup. Tribunal 1943 136. See also courts, organization of~.
Switzerland economy 1-2 47n; neutrality xx 2n 146n 147; half size of Panama lxxxiv. See also Gonzenbach, Adolphe (Swiss chargé.)

T

Tapia, Judge Alejandro 134
Tedman, Frank 188
Tejada J., Capt. Carlos Enrique 62 65
Tejeira, Gil Blas 64
Terán Albarracín, Gov. Rafael 72
Tessin (Swiss canton). See Vairano colony.
Testa, Ernesto 56
Thompson, Ambrose W. xlin
Ticino (Swiss canton). See colony, Vairano.
Torrijos Herrera, Omar becomes dictator xxvin; election 1984 lxvi; Torrijos-Carter Treaty lxvi lxx; completes militarization lxxiii; dies in plane crash lxvi; Holocausto en Panamá, responsibility for~ 179; Miró assassination 69n
transportation, public xxii-xxiii
Troetsch, R. Alejandro Die Brücke, in~ 222; Lehner disloyal to~ 210-11; provides repatriation bond 25; visited by Morf 25
Tropenheimat: Panamá-Mexiko. See Zimmermann, Werner.
Turner, Domingo H. 56

U

U.S. intelligence. See intelligence services, U.S.
U.S.-Panama relations Arnulfo Arias's resistance to U.S. xviii xlviii lii-liii lvii; Canal Zone sovereignty conflict xxiii l lvi; invasion 1989 xxiv lxxii;

Pma. military, U.S. military, DEA, Reagan adm. close lxix*ff*; protectorate status xix; demands anti-German measures lvi*ff*, concessions xix xlviii lvi; U.S. Sen. reluctant to hand Canal to military lxvi; upper classes favor U.S. lv*ff*; U.S. approves anti-Arias coup li lxv, *Acción Comunal* coup xlvii; U.S. trains military, police lxxiii
Ubico y Castañeda, Jorge (Pres. Guatemala) 60n 61 64
ultimatums 92-3 106; Arias's responsibility for 107-9 216n; coded telegram authorizing~ 137; delivery of~ 136 141; text 125-6; Huff orders~ 141
United Fruit Co. 56n 60n 70. *See also* **Chiriquí Land Co.**
United Liberal Party 55
Urriola, Bolívar (policeman) exonerated 150

V

Vairano colony. *See* **colony, Vairano.**
Valderrama, Lt. Col. (Gen. Supt. Police) Nicolás 63
Valdés, A.R. (Instructor Gen. Of Police) 59-60n
Vallarino, Capt. Bolívar military rank 65
Vásquez Díaz, José María, (prosecutor 1st Sup. Trib.) 137
Vásquez, Sup. Ct. Justice Publio 121
Virgilio (ship) 197; infant named for~ 5n; landing at Cristóbal Dec. 31, 1938 28
Volcán (name) 16n
von Winter. *See* **Winter.**

WXY

Wachter, Emil 170-1 228; *Holocausto en Panamá*, in~ 188-9
Wachter, Sophie. *See* **Müller** (later Wachter), Sophie, *née* Baumann.
Waser, Alfred *31 39 50 205* 200 213; named receiver 159; mismanagement 163; present at inventory 160; Sophie, Robert Müller live with 170
weapons *102*; colonists unarmed 81 83 150; colony inspected for 81; flawed forensic examination of~ 125 130-5 137; government claims colonists armed lxxxii 74 81 84-5 90 125 142-3 150-1 217; Haug searched for 216; Häusle carrying machete 93 141; La Chorrera, La Laguna, Gariché uprisings 1940-41 56-7 107; Lehner claims weapons "spiritual" 141; police weapons 88-9 93-4
Wehrli, Bertha 198
Wehrli, Viola *162 220*; background 4-5; believes Lehner responsible for deaths xlin; cares for Böps (Roberto Müller) 170; death of son 26n 158 197 219-20; deposition (Swiss investigation) 158n; divorce 4 5n 210 219n; *Holocausto en Panamá*, in~ 189; injuries 96 100 103; present at inventory 160; marries Meinrad Fassler 170n; returns to Switzerland 170; visa 25. *See also* **Rieser,** Georg; **Rieser,** Virgilio Columbio.
Weil, Raymond 168
Werren family 4; spoke Spanish 47; visa 25
Werren, Cornelia xli *162 218*; children live in Chiriquí 169; *Die Brücke*, in~ 223; *Holocausto en Panamá*, in~ 181 189; injuries 100; marries Gustav Haug Jr. 169 172; retracts statement 123
Werren, Gottfried xl 4 *96*; assumes leadership 159; deposition 123; *Die Brücke*, in~ 223 229; responsible for supplies, heat 40-1 204; affected by teargas 100; Lehner rejects advice of~ 123; loses wife, daughter 157; photos used in cover-up 103; present at inventory 160; *Holocausto en Panamá*, in~ 189; tied up, jailed after massacre 97 216; uninjured 96 113 142 217
Werren, Klara (mother) 4; buried at Volcán 99 124; death of~ lxxxii 217; *Die Brücke,* in~ 223 229; denied access to Klärli's childbed 209; *Die Brücke,* in~ 223; *Holocausto en Panamá,* in~ 181 189
Werren, Klärli (dtr.) 4; cohabits with Lehner 200-1 211; death of child 210n 217; *Die Brücke*, in~ 223 229; *Holocausto en Panamá*, in~ 181 189; killed inside house 99; photo used in

cover-up 103; pregnancies 41n 206 207n 208-9; remains desecrated by CNN 172; scalding of Loni Morf, at~ 207

West Indians in Panama lii 20 58; efforts to expel 53-54; immigration barred 24n

Wilson, U.S. Amb. Edwin C. reports coup lxv

Winter, Hans von (German *Chargé d'Aff.*) cable to Berlin 87 109-11; dealings with Pma. Min. For. Rel. 138*ff* 144-5; *Holocausto en Panamá*, in~ xxxii; note re Mixed Commission 133 138 143

World War I internments during 31n; Switzerland, in~ 1-2

World War II xviii 110n 143n; Arias mistrusted lxviii; colonists flee 2; Haug awaits news of~ 204; invasion of USSR xxxii; *Holocausto en Panamá*, in~ xxxiii 178-9; internments during~ xix 34-7 204; Lehner predicts outcome 217; Panama declares war xxxi*n* lix 73 145; U.S. campaign against emigrants during~ xxxviii xliv 34-6; war preparations xix lvi lix lxii 73 111. *See also* SCADTA (airline), SEDTA (airline).

Z

Zimmermann, Werner 14n 196

Zulauf, Verena 22 26

ABOUT THE AUTHOR

DR. CARLOS HUMBERTO CUESTAS GÓMEZ, formerly presiding judge of the Third Appellate District of Panama and Secretary-General of the Supreme Court of Justice, has returned to the Superior Tribunal bench in the Third District (Chiriquí). He earned his law degree from the University of Padua in Italy in 1978, and has engaged in post-graduate studies at the Universidad Santa María la Antigua (where he also taught) and the University of Panama. As a legal scholar, historian and novelist, Dr. Cuestas has written numerous articles on legal subjects, historical novels and monographs related to the history of his native province. He resides with his wife Raffaella in Altos de Boquete.

His maternal grandfather was the first investigating prosecutor in the Cotito case in 1941.

ABOUT THE EDITOR AND TRANSLATOR

DAVID M. FISHLOW, born in 1943, spent his childhood in New York City and his high school and college years in Claremont, CA. During the summer of 1961, he was a Good Humor®, though not particularly good-humored, ice cream man in eastern Los Angeles, a formative period in which he learned to say *chocolate, vainilla, fresa, frambuesa, naranja and cereza*. He came to Panama in the U.S. Peace Corps in 1964 and expanded his vocabulary substantially.

After returning to the United States in 1966, he served as editor of *El Malcriado*, the newspaper of the United Farm Workers in Delano, CA; published *¡Ya Mero!*, a community newspaper in the Lower Rio Grande Valley of Texas; served as a staff member of the American Civil Liberties Union, press secretary to the Attorney General of New York State, press secretary to Hon. David Dinkins in the 1989 New York City mayoral campaign, and as a certified interpreter/translator in the California state courts. Since 1993, he has lived most of the time on a small farm in Volcán, Chiriquí.

His maternal grandfather was a brick-layer in the Bronx.

In einem gemeinsamen Grab 200 Meter von diesem Punkt, auf dem Bauernhof erbaut von Karl and Margarethe Schmieder, liegen die Überreste von zehn der zwölf Schweizerischen und Deutschen pazifistischen Opfer, die in der brutalen Polizei-Massaker, die in den frühen Morgenstunden des 7. Juli 1941, stattgefunden erschossen wurden, während der ersten Amtszeit von Präsident Arnulfo Arias Madrid. In ihrer Erinnerung, dass von den beiden Opfern in Volcán begraben, wie auch an die acht Verwundet, haben ihre Nachkommen und Freunde dieses Denkmal im Jahr 2014 errichtet.

A 200 metros de este punto, en la finca fundada por Karl y Margarethe Schmieder, yacen en una fosa común los restos de diez de los doce pacifistas suizos y alemanes, víctimas de la brutal masacre policial perpetrada en tempranas horas del 7 de julio de 1941, durante la primera presidencia de Arnulfo Arias Madrid. En homenaje a ellos, los dos caídos sepultados en Volcán, y los ocho heridos, sus descendientes y amigos han erigido este memorial en el año 2014.

In a common grave 200 meters from this point, on the farm founded by Karl and Margarethe Schmieder, lie the remains of ten of the twelve Swiss and German pacifist victims gunned down in a brutal police massacre in the early morning hours of July 7, 1941, during the first presidency of Arnulfo Arias Madrid. In their honor, that of the two victims buried in Volcán, and the eight wounded, their descendants and friends have erected this memorial in the year 2014.

Plaque at roadside, near the gate of Cotito Farm.

עליהם השלום – PEACE UPON THEM